The
FINGER LAKES
Book
A Complete Guide

Children watch the old wooden wheel turn at New Hope Mills on the west side of Skaneateles Lake.

THE
FINGER LAKES
BOOK
A Complete Guide

SECOND EDITION

Katharine Delavan Dyson

Berkshire House
Woodstock, Vermont

ISBN 1-58157-069-4
ISSN 1548-4017

Front cover photo of Watkins Glen Dock © Pat and Chuck Blackley
Back cover photos by Katharine Delavan Dyson; author's photo by Chickadee Lane Photography
Interior photos by Katharine Delavan Dyson
Cover design by Jane McWhorter
Interior design and composition by Dianne Pinkowitz
Maps by Ron Toelke

Published by Berkshire House, an imprint of The Countryman Press, P.O. Box 748, Woodstock, Vermont 05091

Distributed by W. W. Norton & Company, Inc., 500 Fifth Avenue, New York, NY 10110

Manufactured in the United States of America

10 9 8 7 6 5 4 3 2 1

No complimentary meals or lodgings were accepted by the author and reviewers in gathering information for this work.

Berkshire House's
Great Destinations travel guidebook series

Recommended by *National Geographic Traveler* and *Travel & Leisure* magazines.

[A] crisp and critical approach, for travelers who want to live like locals.

— *USA Today*

Great Destinations™ guidebooks are known for their comprehensive, critical coverage of regions of extraordinary cultural interest and natural beauty. The authors in this series are professional travel writers who have lived for many years in the regions they describe. Each title in this series is continuously updated with each printing to insure accurate and timely information.

Neither the publisher, the authors, the reviewers, nor other contributors accept complimentary lodgings, meals, or any other consideration (such as advertising) while gathering information for any book in this series.

Current titles available:
The Adirondack Book
The Berkshire Book
The Charleston, Savannah & Coastal Islands Book
The Chesapeake Bay Book
The Coast of Maine Book
The Finger Lakes Book
The Hamptons Book
The Hudson Valley Book
The Monterey Bay, Big Sur & Gold Coast Wine Country Book
The Nantucket Book
The Napa & Sonoma Book
The Santa Fe & Taos Book
The Sarasota, Sanibel Island & Naples Book
The Shenandoah Valley Book
The Texas Hill Country Book
Touring East Coast Wine Country

If you are traveling to, moving to, residing in, or just interested in any (or all!) of these enchanting regions, a Great Destinations guidebook is a superior companion. Honest and painstakingly critical, full of information only a local can provide, Great Destinations guidebooks give you all the practical knowledge you need to enjoy the best of each region. Why not own them all?

To the memory of my father, William H. Delavan,
who grew up in Seneca Falls and moved to Skaneateles,
where he raised his family. I remember our walks in the fall along
leaf-strewn paths, sled rides down our backyard to the lake,
and sailing, swimming, and burying him up to his neck in piles
of sand on our little beach. His love and great enthusiasm for the
Finger Lakes area live on to brighten my world.

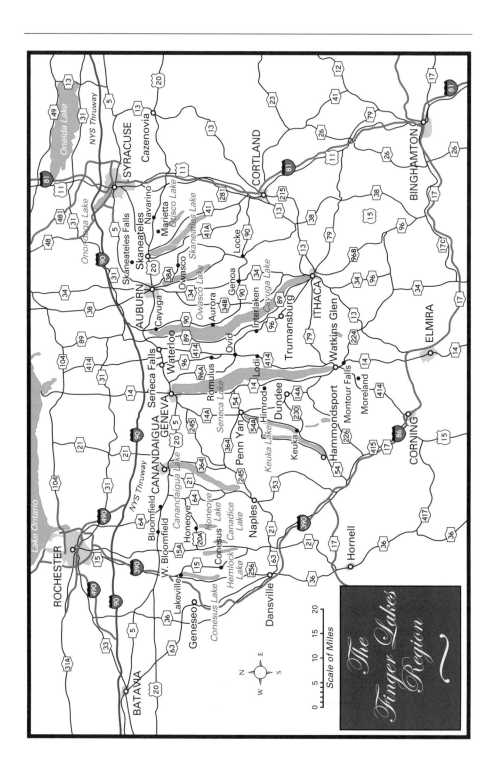

The Finger Lakes Region

Scale of Miles

0   5   10   15   20

Contents

CHAPTER ONE
Imprint of the Spirit
HISTORY
17

CHAPTER TWO
Highways, Byways, and Waterways
TRANSPORTATION
24

CHAPTER THREE
Picture Perfect
SKANEATELES, OWASCO, AND OTISCO LAKES
35

CHAPTER FOUR
Vineyards, Colleges, & Museums
CAYUGA LAKE
80

CHAPTER FIVE
Deep Waters and Gorges
SENECA LAKE
134

CHAPTER SIX
Split Personality
KEUKA LAKE
171

CHAPTER SEVEN
Scenic Vistas and Small Town Charm
CANANDAIGUA LAKE
Canadice, Conesus, Hemlock, and Honeoye Lakes
200

CHAPTER EIGHT
Gold Medal Grapes
WINERIES
239

CHAPTER NINE
Host Cities
SYRACUSE, CORTLAND, ELMIRA, CORNING, AND ROCHESTER
256

CHAPTER TEN
Finger Lakes Facts and Figures
INFORMATION
283

Acknowledgments

In the process of researching, writing, and updating this book, I continually meet people who go out of their way to help me.

First I must thank my publisher, Jean Rousseau, for believing this project would work and for giving me the time and resources to do it properly. I also want to thank Dale Evva Gelfand, Jennifer Thompson, and Philip Rich at Berkshire House, who were indispensable in providing thoughtful input, patience, kindness, and support throughout the many months it takes to write and update the book.

As I explored the Finger Lakes from lake to lake, town to town, filling up my car with brochures, flyers, menus, and other materials, I want to thank those who helped me along the way: Alexa Gifford, president Finger Lakes Tourism; Gene Pierce of Glenora Wine Cellars; and Barbara Adams of the Seneca Wine Trail.

I am grateful to Carol Kammen, Historian and Senior Lecturer, Department of History, Cornell University, for giving me input and resources to complete the history segments. I also must thank Idelle Dillon, executive director of the Yates County Genealogical and Historical Society, for providing a wealth of historical information on Yates County; Moe Koch, of Seneca County Tourism; and Valerie Knoblauch, director of the Ontario County Tourism Board, who gave me an insider's tour of her region as well as valuable insights into the history and happenings in the area.

I appreciate the help I received from many others, including Eva Mae Musgrave, owner of The Edge of Thyme and secretary of the Finger Lakes B&B Association; Pauline Weaver, Weaver-View Farms, Penn Yan, who gave me new insight into the Amish/Mennonite people in the region; and Peter Jemison, director of Ganondagan State Historic Site, Victor, who helped me better understand the history, contributions, and place of the Native American people in the Finger Lakes.

Also thanks to Carol Eaton of the Syracuse Chamber of Commerce, who opened my eyes to the many interesting things in Syracuse; Pat White of the Steuben County Conference and Visitors Bureau; Meg Vanek of Cayuga County Tourism; Sue Dove of the Skaneateles Chamber of Commerce; and Jim Dempsey of the Cortland County Visitors Bureau. Another big thanks goes to Diane Wenz, a Geneva native and friend, who gave up many hours to show me her "hometown," and Jeanne Pinckney for help on Auburn.

As I drew on the local knowledge and expertise of family and relatives, a hearty thank you goes to Nelson "Pete" and Edith Delavan for their help on Seneca Falls; to Byron and Caroline Delavan for sharing their thoughts on Canandaigua; to my brother Bill Delavan and his wife, Terry, for insider's information on Syracuse; and to my sister, Holly, who spent some exhausting hours driving with me and writing down special things as we went along. The hospitality and "camping rights" bestowed on me by my son Christopher and his wife, Cathy Pinckney, as well as my son Doug and his wife, Georgina, in Skaneateles made my job so much easier.

I loved having my five- and seven-year-old grandchildren, Maddy and Dougie Pinckney, along on several excursions to test out the kid-friendly sites and pose patiently for pictures. My heartfelt thanks goes to my husband, John, who encouraged me month after month to do what I had to do to get the job done and patiently endured many evenings of late dinners and general chaos and piles-of-paper overload. I could never have completed this project without his support.

Introduction

As you drive through the rolling hills and valleys of the Finger Lakes, a region of tidy villages like Skaneateles where summer brings Friday-night band concerts and acres of vineyards that blanket the hills, you are mindful that this region is one of the most beautiful on earth. The crystalline waters of more than 11 lakes nestle in the valleys, horses graze in meadows, corn and wheat fields create crazy-quilt patterns across the landscape, waterfalls plunge into deep gorges, and in many places it's open sky country with miles of vistas in every direction.

Summer brings fleets of sailboats tacking from shore to shore; endless fields of tasseled corn, alfalfa, and wheat; and flashes of goldenrod, china-blue chicory, purple horse mint, and buttercups that line the roads, turning dusty as warm weather wanes. Long warm-soft evenings sparkled by the fleeting beacons of lightning bugs are savored.

High school and college football games kick off the orange-red glow of fall, which quickly turns brisk as grapes and apples are harvested and dry bundles of corn stand like sentries in the countryside against deep lapis skies. Winter ushers in drifts of snow and ice-covered trees. Skiers take to the slopes; skaters clear the snow off lakes and ponds and glide onto the ice. Spring blossoms with sweet-scented blue, pink, and white lilacs and tulips, daffodils, and clouds of forsythia; and hundreds of waterfalls burst over outcroppings of rocks, diving to icy pools below, taking your breath away.

Then there are things man has created: picture-postcard villages with expansive lawns; white-clapboard houses with front porches furnished with wicker furniture and window boxes brimming over with petunias, ivy, and geraniums; respected colleges and universities; mansions like Rose Hill in Geneva and Sonnenberg in Canandaigua; the amazing Corning Glass Center; Watkins Glen International Racing Circuity; and a handful of old-fashioned ice-cream parlors, wooden-floored hardware stores, and drive-in movie theaters from the '50s stubbornly hanging in there.

One of the most exciting cities in the region, Ithaca, has a revitalized downtown area, including a pedestrian street lined with trendy cafés, boutiques, art galleries, and gift shops. Cornell University and Ithaca College play a strong role in creating a vibrant atmosphere of continual growth and cultural opportunities.

Other colleges and universities in the Fingers Lakes—Wells College, Hobart and William Smith Colleges, and Keuka College—also contribute greatly to their communities.

Many of the original settlers in the region were farmers, and today a strong farm population still exists. As you drive along country roads, you'll pass billboards promoting farm machinery, tractors and combines parked in fields near barns that easily dwarf nearby dwellings, huge blue Harvestore silos, and a patchwork of plowed fields defined by tightly woven stands of trees and hedgerows. Signs along the road warn of cows or tractors crossing and advertise home-produced products: stacked rows of split firewood, fruits and vegetables, cut flowers, and piles of corn. Always corn. And at the end of the day as the sun melts into the horizon, you are sure to see black-and-white Holsteins crowding the gates, their udders heavy with milk, as they wait for the farmers to take them into the barn and relieve them of their bounty.

The legacy of the past is evident in Moravia, where much 18th-century architecture has been preserved. Auburn is a repository of American history and historic homes. If Native American history is your passion, check out the Ganondagan State Historic Site in Victor, a 17th-century Native American settlement, and Sainte Marie among the Iroquois, a living-history museum in Liverpool.

Many of the pleasant little towns like Homer, Avon, and Dresden are nice places to live but don't necessarily attract passing travelers, nor do they count on transient tourists for their livelihood. Anchored by farmland on either end of the main route that runs through them, these little towns might have a shop or two worth browsing, a barn full of antiques piled helter-skelter, or perhaps a place to eat or a nice B&B. Some shops even post their hours as "open by chance or appointment."

For some, this lack of commercial hype is enough of a reason to come: the promise of a few days escape from the corporate treadmill. In the Finger Lakes the pace is kinder.

This does not mean that there isn't plenty to see and do. There are vineyards to visit, cruises to take, historical sites and attractions such as the Erie Canal Museum and the Women's Rights Park to explore. There are great restaurants, festivals and fairs, beautiful villages and cities, and places to stay ranging from wonderful B&Bs to large hotels and boutique spa resorts. And always, people that smile and greet you warmly even if you are just stopping for a look.

Growing up in Skaneateles and living in this village for more than half of my life, I can trace family roots back six generations. My father was born in Seneca Falls, and relatives live throughout the region from Rochester to Syracuse. As a travel writer I am fortunate to be able to visit places all around the world, from Africa to China to Brazil to Europe. Perhaps because of these experiences, I have been left with a deep appreciation for the Finger Lakes, a part of our world that combines some of the best characteristics of those places that I have enjoyed the most.

Whether traveling through southwestern Ireland with its rolling fields, the Lake District in England, the tented camps and wide-open bush in Botswana, the lochs of Scotland, or the vineyards banked along the Rhine in Germany, I am continually reminded that back home, too, is a place where the hills soothe, lakes dazzle, and the people are warm and comfortable with themselves and where they live. It's a good feeling to know that in our own country, there is such a place as the Finger Lakes.

—*Katharine Dyson*

THE WAY THIS BOOK WORKS

This book covers the region of the Finger Lakes around or within easy driving distance of the eleven lakes, an area that falls approximately inside the perimeter of a rough circle drawn along the New York State Thruway (Interstate 90), Route 81, Route 17, and Route 390 and stretching from Syracuse to Rochester and south to Ithaca. It encompasses 11 lakes (plus a few smaller lakes) in an area of about 90 miles by 60 miles.

A general history of the region opens the book, followed by an overview of the best routes into the area, by land, air, and water. The lake areas are described in five chapters: *Skaneateles, Otisco, and Owasco; Cayuga; Seneca; Keuka*; and *Canandaigua,* which includes Canadice, Conesus, Hemlock, and Honeoye. Within each of these chapters, you will find information about everything from history, lodging, restaurants, recreation, shopping, and cultural attractions. A separate *Wineries* chapter highlights a selection of the area's wineries and vineyards. Features of major cities—Syracuse, Rochester, Corning, Elmira, and Cortland—are described in the *Host Cities* chapter. Ithaca, also an important city, is described in the *Cayuga Lake* chapter. The final chapter, *Information,* gives Finger Lakes facts and figures.

In the Index you will find lodging and dining facilities organized by lake area and listed according to price and type. Every effort has been made to place towns and villages in the chapter that covers the lake (or lakes) nearest to the place. Still, there are coin tosses on some spots that straddle an area almost dead center between two lakes. In this case the index can be your best friend.

Although all information was as accurate as possible as of publication date, we suggest that you call ahead before visiting; circumstances could have changed in the meantime. Please note that many places are open only during the warmer months, usually from mid-April through mid-October.

PRICES

Since the Finger Lakes region is most active with visitors during the warm weather months, you can expect prices to be higher at that time, especially for lodging. In addition to higher prices during the popular months, you may also find that some places require a two- or three-night minimum. Cabin or house rentals may require one week's minimum. Off-season is a different story.

A general price range is given instead of exact prices. Lodging prices are per room, double occupancy, and may or may not include breakfast or other meals. Restaurant prices indicate the cost of a meal for one person including an appetizer or salad, main course, and dessert. Bar beverages are extra.

Lodging price codes:
$: Up to $75 per couple

$$: $76–$150 per couple
$$$: $151–$250 per couple
$$$$: More than $250 per couple

Dining price codes:
$: Up to $10
$$: $11–$25
$$$: $26–$40
$$$$: More than $40
Prices are estimated per person for appetizer and dinner entrée without tax, tip, or alcoholic beverages.

We welcome your comments on the content of the book and any personal experiences you care to share. A major effort was made to include all key historic sites and attractions as well as a wide variety of lodgings, restaurants, retail establishments, and other places of interest. The purpose of this book was not to include every store, every bed-and-breakfast, every restaurant, every shop and so forth, but to give you a guide to the places you should know about along with first-person descriptions and enough information to help you make educated choices. However, if places have been left out that should be considered for the next edition, we would be happy to hear about them.

CHAPTER ONE
Imprint of the Spirit
HISTORY

Cayuga Museum, Auburn

According to legend, when the Great Spirit laid his hands on this land to bless it, the imprints left by his fingers filled with water to form lakes. Hence the "Finger Lakes." You can believe this or the geologists' explanation: More than 550 million years ago, during the Pleistocene Ice Age, glaciers crept through the area from north to south, carving deep slices in the land. The ice pushed the land and rocks southward. Gradually the ice melted, and the glaciers withdrew, leaving shale-bedded valleys of water so deep in some places that their bottoms are below sea level.

As the glaciers receded, the pile up of rocks in the southern ends of lakes like Skaneateles and Cayuga produced fiordlike terrains with steep sides and deep waters, creating perfect microclimates for growing grapes. Spectacular waterfalls like the 215-foot-high Taughannock Falls off the southwestern shores of Cayuga Lake and the deep gorges of Watkins Glen at the southern end of Seneca Lake also resulted from the glaciers retreating.

The glacial landscaping—the lakes, the moraines (debris fields left by glaciers), and the small "kettle lakes" (bowl-like depressions)—created a uniquely stunning landscape and fertile agricultural lands.

The clarity of the water of the Finger Lakes has gained a worldwide reputation. So clean is the water in Skaneateles Lake, some homes and camps along the shores still draw their drinking water directly from the lake. Keuka Lake, too, is known for its exceptionally pure water: Whether you're at the end of a long pier or in a boat on the lake, the water is so clear, it's like looking through glass straight down to the bottom.

FIRST THERE WERE THE NATIVE AMERICANS

One summer day when I was 12 years old, I dove off our dock into Skaneateles Lake. That day the crystal clear water was calm. Swimming out a ways, I looked down. There, half-buried in the sand and shale, I saw a few pieces of pottery. Having learned about the Onondagas who had lived on these shores, I let my imagination freefall: Had I discovered a piece of history? Later, in a canoe, I tried to find that spot again. I never did. To this day I remember that moment and the excitement of my discovery.

Even a brief run through the area will leave no doubt as to the Native-American heritage of the Finger Lakes. Names of lakes, villages, streets, restaurants, inns, and even today's families are derived from tribal language: Taughannock, Ithaca, Montezuma, Genesee, Cayuga . . . the list goes on.

Before the American Revolution in 1775, some 20,000 members of the Haudenosaunee (the Six Nations of the Iroquois Confederacy) lived in communities throughout the Finger Lakes region. In the east were the Mohawk, the warriors and keepers of the eastern door of the Long House; the Onondaga were the fire keepers and the story-belt "secretaries" of the tribes. The Seneca, hunters and keepers of the western door and the largest of the nations, were the most fiercely protective of their territory. There were also the Oneida and Cayuga, the farmers, and later the Tuscarora.

Before the first white settlers found their way along the trails and passageways created by the Native Americans, life in the Finger Lakes was remarkably democratic. The "Great Law" of the Native Americans gave their people free speech, religious liberty, and the right to bear arms to protect the security of each person. The women were influential in society, and the war chiefs were subordinate to the highly respected elected civil chiefs such as Joseph Brant, a Mohawk, and Cornplanter, a Seneca.

In 1794 the Pickering Treaty, an agreement between the United States and the Haudenosaunee (Iroquois Confederacy), marked the beginning of the Native Americans' retreat from their lands. The treaty confirmed the Phelps and Gorham Purchase of 2,600,000 acres east of Genesee for $5,000 plus an annuity of $500 in perpetuity. This treaty was very important to the Haudenosaunee because it established the sovereignty of their nations; from that point on they

---

Mary Jemison

When Mary Jemison's family was attacked by a Shawnee war party in 1758, everyone was killed except two brothers, who escaped and headed south, and 15-year-old Mary, who was captured, adopted as a Seneca sister, and treated as one of their own. As an adult, Mary married a Delaware chieftain, She-nin-jee, and lived with him and his people in Pennsylvania near Gettysburg.

She is said to have loved She-nin-jee and bore him a son known as Buffalo Tom. After her husband was killed while he was hunting, she walked 300 miles north with two of her Seneca brothers to the area now known as Letchworth Park, where she rejoined her adoptive family. Eventually she married an older man, a Seneca named Hiakatoo, who was known to be a fierce but wise warrior. Together they had many children, and in her later days, Mary spoke affectionately of him.

Her final home was along the Genesee River, which runs through Letchworth Park in the western part of New York State, and a statue in the park of Mary Jemison pays tribute to this remarkable woman. One of Mary's several times great-grandsons, Peter Jemison, is director of the Ganondagan Historic Site in Victor.

---

would be considered independent from the United States. Each year on November 11, the signing of the Pickering Treaty is celebrated at the county courthouse, with Peter Jemison and other Native Americans in attendance.

At the Wood Memorial Library in Seneca Falls, you'll find a piece of faded old parchment, the Native Americans' copy of the original Pickering Treaty, signed by Red Jacket, Little Beard, and Cornplanter. A boulder on the courthouse grounds in Canaan marks the place where the signing took place.

The 18th and 19th centuries were turbulent times. Settlers against the natives, natives against settlers. Families on both sides—including women and children—were killed or taken prisoner. Some were tortured. Others, like Mary Jemison, were assimilated into the tribal community.

During the Revolutionary War, General George Washington, believing that the Native Americans were siding with the British, ordered generals Clinton and Sullivan to wipe out Indian activity in the region around Seneca and Cayuga Lakes. In carrying out their assignment, more than 5,000 men with 4,000 horses torched villages and cornfields, cut down trees, and exiled the people. Not a single Indian settlement or field of corn was spared. Their wave of destruction broke the backbone of the Iroquois community.

A plaque on the west side of Cayuga Lake near Burroughs Point reads: site of an indian village destroyed during the sullivan campaign 1779. As reminders of lives past, arrowheads and bits of pottery occasionally turn up in the fields and along lakeshores.

SETTLERS MOVE IN

In the late 1700s people like Job Smith and John Cuddeback drifted into the area, settled down, and became the first settlers in such communities as

Seneca Falls and Skaneateles. Most of these early settlers were farmers who cleared the land and planted crops on the fertile, well-drained soil. Some raised cattle and established dairy farms.

Dwellings then were simple structures built around a central fireplace, perhaps with a beehive oven in the back and sleeping quarters in a loft. Water was hand pumped from wells, and cooking was done in the fireplace using wood for fuel. Pine knots and later whale oil, were burned for light.

In 1781 transportation routes followed trails created by the Native Americans. After the Revolutionary War, when the United States government granted land to officers and soldiers who had fought for independence, the population in the region expanded rapidly.

For a while, especially after the opening of the Erie Canal, which allowed goods to travel easily from the region to New York City's markets, farmers thrived. Businesses developed along the waterways: mills, retail establishments, banking institutions. The most imposing buildings of the period were the grist- and sawmills along rivers and outlets such as on Keuka Lake at Penn Yan.

Most people moved their families into the region during the winter, when the rough roads were frozen hard and smoothed by snow, making it easier going for wagons carrying household goods. With the construction of the Seneca Turnpike in 1803 from Utica to Canandaigua, traffic increased and stagecoaches rumbled across the miles on regular routes. A long bridge built across the northern end of Cayuga Lake meant that travelers on the Great Western Turnpike no longer had to go the long way around Montezuma Swamp. At either end of the bridge, taverns and general stores blossomed, creating mini boomtowns. Today the bridge is gone, and the area known as Bridgeport consists merely of a firehouse, an old cemetery, and a park.

Following the Great Depression of 1929, many farms were abandoned. Some areas, such as the land southwest of Skaneateles Lake, were purchased in the 1930s and replanted by the Civilian Conservation Corps. Today these state forests are used for hiking, biking, and other recreational purposes and are also preserved as open land for wildlife, trees, and unusual plant species.

In the early 1900s, when most buildings were constructed of wood and firefighting equipment and transportation of water were primitive, many villages, including Seneca Falls, Skaneateles, and Geneva, were scarred by major fires. New buildings were built of brick and constructed with firewalls (very visible in the business block along Genesee Street in Skaneateles).

THE ERIE CANAL

One of the most important manmade features of the region was the Erie Canal, at first derided as a major folly. Stretching from Albany to Buffalo, "the Big Ditch," as it was not so affectionately called, took an army of laborers eight years of blasting rock, digging earth, felling trees, and building locks to complete. The first ceremonial shovel of dirt was dug in Syracuse near the spot where the Erie Canal Museum now stands. When the canal opened in 1825, sending a rush of water flowing from Lake Erie and the Hudson River, cannons spaced 5 miles apart along the 363-mile canal heralded this grand event.

It was a brilliant idea, sparked by a man from his jail cell who dreamed of a waterway that would link Lake Erie to the Hudson River. As the story goes, Jesse Hawley, once a man of substance in the freight-forwarding business, found himself languishing in debtor's prison in Canandaigua after his failed attempts to transport grain from farms in the area to the mills in Seneca Falls and finally to New York City. It was too expensive and too treacherous. During his 20 months behind bars, he wrote a series of 14 essays, including one that proposed a better way to move his products: a manmade waterway from Lake Erie to the Mohawk River. He made sketches and wrote several articles detailing how it could be done. Eventually these materials landed in the hands of New York City mayor De Witt Clinton.

Clinton became obsessed with the idea, and in 1817 ground was broken for the new canal. Lacking proper engineering talent, the project became a huge on-the-job-training exercise. Special challenges included constructing locks, developing waterproof cement, blasting through rock, constructing aqueducts across the Genesee River in downtown Rochester and the valley in Pittsford, and solving the problem of keeping the water from drying up in areas prone to drought (feeders were built from lakes and streams).

As one obstacle after another was overcome, American workers developed expertise in engineering. The need for professional schools was met with the founding of Rensselaer Polytechnic Institute in Troy, the Civil Engineering Department of Schenectady's Union College, and the Rochester Institute of Technology.

*Memorial Day Museum,
Waterloo.*

When the canal was completed, goods could be moved from Buffalo to New York City in just ten days instead of six weeks, and a ton of freight cost $10 instead of $100. Products moving easily from western to eastern markets meant that immigrants started coming into the area, and commerce thrived. In 1835 the canal was widened and deepened, and locks were doubled to handle the gridlock from the increasing traffic. Continual improvements over the next few years included rerouting a portion of the canal to incorporate existing rivers and lakes and building a "spur"—the Cayuga-Seneca Canal, which connected the two lakes. In 1918 the Erie Canal became the Barge Canal.

The canal brought new prosperity to the state and especially to the villages along the waterways, including Syracuse, Port Byron, and Seneca Falls. Seven years after it opened, the canal was the main method of travel from west to east. Travelers could go from Buffalo to Albany, then connect with the Post Road, and continue to New York.

Portions of the canal are still open today, and its use as a recreational waterway has replaced its importance as a commercial conduit.

WOMEN'S RIGHTS

Women's rights first appeared on the nation's agenda at a convention held in 1848 at the Wesleyan Chapel in Seneca Falls. Led by the determined duo of Elizabeth Cady Stanton and Lucretia Mott, the convention dealt with such issues as temperance, abolition, suffrage, and dress reform. The Declaration of Sentiments and Resolutions was read to 300 people, including 40 men. In all, 100 people signed the declaration.

Amelia Jenks Bloomer, who was known for appearing in the village in her bloomers, raised many eyebrows. But she persisted in setting a fashion trend of sorts (the Diana Vreeland of her time, perhaps).

Seventy-five years later, in 1923, when the town celebrated the anniversary of the first Women's Rights Convention, my Aunt Lee (Elizabeth) Delavan was one of seven young girls who took part in an outdoor pageant.

A small bronze marker on a building on Fall Street in Seneca Falls marks the location where the women's rights movement all started.

MENNONITES AND AMISH

The central Finger Lakes region is home to more than 300 Amish and Mennonite families who originally came from Pennsylvania. Here, around Seneca, Keuka, and Cayuga Lakes, they continue to practice their strong religious beliefs. Their horse-drawn black buggies occasionally seen on the roads are a reminder that there are still those who by choice live their lives with no electricity, phones, television, or computers. Such things, along with cars, planes, and trains, are seen as threats to breaking up the family unit, corrupting the values they hold dear.

What's In a Name?

Many places in the Finger Lakes have undergone several name changes, sometimes for obvious reasons. For example, Phelps was once Vienna, Hemlock was Slab City, Perry was both Shacksburg and Ninevah, Honeoye was Pitt's Flats, Vincent was Muttonville, and Bristol Springs was first called Cold Springs. Geneva was once Kanadesaga, which translated as "dog town," and Naples was first called Watkinstown.

This does not mean they don't live well. On the contrary; because of their hard work, close-knit families, and sense of community, the Amish and Mennonites most often flourish. They own their own land, are very self-sufficient, take great joy in their children, and make strong contributions to their communities.

Most earn their living through farming and building; some have shops, work in restaurants, and make and sell quilts and other craft items. Most work very hard, live simply, educate their children in one-room schoolhouses until they reach their late teens, and bring up their boys and girls to have a strong work ethic.

FAMOUS FINGER LAKES RESIDENTS

This region has had its share of important and wealthy personalities. Francis Bellamy, who wrote the "Pledge of Allegiance," lived in Mt. Morris; Clara Barton established the first American chapter of the Red Cross in Dansville; Susan B. Anthony was a champion of women's rights; Ezra Cornell founded the college of the same name in Ithaca. Residents of Auburn have included abolitionist Harriet Tubman; Theodore Willard Case, founder of 20th Century Fox; and William H. Seward, governor of New York and the man responsible for the purchase of Alaska. Mark Twain lived in Elmira, and Amelia Bloomer of bloomers fame was born in Homer.

CHAPTER TWO
Highways, Byways, and Waterways
TRANSPORTATION

Farms near Cortland

With the Finger Lakes region just a one-day drive (about 300 miles) from about 50 percent of the population of the United States, many visitors arrive by car. Some, however, come by rail via **Amtrak**, whose route across New York State roughly follows the east-west route of the New York Thruway from Albany to Buffalo. Finger Lakes area stations are in Syracuse and Rochester. And airports in Syracuse, Rochester, Ithaca, Elmira/Corning, and Binghamton link the region to the rest of the world. Finally, the Greyhound/Trailways bus system offers point-to-point service throughout all the major cities (800-231-2222).

Approximate distance to the center of the Finger Lakes Region:

From Albany: 214 miles
Buffalo: 138 miles

New York City: 295 miles
Rochester: 55 miles
Washington D.C.: 337 miles

Approximate miles between key cities:

Corning–Albany: 206
Corning–Boston: 373
Corning–New York City: 267
Corning–Rochester: 103
Corning–Syracuse: 99

Syracuse–Albany: 136
Syracuse–Boston: 299
Syracuse–Buffalo: 147
Syracuse–Corning: 90
Syracuse–New York City: 253
Syracuse–Philadelphia: 255
Syracuse–Toronto: 248
Syracuse–Washington, D.C.: 350

Rochester–Albany: 232
Rochester–Buffalo: 78
Rochester–New York City: 360
Rochester–Philadelphia: 351
Rochester–Syracuse: 91

Penn Yan–Buffalo: 100
Penn Yan–New York: 250
Penn Yan–Philadelphia: 250
Penn Yan–Syracuse: 75
Penn Yan–Toronto: 150

BY CAR

Many roads follow old Native American trails and go along waterways. For example, Route 5, which runs east-west through the region and becomes Route 5 & 20 much of the way, was once a Native American footpath only about 18 inches wide and blazed by hatchet notches on trees. The Great Central Trail led to the longhouse on the shores of Onondaga Lake. A cavalcade of colonial settlers, French priests, traders, explorers, adventurers, and pioneers widened the trail as their wagons rumbled along the routes.

FINGER LAKES ACCESS

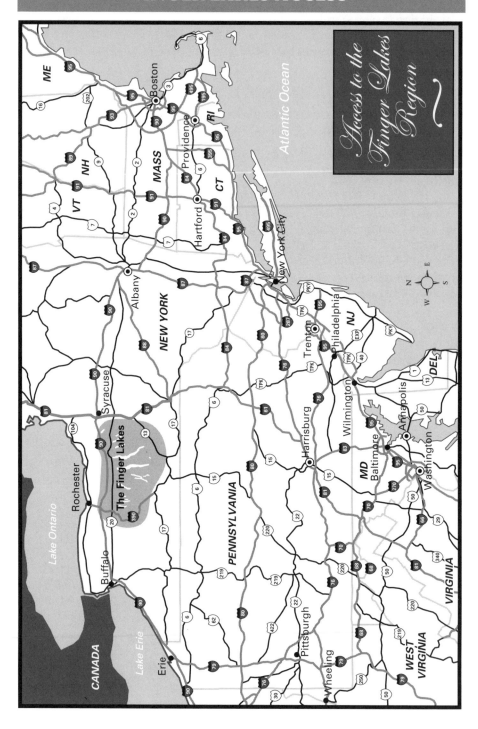

East-West Routes

Major east-west routes include scenic Route 17, the New York Thruway (Interstate 90), and Route 20 and Route 5 & 20. From New York City, it's about a four- or five-hour drive to the easternmost part of the Finger Lakes following these routes.

Interstate 86: From Jamestown to Orange County just north of New York City, this divided highway offers rest areas and picnic areas along the way. Although I-86 seems to be continually under repair at various points, for the most part the surface is good, and the scenery along the rivers and through the Catskills and southern tier of the state to Erie, Pennsylvania, makes it well worth going this way unless you are into high-speed driving (speed limit is 55 mph). Gas stations and other services are well marked on the route.

The New York Thruway (Interstate 90): This limited-access divided toll road runs along the top third of the state from Albany to Buffalo and south to Erie. It's rather boring but efficient, with a speed limit of 65 mph in many sections. Service areas are at regular intervals about every 15 to 20 miles.

Route 20: The old route used extensively before the Thruway was built links Albany to Buffalo. It runs right through the center of many of the most beautiful towns in the Finger Lakes. If you have the time—village speed limits and stoplights will slow your pace—but want to capture the flavor of the region, I recommend that you take this route. Major towns along Route 20 include Skaneateles, Auburn, Seneca Falls, Waterloo, Geneva, and Canandaigua. Feeders into the lake roads and vineyards run off this route.

North-South Routes

Major north-south routes are Interstate 81 bordering the eastern lakes region and Route 390 going from I-86 to Rochester.

Interstate 81: Running along the easternmost border of the region, this divided highway has fair to good roads and well-marked exits. Two lanes run each way along most of the route, and some portions allow 65 mph driving. Picnic areas and services are available along the highway.

The New York State Canalway Trail: More than 230 miles of multiuse recreational trails crisscross the Finger Lakes region. Most are adjacent to the state's canals or run along remnants of original canals no longer in use. The typically flat terrain provides excellent biking for all levels of skills. Those who want to fill in the gaps of the entire 524-mile canal system can use New York State Bike Routes 5 and 9, which run north and west along current state roads.

Route 15: Runs from Washington, D.C., through central Pennsylvania, Harrisburg, and through the heart of Amish country to Corning.

Interstate 390: Skirts the western part of the region from I-86 to Rochester.

BY WATER

Erie Canal

Running east-west from Albany to Buffalo, the New York State canal system contains 524 miles of canal and waterways connecting Albany, Utica, Syracuse,

---

Chartering a Canal Boat

Erie Canal Cruise Lines (800-962-1771; www.canalcruises.com; PO Box 285, Cape Vincent, NY 13618) Half-week and full-week charters on the Erie Canal are available from $1,500. Up to six adults are included in the fare, along with linens, fuel, housewares, lock fees, itinerary, and applicable tax. The 40-foot custom-built canal cruiser features two private suites with a vanity, toilet, and access to the shower, a dinette that converts to a full-size berth, and a fully equipped galley. The boat is air-conditioned and there is a television/VCR and CD/cassette player. Social and lounging areas are located aft and on the top deck. The knotty-pine interior of the boat has a homey feeling with curtains on the windows.

You can begin your trip in Seneca Falls on the Cayuga-Seneca Canal, where you will experience the double lock, lifting you 50 feet in back-to-back lock chambers. You'll join the Erie Canal just beyond the Montezuma National Wildlife Refuge. A 200-mile bike and hiking path traces the original Erie Canal towpath. You can also start in Fairport, southeast of Rochester, and cruise west toward Pittsford and Lockport.

Mid-Lakes Navigation Company (315-685-8500, 800-545-4318; www.mid-lakesnav. com; PO Box 61 • Skaneateles, NY 13152) Mid-Lakes offers two- and three-night canal cruises with accommodations at ports along the way. For example, the 40-passenger *Emita II*, which sails from Buffalo to Syracuse and Albany, has a bar, a library, an open front deck, and an upper deck.

For those who prefer to captain their own boat, Mid-Lakes charters Lockmaster canal boats ranging from 33 feet to 44 feet long and 10 feet wide, with a top speed of about 6 mph. The boats are fairly simple to operate, and you can navigate the locks in about 20 minutes. Each comes with a fully equipped galley, VHF radio, ice cooler, gas range, refrigerator, binoculars, linens, cleaning supplies, and two bicycles. Some have two cabins. Weekly charters are available. Starting at Cold Springs harbor near Syracuse, you can choose to cruise three different canals. One of the most popular is the Cayuga-Seneca Canal; tie up in Seneca Falls for the night.

Low Bridge Charters (585-352-9825, 866-352-9825; www.lowbridgecharters .com; PO Box 245, Spencerport, NY 14559) European-style bareboat charters.

Rochester, and Buffalo. Systems include the Erie Canal, the Champlain and Oswego systems, and the Cayuga-Seneca Canal built in 1821 to connect the two lakes. Great destinations for day trips, weekend excursions or to serve as connecting points to other waterways, the New York State canals are usually navigable April through November. The system has 60 locks, making it possible for canal boats and pleasure craft to go across the entire state by water. Boat launches are located at points along the way. Two-day permits as well as seasonal permits are available ($5 to $100). For more information, contact the NYS Canal System: 518-471-5011; 800-4CANAL4; www.canals.state.ny.us.

Boating

In line with the Federal Boating Act, every boat using auxiliary power must be registered and numbered. Licenses are issued for a three-year period.

Those bringing in boats from other states do not need to get a license for 90 days, provided these boats are numbered according to federal law. If you don't have a proper registration, you need to get one. Contact the Department of Motor Vehicles, Division of Motor Vehicle Regulation, Empire State Plaza, Albany, NY 12228. A free pocket guide and map brochure on the Canal and Lakes System is available by calling 800-KIT-4-FUN.

Speed limit is 5 mph within 100 feet of shore, except on Canandaigua and Keuka Lakes, where the limit is extended to 200 feet from shore.

ARRIVING AT HOST CITIES

CORNING

By Air

Elmira/Corning Regional Airport (607-739-5621; Exit 51 on Route 17, Corning, NY 14830) Scheduled air services with **USAirways** and **Northwest Airlines.** Corning is also about equal distance from the Syracuse and Rochester airports.

By Train

Corning is about equal distance from the Rochester and Syracuse **Amtrak** stations. The distance is approximately 75 miles in either direction.

Rental Cars

Avis, Hertz, and **National** car rentals are available at the airport.

ELMIRA

By Air

Elmira/Corning Regional Airport (607-739-5621; Exit 51 on Rte. 17, Corning, NY 14830) Scheduled air services with **USAirways** and **Northwest Airlines.** Elmira is also about equal distance from the Syracuse and Rochester airports.

By Train

Elmira is about equal distance from the Rochester and Syracuse **Amtrak** stations. The distance is approximately 75 miles in either direction.

Rental Cars

Avis, Hertz, and **National** car rentals are available at the airport.

ITHACA

By Air

Tompkins County Airport (607-257-0456; www.tompkins-co.org/airport or www.co.tompkins.ny.us/airport/airport.hmtl; 72 Brown Rd., Ithaca, NY 14850) The airport is served by **USAirways,** with jet service to Pittsburgh and 45 other daily flights to Philadelphia, New York City, and Boston. The airport has a café, conference room, computer/fax/modem jacks, and a limousine shuttle.

By Train

Ithaca is about 47 miles from the Syracuse **Amtrak** station.

Rental Cars

Avis and **Hertz** rental cars are available at the airport terminal.

ROCHESTER

By Air

Greater Rochester International Airport (585-464-6000; www.rocairport.com; 1200 Brooks Ave., Rochester, NY 14624) On the south side of Rochester, 15 minutes from downtown, the airport has one main terminal with two concourses.

More than 220 flights a day fly to 22 cities nationwide. On-site services include shuttles to the hotels, car rentals, taxi and bus service, sheltered parking garage, business center, meeting rooms, restaurants, and gift shops.

Rochester Shuttle Express (888-663-3770, 585-663-3760) Round-the-clock, door-to-door service between your home and the Greater Rochester International Airport. The shuttle also offers mini tours of Rochester and trips to Niagara Falls, Buffalo, and Toronto.

By Train

Amtrak Station (800-USA-RAIL, 800-872-7245; www.amtrak.com; 320 Central Ave., Rochester, NY 14605) Services: ticket sales, Quik-Trak Ticketing Machines, checked baggage. The trip to New York City takes about 6.5 hours; the run from Rochester to Syracuse is 1 hour 16 minutes.

By Bus

The Regional Transit Service (RTS) (585-288-1700, 888-288-3777; 187 Midtown Plaza, Rochester, NY 14604) A quick, convenient way to get around. New York State **Trailways** and **Greyhound** bus terminals here.

By Car

A color-coded sign system aids drivers in navigating downtown Rochester: Convention Center=red, Eastman Theatre=blue, Shopping=orange, Strong Museum=brown, War Memorial=green. Auto rentals —**Alamo, Americar, Avis, Budget, Enterprise, Hertz, National,** and **Thrifty**—are at the Greater Rochester International Airport and other outlets.

By Taxi

Taxis can be found at the airport, bus station, train terminal, hotels, and on call.

SYRACUSE

By Air

Syracuse Hancock International Airport (315-454-4330; www.syrairport.org; Rte. 81, Exit 27; mailing address: 1000 Colonel Eileen Collins Blvd., Syracuse, NY 13212) More than 270 passenger flights arrive and depart daily from the airport, which is serviced by six major airlines and three commuter lines.

By Train

William F. Walsh Regional Transportation Center (General information: 315-478-1936; 131 P&C Pkwy., Syracuse NY 13208) Services include ticket sales, checked baggage. Amtrak (800-USA-RAIL; 800-872-7245; www.amtrak.com) provides rail-passenger transportation for an East Syracuse terminal with eight daily departures. The trip to New York City takes about 5.25 hours.

Ontrack (315-424-1212) Originally started to get Syracuse University students around, Ontrack has expanded its services to include an extensive network of routes through historic areas, fall foliage tours, even cowboy holdups and a Santa's train.

By Bus

Greyhound/Trailways (800-231-2222; 131 P&C Pkwy., Syracuse, NY 13208) Located in the same transportation terminal as Amtrak.
Centro Bus/Central New York Transportation Authority (315-442-3333) provides public transportation in the city and to the suburbs. **Onondaga Coach, Greyhound, Syracuse & Oswego,** and **Trailways** also have intercity passenger service.

By Taxi

Taxis can be found at the airport, bus station, train terminal, hotels, and on call.

By Water

The Port of Oswego on the southeast shore of Lake Ontario is 34 miles northwest of Syracuse. The New York State canal system encompasses 524 miles and runs east-west across the state, linking the Niagara River with the Hudson River. The Onondaga Lake Barge Canal Terminal is just north of Syracuse.

By Car

Alamo, Americar, Avis, Budget, Enterprise, Hertz, National, and **Thrifty** auto rentals are available at Hancock International Airport and other outlets.

SCENIC ROUTES

The entire Finger Lakes region is laced with roads and highways that provide some of the most scenic views in the country. Here are some suggestions.

Keuka Lake

Shoreline Route: Route 54A, which runs 22.6 miles from Penn Yan to Hammondsport along the westernmost shore, clings closely to the shoreline, winding and twisting around coves and rock outcroppings. For this reason it is considered one of the most scenic drives in the world. Several restaurants are along the route with open decks close to the water.

Middle Road Overlook: Middle Road, along with Routes 74/76, runs through the hillside vineyards, revealing stunning views of the lake. I suggest you do a loop, going one way on Route 54A and returning on Route 76, Middle Road and 74. Going south from the northern end, Route 54A splits at Branchport. Go right on Italy Road, then left on 74/76. Follow the signs to Dr. Frank's Vinifera Wine Cellars, Heron Hill Winery, and Bully Hill, which will jog you over to Middle Road and south to Hammondsport. Return along 54A, where you will get so close to moored boats, you'll be able to read their names.

East Bluff Drive and Skyline Drive: These roads run between the Y branches of Keuka Lake. At the crook of the Y are spectacular views of the lake in all directions.

New York to Finger Lakes Interstate 86: This has been designated as one of the most scenic highways in the country. The highway winds through the Catskills and along many gushing, rugged streams.

Canandaigua Lake

Lake Loop: Starting from Routes 5 & 20 in Canandaigua, take Route 364 south. After about 13 miles, go straight on West Avenue, then take a quick left

*Cows grace the Finger Lakes'
countryside.*

onto Coward Cross Road, then a quick right at the stop sign on Route 245 south
into Naples. At the end of Route 245, take a right onto Route 21, and go north,
back into Canandaigua. Stop in Naples to visit the Arbor Hill Grapery and Widmer's Wine Cellars.

Cayuga Lake

Lake Loop: Take Route 90S off Route 20, drive down the eastern shore of
Cayuga Lake, stop at Aurora for a bite to eat or shopping, continue on to Ithaca
at the southern end of the lake, and then return along the western shore past
Taughannock Falls to reconnect with Route 20. This loop around the lake can
take a couple of hours or a whole day if you stop for lunch and check out the
vineyards and attractions along the way.

New Scenic Byway: The whole lake is circled by this byway, starting with
Route 20 to Route 34B, then on Route 34 into Ithaca. It continues on Route 89 to
Route 5 & 20 and the Montezuma Wildlife Refuge.

Conesus Lake

Lake Loop: From Lakeville, go west on Route 20A, then left onto Route 256
(West Lake Road) Follow this to south end of the lake, and then turn left onto
Slyker Hill Road and left again onto East Lake Road. Go north back to Lakeville.
Round-trip is about 19 miles.

Skaneateles Lake

Lake Loop: From Route 20 in the village, take Route 41A south along West
Lake Road. You'll pass Mandana and New Hope on your way to the south end
of the lake. At New Hope watch for Glen Haven Road, and turn left. Turn right
at the T junction, and continue on Glen Haven Road. Turn left at the stop sign,
Route 41A, and go north along the east side of the lake back to the village. You'll
enjoy many lake views and pass several farms. Fun stops along the way include
New Hope Mill in New Hope (closed now, but stop to photograph a small covered bridge and working water wheel) and the old Glen Haven Hotel (watch for
sign). Round-trip is about 40 miles.

CHAPTER THREE
Picture Perfect
SKANEATELES, OWASCO, AND OTISCO LAKES

The business area and St. James Episcopal Church are located on the shores of Skaneateles Lake.

Close to Syracuse and the most eastern of the Finger Lakes, Skaneateles, Otisco, and Owasco are all quite different in style and spirit.

SKANEATELES LAKE AND SKANEATELES

At 16 miles long and just 1 to 2 miles wide, Skaneateles Lake lives up to the meaning of its name, "long lake." Tucked in and around the lake are the small villages of Skaneateles at the north end, Mandana and New Hope on the west side, Glen Haven at the south end, and Spafford and Borodino on the east side. Because of its depth—up to 350 feet—the color of the water can change dramatically from deep cobalt to brilliant turquoise. Set against this

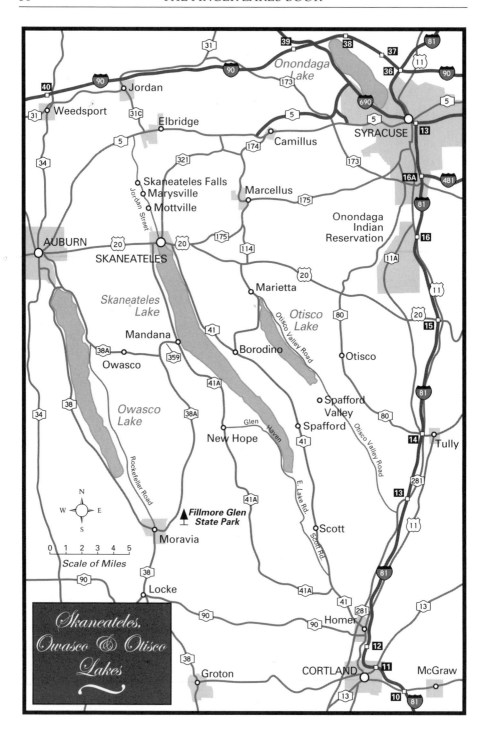

stunning backdrop, the white sails of boats gliding noiselessly through the water are a magnificent sight.

Nestled around the northern end of the lake, Skaneateles —18 miles southwest of Syracuse—reigns as the prima donna of Finger Lakes villages. Time and wise local policies have dealt kindly with it over the years. This pampered and prosperous picture-perfect place—about 2,800 in the village, 4,800 in the town—attracts doctors, contractors, academics, manufacturers, lawyers, sales representatives, and other affluent types who vie for choice and pricey homes that fan out around the northern tip of the lake, up the hills behind Genesee Street and along the shoreline. Summer brings a constant flow of tourists into town.

Many white and a few multihued Victorian and colonial houses—some with cupolas, others with wide porches furnished with wicker rockers—line tree-shaded streets. (It is interesting to note that early records indicate the first houses in town were painted red.) Homes are impeccably maintained, and many are of historic interest, including a handful that were stops on the Underground Railroad, safe havens for runaway slaves.

A few years ago Skaneateles hit the national news for its stress-free-environment program. Those parked along Genesee Street (the main drag) had no reason to panic if their meter time had run out: The meter police would simply drop in an extra coin for them so that they would have more time to shop, eat, and linger—a very user-friendly policy.

Throughout the year, Skaneateles provides an array of hometown fun, especially in the summer when streets and sidewalks could almost be described as congested. Every Friday evening by the water in Clift Park, a community band plays from the round gazebo, entertaining villagers with rousing Sousa marches, show tunes, and other upbeat music. Sunday afternoons in July and August find polo matches in a field off West Lake Road, the last weekend in July is the Antique and Classic Boat Show, and every weekend in August, the Skaneateles Musical Festival showcases music under the stars.

At Thanksgiving the Turkey Trot offers a fun run for charity; at Christmastime Dickens characters stroll the sidewalks, greeting shoppers. Memorial and Labor Day weekends roll out old-fashioned parades, parties, games, rides, and fireworks.

The village has three lakeside parks: Clift Park, Thayer Park, and Shotwell Park as well as Austin Park on the north end of town with tennis courts and ball fields. The Skaneateles Community Center and Allyn Arena offer amazing sports facilities, especially when you consider the size of the town. There is an Olympic-size pool along with four other pools, some with impressive water features including a giant slide and the kinetic waterworks, plus there's a state-of-the-art ice arena, the second ice arena in town. A small ski area is just outside town.

Shopping in the village is a treat. Genesee Street, with its brick sidewalks, brick buildings, and period lighting, is lined with interesting boutiques, craft shops, galleries, and cafés. Old-time favorites like the Hitching Post and Rid-dler's news store have been joined by sophisticated newcomers such as Paris Flea, a gift shop tucked under the new Village Inn—also decorated with French flair.

What industry there is in Skaneateles is located on the fringes of town. One of the most respected companies—named by *Fortune* magazine as one of the best places to work in the U.S.—is the Skaneateles Falls–based Welch Allyn, Inc., a medical instrument and fiber optics company. Welch Allyn, which has branched out to other parts of the country, is a major employer of people in the area. An-other home-grown company, a wooden toy company founded by Marshal Larrabee in 1936 as Skaneateles Handicrafters, is known for its high-quality hardwood pull trains, blocks, and toys. When Larrabee sold the company to the German-based company Habermaass in 1980, the product name was changed to T. C. Timber. Although the manufacturing of the toys is no longer done in Skaneateles, the company maintains a sales office and store at its location on Jordan Road.

Skaneateles: Growth and Development

In 1791 Skaneateles contained 41 military lots given to Revolutionary War soldiers, surveyors, and early settlers as compensation. The land the village now occupies was originally lot #36 purchased by Jedediah Sanger, who con-structed a log dam in 1797 in the center of town where the outlet from the lake flowed under a bridge and the main street. The increased water flow created power to operate a grist- and sawmill. The historic landmark is still there, but its fate is uncertain as of this writing. For a few years the Old Stone Mill was the site of a restaurant and pub, but more recently it has been unoccupied. In 2003 the building was purchased by Skaneateles developer Rick Diamond, lending renewed hope that the old building will be restored. Although as of this writing plans were not firmed up as to how the building would be used, Diamond is considering combinations of retail, residential, and office space including rent-ing the space to the town and village governments for consolidated offices.

In 1794 John Thompson settled on military lot #18, and that same year Abra-ham A. Cuddeback took a 43-day wagon journey from Orange County, New York, to Skaneateles, bringing his wife, 8 children, 3 yoke of oxen, 1 horse, and 12 cows. He built a log cabin on a heavily wooded piece of land on the west side of the lake, and more families followed.

An ideal location to attract settlers, Skaneateles was at the junction of east-west major routes, Route 20, the Cherry Valley Turnpike, and the Great Genesee Road, which followed the old trail used by Native Americans from Utica and Canandaigua. (Later the 1800 Seneca Turnpike improved the same road.)

This land held much promise. The outlet to the lake provided water power for mills and other industries; the soil was fertile for such crops as corn, beans, and wheat; and the lake not only supplied settlers with water, but also the scenery soothed the soul. Gradually the town grew; tanneries, bark mills, distilleries, cigar makers, blacksmiths, and other businesses opened up, some clustered around Mottville, just north of the village center. Farms blossomed, specializing in crops like tobacco for cigars, cabbages for sauerkraut, and teasels for the cloth industry.

Skaneateles's first store was opened in 1803 by Winston Day, and by 1830 there were seven stores, a Masonic Hall, three hotels, two sleigh and carriage factories, five flour mills, six saw mills, two iron foundries, and one brass foundry.

Teasels

For more than a hundred years, virtually all teasels cultivated in American came from the Skaneateles area and nearby Marcellus. Teasels look like thistles, but the stiff natural awns (hooks) on the burr head grow down. This feature made the teasel an excellent "tool" to raise the nap of woolen cloth. As a reminder of this once-important industry, a few buildings used to store the crop still stand, and some of these old teasel barns have been converted into private residences. One is on East Street; another on a side road off Academy Street.

The sprawling blue Sherwood Inn that dominates the lakefront on the west end of the village started life as Isaac Sherwood's Tavern in 1806, welcoming travelers arriving by stagecoach. A man of both large proportions and vision, Sherwood also owned the Old Mail Line stagecoach company, which carried mail between Utica and Canandaigua. More than 15 stages stopped daily at the Sherwood on their route.

Over the years the hotel expanded and changed names from Sherwood's Tavern, to Lamb's Inn, Houndayaga House, Packwood's National Hotel, Packwood House, Kan-Ya-To-Inn ("beautiful view"), and back to the Sherwood Inn, thanks to Chester (Chet) Coates, one of the previous owners, who lived in a wing on the second floor with his wife and daughters. Today the Sherwood Inn is owned by William Eberhardt.

Carriage and boat building were very important to the village's early economic growth. Carriage builders included Seth and James Hall, John Packwood, and former blacksmith John Legg. Boat companies founded here included the Bowdish Boat Company, the Edson Boat Company, and George Barnes' Skaneateles Boat and Canoe Company, where the first Lightning Class sailboat was built. The Lightning in those days was a 17-foot double-planked centerboard-keel wooden boat. Today a lighter version in fiberglass is a popular recreational craft on the lake. The tradition of boatbuilding in the area has been reborn with the recent opening of the Skaneateles Wooden Boat Company on Mill Road in Mottville.

In the late 1800s Syracuse, 18 miles to the northeast, started tapping into the lake for its drinking water. The water in the outlet slowed down, waterwheels turned more sluggishly, and industry was curtailed. Although Skaneateles Lake is known for its purity, a critical period for the village occurred in the 1920s, when Syracuse's withdrawal of water brought the lake level to a dangerously low point, upsetting the sewage system. A typhoid epidemic broke out when the water became contaminated, and village leader Charles Major Sr. had to have water piped into the community.

THE COMING OF THE RAILROAD AND STEAMBOATS

In 1840 a railroad with horse-drawn cars shuttled passengers back and forth between the village and Skaneateles Junction 5 miles north of town, where they could connect to the Syracuse-Auburn Railroad. The Skaneateles Railroad, a steam line, was launched in 1865, replacing the equine version. The line was so short that when some became concerned about snow and rain, one man replied, "Hell, build a roof over it."

Passengers would catch the train in Syracuse or Auburn and change trains at Skaneateles Junction, often in the summer months, enroute to their homes or resorts on the lake. Passenger service was discontinued in 1931, and the railroad was abandoned in 1982.

Around 1900 the Auburn and Syracuse Electric Trolley began shuttling people between cities. Both the train and later the trolley tied into the lake steamboats. The first steamboat, the 80-foot *Independent,* began carrying passengers up and down the lake in 1831, and was later joined by the 40-foot *Highland Chief,* the *Homer,* the *Ben H. Porter,* the 180-foot *Glen Haven, Ossahinta,* and *City of Syracuse-on-the-Lake,* which carried passengers to the south end of the lake to Glen Haven, where there was a spa-style resort and a small village with a hotel, restaurant, and a couple of stores. The hotel is gone; a small community and a lakeside restaurant remain.

Judge Ben Porter *offers sightseeing and dinner cruises on Skaneateles Lake.*

Large steamboats ceased to exist in 1917, but smaller boats took up the slack for such important services as mail delivery to the lake-bound cottages. Mailboxes were placed on the end of docks, and the mail boat would cruise alongside and deposit the mail all around the lake. Sometimes passengers packed lunches and went along for the ride. Today this practice continues on the U.S. Mailboat Cruise operated by Mid-Lakes Navigation Company.

Among the early boat operators were Mr. A. J. Hoffman who ran the *Florence*, and the Stinsons, who ran the Stinson Boat Line from 1938 until 1968, when the boat *Pat II* was sold to Peter Wiles of Mid-Lakes. Today the *Judge Ben Wiles*, a handsome double-decker diesel craft resembling the old steamboats, offers dining and sightseeing cruises on Skaneateles Lake, and *Pat II* remains in service. Over the past 30 years, Mid-Lakes has branched out from Skaneateles with a lake and canal boat operation throughout the Finger Lakes.

Big Doings in Skaneateles

"We haven't had this much excitement since Banjo Greenfield's son, Dozer, towed his double-wide through town, and they had to raise the streetlights." (Matt Major referring to the impending arrival of President Bill Clinton and first lady, Hillary, who came to vacation on the lake in 1999.)

FAMOUS VISITORS AND RESIDENTS

Famous visitors to Skaneateles have included Revolutionary War hero Marquis de Lafayette; statesman and orator Daniel Webster, who visited in 1825; and General Jonathan Wainwright, who was feted in his wife's hometown in one of the grandest parades the town has ever seen, when he returned from a World War II concentration camp. Most recently, during Bill Clinton's presidency, the Clintons vacationed here at a private home on East Lake Road

Skaneateles was the home of several Roosevelts. Nicholas Roosevelt lived in town from 1831 to 1854. His relative Samuel Montgomery Roosevelt and later his son, Henry Latrobe Roosevelt, spent summers in an imposing pillared Greek-Revival mansion called Roosevelt Hall. Famous guests included Theodore as well as Franklin and Eleanor Roosevelt. The Roosevelts would often bring showgirls to the property to perform on a grassy flat stage near the shore; friends and guests enjoyed the entertainment from seats set on the tiered hillside facing the lake.

William H. Delavan, who purchased the home in 1942, renovated the mansion and restored a large conservatory-style greenhouse filled with tropical trees and flowers. After Delavan sold the estate in 1959, the new owner, Dennis Owen, divided the 20 acres of land into a few building lots. Today the greenhouse is gone, and the property contains a handful of luxury homes. Owen, who brought his family up in the mansion, deeded the property to the Catholic

Diocese, and it was occupied by the Christian Brothers until recently, when it was sold and is once again a private residence.

GONE WITH THE WIND

Over the years a number of activities have risen and fallen in popularity. Once hot, now gone, are horse racing, ice boating, roller skating, and Microd racing. Microds were an interesting phenomena. From 1954–1965 young boys, with help from their dads and the Robinson family who built the first prototype in their barn, constructed miniature automobiles made of plywood and powered by lawn-mower engines. All summer long weekly races were held on the track where the Allyn Arena now stands. Each car was sponsored by a member of the business community. If you think Little League baseball gets competitive, you should have seen *this* crowd. The sidelines were jammed with people cheering on their favorite cars as they raced around the track.

Summer-stock theater was another favorite pastime. When the Lyric Circus came to town in 1952 and erected its huge blue tent on a site just east of the village, professional actors, actresses, and musicians from New York would perform in a summer series of musicals on a round stage surrounded by tiers of seats. Residents got involved in many aspects including marketing, financing, and ushering. But in the late '50s attendance declined. The final blow came from a hurricane, which toppled the tent; by 1960 the theater had shut down.

OWASCO LAKE AND AUBURN

The largest populated area in this three-lakes region, the city of Auburn, is 2.5 miles north of Owasco Lake. *Owasco* is a Native American word meaning "the crossing." Those passing through town along Route 20 do not get so

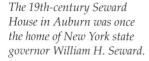

The 19th-century Seward House in Auburn was once the home of New York state governor William H. Seward.

much as a peek at the 12-mile-long deep-blue lake, so reward yourself with some magnificent views of the water by taking a detour via Lake Avenue to Emerson Park.

Owasco Lake is surrounded by rolling farmland, lakeside homes, and camps as well as several impressive large homes on the east side of the lake. At the southern end is Moravia, a small village of 19th-century homes and long-time residents. One of its biggest assets, Fillmore Glen State Park, is blessed with nature trails, picnic areas, deep gorges, and waterfalls. Moravia is the birthplace of our 13th president, Millard Fillmore, and childhood home of John D. Rockefeller. A blue historical marker notes the place where Rockefeller's house once stood.

Auburn has exceptional art and historical museums as well as more than 200 homes and buildings of architectural interest. Established in 1793, Auburn was once a busy, growing city. In the early 1900s, small manufacturing companies made their headquarters here producing products such as shoes, rope, and farm machinery. In the last 50 years most of these companies have moved out, leaving behind a slower-paced, perhaps less-affluent town but still one with a great deal of charm, offering a pleasant, affordable style of living, a fine lake, and a handful of lovely parks.

Tree-shaded neighborhoods of substantial turn-of-the-20th-century houses with wide front porches leading to sidewalks recall the days when Auburn was on the move. In particular the South Street area, a National Register Historic District, is home to several important buildings, including the Seward House, former residence of William H. Seward, governor of New York, Lincoln's secretary of state, and the man responsible for purchasing Alaska for $2 an acre (at the time it was called "Seward's Folly"). Harriet Tubman's modest dwelling and the home she built for her mother is farther down the street on the edge of town. Tubman, a Maryland slave, escaped to the north, where she became a leader in the Underground Railroad movement, hiding runaway slaves until they could find freedom in Canada.

Auburn Prison

Looming in a corner of the city, the gray walls of the Auburn Correctional Facility, a maximum security prison, continue to draw curious onlookers. Site of the first electric chair (now a museum piece) and the place Chester Gillette of *An American Tragedy* was put to death, the prison is an important part of Auburn's history and still in operation.

On summer evenings concerts take place in Hoopes Park, with its pretty pond and spouting fountain. In Emerson Park the Merry-Go-Round Playhouse stages professional musical productions in a building that formerly housed a fabulous carousel, which my children loved to ride on—it had a real brass ring and splendid wooden horses. The carousel seemingly disappeared overnight when it was sold and quietly moved out of state. An amusement park and games arcade, once a source of family fun in the park, is also gone, but the large pavilion—formerly the scene of many a big-band cotillion—still exists and is often rented out for weddings and other large parties and events.

Auburn's shopping activity has largely moved from Genesee Street to the Fingerlakes Mall outside the village center, and indeed a bypass road encourages that movement. Insurance companies, banks, real-estate offices, and other businesses have taken the spaces once occupied by retail stores. The whole area is neat and businesslike, but still some retail establishments in the old center such as Nolan's Sports Store and the Liberty Store continue to hang in there, and a few restaurants like Parker's, a bistro-style café, and the eclectic Kangaroo Court bar and restaurant continue to attract loyal patrons to the once thriving "downtown."

OTISCO LAKE

The easternmost lake, Otisco, is small and quiet. The largest village, Amber, on the east side, has only a few stores and homes. At the northern end water spills over a dam into a river. Just 6 miles long, Otisco is surrounded by wooded hills—a pretty place for a drive or a picnic. Better yet, if you have a canoe in tow, it's a perfect lake for paddling. Other than a couple of snack stands, Footprints restaurant on the water, and marinas, there isn't a whole lot more going on here.

LODGING

Although the Sherwood Inn, the Lady of the Lake, the new Packwood House, and Hobbit Hollow all have views of Skaneateles Lake, there are no places to stay directly on the water. Lodging choices range from country inns and a smart new resort-spa to bed-and-breakfasts, two small in-town hotels, and '50s-style motels; a few chain hotels are in Auburn. Syracuse, about a half hour drive from Skaneateles and Auburn, has a wider choice of accommodations (see Chapter Nine, *Host Cities,* for more information about Syracuse lodgings).

LODGING RATES
$: Up to $75 per couple $$$: $151–$250 per couple
$$: $76–$150 per couple $$$$: More than $250 per couple

Skaneateles

INNS AND HOTELS

THE BIRD'S NEST MOTEL
Innkeepers: Patricia and
   Eugene Creech.

On the edge of Skaneateles, this is your basic motel, with 17 rooms, 10 junior suites, and 3 ef-

315-685-5641.
www.thebirdsnest.net.
1601 E. Genesee St.,
   Skaneateles, NY 13152.
On Rte. 20.
Rooms: 30 rooms, suites,
   apartments.
Open: Year-round.
Price: $–$$.
Credit Cards: Most major.

MIRBEAU INN AND SPA
Innkeeper: Joachim Ohlin.
315-685-5006,
   877-MIRBEAU;
   fax 315-685-5150.
www.mirbeau.com.
851 W. Genesee St.,
   Skaneateles, NY 13152.
Rooms: 34 rooms, cottages,
   suites.
Open: Year-round.
Price: $$$$.
Credit Cards: Most major.

ficiency apartments, all on ground level. Nothing fancy but clean and cheap. Cool off in the outdoor pool tucked between Route 20 and the parking area: not scenic but useful.

Tucked into a hillside on the edge of Skaneateles, the new resort Mirbeau is targeting affluent travelers with a full-service spa with 10 treatment rooms and a choice of a wide variety of therapies. An elegant resting area is modeled after a Roman bath, with soft lighting, columns, lovely wall frescoes, soft comfortable chaises, and radiant-heated floors. European in feeling, Mirbeau has ochre stuccoed walls with blue trim and shutters, high-pitched tilelike roofs, arched windows, and massive 300-year-old timbers that have been designed into the buildings.

Rooms face inward around a pond reminiscent of Monet's water garden at Giverney. There is an arched bridge, water iris, and many other flowers and shrubs. Arched iron trellises with climbing roses and wisteria create a romantic entry to many of the cottages. A grove of tall trees, wildflowers, and a few benches beckon to those who want some quiet time; a meditation trail and tea house are to come. A valet escorts you to your room and helps you with whatever you might need, including golf tee times or dinner reservations.

Guest rooms are spacious and superbly appointed. Fabrics were designed in France; linens, including Frette, come from Italy, and duvets are filled with Canadian down. Armoires with fine inlays, period pieces, antiques, and fireplaces add to the ambiance. Many rooms have beamed ceilings and are painted in deep red or gold. Each room has a fireplace and a patio or balcony with wrought-iron table and chairs. Baths come with deep French soaking tubs on feet, large showers, and double vanities. The sound system is Bose with a CD player. Some of the public rooms are painted by hand in deep ochre; one has a ceiling border of grape vines. The dining room features "Mirbeau Estate Cuisine"—see "Restaurants" for more information.

PACKWOOD HOUSE
Innkeeper: William
   Eberhardt.

This handsome new three-story brick building, built on the site of the old post office, affords some wonderful views from the windows and bal-

800-374-3796; 315-685-3405;
fax 315-685-8983.
W. Genesee St., Skaneateles,
NY 13152.
Rooms: 19.
Open: Year-round.
Price: $$–$$$.
Credit Cards: Most major.

conies of the lake-facing rooms. On the first level are retail shops; rooms and suites are on the second level. Amenities include minifridges, TVs, and complimentary continental breakfast (or you can go next door to the Sherwood Inn for your wake-up meal.)

SHERWOOD INN
Innkeeper: William
Eberhardt.
315-685-3405,
800-3-SHERWOOD;
fax 315-685-8983.
www.thesherwoodinn.com.
26 W. Genesee St.,
Skaneateles, NY 13152.
On Rte. 20.
Rooms: 24.
Open: Year-round.
Price: $$–$$$.
Serving: Continental B, L, D.
Credit Cards: Most major.

Located on the southern end of the lake just across from a waterside park, this historic inn—built in 1807 and once a stagecoach stop—is a rambling three-story blue building right in the center of town and shops. This grand old building is now even better, thanks to an extensive renovation of both public and private rooms. Many rooms now have gas fireplaces and whirlpool baths. The inn has an enclosed wide veranda and a publike bar, and all rooms and suites are different; some overlook the lake, others the backyard and parking lot (these views may not be the greatest, but the rooms are very quiet). Decor is eclectic colonial, with a bit of early American and Victorian thrown in. One of the best views in the house is from room #28, a second-floor corner room overlooking the lake and the village. The third-floor rooms tend to be more serene. Eat in the dining room or tavern.

**THE SKANEATELES
HOTEL**
Innkeepers: Curtis and Tony
Feldman.
315-685-2333.
www.skaneateleshotel.com.
12 Fennell St., Skaneateles,
NY 13152.
Rooms: 6.
Open: Year-round.
Price: $$–$$$.
Credit Cards: Most major.

Located in a fully renovated building in the village, this boutique hotel offers rooms that are all somewhat different from one another. Two have over-sized Jacuzzis, and one is handicapped accessible. There is an honor kitchen as well as a washer and dryer. The inn has no restaurant facilities but does offer snacks. It is within walking distance of the lake and the village center.

SKANEATELES SUITES
Innkeepers: Curtis and Tony
Feldman.
315-685-7568.
www.skaneatelessuites.com.
PO Box 912, Skaneateles,
NY, 13152.

These motel-style bungalows on Route 20 just outside the village feature six spacious suites with kitchenettes, sitting and dining areas, and sliding-glass doors. The Honeymoon Suite has an in-room whirlpool tub and private patio. Complimentary breads, beer (two), and soda (two) are included in

On Rte. 20.
Rooms: 6.
Open: Year-round.
Price: $–$$$.
Credit Cards: Most major.

the rate. Also on the property is a four-bedroom house, popular with families. Housekeeping services are provided.

Antique cars in front of the Sherwood Inn, a historic town landmark.

VILLAGE INN
Innkeeper/Owner: John
  Pidhirny.
800-374-3796; 315-685-3405.
www.villageinn-ny.com.
25 Jordan St., Skaneateles,
  NY 13152.
Rooms: 4.
Open: Year-round.
Price: $$–$$$.
Credit Cards: Most major.

You're right in the center of town, yet once you slip into your room, you'll enjoy total privacy and quiet. Each room in this newly renovated European-styled hotel, which is housed in an historic corner building in the village, has a fireplace, whirlpool bath, minifridge, and Old-World-charm decor. The Terrace Room on the third floor has a balcony with a lake view, the Cottage Room has a rustic exposed brick wall, the English Estate Room transports you to the English countryside, and the sunny French Country Room is decorated in red-and-yellow toile. Rooms open onto a lounge and breakfast area where a continental breakfast is served, or you can have a full breakfast in the Sherwood Inn, a five-minute walk away. Want to pick up a special gift? Paris Flea is on the ground level.

WHISPERING WINDS
MOTEL
Innkeepers: Rita and
 Richard Drake.
315-685-6056.
www.skaneateles.com/
 whisperingwinds.
PO Box 944, Skaneateles,
 NY 13152.
On Rte. 20.
Rooms: 12
Open: May–Oct.
Price: $–$$
Credit Cards: Most major

A neat and efficient motel just west of the village. Each comfortable unit has a private carport, air-conditioning, cable TV, telephone, and refrigerator. There is also a heated outdoor pool.

BED & BREAKFASTS

ARBOR HOUSE INN &
SUITES
Innkeepers: Tom and Nancy
 Shaver.
315-685-8966, 888-234-4558.
www.arborhouseinn.com.
41 Fennell St., Skaneateles,
 NY 13152.
Rooms: 7 with private baths.
Open: Year-round.
Price: $$$.
Credit Cards: Most major.

This mid-19th-century brick Federal-style house is across from a supermarket and just a five-minute walk to the lake and the center of town. Four rooms and a two-room suite come with private baths—four with Jacuzzis and two with gas fireplaces; two additional rooms are located in a renovated Teasel barn. All are air-conditioned and beautifully furnished with a combination of antiques and reproductions as well as oriental rugs. Breakfast is served in the dining room or on the sun porch, and there's a wet bar in the kitchen. Nonsmoking.

BLUE WILLOW INN
Innkeepers: Kebbie and
 Ken Rosenberg.
315-685-1101; 800-BWillow.
www.thebluewillowinn.com.
4423 State Street Rd.,
 Skaneateles, NY 13152.
Rooms: 4; 3 with shared
 baths, 1 with private bath.
Open: Year-round
Price: $–$$
Credit Cards: most major

Located 3.5 miles from the center of town, this country inn overlooks rolling countryside. The white country farmhouse has a nice front porch with Adirondack chairs and is whimsically furnished with a combination of hand-painted furniture, antiques, oriental rugs, and double, queen, and king-sized beds. You can relax on the backyard patio, and enjoy a full country breakfast served in the dining room. The most romantic and largest room is the Blue Willow Room, which has a four-poster bed.

HUMMINGBIRD'S HOME
Innkeeper: Sabina
 Ciszewski.

Set in beautiful gardens just a bit out of the village, this gracious, circa 1803 colonial home with original plank floors is decorated with colonial-

315-685-5075, 866-207-1900.
www.hummingbirdshome
  bandb.com.
4273 W. Genesee St.,
  Skaneateles NY 13152.
Corner Rte. 20 and County
  Line Rd.
Rooms: 4 with private baths.
Open: Year-round.
Price: $–$$.
Credit Cards: Most major.

period furniture and antiques and wallpaper, oriental carpets, and artwork. All rooms are air-conditioned, some have fireplaces, one has a Jacuzzi. A
full gourmet breakfast is served in the dining room,
and complimentary beverages are provided. Children are welcome.

THE GRAY HOUSE

Innkeepers: Val and Bob
  Gray.
315-685-0131.
www.gray-house.com.
47 Jordan St., Skaneateles,
  NY 13152.
Rooms: 4, including 2 suites;
  all with private bath.
Open: Year-round.
Price: $–$$.
Credit Cards: Most major.

Just one block from Genesee Street, the main shopping area, and the lake, this beautifully decorated
Victorian home has two large living rooms, air-
conditioning, two porches, and gardens. Two suites
have queen-sized beds and sitting rooms. A full
breakfast is served.

Their adjacent property, the 1840 "Little Gray
House," is available for weekly or monthly rental
and offers two apartments with full kitchens and
whirlpool baths. Included in the apartments are
cable TVs, VCR, CD player, air-conditioning. A fully
equipped laundry room is also available to guests,
as are a large porch and large backyard for yard
games and picnicking.

HOBBIT HOLLOW FARM
BED & BREAKFAST

Innkeeper: Celeste Holden.
315-685-2791;
  fax 315-685-3426.
www.hobbithollow.com.
3061 W. Lake Rd.,
  Skaneateles, NY 13152.
Rooms: 4 with private
  baths.
Open: Year-round.
Price: $$–$$$$.
Credit Cards: Most major.

Set high on 320 hillside acres overlooking the lake
just five minutes from the village center, this
beautifully furnished 100-year-old colonial house
has all the amenities of a lovely private home—
which it once was. Rooms overlook horses grazing
in white-fenced fields and, beyond them, vineyards
and the lake. Each room has beautifully polished
floors, and the appointments are elegant—gilt mir-
rors, oriental carpets, white-painted deep moldings,
hand-painted murals, and matelassé and Frette
linens. The Master Suite faces the lake and horse sta-
bles and contains a four-post king-sized bed, fire-
place, two-person whirlpool, and a private veranda
furnished with wicker chairs and tables. The Chan-
ticleer Room, which also overlooks the lake and fields, is decorated in French
country and is spacious and sunny. It has a queen-sized pencil four-post bed
and European soaking tub. A full breakfast is served in the elegant yellow din-
ing room.

Swimming is popular off the shores of Clift Park in Skaneateles.

LADY OF THE LAKE
Innkeeper: Sandra
  Rademacher.
315-685-7997, 888-685-7997.
www.ladyofthelake.net.
2 W. Lake Rd., Skaneateles,
  NY 13152.
Rooms: 3 with private baths.
Open: Year-round.
Price: $$-$$$.
Credit Cards: Most major.

An ideal location on the corner of Genesee Street and West Lake Road within a block of the lake, park, and shopping area, this 19th-century Victorian house features such details as a spacious front porch just made for rocking, stained-glass windows, a gracious wide staircase, and lovely parlor and dining rooms. Guest rooms are each different and furnished with a collection of period furniture and antiques. The Stella, the largest room, has a white-iron king-sized bed set into an alcove, where you get a peek at the lake. Full breakfasts are served.

Owasco Lake and Auburn

HOLIDAY INN
Manager: Linda Knight.
315-253-4531;
  fax 315-252-5843.
www.holiday-inn.com/
  auburnny.
75 North St., Auburn, NY
  13021
Corner Rte. 34 and Rte. 5 &
  20.
Rooms: 165.
Open: Year-round.
Price: $$-$$$.
Credit Cards: Most major.

Centrally located in the business part of town, this is a popular choice with those on the road. The 165 rooms were renovated a couple of years ago and are comfortable; some come with Jacuzzis, and some overlook the courtyard. There is a very nice indoor pool and courtyard, and for an area that can get some rather cold weather, that's a big plus. Some locals have been known to check in with their kids for the weekend for some relaxation and swimming. There is also a fitness center, business center, restaurant, game room, and lounge. Breakfast is served daily; McMurphy's Irish Pub and Restaurant offers lunch and dinner daily and entertainment on selected weekends, and the Falls Room is open for breakfast. A convention center and meeting rooms can accommodate up to 700 people.

MICROTEL INN AND SUITES
Manager: Jackie Lewis.
315-253-5000, 888-771-7171.
12 Seminary Ave., Auburn, NY 13021.
Rooms: 79.
Open: Year-round.
Price: $–$$.
Credit Cards: Most major.

Located in the center of town on Route 5 & 20, the hotel makes a good base for those on business. It features suites with separate living rooms and kitchenettes equipped with microwaves and refrigerators. Furnishings are modern and efficient. Amenities include dataports, voicemail, cable TV, guest lounge, and a fitness center. A complimentary breakfast is included in the rate Monday through Friday.

SPRINGSIDE INN
Innkeepers: Sean and Beth Lattimore.
315-252-7247;
fax 315-252-8096.
www.springsideinn.com.
6141 W. Lake Rd., Auburn, NY 13021.
On Rte. 38.
Rooms: 8 with private baths.
Open: Year-round.
Price: $–$$.
Credit Cards: Most major.

With new owners, this four-story mid-1800s frame inn, believed to have once harbored runaway slaves who were hidden in the house and the thickets behind, was originally built as a boarding school and in subsequent years used as private residence, summer resort, and, finally, year-round hotel. Now it is getting a much-needed infusion of loving care. The inn's new owners have dramatically renovated the rooms as well as the public areas and grounds. Hanging flower baskets decorate the porch, a perennial garden and path lead to a gazebo beside a pond, and the sunny, intimate breakfast room is a perfect place to enjoy the complimentary breakfast that comes with the room rate. Rooms are beautifully decorated, many with toile and Waverly-style flowered wallpapers and fabrics. Four-poster canopy beds, wet bars, Jacuzzis for two, and polished wood floors have brought new life into the accommodations. Springside is also well-known as a place to eat and for group functions, especially weddings.

RESTAURANTS

Whereas Otisco Lake offers only a handful of seasonal restaurants and snack bars, Auburn on Owasco Lake and Skaneateles are quite a different story. Places to eat range from the pricey and elegant Mirbeau and Rosalie's in Skaneateles to more casual restaurants like the Blue Water Grill on Skaneateles Lake, Doug's Fish Fry just a block away, and the family-owned and run Mandana Inn—famous for its scrod—farther down the lake. Auburn also offers a number of excellent steak houses, Italian-style cafés, and long-established restaurants, including Balloons and Lasces.

Anyone who has passed through Skaneateles, if only briefly, usually remembers Krebs. Located on Genesee Street in a modest two-story clapboard house with a large front porch, this restaurant has been famous for its bounteous family -style meals since it was founded by Cora and Fred Krebs in 1899.

Prices are estimated per person for appetizer and dinner entrée without tax, tip, or alcoholic beverages.

$: Up to $10
$$: $11–25
$$$: $26–40
$$$$: More than $40

Skaneateles Lake and Skaneateles

BLUE WATER GRILL
315-685-6600.
11 W. Genesee St.,
  Skaneateles, NY 13152.
Open: Daily 11:30–10,
  depending on season.
Price: $–$$.
Cuisine: Bistro American.
Serving: L, D.
Credit Cards: Most major.

One of the hot spots in town, Blue Water Grill is the place where locals head when they don't want to cook. The sandwiches are huge—I always share with whoever is game to do it. In the warm weather, ask to sit on the deck. It's right on the outlet to the lake, so you get a good water view; you can practically pull up in your boat and tie up just below the deck. The menu is loaded with good things like grilled chicken pesto wrap, turkey wrap—lots of wraps—hamburgers, ravioli, fajitas, BBQ chicken, steak sandwiches, and nachos. Vegetarians will find plenty of tempting items, too. I especially like the pizza topped with fresh basil, tomatoes, and mozzarella. The grill features a good selection of beer and wines along with shooters from the freezer. Sauza Commemoritivo Tequila? Now, there's a challenge.

DOUG'S FISH FRY
315-685-3288.
8 Jordan St., Skaneateles,
  NY 13152.
Open: 11am–10pm in-
  season; closes earlier off-
  season.
Price: $–$$.
Cuisine: Chicken, seafood.
Serving: L, D.
Credit Cards: No.

They line up around the corner in the summertime for what some consider the best fish and chips outside of England. It all started in 1982, when Doug Clark opened up on a side street in a small place with just two booths and a narrow counter with a couple of stools. The original place is still the heart of the operation, but now you can take your meal to an adjacent antique brick building, where there are tables and chairs; in the summer there is a roped-off picnic area in the parking lot, where you can eat and mingle with locals and tourists alike. I always look forward to the fish sandwich ($4.39 or $6.80 with fries and slaw). There is also Doug's dippin' chicken dinner at $6.80, shrimp, scallops, lobster, clams, and sometimes frog legs. Also good are the homemade chowder, onion rings, franks, draft beer, and soft and hard ice cream. New owner Mark Teasdale-Edwards says he doesn't plan to change a thing. "If it isn't broken, why fix it?" he says.

The Glen Haven boat launch is located at the southern end of Skaneateles Lake.

THE GLEN HAVEN
607-749-3779.
www.skaneateles.com/
  glenhaven.
7434 Fair Haven Rd.,
  Homer, NY 13077.
Open: Mother's Day
  through September.
Price: $–$$$.
Cuisine: Casual fine dining.
Serving: L (weekends), D.
Credit Cards: No.

Located at the south end of Skaneateles Lake, the Glen Haven operates one of the few boat launches in the area, so you can arrive by boat and eat on the deck overlooking the lake. Chris and Susan Beaudry, who have owned the four-story building for close to 25 years, will tell you that in 1900 it served as a tearoom for wealthy ladies and during Prohibition was converted to a speakeasy. Today this casual, fun restaurant serves things like wood-grilled salmon, jerk pork, and blackened steak, along with pasta dishes, black-bottom key-lime tarts, and dinner salads. Call for directions: It's not easy to find unless you're coming by boat.

THE INN BETWEEN RESTAURANT
315-672-3166.
2290 W. Genesee Tpke.,
  Camillus, NY 13031.

Knotty-pine walls with an eclectic mix of furnishings and pastel-colored wall coverings and fabrics set the mood in this cheery restaurant housed in a well-maintained Colonial house with three fire-

On Rte. 5.
Open: Tues.–Sat. from 5,
  Sun. from 2, closed Mon.
Price: $$–$$$.
Cuisine: Continental.
Serving: D.
Credit Cards: Most major.

places. Meals are artfully presented and feature such items as baby rack of lamb, fresh seafood, and veal dishes.

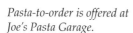

Pasta-to-order is offered at Joe's Pasta Garage.

JOE'S PASTA GARAGE
315-685-6116.
28 Jordan Rd., Skaneateles,
  NY 13152.
Open: Daily 11–10.
Price: $.
Cuisine: Italian American.
Serving: L, D.
Credit Cards: Most major.

Named after owner Gary Robinson's son, Joey, this new Italian-American bistro-style eatery is destined to become one of the village's hottest restaurants. It has everything going for it: an historic location in a 19th-century stone building—which has known life as a carriage and sleigh factory, a blacksmith shop, and most recently, Paul Trabold's garage—an enthusiastic owner with a successful track record with the high-end Rosalie's Cucina, a creative menu where you can build your own pizzas and pastas and just about everything costs less than $10, and a cozy *taverna*-like dining room with ochre tile floors, beams, and a pizza oven that bakes like the old wood-fired ones. Everything is made from scratch under the direction of Chef John Gow, who formerly held the position of sous chef at Rosalie's. House specialties include vegetable lasagna, grandma's stuffed peppers, fresh oysters cornmeal crusted and fried, chopped clams steamed in white wine and garlic, and a to-die-for Dee-licious Garage Salad (named after Gary's wife, Dee) with fresh spinach, raspberries, candied walnuts, sweet red onions and gorgonzola tossed in a warm balsamic vinaigrette. For those in a rush, a takeout window lets you drive up and get your order without leaving your car. There are no reservations, but you can stop in, leave your name, and be paged wherever you are by cell phone when your table is ready. Restaurant manager is Becky Mello-Eagan.

JOHNNY ANGEL'S HEAVENLY HAMBURGERS
315-685-0100.
22 Jordan St., Skaneateles, NY 13152.
Open: Daily 7am–8pm, Fri.–Sat. until 10.
Price: $–$$.
Serving: B, L, D.
Credit Cards: MC, Visa, AmEx.

It's the place to be for breakfast eggs and bacon and New Hope Mills pancakes. Lunch and dinner feature half-pound burgers, homemade soups, fish, chicken, hot sandwiches, battered fries, Texas chili, pies, ice cream, beer, and wine. Order and pick up your food from the counter, and take it to one of the long tables with red-and-white checkered tablecloths or to an adjacent room containing an ice cream bar. Some families make breakfast here a Sunday-morning habit. The current owner is Bill Lynn, who took over from the founder, John Angyal.

KABUKI
315-685-7234.
12 W. Genesee St., Skaneateles, NY 13152.
Open: Daily 5–10.
Price: $–$$.
Cuisine: Japanese.
Serving: D.
Credit Cards: Most major.

For all those people who crave Japanese food, at last the Finger Lakes has a winner. One of the newest restaurants in town, Kabuki brings sushi and other Japanese specialties to Skaneateles. The design of this small restaurant is refreshingly clean, modern oriental in flavor but not overdone, with yellow walls, a red ceiling, and soft green accents, setting the tone. Sushi such as the California rolls and Hamachi (yellow tail) is fresh and tasty—you may decide to make a meal out of it. There are many other choices, including the Kabuki roll, which is filled with spicy shrimp and scallions; chicken sate made with marinated chicken that you dip into a spicy peanut sauce; and the miso-marinated sea bass, one of the restaurant's most popular dishes. There is a full-service bar, and takeout is available.

THE KREBS
315-685-5714, 315-685-7001.
53 W. Genesee St., Skaneateles, NY 13152.
Open: Open daily early May–late Oct.
Price: $$$–$$$$.
Serving: D from 6, cocktails from 4, Sun. brunch 10:30–2; Sun. dinner from 4; Sun. cocktails from 12.
Cuisine: Hearty American cuisine and lots of it.
Credit Cards: Most major.

Arguably the most famous restaurant in the Finger Lakes, Krebs has been long known for its eat-all-you-want multicourse prix-fixe dinners. In the foyer, framed letters and signatures of several important guests are displayed, including Franklin Roosevelt, who sat in one of the wicker rockers on the porch, and Charles Lindbergh and George Bernard Shaw. Seven-course dinners are served on linen-covered tables in the rooms on the first floor. Two rooms upstairs, furnished with Victorian settees and chairs, are used for pre-dinner cocktails. Another room contains a bar and dining room for casual dining with a pub menu. Outside, white wrought-iron chairs and tables surrounded by lawns and gardens provide yet another place to sip a drink.

I was pleasantly surprised that even after all these years, most items are still very good and homemade, such as the sticky rolls, soups, and pastries. With most courses, you have two or more choices, including items like shrimp cocktail, soup (the tomato soup was excellent, boasting huge chunks of fresh tomato), and the lobster Newburg, which was loaded with lobster. The main course is served family-style, a parade of dishes heaped with fried chicken, roast beef with horseradish sauce, mashed potatoes, yams, and other comfort foods; seconds are available, though with several courses already behind you, I can't believe anyone would ask for more.

Reservations are desirable.

MANDANA INN
315-685-7798; 315-685-6490.
1937 W. Lake Rd., Mandana, NY 13152.
Open: Apr. 1–Dec. 31, Mon., Wed.–Sat. 5–10, Sun. 3–8:30, closed Tues.; winter open Wed.–Sat. 5–10, Sun. 3–8:30, closed Mon. and Tues.
Price: $$.
Cuisine: Seafood, steak, Black Angus beef.
Serving: D.
Credit Cards: Most major.

This casual, long-established family-owned and operated restaurant is located on the west side of the lake on Route 41A. I grew up with a strong dislike of fish until I was talked into eating the scrod here: Mandana Inn is famous for this dish prepared with a broiled crumb topping. I've been hooked on fish ever since. The homey interior, which has changed little over the past 30 years, is furnished with pine tables and chairs and contains two dining rooms and the Cherry Pub.

MARIETTA HOUSE
315-636-8299.
Rte. 174S, Marietta, NY 13110.
Open: Apr.–Jan. 1, Fri. and Sat. from 5pm.
Price: $$.
Cuisine: American.
Serving: D.
Credit Cards: Most major.

Just north of Otisco Lake, you'll find this large restaurant, one of the best features of which is the beautiful brick patio and gazebo set in gardens: a perfect setting for a wedding or special occasion. The facility can accommodate up to 250 guests. The dining room and pub are open for dinner on weekends; it's open year-round for weddings and functions.

MIRBEAU
877-MIRBEAU, 315-685-5006; fax 315-685-5150.
www.mirbeau.com.
851 W. Genesee St., Skaneateles, NY 13152.
Open: Daily.
Price: $$$–$$$$.

Chef Edward J. Moro comes from Hotel Hersey and is already chalking up an impressive track record here. Those who have eaten at Mirbeau feel the cuisine is worth the price tag: a four-course dinner is $52, and a five-course meal is $58. Choices include butter-roasted Maine lobster tail with melted leeks and carrot ginger sauce, Fallow Hollow Farm

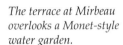

The terrace at Mirbeau overlooks a Monet-style water garden.

Cuisine: Seafood, beef.
Serving: B, L, D.
Credit Cards: Most major.

venison with apple conserve, rosemary fingerling potato and sour-cherry sauce, and wild-berry soufflé. Lunch and breakfast choices are equally tempting. My recommendation: Pick a special evening, reserve a table on the terrace, and enjoy a splendid dinner. Perhaps start with a warm potato and goat-cheese terrine with baby arugula, champagne vinegar, and olive oil, followed by Chesapeake Bay soft-shell crab with spicy corn, red pepper, and fennel coulis, then charred beef tenderloin with foraged mushrooms and truffle mashed potatoes, or perhaps Scottish salmon with crispy rosti potato cake and littleneck clam chowder climaxed by a wild-berry soufflé.

ROSALIE'S CUCINA
315-685-2200
841 W. Genesee St.,
    Skaneateles, NY 13152.
Open: Daily Mon.–Thurs.
    and Sun. 5–9, Fri. and Sat.
    5–10.
Price: $$$.
Cuisine: Italian.
Serving: D.
Credit Cards: Most major.

This adobe *taverna*-style restaurant was built by Philip Romano in memory of his sister, Rosalie. The menu begins, "We are very proud of our chefs, wait staff, bartenders, and all of our crew for keeping Rosalie's legacy alive and her *cucina* filled with great food, friendly service, and, most important, happy guests." This restaurant lives up to its promise, now under the ownership of Gard Robinson. Although one person commented, "The best place to eat when someone else is buying," the higher-than-average prices for the area don't seem to faze the continuous stream of people who come here to eat. The Italian cuisine is excellent and plentiful. It's upper-crust Italian (which seems a tad out-of-place in such a traditional central New York village), but who's to care. Rosalie's is wildly popular among those looking for a special meal, including rich pasta dishes, good breads, succulent meats, and pizza from a wood-fired oven. Among the pasta specialities are far-falle con pollo (bowties, chicken, pancetta, asiago cream, red onions, and peas) and risotto con funghi (arborio rice, with portabella and shiitaki mushrooms, parsley, and reggiano). For your main course you might order arrosto con porc (slow roasted pork, oregano, garlic, and cannellini beans) or aragosta alla Rosalie (grilled lobster tails, orzo, spinach, and artichokes). An extensive wine list ranges from a $19 White Zinfandel to a $120 bottle of Cuvée Dom Perignon. Reservations are taken for parties of six or more.

SHERWOOD INN
315-685-3405,
  800-3-SHERWOOD;
  fax 315-685-8983.
26 W. Genesee St.,
  Skaneateles, NY 13152.
Open: Year-round.
Price: $–$$ tavern, $$–$$$
  dining room.
Cuisine: American.
Serving: B, L, D.
Credit Cards: Most major.

The Sherwood—located on Route 20—has three places you can eat: the main dining room, the lakeside enclosed porch, and the tavern. The ambiance is traditional in the dining room; the tavern is more casual and resembles an English pub with a long bar, a few booths, and tables. Menu items in the dining room include such classics as grilled duckling with red onion apricot relish; filet mignon sautéed with shallots, red wine, and wild mushrooms; parmesan-crusted halibut filet; and grilled Atlantic salmon with orange butter, served with lobster mashed potatoes. Tavern fare is more basic: grilled chicken sandwich, portabella ravioli, Caesar salad, and tavern burgers. Often on weekends there is live music in the tavern.

CASUAL FOOD

Grammie's Breakfast Tea Room & Gift Shop (315-636-8111, 607-749-6434; 1126 Woodworth Rd., Skaneateles, NY 13152; off Rte. 41) It's 11 miles down East Lake Road out of Skaneateles, and you have to watch for the sign on the right side of the highway where you turn towards the lake on Woodworth Road, but it's worth the trip. Typically, breakfast tea includes tea or gourmet coffee, crêpes, scones, breads, fresh fruit condiments, lemon curd, jams, and Arbor Hill Claret Wine Sauce. Grammie's Victorian tea treats you to coffee or tea, scones, lemon curd, fruit, cucumber sandwiches, feta cheese spread, and dessert. Open Tues., Thurs., Fri., Sat. 11–4. Call ahead for reservations.

Morris's Grill (315-685-7761; 6 W. Genesee St., Skaneateles, NY 13152) Anyone who ever grew up in Skaneateles knows about Morris's. It's the ultimate hangout bar and meeting place—and they serve food, too.

Patisserie (315-685-2433; 4 Hannum St., Skaneateles, NY 13152) There are just a few tables on a patio in this delightfully small bakery shop tucked into a corner behind the Sherwood Inn. Freshly made breads, cakes, pies, and pastries, along with coffees and teas.

Skaneateles Bakery (315-685-3538; 19 Jordan St., Skaneateles, NY 13152) Homemade bakery products and good coffee bring locals in for breakfast and light lunches. Specialties are doughnuts, sandwiches, soups, and rolls. Not much in the way of ambiance—unless you like to watch people outside walk by through the large front windows. Doughnuts—especially the ones they call "headlights," with white frosting—are yummy and death on diets. Cookies, cakes, and other bakery products, too. A village institution. Open Mon.–Sat. 6am–5:30pm.

Skan-Ellus Drive-In (315-685-8280; 1659 E. Genesee St., Skaneateles, NY 13152; junction Rtes. 175 & 20) A snack bar with indoor seating area offering ice cream, deli sandwiches, burgers, hot dogs, and fries. It's been around for more than 30 years, and it's still going strong. Open daily 10–9; later in summer.

Sweetwater Café (315-685-6600; 9 W. Genesee St., Skaneateles, NY 13152) An extension of the Bluewater Grill, this new shop offers ice cream and dessert, such as fresh pastries, as well as early morning continental breakfast, light soups and salad. Open daily 8am–10pm.

Valentine's (315-685-8804; 18 West Genesee St., Skaneateles, NY 13152) When I just have to have pizza, I come here. They also have calzones, subs, wraps, and salads along with beer. And they deliver.

Owasco Lake and Auburn

RESTAURANTS

BALLOONS
315-252-9761.
65 Washington St., Auburn, NY 13021.
Open: Tues., Wed., and Thurs. 5–9:30pm, Fri. and Sat. 5–10pm, Sun. 5–9pm.
Price: $–$$.
Cuisine: Hearty American; steaks.
Serving: D.
Credit Cards: Most major.

This small steak house, which lies in the shadow of the Auburn prison, is still delivering good food at reasonable prices. Many of the waiters have been here long enough to seem immortal. Specialties include prime rib, steaks of all kinds, and salads. It's small and intimate. Bring your appetite.

CASCADES
315-497-1602.
Rte. 38 Cascade on Owasco, Moravia, NY 13118.
Open: Year-round.
Price: $–$$.
Cuisine: American, seafood.
Serving: L, D.
Credit Cards: Most major.

It's a casual, fun place to come. Pull up by boat, or come by car. Eat overlooking the lake on the open deck or inside. Great hamburgers, sandwiches, chicken, and salads.

CURLEY'S RESTAURANT
315-252-5224, 315-252-5277.
96 State St., Auburn, NY
  13021.
Open: Mon.–Sat. 11–2,
  Mon.–Thurs. 5–9, Fri. and
  Sat. 5–10; tavern menu in
  bar all day.
Price: $$–$$$.
Cuisine: Italian, pub fare,
  steaks, seafood.
Serving: L, D.
Credit Cards: Most major.

A long-time winner among locals, Curley's has been serving food and drink to patrons since 1934. Weekends often offer some entertainment. Ask to sit on the outdoor deck in the summertime.

**SWABY'S KANGAROO
  COURT**
315-258-9693.
6 South St., Auburn, NY
  13021.
Open: Mon.–Sat. 3pm–2am,
  Sun. 4pm–2am.
Price: $.
Cuisine: Pub, sandwiches.
Serving: D.
Credit Cards: Most major.

S waby's looks like it's been here since the late 1800s. The decor is eclectically odd and includes artwork, gilt chairs, a ship's figurehead, wooden arms, fans, globes, model dinosaurs, an old electric chair, and barber chairs along the bar. There are lots of interesting antiques and memorabilia—a real trip. Great beer and pub food complete the picture.

DAUT'S
315-252-7175.
10 E. Genesee St., Auburn,
  NY 13021.
Open: Mon and Tues. 4–10;
  Wed. and Thurs. 11–10;
  Fri. and Sat. 11–11.
Price: $$.
Cuisine: American.
Serving: L, D.
Credit Cards: Most major.

It feels like an old-time bistro but new windows have given the former Riordan's a lighter look. A well-rounded menu includes steak, prime rib, pasta, seafood, and chicken dishes along with generous-sized salads. Be sure to check out their Mexican Night. There is both a dining room and a more casual pub.

LASCA'S
315-253-4885.
252-258 Grant Ave., Auburn,
  NY 13021.
On Rte. 5.
Open: Tues.–Thurs. 5–9, Fri.
  and Sat. 5–10, Sun. 4–9.
Price: $$–$$$.
Serving: D.
Cuisine: Italian.
Credit Cards: Most major.

E njoy huge portions: If you don't go home with leftovers, you'll be disappointed. Specialities include deep-fried scallops, shrimp scampi, Gramp's eggplant parmigiana, and chicken piccata. For an appetizer, try the antipasto Nicholas or deep-fried mushrooms. Entrées come with salads, vegetable, and potato, rice, or pasta. A good deal.

**PARKER'S GRILL AND
  TAP HOUSE**
315-252-6884.
129 Genesee St., Auburn,
  NY 13021.
Open: Daily
  11am–midnight.
Price: $.
Cuisine: Bistro style.
Serving: L, D.
Credit Cards: Most major.

One of the few restaurants on Genesee Street in the heart of the business district, Parker's is the newest kid on the block and packed at lunch time. In addition to a long bar, there are regular tables, high-top tables, and booths plus Tiffany-style lamps and lots of wood trim. Although I found the service a bit on the casual side, the servers were friendly, and food was good pub style—finger foods, hamburgers, Philly steak sandwiches, pita pockets, and soups—plus 20 beers on tap.

**THE PIONEER
  RESTAURANT**
315-252-9721.
3191 E. Genesee St., Auburn,
  NY 13021.
Open: Tues.–Sat., Sun. 12–8.
Price: $–$$.
Cuisine: Basic American.
Serving: D, Sun. L.
Credit Cards: Most major.

A long-time favorite of locals, and I had to include it for old time's sake. You can't eat here and not try its crispy-fried foods. Popular with families and very homey—they sell a lot of turkey dinners. The decor hasn't changed much in 50 years, and the outside looks like it could use a facelift. Seniors love it. If you're not into grease, this may not be your place.

SPRINGSIDE INN
315-252-7247;
  fax 315-252-8096.
www.springsideinn.com.
6141 W. Lake Rd., Auburn,
  NY 13021.
Open: Apr.–Dec., Tues.–
  Thurs. 5–9, Fri. and Sat.
  5–10, Sun. 10:30–7;
  Jan.–Mar., call for hours..
Price: $$–$$$.
Cuisine: Classic American.
Serving: D, Sun. brunch.
Credit Cards: Most major.

An institution in Auburn on Route 38, this red-painted inn with its rambling porches and awnings offers you several dining choices. Dine in the cozy pub room or in the cathedral-ceilinged dining room decorated with turn-of-the-20th-century lamps and English carpets where the menu features traditional hearty items such as roast beef, baked Virginia ham, baked chicken, lobster Newburg, duck flambé, and popovers. Salads use local produce in season, and the inn prepares its own salad dressing. A variety of rooms are available to accommodate intimate dinners as well as large functions.

CASUAL FOOD

Hunter's Dinerant (315-255-2282; 18 E. Genesee St., Auburn, NY 13021) One of the last of its kind, Hunter's has been serving customers all hours of the day and night for more than 50 years. Try the homemade pies and puddings as well as the meatloaf, mashed potatoes, and other comfort foods. Open 24/7.
The Mahogany Table (315-258-5288; 130 Genesee St, Auburn, NY 13021) Ethnic comfort food.

McMurphy's Authentic Irish Pub & Restaurant (315-253-4531; 75 North St., Auburn, NY 13021; at the Holiday Inn) Good Irish food and beer, burgers, sandwiches, steak, and seafood. Try the Shepherds Pie or Cousin Katie's Guinness Stew.

Parisi's Bistro at Five Points (315-252-7511; 50 Arterial West, Auburn, NY 13021; on Rte. 5 & 20) A cozy place with good Italian fare.

Reese's Dairy Bar and Mini Golf (Rte. 5 & 20, west of Auburn) A candy-colored dairy bar and miniature golf links with picnic tables. Ice cream, hamburgers, and other snack foods.

Wegman's (315-255-2231; 40–60 Genesee St., Auburn, NY 13021) A cappuccino and latte bar is in this full-service grocery store. Buy a dessert, bagel, or sub, and head to the seating area. Open 24/7.

Otisco Lake

The Otisco Lake outlet.

FOOTPRINTS ON THE LAKE
315-636-8255.
2437 Rte. 174, Marietta, NY 13110.
Open: Tues. to Thurs. 5–9; Fri. and Sat. 5–10; Sunday brunch 11–2; Sun. dinner 5–9.
Price: $–$$$.
Cuisine: American.
Serving: D, B.
Credit Cards: Most major.

Boats can dock at this casual lakeside restaurant, where you can sit on the large deck outside or in the main dining room. Enjoy lobster, steak, seafood, and other family favorites. On Sunday, a live jazz group plays for a champagne brunch.

CASUAL FOOD

Lake Drive-Inn (315-636-8557; corner Otisco Valley Rd. and Otisco Rd., Marietta, NY 13110) A snack stand with picnic tables and small indoor area offering ice cream, hot dogs, hamburgers, fries, pizza, and other quickfood. Open in summers Wed.–Thurs. 12–9, Fri. and Sat. 12–10, Sun. 12–8.

Chief Logan

Where Auburn now stands was once a Native American village, the home of Logan (Tah-gah-jute). A sachem of the Shamokins and Cayuga tribes, Logan was known as a peaceful and wise man. Because of his great oratorical skills and good sense, he often represented the Six Nations at powwows with whites. This all changed when his entire family was brutally slaughtered by a renegade band of settlers. Lashing out in retribution, he took the lives of several white families, although it is said he did not allow his warriors to apply torture to the victims, at that time a common practice among his people. Logan is buried in Fort Hill Cemetery in Auburn, where his grave is marked by a limestone obelisk.

CULTURE

Skaneateles Lake and Skaneateles

Skaneateles Festival (315-685-7418; 97 E. Genesee St., Skaneateles, NY 13152) The music of Mozart, Bach, Bartok, Prokofiev, and other great composers are showcased in a series of chamber music concerts in various locations, including Brook Farm at 2870 West Lake Road, where you can sit under the stars (bring lawn chairs, blankets, and flashlights); the First Presbyterian Church and Marcellus High School KidsFest performances are also given. Single tickets $19–$25; season subscription $130–$190.

John D. Barrow Art Gallery (315-685-5135; 49 E. Genesee St., Skaneateles, NY 13152; in the village library) Presented is the life's work of one of the area's most prolific 19th-century poets and painters, including numerous oil portraits and early scenes of the area. This exhibit should be of interest to anyone who likes local history. Open July and August, Mon.–Sat. 12–4; Jan.–Mar., Sat. 2–4. (Or ask the librarian on other days, and you might get a peek.)

The Creamery and Skaneateles Historical Society (315-685-1360; 28 Hannum St., Skaneateles, NY 13152) Once the place farmers came to sell their milk, cream, butter, and other dairy products to the public, this 100-year-old building now houses the local historical society as well as hundreds of artifacts, a research and archives department, gift shop, and meeting room. Open summers Thurs.–Sat. 1–4; the rest of the year Fri. 1–4 or by appointment.

Owasco Lake and Auburn

MUSEUMS, EXHIBITS, AND HISTORIC SITES

Cayuga Museum and the Case Research Laboratory (315-253-8051; fax 315-253-9829; www.cayuganet.org/cayugamuseum; 203 Genesee St., Auburn, NY 13021) Permanent and changing exhibits about life in Cayuga country are attractively displayed in the Willard Case mansion (circa 1840). Case, an important inventor of his time, perfected the tube that made sound movies possible. In fact, the first commercially successful system of sound film was invented in the Case Research Lab in 1923. See a Tiffany window, Bundy clocks, Victorian-era furnishings, and a 1928 Movietone news film along with other memorabilia. It's also a great place to learn about Native American art.

Cayuga-Owasco Lakes Historical Society Museum (315-497-3906; 14 W. Cayuga St., Moravia, NY 13118) The "History House" is a treasure trove of more than 500 items, focusing on local history and genealogy. Most of the pieces on display have been donated by area citizens. Call for hours.

Fort Hill Cemetery (315-253-8132; 19 Fort St., Auburn, NY 13021) Several important Auburn people are buried in this cemetery, which around 1100 was used as a fortress by the Iroquois and Cayuga tribes. The remains of the last fortifications are still evident, and a monument to Chief Logan, one of the great Native American leaders, is in the cemetery. Other prominent leaders buried here include William H. Seward, whose grave is on a slight hill near the Wadsworth and Aikin family monuments, and Harriet Tubman. To find her grave, from the Fort Hill entrance, keep right along the lower border of the cemetery, and look on your left when you round a bend. Her stone is under a tall pine, flanked by two small shrubs.

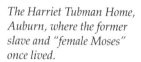

The Harriet Tubman Home, Auburn, where the former slave and "female Moses" once lived.

Harriet Tubman Home (315-252-2081; hthome@localnet.com; www.nyhistory .com/harriettubman;, 180 South St., Auburn, NY 13021; on Rte. 34) This is the museum and home of Harriet Tubman, a heroic woman and former slave from Maryland often called "the female Moses" and the "Joan of Arc" of her race. She made 19 dangerous trips south to rescue more than 300 slaves. During the Civil War, she became a Union spy, scout, and nurse, bringing 700 of her people from plantations to join the Union army. The house she built for her mother and small hospital is open and contains Tubman's sewing machine, her coal stove, a number of pieces of furniture, linens, and other memorabilia. A modest museum is also on the property. Although her private home is also here, it is not yet open to the public. Every year more than 2,000 people from the A.M.E. Zion Church Connection (African Methodist and Episcopal) make an annual pilgrimage to the site over Memorial Day weekend. Open Feb. 1-Oct. 31, Tues.–Fri. 10–4, Sat. 10–3; Nov.–Jan. by appointment. Admission: adults $3, seniors $2, children under 16 $1.

Schweinfurth Memorial Art Center (315-255-1553; fax 315-255-0871; smac@ relex.com; www.cayuganet.org/smac; 205 Genesee St., Auburn, NY 13021) An extensive museum displaying all periods and kinds of art. There are six major shows a year, including the annual "Quilts=Art=Quilts," "Made in New York," "Both Ends of the Rainbow" (children's and seniors' artwork), and other fine-arts exhibitions, revolving exhibits, and crafts shows. The museum has an excellent gift shop, with several one-of-a-kind items on sale and offers a number of classes, lectures, and trips. The facility is state-of-the-art and a great asset to the city. Open Tues.–Sat. 10–5, Sun. 1–5.

Seward House (315-252-1283; www.sewardhouse.org; 33 South St., Auburn, NY 13021) Griffins flank the entrance of this museum and imposing early 19th-century home of William H. Seward, New York governor, U.S. senator, and secretary of state under Presidents Lincoln and Johnson. Seward was instrumental in the purchase of Alaska and one of the founders of the Republican Party. The museum contains period and Civil War pieces, and there is a lovely garden and gazebo. Guided tours are given Feb.–Dec. Open July 1-Oct. 14, Tues.–Sat. 10–4, Sun. 1–4; off-season Tues.–Sat. 1–4; closed Mon. and all Jan. Admission $3.25.

Ward W. O'Hara Agricultural Museum (315-253-5611; www.cayuganet.org /agmuseum; 6880 East Lake Rd., Auburn, NY 13021; at Emerson Park and Rte. 38A) This is much more than a museum of important farm implements and tools circa 1800–1930. There is a blacksmith shop, general store, woodwork shop, cooperage, 1900 country kitchen, and veterinarian's office. Special events include a draft horse show, antique tractor rodeo, miniature horse and pony show, and dairy and old ways days. Children will enjoy the "Try & Touch" exhibits. Open June, Sat. and Sun. 11–4, July–Aug. daily.

Willard Memorial Chapel (315-252-0339; 17 Nelson St., Auburn, NY 13021) This is the only complete and unaltered Tiffany chapel in the country. It is constructed of gray limestone and red sandstone in the Romanesque Revival style of architecture; the Tiffany interior contains a 9-paneled rose window depicting religious symbols and figures, a 3-paneled stained glass window, 14 opalescent nave windows, 9 leaded glass chandeliers, a memorial mosaic bronze and gilt tablet, mosaic floors, a jeweled pulpit, and gold stenciled furniture and ceiling. It's simply dazzling. The Tiffany Summer Concert Series takes place in the chapel every Wednesday at noon July and August. Open Tues.–Fri. 10–4 or by appointment; closed holidays. Admission $2.

Photo Ops

Skaneateles Lake: One of the best views of the deep blue lake is from a spot about 2.8 miles north of Scott on Route 41.

Carpenter's Falls: To find the 100-foot falls near New Hope, go 11 miles south on the west side of Skaneateles Lake to Apple Tree Road (mile marker 14), bear left at the fork, and cross over the falls at the east-west escarpment. If you want to walk down to the bottom of the gorge, there is a quasi trail—not maintained but well worn. Wear good hiking shoes as the going can get rough. But once you reach the bottom, there is a wonderful level place perfect for a picnic. Wade in the water for a great view of the falls.

New Hope Mills: Hardly a blink in the road along the west side of Route 41A—watch for a small sign, NEW HOPE MILLS, just past Mandana going south. The old mill wheel still turns, although we're told that for a while, at least, the grinding of grains has been curtailed. The shop, housed in a weathered barn, is filled with flour products, organic grains, spices, honey, and other locally produced items.

Otisco Lake: Taking East Lake Road from Skaneateles, go left on Eibert Road 2 miles from Route 41. As you round a corner and pass a 10-mph sign, you'll get an expansive view of the lake ahead.

THEATER

Auburn Players Community Theater (315-258-8275; Empire State College–State University of New York, 197 Franklin St., Auburn, NY 13021) Drawing from local talent, this group offers four productions a year.

Finger Lakes Drive-In (315-252-3969; Clark St., Auburn, NY 13021; Rtes. 5 & 20) One of the few remaining outdoor movie theaters left in the region. Now offering first-run movies. Open seasonally.

Merry-Go-Round Playhouse (315-255-1785, 800-457-8897, off-season 315-255-1305; PO Box 506, Auburn, NY 13021; in Emerson Park, Rte. 38A) Four Broadway musicals come to the Finger Lakes each summer. Productions such as *42nd Street* and *Annie Get Your Gun* are held in the former carousel pavilion in Emerson Park. On the drawing board are plans for a major expansion that will increase seating capacity from 364 to 525. Ticket prices are $19 to $26.

RECREATION

Skaneateles Lake and Skaneateles

Skaneateles Community Center (315-685-2266; 97 State St., Skaneateles, NY 13152) One of the best and biggest (two stories, 11,000 sq. ft.) sports facilities in central New York, this new complex houses the W. G. Allyn Arena, a full-size heated ice arena; the Mary H. Soderberg Aquatic Center, with 5 pools including a plunge pool, an 8-lane competition pool, and a 12-person hot tub; professional-style locker rooms; dressing room for the Skaneateles figure skating club; track; second-floor viewing area over the rink; workout rooms; Community Room; dining concessions; game room; pro shop; and offices. A full calendar of programs and events is offered throughout the year. Also on the property is the older ice rink, the Austin Park Pavilion, that's still utilized for skating and events. Annual memberships are available ranging from $47–$639; day fees are $4–$6.

BIKING

Skaneateles Lake Loop (40 miles): Starting from the village, go south on West Lake Road, then continue on Route 41A to Glen Haven Road. Return to the village by cycling north on Route 41. Key stops along the way include New Hope Mills (just south of Mandana on Route 41A), Glen Haven at the end of the lake, and Borodino on Route 41.

BOATING

Skaneateles Sailing Club (315-685-7541; 2745 E. Lake Rd., Skaneateles, NY 13152) Located on the east side of the lake in a protected cove, this club holds informal races weekly and other sailing events. There is a membership fee and fee for boat storage or mooring. Members can use the clubhouse and dock facilities. The club was founded by longtime expert sailors Janet and Richard Besse.

CRUISES

Mid-Lakes Navigation Company (315-685-8500, 800-545-4318; www.mid-lakesnav.com; 11 Jordan St., PO Box 61, Skaneateles NY 13152) Celebrating 35 years of service, Mid-Lakes Navigation Company offers a variety of cruises on Skaneateles and on New York State's canal system. On Skaneateles Lake, two boats—the double-decker *Judge Ben Wiles* and the *Barbara S. Wiles,* a smaller classic wooden craft—feature two-hour lunch ($20) and three-hour dinner cruises ($37), one-hour sightseeing excursions ($8), wine-tasting cruises, a three-hour Sunday brunch lake outing ($31), a 32-mile, three-and-a-half hour U.S. Mail Cruise ($17) delivering mail to camps around the lake (reserve a box lunch or bring your own), and special group cruises. The dinner cruise gives you a choice of four entrées plus a glass of champagne. Mid-Lakes also offers cruises departing Syracuse, Albany, and Buffalo on the Erie Canal. Two- and three-day cruises with meals and accommodations are also offered. For those who want to go it alone, canal boats are available for charter.

The old boathouses continue to serve boaters on Skaneateles Lake.

MARINAS AND LAUNCHES

Glen Haven (607-749-3779; 7434 Fairhaven Rd., Homer, NY 13077) Public launch and docking facilities; restaurant on premises.

New York State Launch (3 miles on West Lake Rd. from village) Public launch.

Skaneateles Marina (315-685-5095; fax 315-685-1738; 1938 West Lake Rd., Mandana, NY 13152) Full service marina, services, ship store, gas, pontoon boat rental.

Sailboat Shop (315-685-7558; 1322 E. Genesee St., Skaneateles, NY 13152) Sailboat and canoe rentals and sales.

Town of Skaneateles Boat Launch (315-685-3473, Rte. 41A, Mandana, NY 13152).

GOLF

Most golf courses in the region are open from about April 1 through November 1.

The Midlakes Club (315-673-4916; Bockes Rd., Skaneateles, NY 13152) 18-hole public course overlooking the lake.

Foxfire at Village Green (315-638-2930; 1 Village Blvd., Baldwinsville, NY 13027) Near Syracuse, the well-manicured par-72 championship Foxfire wanders through a community of homes and condos. Elevated tees, narrow fairways, water, and bunkers make it a challenge. A round of golf, including cart and lunch, is priced from $29. There is a driving range on the property.

The Links at Sunset Ridge (315-673-2255; Rte. 175, Marcellus, NY 13108) This young course is fairly flat, with high roughs designed to resemble a links layout. Jeff Clark, head professional, points out that the tees are gender-neutral: Where you tee off from depends on your handicap; i.e., if your handicap is less than 12, you tee off from the orange or black tees; 12 to 25, you drive from the green tees; and more than 25, from the gold tees. Water comes into play on four holes, and the course is well bunkered. Greens fees are $19, $26 with cart on weekdays; on weekends $22, $32 with cart.

Radisson Greens Golf Club (315-638-0092; 8055 Potter Rd., Baldwinsville, NY 13027) A Robert Trent Jones course that's high on quality, low in greens fees (less than $45 with cart). Tough par fives and great greens and fairways. A good bet for better players.

West Hill Golf Course (315-672-8677; 2500 W. Genesee Tpke., Camillus, NY 13219) One of the best par-three courses in the state. A virtual arboretum, West Hill has an enormous variety of trees planted along the fairways. The front nine is much easier and less dramatic than the back nine, which has a lake that brings water into play on several holes. Greens fees are $13; a half cart is $7. If you're going to play more than three rounds, buy the $25 yearly membership fee. Greens fees drop to $9 per round for members.

HIKING

Baltimore Woods (315-673-1350; From Skaneateles center, take Rte. 20 east, left on Rte. 175, Lee Mulroy Rd. Take another left on Bishop Hill Rd. to the upper parking area and pavilion.) Several loop trails from 0.25 to 0.7 mile are laced through this 170-acre area owned by Save the Country and operated by Centers for Nature Education. Moderately difficult trails go up and down hills, across brooks and flood plains, through woods and fields. The Violet trail contains a 0.3-mile maze containing labeled plantings of wildflowers and plants.

Bear Swamp State Forest (607-753-3095 ext. 217; to find the long loop, going south on Rte. 41, turn left on Iowa Rd. after Reynolds Rd., and take the first left on Bear Swamp Rd. to the parking area on the right. To find the short loop, going south on Rte. 41A, after Reynolds Rd., turn left on the next un-marked dirt road and look for a DEC sign on the right side of Rte. 41A; park where you see the trailhead near a wooden kiosk.) Off the southeast end of Skaneateles Lake, this 3,316-acre state forest is home to 13 miles of well-marked trails. Take the rather difficult 3.4-mile loop or the longer and also difficult 7.8-mile loop. Both go through forests of pine and spruce, over streams and bridges, and up and down hills, some steep.

Cayuga County Erie Canal Trail (315-253-5611; starts just east of Port Byron off Rte. 31 at Randolph J. Schassel Village Park) You can take a 9.3-mile walk (one way) along the former towpath and abandoned canal bed, or tie into another 14.8 miles through Erie Canal Park in Camillus for a 20-mile (round-trip) walk. The walking, although rough in places, is pretty level and easy except for a few rough places, but it will take you a good part of a day to do it. One of the highlights is Lock 52 west of Port Byron. This trail is available to hikers, bikers, and horseback riders.

Charlie Major Nature Trail (315-685-3473; from center of village on Rte. 20, go north on Jordan St., then left onto Fennell Rd. Look for a parking area and NA-TURE TRAIL sign just after Old Seneca Turnpike.) A prominent Skaneateles leader from the 1950s through the 1990s and a great advocate of hiking, Char-lie Major came up with the idea for this 1.6-mile easy trail that follows an abandoned rail line. Partway down, look for the falls on your right, and take the path that goes across some large foundation stones to the falls. There you'll find a perfect place to stop and have a picnic right over the water as it spills over the rocks.

OTHER ATTRACTIONS

Carpenter's Brook Fish Hatchery (315-689-9367; Rte. 321, Elbridge, NY 13060) See the hatchery where thousands of brown, rainbow, and brook trout eggs are hatched, and the small fish are put into ponds to grow. Picnic tables, workshops (by reservation), and fishing programs (for senior citizens and special needs groups).

Polo Matches (Off W. Lake Rd., turn right on Andrews Rd., Skaneateles) Polo held Sundays at 3pm during July and August. Small parking fee.

Skiing: Greek Peak (800-955-2754; http://www.greekpeakskiclub.org); Skan-eateles Family Ski Hill (315-636-8486) open to winter ski members; Song Mountain Ski Center (315-696-5711).

Owasco Lake and Auburn

BIKING

Owasco Lake Loop: A 32-mile loop around the lake starting at Emerson Park, going south on Route 38 along the west side of the lake, to Moravia and Fillmore Glen and returning north on Route 38A. Key stops include Moravia and Fillmore Glen. Bring your suits for a swim in Emerson Park at the end of your trip.

Sailing is a major sport on Skaneateles Lake.

BOATING

Lake Country Outdoors (315-497-3006; PO Box 444-1541, Moravia, NY 13118; on Rte. 38) Full services and launching facilities.

Trade-A-Yacht Marina (315-258-9096; 147 Pulsifer Dr., Auburn, NY 13021) Sales and service.

GOLF

Arnold Palmer Golf (315-253-8072; Gates Rd., Auburn, NY 13021; off Rte. 5) Bring the family. Driving range, miniature golf, batting cages, game room, and snack bar.

Dutch Hollow Country Club (315-784-5052, Benson Rd., Auburn, NY 13021) When you play Dutch Hollow Country Club, a ten-minute drive from town, remember your retriever: There's water, water everywhere. Dutch Hollow Brook comes into play on 8 holes, and the 14th, par three, can beat you up if you miss the 130-yard drive and land in the gully that lies between the tee and the green. Be prepared for lots of ups and downs; it's hilly. Several clinics are offered each year.

Fillmore Golf Course (315-497-3145; Tollgate Hill Rd., RR 1 Box 409, Locke, NY 13092) This is a pretty basic public course with the advantage of its location in Fillmore Glen. The 18-hole course is open seasonally. There are riding carts, a pro shop, and a snack bar. Greens fee are about $11.

Highland Park Country Club (315-253-3381, Franklin St., Auburn, NY 13021) Popular with locals, this semi-private, well-maintained course has its share of quirky holes and lovely views of the countryside. It is considered one of the better courses in the area.

Indian Head (Rte. 5 and 20, Auburn, NY 13021) A public 18-hole course. Rather flat and not too exciting but a good place for beginners.

HIKING

Auburn-Fleming Trail (315-253-5611; from Rtes. 5 & 20 in Auburn, go south on Columbus St., and park on Dunning Ave. just after Clymer St.) This straight 2-mile dirt-and-stone up-and-back trail is an easy walk along an old tree-lined railroad bed just west of the northern end of Owasco Lake.

Fillmore Glen State Park (315-497-0130; just off Rte. 38 south of Moravia; use the back parking lot.) Near the south end of Owasco Lake are three 1.8-mile (one way) moderately difficult dirt trails in this 938-acre magnificent gorge and valley. The trails start in the valley and rise 349 feet to a dam. The North and South Rim Trails follow the rims of the gorge; the Gorge Trail goes along Dry Creek (which is actually not dry at all). At the turning point of the trails is a two-level dam. The lower pool of water is great for swimming. The Gorge Trail is a perfect one for young children, level and safe with smaller waterfalls and walls of layered shale all along the way (a "prehistoric library.") Check out the Cowsheds, a cavern carved out of rock by a tumbling waterfall. The scenery—deep-cut gorges, forests, streams, ponds, and great boulders and rock formations—is wonderful.

PARKS, NATURE PRESERVES, AND CAMPING

Casey Park (315-253-4247; N. Division St., Auburn, NY 13021) A multipurpose sports and recreation facility, with tennis courts, Olympic-sized swimming pool, and biking and walking trails. Picnic areas, playgrounds, horseshoe pits, and bocce courts.

Emerson Park (315-2553-5611; Rte. 38A, Auburn, NY 13021) A large, sprawling grassy park on the shores of Owasco Lake. Swimming, beaches, boat launches, picnic facilities, playgrounds, bathhouse, and a restored pavilion. Also on grounds is the Cayuga County Agricultural Museum.

Fillmore Glen State Park (315-497-0130; Rte. 38A, Moravia, NY 13118) A lovely, deep limestone-and-shale glen comprising 857 acres, with many waterfalls, nature trails, 60 campsites, three cabins, picnic pavilions, ball fields, and swimming pool. The original factory where the first cast-iron plow was invented by Jethro Wood is still standing near the falls.

Montezuma National Wildlife Refuge (Rte. 5 and 20; west of Auburn) A rich ecological environment and haven for birds and other wildlife. Trails, roads, observation tower, and visitor center make this exceptional resource easily accessible.

Enjoying a refreshing drink at the stone fountain in Clift Park, Skaneateles.

OTHER ATTRACTIONS

Balloon Rides (Sunset Adventures: 315-252-9474; www.fingerlakesballooning .com; Box 6863, RD 5, Beech Tree Rd., Auburn, NY 13021) Drift in a colorful balloon over the Finger Lakes. Balloons depart at sunrise or about one and a half hours before sunset. Price: $135 per person for a one-hour flight and champagne.

Cayuga County Fairgrounds (315-834-6606; www.dirtmotorsports.com; 1 Speedway Dr., Weedsport, NY 13166; Rte. 31) A variety of events are staged here throughout the year, such as fairs, dirt-track motor races, demolition derbies, monster-truck competitions, agricultural exhibits, horse shows, concerts, and arts and crafts. It is the home of Dirt Motorsports Hall of Fame and the Classic Car Museum, containing vintage racing vehicles and memorabilia (315-834-6667).

Falcon Park (315-255-2489; 130 N. Division St., Auburn, NY 13021) See super baseball and enjoy a hot dog in a 2,044-seat baseball stadium where the Auburn Doubledays, a Class A farm team for the Houston Astros (in the NY–Penn League) play June through September. The team is named after Abner Doubleday, baseball's legendary founder, who grew up in Auburn.

Otisco Lake

Otisco Lake Marina (315-636-8807; Amber-Preble Rd., Marietta, NY 13110) Boat sales, service, rentals, and storage.

SHOPPING

No doubt about it: *The* shopping mecca of the area is Skaneateles. The attractive brick sidewalks and period lighting that line Genesee Street, the main street, are lined with upscale gift shops, art galleries, boutiques, antiques shops, and cafés that invite you to stop and linger. When you need a break, you need only stroll down to either end of the street for a lake break on a wooden bench by the water.

A few shops are worth visiting on the western end of the area, up Jordan Street and around the corner past the Sherwood Inn, where there is a marvelous clothing store and bakery tucked into quarters in a big old house.

Except for the Finger Lakes Mall and a few bright lights in the former retail district such as Aardvarks & Zippers and Swaby's Kangaroo Court, Auburn doesn't offer much in the way of a major shopping experience.

Skaneateles and Skaneateles Lake

ANTIQUES

New Hope Antiques was once an 1820s farmhouse.

New Hope Antiques (315-497-2688; 5963 New Hope Rd., New Hope, NY 13118) China, books, paintings, jewelry, collectibles, and memorabilia are displayed in a newly restored 1820s farmhouse house. Open summers daily 11–5; closed Tuesdays. (Call ahead as the shop is closed the odd week.)

Skaneateles Antique Center (315-685-0752; 12 E. Genesee St., Skaneateles, NY 13152) You can spend hours browsing through the antiques and collectibles of more than 30 dealers located on two floors. Find furniture, pottery, books, jewelry, linens, lighting, primitives, militaria, coins, decorative arts and crafts, accessories and other things. Open Mon.–Sat. 10–5:30; Sun. 12–5.

White & White (315-685-7733, 18 E. Genesee St., Skaneateles, NY 13152) Stephen and Beverly White continually look for unique antiques, both furniture pieces and collectibles. Most are high-end items. Open Mon.–Sat. 10–5.

ART AND BOOKS

Long Lake Gallery/Skaneateles Framing Company (315-685-9260; www.skane atelesframeco.com; 5 Jordan St., Skaneateles, NY 13152) Represents more than 30 Central New York artists selling regional paintings, prints, and other artwork. The gallery also does framing.

McCarthy's Finger Lakes Photography and Gallery (315-685-9099; www.john francismccarthy.com/the_artist.htm; 9 Jordan St., Skaneateles, NY 13152) A fine selection of regional books, posters, notes, prints, and gifts by noted photographer John McCarthy.

CHILDREN'S AND TOYS

Frog Alley Toys (315-685-0359; 22 Jordan St., Skaneateles, NY 13152; in the Village Square Bldg.) This fun shop contains a delightful assortment of toys, books, plush animals, games, science kits, building blocks, and even candy.

The Kinder Garden (315-685-2721; 3 E. Genesee St., Skaneateles, NY 13152) Lovely children's clothes and toys, including frames, stuffed animals, kiddie banks, pictures, and games.

T. C. Timber/Haba U.S.A. (315-685-6660, 4407 Jordan Rd., Skaneateles, NY 13152) Formerly Skaneateles Handicrafters, this company has inherited a strong tradition of wooden trains and toys. Their hardwood tracks, trains, and other butter-smooth wooden toys are about the best you'll find anywhere in the world. T. C. Timber is available in good quality toy stores, but here on Saturdays from 10am–1pm, you can load up on engines, train cars, and other toys .

CLOTHING

Bella Blue (315-685-3272; 32 W. Genesee St., Skaneateles, NY 13152) Trendy women's clothes, shoes, and accessories.

cate&sally (315-685-1105; 58 E. Genesee St., Skaneateles, NY 13152) Chic, sassy and sophisticated women's apparel, including cardigans, shoes, collections, separates, hats, and colorful sundresses.

CRAFTS

The Cat's Whiskers (315-636-8284; 1477 Willowdale Rd., Skaneateles, NY 13152) This shop specializes in arts, crafts, quilts, folk art, and prints. Open Tues., Thurs. Sat. 11–5.

Elegant Needles (315-685-9276; 5 Jordan St., Skaneateles, NY 13152) Everything for those who want to knit, crochet, needlepoint, etc. Fine yarns by Rowan, Classic Elite, Dale of Norway, and Renaissance. Handknit Norwegian sweaters.

FOOD and WINE

Beak & Skiff Apple Hill (315-677-5105; www.beakndskiff.com; 4472 Cherry Valley Tpke., Lafayette, NY 13084; on Rte. 80 off Rte. 20) It's hard to know whether to put this one under food or family entertainment. It's both. Beautiful apple orchards hang heavy with several varieties of apples from late summer through October. You can pick your own apples, arriving at the best picking spots via the farm's tractor-drawn wagon. Children will love the corn maze and goat-and-sheep pen. There are picnic tables, a large retail store packed with apple-oriented and other items, from colorful candles to children's hand-knit garments, and a snack stand is open on weekends. (Call or visit their website first for information on picking and snack-stand operations.)

Burdick Sugarbush (315-685-5501; Hencoop Rd., Skaneateles, NY 13152; off Rte. 41A) See maple syrup being tapped from the trees; farm animals.

Essentially Bread (315-689-1200; 245B E. Main St., Elbridge, NY 13060) This is the place to come for pastries and artisan breads made from scratch. Varieties include sourdough, semolina, raisin walnut, peasant, mozzarella and dill, bacon and cheddar, ciabatta, and potato and onion.

Farmers' Market (Austin Park Pavilion, Skaneateles, NY 13152) A variety of farmers and bakers bring their wares to this open market. Right of the back of their trucks you can buy vegetables, fruit, flowers, herbs, cheese, and breads. Held each Thursday afternoon during the summer months, 3:30–6:30.

Goat Hill Farm (315-655-3014; goathill@dreamscape.com; 2915 Gulf Rd., Manlius, NY 13104; a right off Rte. 20 east of Skaneateles just past Pompey Center,) More than 150 goats are milked twice a day on this 57-acre goat farm owned by Steven and Jennie Mueller. Products for sale include goat cheese. Open noon–7.

King Ferry Winery (315-685-2009; 800-439-5271; www.treleavenwines.com; 22 Jordan St., Skaneateles, NY 13152; in the Village Square Bldg.) This wine shop features Treleaven wines, Chardonnay, and other wines produced using European techniques. Wine-tasting room and gift shop. Open Mon.–Fri. 11–6; Sat 10–6; Sun. 12–5.

New Hope Mills (315-497-0783; RD#2, off Glen Haven Rd., north of Mandana just off 41A) A small country mill store and museum specializing in stone-ground grain products, unbleached and enriched products such as bulgar, baking supplies, fruits and nuts, honey, potato flour, and pancake mixes. No fancy packaging, but you can't beat the prices: A 1-pound package of buttermilk pancake mix is $1.50; 5 pounds $2.60; 2 pounds of oat bran is $1.50; 5 pounds of buckwheat $3. Open Apr.--Dec. Mon.–Fri. 9–4, Sat. 9–3; Jan.–Mar. Mon.–Fri. 9–4, Sat. 9–noon.

Rhubarb (315-685-5803; 59 E. Genesee St., Skaneateles, NY 13152) Located in a former book store, this shop is a treasure trove for those who love to cook. It contains all kinds of kitchen gadgets, cookbooks, gourmet foods, cutlery, aprons, espresso makers, cookware, and salsas.

Rosalie's Bakery (315-685-2200; 841 W. Genesee St., Skaneateles, NY 13152) The aroma of freshly baked bone bread and biscotti draw you into the back of Rosalie's Cucina. They also make desserts, wedding cakes, Hawaiian fruit bread, and other goodies. Open Mon.–Sun. 10–6.

Tierra Farm Café-Bakery (315-496-2602; 6407 Glen Haven Rd., New Hope, NY 13118) Find organic vegetables, a café—offering specialty pizzas, ice cream, and vegetarian entrées—and a bakery on a working farm. Sculptures by the owner are located on the grounds.

Vermont Green Mountain Specialty Company (315-685-1500; 50 E. Genesee St., Skaneateles, NY 13152) I dare you to come in here and leave empty-handed. There are just too many good things all around: handmade chocolates, gourmet coffees and foods, old-fashioned lollipops, cookies, cakes, and other pastries, and gift baskets and novelties. Open Mon., Wed.–Sat. 6:30am–7pm; Tues. 6:30am–5pm, Thurs. and Fri. 6:30am–9pm in summer; Sun. noon–6pm.

The Village Bottle Shop (315-685-5197; 18 W. Genesee St., Skaneateles, NY 13152) A fantastic array of wines and spirits are displayed in a handsome period setting.

GIFTS

Aristocats and Dogs (315-685-4849; www.aristocatsanddogs.com, 62 E. Genesee St., Skaneateles, NY 13152) The stars in the shop are the one or two kittens up for adoption through the SPCA. All the merchandise is cat or dog oriented. There are collars, ceramics, toy animals, even a doggy life preserver.

Chestnut Cottage (315-685-8082; 75 E. Genesee St., Skaneateles, NY 13152) This store, which rambles through rooms that were once a private home, contains a wealth of Christmas ornaments and wreaths. There are also many red-white-and-blue Americana-style items.

The Country Cabin (315-685-3032; 6 Jordan St., Skaneateles, NY 13152) Early-American-style gifts, crafts, cheese, pottery, and exceptional hand-crafted gifts and seasonal items.

1st National Gifts (315-685-5454; 2 E. Genesee St., Skaneateles, NY 13152) It's housed in the lofty former bank building, hence the name. Lots of souvenir and local items set up in gift stations.

Gallop On Saddlery (315-685-5232; www.galloponsaddlery.com; 38 E. Genesee St., Skaneateles, NY 13152) Filled with equestrian items: clothes, stuffed and toy horses, saddles, gifts, T-shirts, and more.

The Hitching Post Gift Shoppe (315-685-7304; 2 W. Genesee St., Skaneateles,

NY 13152) Since 1957 this corner gift shop has been doing a brisk tourist trade. It's the place to go for cards, pewter, early-American items, candles, brassware, and souvenirs. It also has an assortment of good books.

Imagine (315-685-6263; 8 E. Genesee St., Skaneateles, NY 13152) The merchandise lives up to its name. Find dazzling handblown glass, pewterware, silver jewelry, puzzles, oil lamps, prints, charms, and other interesting things.

Paris Flea, a shop filled with accessories and one-of-a-kind gifts and antiques.

Paris Flea (315-685-7228; 23 Jordan St., Skaneateles NY 13152) A new, sophisticated boutique-style gift shop selling a fine mix of antiques and very unusual new items from glassware and china to small furniture pieces.

Pomodoro (315-685-8658; 877-POMODORO; 61 E. Genesee St., Skaneateles NY 13152) As you enter, you'll see a sign that says: YOUR HUSBAND CALLED; SAID TO BUY ANYTHING YOU WANT. This should not be a problem if you like primitive art, candles, ornaments, candies, cards, and other unique gifts. There are also several brand-name collectibles such as Mary Engelbreit, Land and Wise, and Portmeirion.

The White Sleigh Christmas Shoppe (315-685-8414; 1 W. Genesee St., Skaneateles, NY 13152) Everything here is for Christmas: Dickens's Village, Byers' Carolers, Old-World Santas, trees full of ornaments, and candles.

Owasco Lake and Auburn

ANTIQUES

Auburn Antiques (315-252-9701, 255-1458; 7 Arterial E., Auburn, NY 13021; on Rte. 5) Packed with all sorts of stuff, from antique hockey sticks, jewelry, and glass to memorabilia and furniture. A fun browse with hidden reassures possible. Open Tues.–Sat. 11–5, Sun. and Mon. by chance.

FOOD

Grisamore Farms (315-497-1347; grisamorefarms@a-znet.com; 749 Cowan Rd., Locke, NY 13092; off Rte. 90 between Locke and Genoa south of Moravia) This is a large complex, with fields, greenhouses, farm store, and Christmas shop. Pick your own strawberries, blueberries, raspberries, apples, cherries, vegetables, and pumpkins, and cut your own Christmas trees. In the fall there are hayrides, a Halloween maze, and a working cider press. Open May–Oct., Mon.–Fri. 8–7, Sat. 8–5, Sun. 10–5; Nov. and Dec., Mon.–Sat. 9–5, Sun. 10–5.

MALLS

Fingerlakes Mall (315-255-1188; PO Box 7128, Auburn, NY 13021; Rtes. 5 & 20) More than 50 specialty stores, restaurants, and department stores.

For More Information

Cayuga County Office of Tourism: 315-255-1658, 800-499-9615; www.tourcayuga .com; 131 Genesee St., Auburn NY 13021.

City of Auburn Historic Sites Commission: 315-258-9820, 877-343-0002; c/o Cayuga County Office of Tourism (see above).

Fnger Lakes Tourism: 315-536-7488; www.fingerlakes.org; 309 Lake St., Penn Yan, NY 13427.

Skaneateles Area Chamber of Commerce: 315-685-0552; Skaneateles-chamber@ worldnet.att.net, www.Skaneateles.com; 22 Jordan St., PO Box 199, Skaneateles NY 13152.

CHAPTER FOUR
Vineyards, Colleges, & Museums
CAYUGA LAKE

Chartered boats cruise the waters of the Cayuga-Seneca Canal.

Anchored on the southern end by Ithaca, home of Cornell University and Ithaca College, and at the north by Seneca Falls, birthplace of the women's rights movement, Cayuga Lake is the longest of the Finger Lakes (40 miles) and the second deepest (435 feet). It is also the lake closest to sea level, with an elevation of 384 feet.

To get an overview of this beautiful body of water, drive around it—or even bike the distance. On your trip around the lake, you'll pass many permanent homes and a large number of summer camps and houses, and in places the road comes very close to the water. You'll pass through small villages like Union Springs, Cayuga, and Ludlowville on the east side and Trumansburg, Interlaken, Sheldrake, and Canoga on the west side. The Wells College town of Aurora is at the midpoint on the eastern shore. Recently this delightful little town

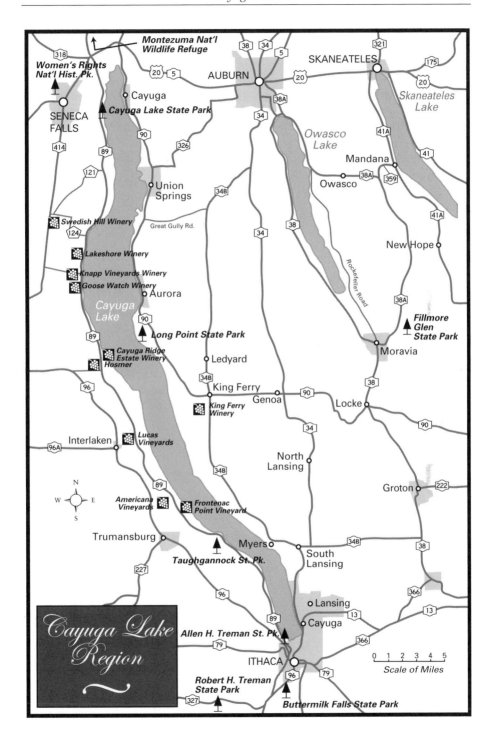

Montezuma Nat'l
Wildlife Refuge

Women's Rights
Nat'l Hist. Pk.

SKANEATELES

SENECA
FALLS

Cayuga

Cayuga Lake State Park

AUBURN

Skaneateles
Lake

Owasco
Lake

Mandana

Union
Springs

Owasco

Great Gully Rd.

Swedish Hill Winery

Lakeshore Winery

Knapp Vineyards Winery

Goose Watch Winery

Aurora

New Hope

Cayuga
Lake

Rockefeller Road

Long Point State Park

Fillmore
Glen
State Park

Cayuga Ridge
Estate Winery
Hosmer

Ledyard

Moravia

King Ferry

Genoa

Locke

King Ferry
Winery

Lucas
Vineyards

Interlaken

North
Lansing

Groton

Americana
Vineyards

Frontenac
Point Vineyard

Trumansburg

Myers

South
Lansing

Taughgannock St. Pk.

Lansing

Cayuga

Cayuga Lake
Region

Allen H. Treman St. Pk.

ITHACA

Robert H. Treman
State Park

Buttermilk Falls State Park

N
W   E
S

0 1 2 3 4 5
Scale of Miles

underwent some dramatic changes, from a major renovation of the historic Aurora Inn to significant upgrades in its downtown buildings and businesses.

Many of the lake's hills are embossed with vineyards marching down to the water's edge. Dramatic waterfalls spill over rugged cliffs and down into deep pools, and rivers gush through gorges carved by ancient glaciers. Hikers, bikers, and all those who appreciate nature can enjoy these spectacular natural assets in the parks that lie around the lake, particularly near the southern end.

Cayuga means "boat landing" in Native American—a name that is still most appropriate, judging by the number of cabin cruisers on the lake. Because of the lake's access to the New York State canal system via the Cayuga-Seneca Canal, Cayuga harbors many boats, large and small, since the possibilities for long-distance cruising are endless.

ITHACA

Ithaca, one of New York State's most energized cities, is bustling with activity from the colleges as well as tourism. Yet its neighborhoods provide a low-key small-town ambiance for Ithaca's close to 30,000 residents, a number that swells by almost 25,000 when Cornell University and Ithaca College are in session.

The two schools are, in fact, Tompkins County's largest private employers: Cornell has a workforce of 8,600; Ithaca 1,300. Cornell, with its prestigious Ivy-League reputation, is an educational leader, particularly in the fields of veterinary medicine, hotel management, biotechnology and agriculture, and life sciences. Ithaca, the largest private residential college in the state, is known for its strong programs in music, communications, and health science.

Much of the commercial action takes place in the center of the city known as the Commons, a pedestrian-only shopping and recreational area with a mix of boutiques, specialty shops, art studios, restaurants, bars, cafés, and offices. It's a very upbeat, hip area worth exploring.

The city also has a thriving arts community, with several theaters, galleries, and museums. In Ithaca, something seems to be going on every night—a play, a concert, a poetry reading, or an opening of a new art exhibit. Much of the action takes place in and around the colleges. A new program is designed to develop Ithaca's downtown as a center for the arts. In this direction, the outdoor sculpture exhibition "Art in the Heart of the City" has been installed on the Commons and Cayuga Street. Renovations are also ongoing in Ithaca's historical scene. For example, the old State Theater recently reopened after a major restoration and is now the venue for ongoing cultural performances. And for outdoor enthusiasts, three major state parks with 150 waterfalls are all within a 10-mile radius of town. There are also plenty of biking and hiking trails and great lake fishing.

Helping Ithaca to flourish is its accessibility. The Ithaca/Tompkins Regional Airport, which is served by USAirways, is only about 10 minutes from Ithaca's city center.

ITHACA'S BEGINNINGS AND GROWTH

The first residents of the area that is now the city of Ithaca were the Cayuga. They farmed the fertile lands around the southern end of the lakes that lay between the swampy flats and the steep hills. In 1779, when General Sullivan swept through on his mission to destroy the Native American villages, the men were impressed by the vast cornfields and orchards. When military land tracts were awarded in the late 1700s, offered by New York State to soldiers who had served in the Revolutionary War, some of these men, including Jacob Yaple, Isaac Dumond, and Peter Hinepaw, returned to build their log cabins on lot 94, on the beautiful lands they had seen 10 years before.

Land was cleared, gristmills were built on Cascadilla Creek, and by 1800 the area was buzzing with activity—so much so that some referred to it as "Sin City." At this time Simeon DeWitt, the state surveyor general, acquired much of the land. In addition to dividing the land into lots and putting them up for sale at most reasonable prices, DeWitt drew up a plan for the town and in 1804 named it Ithaca because of its location within the town of Ulysses. (The ancient Greek hero that *that* town was named after hailed from the island of Ithaca.)

By 1810 the population was up to 250, and the town boasted 38 houses, a post office, hotel, schoolhouse, stores, and a library as well as a doctor, lawyer, and miller. The First Bank of Newburgh opened up in a frame building in 1815, now on East Court Street. In 1817 Ithaca became the seat of a new county—Tompkins—and the freewheeling town sobered up and knuckled down to serious business. After all, as a county leader, it had a new image to establish and uphold.

In the subsequent years, many factors contributed to Ithaca's growth. The *Enterprise,* a steamboat, was launched on the lake in 1821, and the boats that followed, like *Telemachus* and *DeWitt*—along with the daily service provided by the stagecoach system—helped Ithaca develop a strong commercial base. By

Ball field at Cornell University, Ithaca.

1830 the population had swelled to 3,592. The railroads arrived in 1842, further enhancing the transportation of goods and passengers in and out of the region. An electric street railway system was established in 1884, eventually linking the hills and the flats.

EDUCATION

The community emphasis on education was launched in 1823, when the Old Academy opened its doors. Then in 1865 Ezra Cornell, who had made a fortune in the telegraph industry, donated a public library to the county, and, with help from the Morrill Land Grant, he went on to establish Cornell University in 1868 on farmlands on East Hill.

In 1892, when local violin teacher William Grant Egbert rented four rooms and arranged to teach eight students, another important educational institution was created: the Ithaca Conservatory of Music. Gradually it expanded its curriculum and was chartered as a private college in 1931. It changed its name to Ithaca College and in 1960 moved to its present site on South Hill.

Other schools in Ithaca include Tompkins Cortland Community College, which started in Groton and moved to Dryden in 1974, and a branch of Florida Lakes School of Massage, which came to town in 1994.

RENEWAL AND PRESERVATION

The 1950s and 1960s saw out-of-town shopping malls draw people out of the city center, and the business district deteriorated. But by the end of the '60s, a massive urban-renewal program brought new life into the inner city. To make room for the new buildings, entire city blocks were cleared. Unfortunately in the process of a most ambitious program, several buildings of historic interest were razed, including the Old City Hall, circa 1843. The resulting uproar from historic preservationists put the brakes on further destruction of noteworthy structures and spurred the formation of the Historic Ithaca organization.

In 1974 Ithaca Commons was created, a pedestrian zone of shops, offices, restaurants, and other commercial businesses. Older structures were rehabilitated, including the Clinton House, Clinton Hall, and the DeWitt Mall, as well as neighborhood houses. Joseph Ciaschi deserves credit for purchasing, saving, and renovating the Clinton Block and Clinton House in 1985.

SENECA FALLS

Seneca Falls—which is actually closer to Cayuga Lake than to Seneca Lake— has played a surprisingly strong role in a number of developments. Home of the first pump, the first fire engine, and site of the first women's rights conventions, this quiet, modest-sized village has seen periods of both rapid growth and decline.

The main business district in Seneca Falls.

Seneca Falls was the site for the classic movie *It's a Wonderful Life,* its village park at Christmastime becomes a magical fairyland of trees and buildings outlined in lights. In the past, Karolyn Grimes, who played "Zuzu" in the movie, has visited the town to take part in the holiday festivities and autograph books at a signing. Seneca Falls, she says, remains close to her heart.

Today Seneca Falls appears to be on the upturn. The revitalization of the Cayuga-Seneca Canal area which runs behind the main business district, the opening of a new museum, the Seneca Museum of Waterways and Industry, and other historical sites and parks in town make this a place worth visiting. Goulds Pumps, a major local industry with roots in the past, continues to employ many people in the area.

NATIVES, SETTLERS, AND ENTREPRENEURS

In the center of the hunting grounds of the once powerful Haudenosaunee (six nations of the Iroquois Confederacy), Seneca Falls was the first town to be settled in the wilderness between Utica and Buffalo. Then it was called *Sha-se-onse,* meaning "swift waters." And, indeed, the rapids running in the Seneca River created the waterpower for the mills and other businesses, shaping the growth and character of Seneca Falls.

The first "official" white settler, Job Smith, came to the area in 1787. He was a man of questionable character, and there were suspicions among some that he was fleeing from justice. He existed by trading with the Native Americans, assisting travelers over the falls, and eating wild game, river salmon, and corn. Later Smith would move to Waterloo and marry a Miss Gorham.

When General Sullivan swept through the region on his mission to destroy the Native-American villages, with his army was Lawrence Van Cleef. When Van Cleef first saw the lake, the story goes, he was so taken by its beauty that he planted his poplar staff in the ground, vowing to return. When he came back ten years later in 1789, the staff had grown into a tree. Van Cleef, who came from Albany, settled with his family near that tree, which stood for more than 100 years. When it came down in a storm, a piece of it was preserved. That piece of wood can now be seen in the Seneca Falls Historical Museum.

For a while Van Cleef and Smith partnered in a business to transport goods and boats around the falls. Then Van Cleef began to make boats and became well known for his skill at piloting craft over the rapids. He was generous, well liked, and one of the early entrepreneurs. He kept the first tavern in his log home and built the first frame building for his family. (The Parkus family from Connecticut then moved into Van Cleef's log cabin.)

Others followed. Records show that several lots were sold as early as 1796, and it is believed that the first sawmill was built about 1794. Seneca Falls was growing up. A log schoolhouse was built in 1801, employing Alexander Wilson as the first teacher. Dr. Long, the first village physician, settled here in 1793 and the First Presbyterian Church was organized in 1807. In 1814 G. V. Sackett, Seneca Falls's first attorney, opened his law office, completing the village's professional roster of "doctor, lawyer, merchant, chief."

Colonel Wilhelmus Mynderse, who had constructed a house, established a store, and built the Upper Red Mills in 1795, constructed the Red Mills on the lower rapids in 1807. The company was known as the Bayard Company. By 1825 the Bayard land also contained a few small farms, a cooper shop, blacksmith shop, and a community of about 300 people.

By 1818 locks allowed boats to avoid the rapids; 10 years later the Cayuga-Seneca Canal was tied into the Erie Canal, opening vast transportation possibilities for goods and produce originating in Seneca Falls.

As people came and stayed, additional businesses developed, mostly along the river where there was water power. But because of the attitude of the Bayard Company, Seneca Falls did not develop more mills and businesses more rapidly at this time. The company controlled the water power in Seneca Falls and, fearing competition, refused to sell any portion of the land. Thus rival villages along the river developed, and Seneca Falls, with its wonderful natural assets, was left to flounder. It was only in 1825, when the Bayard Company fell on hard times, that it was forced to divide its property and sell its holdings.

During his time with the Bayard Company, Colonel Mynderse had amassed great wealth, thanks to his network of business connections, and was a man of great influence in Seneca Falls—in 1832 he donated land to build the Seneca Falls Academy. He died in 1836, leaving his family a large fortune.

Other early businesses included paper mills, a cotton factory, knitting mills, a clock factory, stone flouring mills, a harness shop, hotels, carriage makers, lumber mills, and leather, tool, and woolen mills, including the successful Seneca Knitting Mills. One of the most important operations came to Seneca Falls in 1839: pump manufacturing. In 1855 Mr. Birdsall Holly received a patent for his rotary pump and engine, which would gain a worldwide reputation for its use in building steam fire engines.

WOMEN'S RIGHTS

On April 23, 1831, Seneca Falls was incorporated as a village. Twenty years later the village was gaining a reputation in the state and beyond for dealing with social and religious reform issues, including abolition of slavery, temperance, and women's rights. One of the earliest gatherings for women's rights in the United States was a convention in 1848 at the Wesleyan Chapel in Seneca Falls, organized by Elizabeth Cady Stanton and Lucretia Mott. The Declaration of Sentiments and Resolutions, based on the Declaration of Independence, was read to the assembly, asserting that women and men should be treated equally and that women should have the right to vote. The site of the convention and Elizabeth Cady Stanton's Greek-Revival home are now part of the Women's Rights National Historical Park.

A photo of Stanton, her daughter, and granddaughter is part of the archives of the Seneca Falls Historical Society. Even as a grandmother, Stanton, with her white finger curls, shawl, and full face, still has the look of one fiercely independent and committed.

FIRE AND GROWTH

A devastating fire took place in the summer of 1890—a cruel irony, as it occurred in the town that had given the world its first fire engine. Starting in the center of the business area, the flames fanned out, ultimately destroying 67 stores, residences, and offices, leaving half of Main Street in ashes. The buildings were rebuilt, and Seneca Falls continued to grow. In 1860 the population was reported to be 4,000.

During the early 20th century, travel on the lake was by steamboat. Vessels such as the *Kate D. Morgan,* the *T. D. Wilcox,* and the grand *Frontenac* plied the waters between Ithaca and Cayuga. On July 26, 1907, encountering stormy weather, the *Frontenac* caught fire. The captain steered the ship toward shore, running it aground about three-quarters of a mile north of Levanna. Panic set in, and eight people drowned. The charred remains of the ship still show just above the lake's surface, a grim reminder of the tragedy.

In 1915 the old Cayuga-Seneca Canal was widened, the smaller locks were replaced with two larger locks, and the area known as "The Flats" was flooded, becoming Van Cleef Lake, to be used as a reservoir for the locks. In the process, more than 115 industrial buildings and 60 homes ceased to exist. It is appropriate that the lake was named after Van Cleef; it was on The Flats that he built his first dwelling.

AURORA

The new terrace of the Aurora Inn overlooks Cayuga Lake.

Founded on the site of the Cayuga village *Deawendote*, which means "village of constant dawn," Aurora is on the eastern shore of the lake. Many of the buildings in this delightful college town, including Wells College, are listed in the National Register of Historic Places.

In addition to the fantasy-filled pottery, furniture, and glass studios of MacKenzie-Childs just north of the village center, Aurora Place is a complex of shops housed in the center of town in newly renovated vintage buildings. In fact, it seems that most of the downtown area of Aurora has undergone a dramatic renaissance, including The Aurora Inn, an important Aurora institution and a village landmark that has been brought back to its original 1833 Federalist design. Much of the work has been funded by the Pleasant T. Rowland Foundation, which received its major monies from a former Wells graduate.

Some very special visitors apparently find Aurora highly desirable. About mid-October, the skies above Cayuga Lake shimmer with the arrival of more than 500,000 wild geese heading south from Canada for the winter. Some 80,000 of these birds stay put and make the shores around Aurora their winter headquarters.

INTERLAKEN

Its former names—McCall's Tavern, Farmer Village, and Farmer—tell the tale of its origins: a simple community with a strong farming population. Incorporated in 1904 as Interlaken, the village has grown along Route 96 on the western side of the Cayuga Lake north of Trumansburg. The Hinman Memorial Library, Interlaken Historical Society, the Farmer's Museum, and many family-owned businesses line Main Street.

Interlaken would be a perfect movie set for a typical down-home village. Here they roll out American Legion breakfasts, parades, Old Home Day, an antique car show, and a flurry of flea markets.

TRUMANSBURG

Also on the west side of Cayuga Lake, about 10 miles north of Ithaca, is the pleasant village of Trumansburg. Founded in 1792 by Abner Truman, his namesake now has a population of about 1,600 people and is adjacent to the spectacular Taughannock Falls State Park. The village is home to a number of historic houses and buildings as well as several unique shops, such as Black Sheep Designs, The Blue Heron Gallery, and T-Burg Toys. The Trumansburg Conservatory of Fine Arts provides educational opportunities for all ages, and the annual Trumansburg Fair held in August is a week-long festival, featuring a demolition derby, horse pulls, colt stake and harness racing, a draft horse show, a firemen's parade, and fireworks.

LODGING

Most of Cayuga Lake's places to stay are in Ithaca at the southern tip, Seneca Falls on the northern end, and Aurora on the eastern shore. Small inns and B&Bs are scattered in or near the vineyards that ring the lake, and several '50s- and '60s-style motels can be found along Route 5 and 20. The largest hotels include the Holiday Inn Executive Tower in Ithaca, the Statler Hotel right on Ithaca's Cornell campus, and the new Courtyard Marriott. Major historic inns include the Aurora Inn and Taughannock Farms Inn. For fun, try the Station Restaurant Sleeping Cars, with accommodations in old railroad cars, in downtown Ithaca.

LODGING RATES
$: Up to $75 per couple
$$: $76–$150 per couple
$$$: $151–$250 per couple
$$$$: More than $250 per couple

Ithaca Area

HOTELS AND RESORTS

**BEST WESTERN
  UNIVERSITY INN**
Manager: Terry Terry.
607-272-6100.
www.bestwestern.com.
1020 Ellis Hollow Rd.,
  Ithaca, NY 14850.
At East Hill Plaza.
Rooms: 101.
Open: Year-round.
Price: $$$.
Credit Cards: Most major.

Next to Cornell University, the hotel is just 15 minutes from the Tompkins County Airport. Rooms are all on one level and are newly redecorated in pleasing beige and mauve colors. All rooms come equipped with refrigerators, televisions with VCRs and HBO service, wireless Internet service, coffeemakers, and irons/ironing boards. Some rooms have cathedral ceilings. Executive rooms offer microwaves, data ports, and gas fireplaces. There is an outdoor pool and an exercise room with 24-hour availability. Rates include continental breakfast and shuttle service to everywhere in Ithaca. This is a convenient, comfortable place, but there is nothing remarkable about the grounds or setting.

**COURTYARD BY
  MARRIOTT**
800-228-9290.
www.courtyard.com/ithcy.
29 Thornwood Dr., Ithaca,
  NY 14850.
Rooms: 106.
Open: Year-round.   .
Price: $$–$$$.
Credit Cards: Most major.

Located in the Cornell Business I Technology Park, Courtyard by Marriott was designed to bring business travelers state-of-the-art amenities, such as dual-line speaker phones with dataport and voicemail, and high-speed Internet access. The rooms are air-conditioned and come with climate control, coffeemaker, hair dryer, and iron/ironing board. There is an indoor pool, whirlpool and exercise facility along with a guest laundry, business services, restaurant, and conference room.

EMBASSY INN
Manager: Nick Patel.
607-272-3721, 607-272-3722.
1083 Dryden Rd., Ithaca, NY
  14850.
On Rte. 366.
Rooms: 25.
Open: Year-round.
Price: $–$$.
Credit Cards: Most major.

Conveniently near the airport, downtown Ithaca, and the colleges, this is a straightforward motel with one- and two-story buildings. It is a bit off the street and with a lawn in front, so it is quiet. All the rooms have been recently redecorated, from carpets and wallpaper to bathrooms. Rooms are air-conditioned and come with cable TV, Posturepedic beds, and courtesy coffee. Some rooms have two double beds, other have a queen bed, and a few have kitchenettes and a sitting area.

**HOLIDAY INN-
  EXECUTIVE TOWER**
Manager: Joseph Kelly.

Location, location, location. This full-service hotel is right in the heart of Ithaca, one block from the Commons and within sight of East Hill and the Cor-

607-272-1000,
800-HOLIDAY;
fax 607-277-1275.
www.hiithaca.com.
222 S. Cayuga St., Ithaca,
NY 14850.
Rooms: 181.
Open: Year-round.
Price: $$–$$$$.
Credit Cards: Most major.

LA TOURELLE COUNTRY INN
Innkeeper: Leslie Leonard.
607-273-2734;
fax 607-273-4821.
www.latourelleinn.com.
1150 Danby Rd., Ithaca, NY
14850.
Rooms: 35.
Open: Year-round.
Price: $$–$$$.
Credit Cards: Most major.

THE STATLER HOTEL
Managing Director: James
Hisle.
607-257-2500, 800-541-2501;
fax 607-257-6432.
www.hotelschool.cornell
.edu/statler.
11 East Ave., Cornell
University, Ithaca, NY
14850.
Rooms: 150,
Open: Year-round; closed
major holidays (follows
Cornell schedule),
Price: $$$–$$$$.
Credit Cards: Most major.

nell University campus. The rooms are continually being redecorated, and the current themes are French and cherry. The hotel has a restaurant, lounge, indoor pool, and fitness center. Rooms are equipped with irons/ironing board, coffeemakers, hair dryers, air-conditioning, and in-room movies. Cornell University, Ithaca College, and airport shuttles are complimentary.

This is not your typical hotel. Set on 70 acres, with hiking trails, two tennis courts, and a patio, La Tourelle looks and feels decidedly European. Each set of rooms has its own character. Queen-sized bed rooms have Mexican wood furniture and dark-green carpet; king rooms are larger, with light Haitian wood furniture and peach carpets. Some rooms have two king beds, others two queen beds. Honeymooners might ask for the special accommodations, which come with round beds, mirrored ceilings, disco balls, and Jacuzzis. The large room, including a four-poster king-sized bed, a wood-burning fireplace, and a small balcony, is also popular with romantics. The rooms that overlook the valley have the nicest views; the others face the front yard. Rooms come with refrigerators, televisions/VCRs, movies, phone, air-conditioning, and free morning coffee. The John Thomas Steakhouse is next door, and the inn is 3 miles from the center of town.

If you can't get spit-and-polish service here, you probably can't get it anywhere: The Statler is the teaching hotel of Cornell University's School of Hotel Administration. Located on the Cornell campus, this multi-story hotel has a very businesslike ambiance, with marble floors, dark woods, and solid-color decor. The rooms are modern and have large picture windows with views of the campus and countryside. The Statler offers kitchenette suites, business desk with phone and dedicated data line, cable television, and in-room coffeemakers. Guests have access to the Cornell University athletic facilities, including the Olympic pool. Banfi's restaurant serves breakfast, lunch, and dinner as well as Sunday brunch. The Regent Lounge has a full-service bar and serves casual food.

BED & BREAKFASTS

BUTTERMILK FALLS B&B
Innkeeper: Margie Rumsey.
607-272-6767;
fax 607-273-3947.
110 E. Buttermilk Rd.,
  Ithaca, NY 14850.
Rooms: 5 with private baths.
Price: $$–$$$$.
Open: Year-round.
Credit Cards: None; cash,
  check, or money orders.

This classic white-brick 1820s house is just two miles from the heart of Ithaca, on two acres of landscaping with huge trees and gardens. Set near the entrance to Buttermilk Falls State Park, it's an ideal base for exploring the trails and gorges of the park. The house, which has belonged to six generations of the Rumsey family, is furnished with family heirloom antiques and accessories, along with 16 Windsor chairs and a large pine table that look antique but were actually made by Margie Rumsey's son. Rooms are furnished with queen, king, or twin beds and handmade quilts; one king room has a Jacuzzi, wood-burning fireplace, and nice sitting area. Upstairs there is wall-to-wall carpeting, while downstairs the floors are covered by lovely Persian rugs. All rooms are air-conditioned. Breakfast is served on the screened porch, in the dining room, or even at the picnic table under the large tree in the backyard. The full breakfast includes hot entrées, lots of fruit, and warm muffins and pastries. In the summer you can swim at the foot of the falls and hike and bike; in the winter you can go cross-country skiing. The Rumsey family has a fine collection of antique board games, including Uncle Wiggley, checkers, chess, and others. Margie says she will make every effort to accommodate special requests such as early-morning breakfasts for those who have to leave for the airport early. When she's asked if she takes children, Margie says quietly that though she is finished raising her own children, if the parents agree to watch their youngsters carefully to make sure they do not abuse the precious things that are in the house, then they are welcome. Smokers and pets, however, are not.

THE CODDINGTON GUEST HOUSE
Innkeeper: Denice
  Karamardian DeSouza.
607-275-0021.
www.thecoddington.com.
130 Coddington Rd., Ithaca
  NY, 14850.
Rooms: 3 suites with private
  baths.
Open: Year-round.
Price: $$ (weekly, monthly
  rentals available).
Credit Cards: Most major.

This new guest house in the style of a turn-of-the-century Italian villa is on the border of the Ithaca College campus on South Hill, five minutes from Cornell University and next door to Angelini Centini's Restaurant. All guest rooms have a superb lake views, and two have a private entrance. All rooms give you plenty of privacy, as each accommodation is in a separate wing. The upstairs lodging is a three-room family suite with large bedroom, full kitchen, living room, veranda, and bath. There are three living rooms for everyone to use, including one for reading, meetings, and live music (with a piano); one for media (television, CD player, movies); and one exercise/TV room. The exercise/sitting room doubles as an optional second bedroom to one of the suites for large parties. There are also porches and verandas for enjoying the view. A generous continental breakfast is served in the dining room, and there is an extra kitchen downstairs and refrigerators in all rooms. Tour packages and learning workshops are available. Children are warmly welcomed.

THE EDGE OF THYME
Innkeepers: Prof. Frank and
   Eva Mae Musgrave.
607-659-5155, 800-722-7365;
   fax 607-659-5155.
www.edgeofthyme.com.
6 Main St., Candor, NY
   13743.
Rooms: 5 with both private
   and shared baths.
Open: Year-round.
Price: $$.
Credit Cards: Most major.

Although the house was built in 1860, when John Rockefeller's executive secretary came to town in 1908, Rockefeller's architect transformed the building into a Georgian-style home. Accommodations include a suite with a queen-sized bed and a separate sitting room with a pull-out single bed, two large rooms with private baths, and two rooms that share a bath. The house is decorated with tapestries, quilts, period wallpapers, Oriental rugs, and lots of antiques and family heirlooms. Eva Mae notes that "I have never said no" when, over the years, various family members asked if she would like a particular antique. Her favorite pieces include a rosewood side table with carved lion's feet now in the dining room, a number of lovely paintings, and the original slaw-making machine invented by her great-great grandfather, which now sits in the library. There are also marble fireplaces, a parlor, an enclosed porch and outside porch, a gazebo, and a pergola. One of the house's most charming aspects is the enclosed porch with leaded windows. When they need scraping and repainting, Eva Mae insists on doing the painting herself: "I won't let painters go near them." Apparently the panes alone cost $250 to replace. Located in a quiet rural village on an acre of landscaped grounds, this B&B lives up to its name: The Musgraves have an herb garden that provides extra flavor for the gourmet breakfasts, which might include coddled eggs, baked apples, and apple blueberry tart. And you can expect great food. Eva Mae loves to cook and is the author of *Tastes at the Edge of Thyme* cookbook. The inn welcomes well-behaved children, but no smokers please. Eva also serves high teas with three-days' notice.

**THE ELMSHADE GUEST
   HOUSE**
Innkeeper: Lillie Teeter.
607-273-1707.
402 S. Albany St., Ithaca, NY
   14850.
Rooms: 8, some with shared
   baths, plus an efficiency
   apartment.
Open: Year-round.
Price: $–$$.
Credit Cards: Most major.

This cozy in-town guest house has been welcoming visitors since 1930. If you don't have a car, this would be a good choice. It is right on the Ithaca Transit bus line, just 2 miles from Cornell University and Ithaca College, and only 3 blocks from Ithaca Commons. Three of the rooms have private baths, the rest share. This is a comfortable, clean place to stay, offering good value. One room has twin beds, four have doubles, and the rest are queens; mattresses are good. Furnishings include quilts, chenille spreads or comforters, lots of pillows, and fairly simple furniture—very few antiques are used. Rooms are air-conditioned and equipped with cable television. A hearty continental breakfast is served, often on the first or second floor porches in warmer weather, in the dining room in the winter. There is a guest kitchenette with microwave, refrigerator, and small counter and cupboard. Coffee, a large assortment of teas and snacks, milk, and orange juice are offered. A large hallway is set up with sofa and chairs for guests' use. If you do have a car, off-street parking is available. Children are welcome, but no pets, please.

THE FEDERAL HOUSE B&B
Innkeeper: Diane Carroll.
607-533-7362, 800-533-7362.
www.federalhouse.com.
175 Ludlowville Rd.,
    Lansing, NY 14882.
Six miles north of Ithaca.
Rooms: 4 with private baths.
Open: Year-round.
Price: $–$$$.
Credit Cards: Most major.

One of the more romantic B&Bs in the area, this 1815 inn is steps away from Salmon Creek and Falls. Constructed by Abijah Miller, this house is where William Seward, secretary of state under President Abraham Lincoln, courted his wife, Frances Miller, niece of Squire Miller. Rooms are exquisitely furnished with antiques and artwork, and the house features original woodwork and a hand-carved fireplace. The Lincoln Suite has a queen canopy bed, gas fireplace, and private staircase. The two-room William Seward Suite has a queen bed, fireplace, sitting room with TV/VCR, and a view of the garden and falls. All rooms are air-conditioned. You can relax on one of the porches, or steal some privacy in the gazebo or gardens. A full breakfast is served, and bikes are available for guests' use.

HOUND AND HARE B&B
Innkeeper: Zetta Sprole.
607-257-2821, 800-652-2821.
www.houndandhare.com.
1031 Hanshaw Rd., Ithaca,
    NY 14850.
Rooms: 5 with private baths.
Open: Year-round.
Price: $–$$.
Credit Cards: Most major.

Built by Samuel Boothroyd on military tract property deeded by General George Washington in 1793, this white-brick colonial is steeped in history and tradition. Victorian antiques, laces, and family heirlooms are found throughout the house, along with Queen Anne wing-backed chairs, fresh flowers, and glittering chandeliers and gilt mirrors. Some rooms have brass beds, and all have down comforters, eyelet sheets, down pillows, and air-conditioning. The bridal suite has a Jacuzzi. The guest living room has a fireplace where you can enjoy a spot of tea, and the library is a retreat where you can catch up on your reading. The grounds are beautifully landscaped and contain herb gardens, rose beds, and an old-fashioned lily pond and fountain. It's a good place to come home to at the end of a day of sightseeing or other activities. In the morning you can look forward to bounteous breakfasts served by candlelight in the formal dining room.

LOG COUNTRY INN B&B
Innkeepers: Wanda and
  Slawomir Grunberg.
607-589-4771, 800-274-4771.
www.logtv.com/inn.
PO Box 581, Ithaca, NY
  14851.
Rooms: 5 with private baths.
Open: Year-round.
Price: $–$$$.
Credit Cards: Most major.

It may be a log house, but the amenities are far from basic. Rustic in looks, with soaring cathedral ceilings, massive log walls, and fireplaces yet containing every modern amenity, this house is set at the edge of a 7,000-acre forest. It should appeal to those with a love of the outdoors. A full European-style breakfast may include blintzes or Russian pancakes and a good selection of home-baked breads, pastries, and jams. Enjoy features like a sauna, fireplaces, Jacuzzi, and afternoon tea. Hiking and cross-country trails are easily accessed, as are the vegetable garden and orchard.

ROSE INN
Innkeepers: Sherry and
  Charles Rosemann.
607-533-7905;
  fax 607-533-7908.
www.roseinn.com.
813 Auburn Rd., Ithaca, NY
  14851.
On Rte. 34.
Rooms: 22.
Open: Year-round.
Price: $$–$$$.
Credit Cards: Most major.

This stately Victorian B&B country inn sits on 20 acres amid gardens and lawns. Rooms are in both the main house and in a nearby carriage house. Built in the 1840s, the house is designed around a stunning circular Honduras mahogany staircase that took two years to build by a master craftsman. It extends from the main hall up through two stories to a cupola. There is a piano in the parlor, hand-carved oak doors, parquet floors, high ceilings, and marble fireplaces. Brandy, the inn's dog, is often on hand to give you a friendly greeting. Each room is different, most lavishly decorated. Some rooms feature four-poster beds covered with silky down duvets, and one suite has a Jacuzzi, mirrored armoires, and French doors that open onto a private patio furnished with white wrought-iron furniture. Number 11, the Bridal Suite, has a king-sized bed, down duvet, fireplace, and arched windows overlooking the garden. The library is well stocked (noted was a sizable collection of Dickens), and there are several board games. Outside is a wood swing for two; nearby, a profusely blooming mandevilla climbs a trellis. Amenities include an honor bar, air-conditioning, and televisions in some rooms. Weddings are often held in the formal gardens under a flower-bedecked arbor. The restaurant serves breakfast and dinner Tuesday through Sunday; see the entry in "Restaurants" for more information.

**THE STATION
  RESTAURANT AND
  SLEEPING CARS**
Innkeepers: Terry and
  Barbara Ciaschi.
607-272-2609.
www.ithacastation.com.

Imagine your own private sleeping car: It's on track but doesn't go anywhere. Converted to guest suites in 1998 and designed by architect Claudia Brenner and V. Romanoff and Associates, real honest-to-goodness vintage sleeping cars are decorated in period decor, and much of the original cabi-

806 W. Buffalo St., Ithaca, NY 14850.
At Taughannock Blvd.
Rooms: 3 private sleeper cars.
Open: Year-round.
Price: $$.
Credit Cards: Most major.

netry and interior woodwork is intact. One suite has balloon shades on all the windows, and each car has a private entrance and full bath, phone, cable television, fireplace, air-conditioning, and a coffeemaker. A continental breakfast is included in the rates. Just outside the cars sits a tall fifty-year-old Seth Thomas clock, whose hands are wound every eight days. The cars are next to the restaurant in the former Lehigh Valley Railroad Station. The former waiting room is the main dining room, where you will find chandeliers from the Ithaca Hotel. The benches are from the original waiting room, the tile floor is original, and the rest rooms retain the old marble partitions and hardware. The accommodations could be considered basic but fun.

VERALMA, THE 1850 HOUSE

Innkeeper: Beverly Beer.
607-275-9519.
www.bbithaca.com/veralma.html.
211 Hudson St., Ithaca, NY 14850.
Rooms: 3 with private baths.
Open: Year-round.
Price: $$.
Credit Cards: Most major.

This elegant 1850s Italianate estate, which once belonged to a mayor of Ithaca, features 12-foot ceilings and a striking three-story walnut staircase leading to a cupola. It's an unusual house because it's virtually the same as when it was built in 1850. Rooms are air-conditioned and have either queen or twin beds and are furnished with family antiques and period accessories, some from the owners' great-great grandparents. There is a guest parlor with a marble fireplace, phone and television, formal dining room, a large front porch, and lovely one-acre grounds. A pool and a carriage house complete the setting. A full breakfast is served and features such items as pecan waffles with maple syrup and specialty omelets. This is a light, bright house conveniently near the Ithaca Commons and colleges. The Veralma does not accept smoking, pets, or children under 12.

THE WILLIAM HENRY MILLER INN

Innkeepers: Ken and Lynnette Scofield.
607-256-4553, 877-256-4553; fax 607-256-0092.
www.millerinn.com.
303 N. Aurora St., Ithaca, NY 14850.
Rooms: 9 with private baths.
Open: Year-round.
Price: $$–$$$.
Credit Cards: Most major.

Built as a private home in 1880 by William Henry Miller, Cornell's first student of architecture, the house is richly detailed with stained-glass windows, American chestnut woodwork, fireplaces, and a spacious parlor, dining room, and music room. The house has a wonderful pointed corner tower and Tudor elements. Located in a pleasant residential area just off the Ithaca Commons, guests can walk to shops, theaters, and restaurants. Rooms are beautifully furnished with antiques and period reproductions. For example, Dane's Room, large and sunlit, has a king bed; the Library has a corner fireplace, bookshelves, sitting area, and queen bed.

The Turret, a third-floor room, has a cozy reading alcove and a queen bed; the Retreat has lots of windows and a nice seating area; the Carriage House has two rooms, one with a Jacuzzi, and is ideal for honeymooners or families traveling together since it is quiet and secluded. All rooms have hair dryer, air-conditioning, telephones, cable television. A full candlelit breakfast is served in either the dining room or the adjoining parlor. It might be baked pear with cream and sun-dried cherries or a three-cheese casserole. You can also have a continental breakfast in your room. Early risers can enjoy a fresh cup of coffee and a read of the *New York Times*. In the afternoon tea is served in the parlor; evening dessert is also offered. Children over 12 welcome; pets and smoking are not.

Seneca Falls Area

BARRISTERS
Innkeeper: Judy Austic.
607-387-6860, 800-914-0145.
www.sleepbarristers.com.
56 Cayuga St., Seneca Falls,
NY 13148.
Rooms: 5 with private baths.
Open: Year-round.
Price: $–$$.
Credit Cards: Most major.

Barristers enjoys a beautiful historic setting in an 1888 Colonial-Revival home in the heart of the Seneca Falls historic district. Special features include carved fireplaces, stained-glass windows, handmade quilts, and queen or king beds. Some have whirlpool baths, and one room has a private sitting room with fireplace. Eat breakfast in the formal dining room, or have a continental breakfast delivered to your door. Enjoy the short walk into town to enjoy casual and fine dinning, the shops and museums, and a stroll along the canal promenade. And relax after a day of exploring the region with a cool drink on the front porch.

HUBBELL HOUSE
Innkeepers: Karl and Joanne
Elliott.
315-568-9690.
www.hubbellhousebb.com.
42 Cayuga St., Seneca Falls,
NY 13148.
Rooms: 4 (2 with private
bath, 2 share bath).
Open: Year-round.
Price: $$.
Credit Cards: Checks or
cash only.

This Gothic-style cottage built in 1855 is on Van Cleef Lake in the historic district of town. Filled with authentic Victorian furniture and memorabilia, including electrified gaslights, it invites the visitor to step back in time without sacrificing modern comforts like air-conditioning and showers. Close to museums, the canal, and shops, the house sits on a hillside, so the main rooms are on a middle level along with a lovely wraparound porch. The common rooms include a large double parlor, library, and dining room. The largest room, the Laura Hoskins Hubbell Room, overlooks the lake and dock. It has a large ornate brass California king-sized bed, private bath, Eastlake marble-topped dresser, and commode. The smaller Lottie Pollard Room, featuring five beautifully arched windows in a bay, is full of Jenny Lind furniture and such accessories as a Victorian tea set. This room shares a bath. A full breakfast—served in the dining room by candlelight— includes fresh fruit, homemade breads or muffins, and hot entrées such as croissant à l'orange, Victorian baked toast with light caramel topping and fresh berries, and stuffed French toast. There is a dock, paddleboat, and canoe.

JOHN MORRIS MANOR
Innkeepers: Tony Masullo
 and John Personivus.
315-568-9057.
www.johnmorrismanor.com.
2138 Rte. 89, Seneca Falls,
 NY 13148.
Rooms: 5 (3 with private
 baths including 1
 w/Jacuzzi).
Open: Year-round.
Price: $$.
Credit Cards: Most major.

Set in lovely parklike grounds on more than five acres, John Morris Manor was built in 1838 in the Greek-Revival farmhouse style. Each room is different. For fun, go spacey with a circa-1950s decor of pale-blue silvery wallpaper with Saturn and other starry things and posters of the film *Forbidden Planet*. Romance blooms in the Pool Room, decorated in burgundy and gold and featuring a private entrance to the pool deck, a king bed, and a Jacuzzi. The Rose Room is quietly pretty, with Laura Ashley rosebud sheets, wicker chairs, a country headboard, and a fireplace. Breakfasts are lavish, perhaps an egg-potato frittata, waffles, or scrambled eggs with fresh chives and tarragon. Fresh fruits and homemade jams and jellies are always on the table. This very country classy 11-room house has several public areas, including a screened porch, an in-ground pool and patio, and a TV room, where you can also escape to read a book, sip a cocktail, or simply relax. John Morris is within walking distance of Cayuga Lake. Children over 12 are welcome.

**VANCLEEF HOMESTEAD
 B&B**
Innkeepers: Joice and David
 Fredenburgh.
315-568-2275, 800-323-8668.
www.flare.net/vancleef.
86 Cayuga St., Seneca Falls,
 NY 13148.
Rooms: 3 with private baths.
Open: Year-round.
Price: $–$$.
Credit Cards: Most major.

This two-story clapboard 1825 Federal-style home was built by the first permanent settler of Seneca Falls, Lawrence Van Cleef. Later the house became the residence of Wilhemus Mynderse, one of the village's most influential citizens of his time. In 1837 the house was transferred to Frederick Swaby, another of the village's original industrialists, whose family then occupied the house for over 100 years. It opened as a B&B in 1996. White with black shutters, the house is close to the center of town, and the rooms are attractively furnished with antiques and period reproductions. The living room, decorated in upbeat blues and whites, has oversized chairs and a sofa surrounding the fireplace, plus a piano. The dining room features colorful floral wallpaper and a fireplace. On the first floor, the light, airy Van Cleef Room features a queen bed in a room with a working fireplace and private bath. The Mynderse Room on the second floor has a wonderful king bed and private bath. The corner Swaby Suite has a queen bed with an adjoining sitting room, which has a double bed. The private bath for this room is across the hall. Down comforters cover the beds in winter. A full, hearty breakfast includes a variety of cereals, juices, coffees, and teas as well as fresh fruit, home-baked breads or coffeecake, and a daily special main course, perhaps "from scratch" blueberry buttermilk pancakes, stuffed French toast, waffles with real maple syrup, sausage strata, quiche, and made-to-order omelets, all served with bacon or sausage. There is an in-ground swimming pool, and rooms are air-conditioned. No smokers, please.

Other Area Lodging

The Aurora Inn in Aurora has been restored to its 19th-century grandeur.

AURORA INN AND RESTAURANT
General Manager: Sue Edinger.
315-364-8888; fax 315-364-8014.
www.aurora-inn.com.
311 Main St., Aurora, NY 13026.
On Rte. 90
Rooms: 10.
Open: Year-round.

With the reopening of the Aurora Inn after extensive renovation, this historic landmark hotel evokes the gracious character of the original inn, which was constructed in 1833 in the Federalist style. Owned by Wells College, the inn had undergone a number of changes over the years, including the addition of a large restaurant across the back. This addition has now been removed to allow the spectacular views of the lake to be revealed at the end of the central entrance hall—just like it was in 1833. Ten guest rooms open onto new balconies lo-

Price: $–$$$.
Credit Cards: Most major.

cated across the front and back to replicate the design of the 19th-century building; rear balconies reveal wonderful views of the lake and sunsets. All the rooms have been greatly enhanced, and many have fireplaces, balconies, marble baths, kitchenettes, sitting areas, flat-screen TVs, and whirlpools. There is a new dining room, cocktail lounge, lake-view terrace with romantic hidden fiber-optic lighting on the terrace and in the trees, and a banquet room. Fireplaces that had been bricked over have been opened up, and there are now eight working fireplaces. Artwork that once hung in the inn has been found and restored; woodwork has been either restored or replicated, and a historic mural has been cleaned. Decor by a talented local interior designer is fresh and light yet rich, using Audubon-style etched print fabrics and wallpaper, jewel-like colors, and special pieces such as Asian-style bamboo/rattan beds—a major departure from the dreary colors of the inn's most recent years. The new inn is handicapped accessible and centrally air-conditioned, and fresh-baked muffins and coffee are delivered outside your door each morning.

DRIFTWOOD
607-532-4324, 888-532-4324.
www.fingerlakes.net/
  driftwood.
7401 Wyers Point Rd., Ovid,
  NY 14521.
Rooms: 5 (3 with private
  bath).
Open: April–Nov.
Credit Cards: Most major.

Driftwood has a private swimming area on the beach. And for those who want to arrive by boat, there is a docking area. Three of the rooms have lake views, and there are lawn games,

FOXGLOVE B&B
Innkeeper: Suzanne
  Hoback.
607-844-9602, 888-436-8608.
www.foxglovebnb.com.
28 Main St., Freeville, NY
  13068.
Rooms: 5, 3 with private
  baths, 2 shared; separate
  suite.
Open: Year-round.
Price: $–$$.
Credit Cards: Most major.

This pretty Victorian (circa 1900) with high roof peaks, large porch, and a bay window, is surrounded by gardens, lawns, and nature trails leading past berry bushes to Fall Creek. Here, 100 years ago, the steamboat *Clinton* would carry passengers to the Old Mill and back for five cents. Located in the Greater Ithaca area, Foxglove is on the historic site of Riverside Park, a popular resort in the 1890s, where freethinkers and adventurers came to escape the city's summer heat. Today it is a special place for artists, actors, writers, musicians, photographers, poets, and nature lovers. Performances are often staged in the gardens. At the back of the property a seven-circuit labyrinth, 45 feet in diameter, with gravel paths and more than 600 herb and flower plants, is a good place to meditate, picnic, or just enjoy. The house is furnished with a mix of old and new; rooms are clean and airy and more on the modern than Victorian side (that is, without the usual doodads). The Tiger Lily Room accommodates one to four, with television and private bath with Jacuzzi. The Rose Room has a queen-sized bed, television, and private bath. The Forget-Me-Not Room has a double bed and shared bath, while the Sunflower Room has a queen-sized bed and shared bath. The Dogwood Suite, in a separate building next door, features a king-sized bed, folding futon couch, kitchen, bath with shower and tub, living room with television/VCR, a screened porch, and, of course, a private entrance. The guest rooms are air-conditioned. The library invites guests to play chess, read, or sit by the woodstove. A refrigerator with complimentary beverages is provided, and an eight-person Jacuzzi awaits on the outside back deck. Choose what you want for breakfast the night before.

GOTHIC EVES B&B
Innkeepers: Rose Hilbert
  and Roman Pausch.
607-387-6033, 800-387-7712.
www.gothiceves.com.
112 E. Main St.,
  Trumansburg, NY 14886.
Rooms: 5.
Open: Year-round.
Price: $–$$.
Credit Cards: Visa, MC.

This pretty 1855 Gothic-Revival home is in the historic area of Trumansburg within walking distance of shops and restaurants. Although elegant and furnished with antiques, Gothic Eves is one of the few B&Bs that welcomes children of all ages. Some rooms connect so children can be in the adjacent room; in the yard are swings, picnic tables, and flower and herb gardens. Just behind the house is an elementary school with a large castle playground. In fact, there are young children in the owner's family, so the place can get a bit lively at times. The house is decorated with period fabrics and is air-conditioned. Fresh flowers are everywhere in the summer months; dried flowers and gourds from the garden are used to brighten up the house in the colder months. The rooms are quite large, and four have ensuite baths; the other bath is private but just out in the hall. The king rooms have an iron bed and a cherry sleigh bed, the double room has a brass bed, and the queen rooms feature a four-poster and sleigh bed. A generous breakfast is served with interesting variations on old standbys—for example, a version of eggs Benedict includes lots of fresh vegetables, and most entrées are garnished with fruit or edible fresh flowers from the garden.

ROGUE'S HARBOR B&B
Innkeeper: Eileen Stout.
607-533-3535.
www.roguesharbor.com.
2079 E. Shore Dr., Corner
  Rtes. 34 & 34B, Lansing,
  NY 14882.
Rooms: 6 (4 with private
  baths).
Open: Year-round.
Price: $$.
Credit Cards: Most major.

Although these rooms are in an old inn over the Rogue's Harbor restaurant, a recent insulation program has successfully locked out any noise you might anticipate from the crowd dining downstairs. Rooms are large and all decorated with antiques such as a Victorian marble-topped dresser and sleigh bed. Robes are provided for the two rooms that share a bath; other rooms have private baths. Room #5 is one of the larger rooms, with a king-sized wrought-iron bed and a lovely Maxfield Parrish print on the wall. It also has a daybed for an additional guest. Grounds are not extensive, but the B&B is just a mile from Cayuga Lake and close to vineyards and many antiques shops. A phone and fax as well as a guest refrigerator are in the common area.

SILVER STRAND AT SHELDRAKE
Innkeeper: Maura Stamberger.
607-532-4972, 800-283-3283.
www.silverstrand.net.
7398 Wyers Point Rd., Ovid, NY 14521.
Rooms: 5 with private baths; 3 bedroom/2 bath guesthouse.
Open: Year-round.
Price: $$–$$$.
Credit Cards: Visa, MC.

This restored lakefront Victorian, built in the mid-19th century, has a lovely old porch, five very attractively furnished bedrooms, and a guest cottage. Each room is quite different, but all have private baths, air-conditioning, and private balconies; some have fireplaces. Room #1 has a very bright feeling, with French doors that open onto a private balcony overlooking the lake and furnished with cushioned wicker porch furniture. Room #2, with a private "turret"-style balcony that affords views of over 20 miles of open water, has a dramatic period queen bed, Casablanca fan, writing desk, comfortable reading chair, and a double Jacuzzi. Room #3 is decorated in a Caribbean theme in cool blues and whites and comes with a six-foot double Jacuzzi open to the room, a gas fireplace, and a private circular balcony with two cushioned chaise longues. Room #4 has a private balcony, queen canopy bed, Casablanca fan, comfortable reading chair, and a walnut bureau with marble top—this is the only room without a bathtub, and views of the water are from the porch. Room #6 is open and airy, with windows facing three directions, and features a cherry sleigh bed, Casablanca fan, two comfortable reading chairs, and cushioned seating on a private sun deck. The three-bedroom, two-bath guest house has use of a 150-foot beach with dock, deck, rowboat, and two-person kayak and has a four-person hot tub, pool table, satellite television/VCR, stereo, dishwasher, microwave, washer and dryer, and two decks with gas and charcoal grills. Boats and bicycles are generally available for guest use.

TAUGHANNOCK FARMS INN
Innkeepers: Susan and Tom Sheridan.
607-387-7711, 888-387-7711.
www.T-Farms.com.
2030 Gorge Rd., Trumansburg, NY 14886.
Rte. 89 at Taughannock Falls State Park.
Rooms: 13; 5 rooms, 3 guest houses.
Open: Closed Jan. 2–Apr. 1.

This lovely Victorian country inn, with its porches, cupola, and high-pitched roof, is tucked into a hillside next to Taughannock Falls State Park. Many of the original furnishings brought here in 1873 by the wealthy owner, John Jones, are still in the house. Some pieces came from Philadelphia, others from England and Italy. During the 1930s, Jones deeded most of the sprawling 600-acre estate to New York State for the creation of Taughannock Falls State Park. In 1945 the mansion was sold and became an inn. Of the 13 guest accommodations, all rooms are air-conditioned, and 5 are

Price: $$–$$$.
Credit Cards: Most major.

decorated with Victorian antiques. There are also three guest houses for families and small groups. Some rooms have phones and televisions, some do not. The dining room has exceptional lake views through its long bank of windows.

WESTWIND B&B
Innkeeper: Sharon R. Scott.
607-387-3377;
    fax 607-387-5655.
www.fingerlakes.net/
    westwind.
1662 Taughannock Blvd.,
    Trumansburg, NY 14886.
Rte. 89, .05 mile south of
    Taughannock State Park.
Rooms: 4 with shared baths.
Open: Year-round.
Price: $$.
Credit Cards: Visa, MC.

An 1870 Victorian farmhouse with lovely porches in a setting of meadows, woods, and ponds, Westwind sits on a hillside above the lake. Rooms share baths that have either a clawfoot tub or whirlpool bath and shower. Twin, double, queen, and king-sized beds are available. Full breakfasts are served.

YALE MANOR
Innkeepers: Donna and
    Hugh Cunningham.
315-585-2208.
www.yalemanor.com.
563 Yale Farm Rd.,
    Romulus, NY 14541.
Rooms: 6 (2 with private
    baths; 4 sharing 2 baths).
Open: Year-round.
Price: $$.
Credit Cards: No.

The former manor house of a 2,000-acre farm, this solid concrete dwelling (circa 1908) sits above Cayuga Lake, offering great views from four of the guestrooms as well as the porch and public rooms. You can walk down to the boathouse and swim off the private beach. For romance, ask for the Monticello Rose Room, with a king four-poster bed, private bath, fireplace, and lake views. According to Hugh Cunningham, breakfasts are so filling, "you have to roll people out after they've eaten." But this is a good thing as they can bulk up before hitting the wine trail. Typical breakfast fare includes homemade breads and tartlets, fresh fruits, a hot course like eggs Florentine or stuffed French toast, and homemade jams and jellies. With 10 acres, there is plenty of space to wander: lawn swings and chairs on the porch invite relaxing.

RESTAURANTS

Most college towns offer a wide variety of places to eat, from casual bars to more formal restaurants. Ithaca is no exception and, for its size, has a large number of restaurants in the downtown area as well as closer to the campuses itself. Outdoor dining has blossomed during the past few years in patio courtyards, along the streets, and in Ithaca's pedestrian market area, Ithaca Commons. Seneca Falls has a few places including the historic Pumphouse, and Aurora has a handful of restaurants, including the lakeside Aurora Inn.

Prices are estimated per person for appetizer and dinner entrée without tax, tip, or alcoholic beverages.

$: Up to $10
$$: $11–$25
$$$: $26–$40
$$$$: More than $40

Ithaca Area

ANGELINA CENTINI'S ITALIAN RESTAURANT
607-273-0802.
124 Coddington Rd., Ithaca, NY 14850.
Open: Tues.–Sun.
Price: $-$$.
Cuisine: Italian.
Serving: Tues.–Fri. L, Tues.–Sun. D.
Credit Cards: Most major.

If you eat outdoors in the Grape Arbor Garden—in warm weather, of course—you will get a nice view of Cayuga Lake. Inside it is fine dining with linen tablecloths and candles. Help yourself to the antipasto and salad makings from the gondola serving bar. Almost everything is made in-house, including sauces, pasta, sausage, meatballs, and desserts. It is for this reason that Angelina Centini is popular among locals. Some evenings there is entertainment, such as an accordion player.

ITHACA YACHT CLUB
607-272-9171.
Rte. 89, Ithaca, NY 14850.
Open: May 1–Aug. 31, Tues.–Sun.; Sept.–Oct., Thurs.–Sun.
Price: $$.
Cuisine: American.
Serving: D, SB
Credit Cards: Most major.

This club, which is open to the public for dinner, is of course on the lake. There are picnic areas, swimming facilities, and boat piers.

JOHN THOMAS STEAKHOUSE
607-273-3464.
1152 Danby Rd., Ithaca, NY 14850.
Open: Daily, Sun.–Thurs. 5:30–10, Fri. and Sat. 5:30–11.
Price: $$-$$$.
Cuisine: Steak house.

This 150-year-old farmhouse, set in meadows and gardens, has five dining rooms—two have fireplaces, one is an enclosed porch with many windows and wonderful views of the gardens, and the upstairs lounge and publike room is a favorite among repeat guests. It has lots of beams, a bar, and a fireplace kept burning during the colder winter months. In the summer you can eat outside on the deck. One thing that sets this restaurant apart from

Serving: D.
Credit Cards: Most major.

other steak houses is Mike Kelly, owner and long-time restaurateur. Not only does he age all the prime beef himself, he also cuts it. Great lobster, chicken dishes served with French-style sauces, salmon, and vegetarian dishes are also offered. Priced at the high end of the Ithaca food chain, this is the place to bring your best clients when you're on an expense account or a place to come for that special occasion. Besides super beef and seafood, the restaurant also has an excellent selection of wines, single-malt scotches, and fine bourbons.

JUST A TASTE WINE AND TAPAS BAR
607-277-9463.
116 N. Aurora St., Ithaca, NY 14850.
Open: Mon.–Fri. 11:30–3:30, 5:30–10:30; Sat. & Sun. 11–3, 5:30–11.
Price: $–$$.
Cuisine: Spanish-American.
Serving: L, D.
Credit Cards: Most major.

If you like to order something for yourself and taste a bit of everyone else's meal at your table, you are in luck at this place—that's the whole idea. Tapas are a Spanish tradition of tasting and sharing a variety of appetizer-sized dishes. Just a Taste's menu is so long, you probably should have it faxed to you and check it out before you arrive. You can get unusual items like garlic-and-sherry braised baby octopus with marinara sauce and fried angel hair or quail stuffed with black beans, garlic sausage, and rice with citrus aoli and chard or something simpler like eggplant tomato soup with mint. In the Old Port Harbor.

MADELINE'S RESTAURANT AND BAR
607-277-2253.
215 the Commons, corner of N. Aurora & E. State St., Ithaca, NY 14850.
Open: Daily for dinner 5–10, Fri. and Sat. 5–11; bar open until 12 Mon.–Thurs., until 1 Fri. and Sat.
Price: $$–$$$.
Cuisine: Asian fusion.
Serving: D.
Credit Cards: Most major

This upbeat, stylish bistro decorated with bold artwork offers a menu that features many Asian-style dishes. For example, you can nibble on fresh chilled Asian soybeans (edamame) in the pod—try them, they're really good—or start with poke: fresh seafood served sashimi-style and seasoned with seaweed, chilies, and onions. Entrées might be wasabi herb-encrusted salmon filet with mango salsa served with Asian black beans and sesame oil seasoned bean sprouts or perhaps seared marinated sushi-grade tuna over green-tea rice. You can eat inside or outdoors. Be sure to save room for one of their great desserts.

MAXIE'S SUPPER CLUB AND OYSTER BAR
607-272-4136.
www.maxies.com.
635 W. State St., Ithaca, NY 14850.

This is one of the hottest places in town. If you're craving some Cajun cuisine or soul-satisfying Southern comfort food such as jambalaya, gumbo, Cajun popcorn, crayfish, or crabcakes, come to Maxie's. It's a casual high-energy restaurant decorated in upbeat reds, purples, and lilacs. All the

Open: Sun.–Thurs.
4pm–1am; food served
Sun.–Thurs.
5pm–midnight, Fri. and
Sat. 5pm–1am.
Price: $$.
Cuisine: Cajun, Southern.
Serving: D.
Credit Cards: Most major.

dishes are made from scratch. Especially popular are the raw oysters, clams, and peel-and-eat shrimp. This is a family operation owned by Chick Evans, a graduate of Cornell, and his wife, Dewi. Besides the food, one of Maxie's biggest assets is their great staff of fun, happy people. "People really like to work here," says Karen, Chick's sister, who also helps in the family business. Free music is offered Sunday nights from 8pm when the place fills up with good crowd of people. No reservations. There are eight microbrews on tap and a 50-bottle wine list that continually rotates. Happy hour is from 4 to 6, when raw oysters and clams are half price.

**MOOSEWOOD
RESTAURANT**
607-273-9610.
www.moosewoodrestaurant
.com.
215 N. Cayuga St., Ithaca,
NY 14850
In the Dewitt Mall.
Open: Mon.–Sat. 11:30–2,
café menu 2–4:30; summer
Sun.–Thurs. 5:30–9, Fri.
and Sat. 6–9:30; winters
Sun.–Thurs. 5:30–8:30; Fri.
and Sat. until 9.
Price: $–$$.
Cuisine: Vegetarian; fish on
weekends.
Serving: L, D.
Credit Cards: Most major.

When I received the *Moosewood Restaurant Cooks at Home* cookbook as a gift, I quickly bonded with the kind of food the folks at Moosewood celebrate: healthy low-fat vegetarian items like grains, fresh vegetables, and fruits; bold salsas in place of rich, complex sauces; dishes like Mediterranean lentil salad, roasted pepper humus, north Indian eggplant, Mexican tomato lime soup, risotto with carrots and feta, and fish with tomato-orange salsa. So it was with great anticipation that I sat down at a table on their outdoor sidewalk patio and read the menu. I was not disappointed and found it very difficult to choose just one thing. I finally decided on Thai noodle salad and a tasty orange-based soup. It was served with a wholesome-grained crusty bread. Heaven. Moosewood is a collectively owned business with more than 20 members who all work together to run the restaurant and create the cookbooks. The menu changes often and draws inspiration from regional American cooking as well as ethnic cuisines. Moosewood serves great fresh fish and seafood dishes, homemade soups, salads, and pastas along with natural sodas, juices, beer, and wine. You can eat indoors in one of their two dining rooms or outdoors in season. An adjoining bar and café offers juices, specialty coffees, and a full-service bar. The restaurant is designed with a clean, contemporary look. It's one of my favorites.

ROSE INN
607-533-7905;
fax 607-533-7908.
www.roseinn.com.
813 Auburn Rd., Rte. 34,
Ithaca, NY 14850.

When I first arrived here, I walked right into the kitchen, which is just off the side porch, one of the main entrances. There I found the chef putting the finishing touches on some delectable-looking pastries for the evening meal. I was told that Charles, the owner, was out picking eldberberries, also to be

Open: Tues.–Sun.; jazz club open Fri. and Sat. Apr.–Nov.
Price: $$–$$$$.
Cuisine: Regional gourmet.
Serving: B (with B&B), D.
Credit Cards: Most major.

presented at dinner. That night, dinner served in the formal dining room in front of a fireplace was elegant, indeed: fine china, candles, crystal goblets, and fresh flowers. Offered from the prix fixe menu were such items as pan-seared rare tuna loin, grilled ostrich loin, and pecan-encrusted grilled filet mignon. Fresh herbs grown in the inn's gardens and fruit from their orchards (16 kinds of fruit trees), along with homemade raspberry brandy preserves, often accompany the meal. The rustic Carriage House Jazz Club, also on the grounds, features live entertainment. Dinner is available à la carte. (For the **Rose Inn B&B,** see the entry in "Lodging.")

SIMEON'S ON THE COMMONS
607-272-2212.
224 E. State St., Ithaca, NY 14850.
Open: Daily 11am–1am.
Price: $–$$.
Serving: L, D.
Cuisine: Continental.
Credit Cards: Most major.

Located in a historic 1871 Italianate building, Simeon's opened as a tavern in 1975. Its interior has been restored to its vintage splendor, with lots of wood, glass, and exposed brick. You can eat inside or outside at a small table set on the sidewalk under a canopy. Generous offerings include the scooper salad with tuna fish, chicken served on greens with abundant vegetables and cheese, or the Jeremiah Beebe sandwich, a classic Reuben with all the trimmings. In addition to sandwiches and finger foods, you can order entrées like Jamaican jerk or island satay and pasta. This is a place people come back to again and again; a good spot to see and be seen.

Seneca Falls

DEERHEAD INN
315-568-2950.
2554 Lower Lake Rd., Seneca Falls, NY 13148.
Open: Daily; Mon.–Fri. 11:30–2, Sat. 5–9:30; Sun. 4–9; bar open until closing.
Price: $–$$.
Cuisine: American.
Serving: L, D.
Credit Cards: Most major.

Located next to Cayuga Lake State Park, you enjoy lake views while eating on a glass-enclosed porch. American classics such as prime rib, chicken Oscar, New York strip, and beef filet. This is a casual place where you get a good meal at a fair price. You can arrive by boat, and dock just across the street.

THE GOULD RESTAURANT & LOUNGE
315-568-1282.
108 Fall Street, Seneca Falls, NY 13148.

Circa 1900, with dark-red wallpaper, wood paneling—great for lunch. My sister, a vegetarian judges restaurants on whether there's a good vegetarian selection. A portabello mushroom sandwich, she says, "is way up there in my book." (The mush-

Open: Tues.–Sat. 11–10;
  Sun. 11–3.
Price: $–$$.
Cuisine: American.
Serving: L, D.
Credit Cards: Most major.

room lived a happy life.) She ordered the sandwich and said it was great. They also serve things like steak, beef filet, lobster, and Italian dishes.

HENRY B'S
315-568-1600.
www.henrybs.com.
84 Fall Street, Seneca Falls,
  NY 13148.
Open: Tues.–Sat. 4:30–10.
Price: $$–$$$.
Cuisine: Northern Italian.
Serving: D.
Credit Cards: Most major.

This new supper club in the center of Seneca Falls has quickly gained a reputation for great food and plenty of it. With an emphasis on sharing, side dishes are served family style, and you can order a large or medium portion to go around. An extensive menu includes things like pan-roasted chicken with a lemon-oregano sauce, jumbo pan-seared shrimp, a classic Caesar salad, and a baby greens salad with goat cheese, pine nuts, and kidney beans in a honey-balsamic dressing. Service is excellent as is the food. There is an intimate, New York City feeling to the place, with white tablecloths, brick walls, and up-front wooden bar. Consider it an eating experience.

THE PUMPHOUSE
315-568-9109.
16 Rumsey St., Seneca Falls,
  NY 13148.
Open: Mon.–Sat., bar daily.
Price: $–$$.
Cuisine: American.
Serving: L, D.
Credit Cards: Most major.

On the corner of Oak and Rumsey Streets, this venerable institution has long been known as a family kind of place with games, pool table, and dart machines. There are more than 25 beers to choose from, and the chef/owner prepares interesting but not bizarre dishes, such as fish, seafood, Italian food, and steak items. It's a favorite among locals.

Aurora

AURORA INN RESTAURANT
See listing under "Lodging."

FARGO RESTAURANT
315-364-8005.
Main St., Aurora, NY 13026.
On Rte. 90.
Open: Daily until 2am.
Price: $–$$.
Cuisine: Tavern style.
Serving: L 11–2; pub menu
  evenings (fish on Friday
  nights).
Credit Cards: None; cash
  and checks only.

For years people have waited all week to run down to Jim Orman's Fargo Restaurant for fried fish on Friday nights. They still do. Now with a new look and a new bar in the style of an Irish pub, you can also chow down on wings (Buffalo and otherwise), along with great burgers, sandwiches, and hearty pub food. Enjoy billiards and beer $1.50 and up. Fargo has a front porch that is used for parties and casual dining, and a patio is on the drawing board.

MacKenzie-Childs features a fantasy restaurant filled with eclectic objects.

**MACKENZIE-CHILDS,
THE RESTAURANT**
315-364-9688.
3260 State Rte. 90, Aurora
    NY, 13026.
Open: Tues.–Sun.
Serving: L Tues.–Sun.
    11:30–2; D Fri. and Sat.
    5:30–8:30.
Cuisine: American.
Price: $–$$$.
Credit Cards: Most major.

This two-level restaurant, adjacent to the complex of MacKenzie-Childs shops, is a fantasy of fun and whimsy. Hanging from the ceiling are teapots, desks, a stuffed doll in a chair, tables, birdcages, tasseled chandeliers, broken pieces of pottery, antique cards . . . every surface is covered. Walls, too, are loaded with three-dimensional objects, while the floor is made of cross-sections of tree trunks and limbs, and the railing leading up the stairs is constructed of tree branches. But then, you are here to eat as well as gape, so enjoy a tasty menu featuring salads, soups, and sandwiches for lunch and things like shellfish risotto, roasted boneless quail, and pepper crusted filet mignon for dinner. A bonus: In the summer you can eat outside on the patio, where there is a goldfish pond. If you have small kids along, they'll have something to watch while they wait for their peanut butter sandwich.

Other Area Restaurants

**GLENWOOD PINES
RESTAURANT**
607-273-3709.
1213 Taughannock Blvd.,
  Ithaca, NY 14850.
Rte. 89, between Cass Park
  and Taughannock State
  Park.
Open: Daily 11–11.
Price: $–$$.
Cuisine: American.
Serving: L, D.
Credit Cards: Most major.

This is the home of the Pinesburger, a 6-ounce cheeseburger on French bread served with mayonnaise or Thousand Islands dressing, lettuce, tomato, and onion—all for $3.75. Glenwood has huge windows both up- and downstairs and a screened-in porch affording super views of the lake and countryside. This is a casual place with a very well-seasoned and friendly staff. Owned and run by the Hohwald family for more than 24 years, Glenwood is known for its generous portions of American staples like burgers, spaghetti, steaks, and fish. The fish fries are great.

**ROGUE'S HARBOR
STEAK AND ALE**
607-533-3535.
Corner Rtes. 34 and 34B,
  Lansing, NY 14882.
Open: Tues.–Sat. 11–10, Sun.
  10–9.
Price: $–$$.
Cuisine: American.
Serving: L, D, Sun. brunch.
Credit Cards: Most major.

In this 1830s inn the two dining rooms and pub are decorated with antiques and local memorabilia. In winter the fireplaces are often lit. Enjoy hand-cut USDA choice beef, local wines, microbrew drafts, and fresh seafood and fish. Shrimp and fried calamari are also specialties. Seasonal outdoor dining is on the porch in the front of the building. Prime rib, hand-cut steaks, a wonderful baked salmon, and an excellent pork tenderloin are among the menu items. Everything is made in-house, including sauces, soups, and desserts. The chowder is especially nice. A selection of local wines, 10 microbrews, and imports on draft are available. Upstairs is **Rogue's Harbor B&B;** see the listing under "Lodgings."

**TAUGHANNOCK FARMS
INN**
607-387-7711, 888-387-7711.
www.T-Farms.com.
2030 Gorge Rd.,
  Trumansburg, NY 14886.
Rte. 89 at Taughannock Falls
  State Park.
Open: Mon.–Sat. 5–9, Sun.
  3–8; Nov./Dec. hours
  vary; Dec. open for
  private parties only; open
  to public New Year's Eve.
Price: $$–$$$.
Cuisine: American.
Serving: D.
Credit Cards: Most major.

I remember with great pleasure the times our family dined at this lovely Victorian country inn, whether it signaled the start of summer or the occasion was a grand family outing. The prix fixe menu includes appetizer, salad, entrée, and dessert—all traditional favorites. Plus it's next to the Taughannock Falls State Park. For accommodations here, see the entry in "Lodging" above.

CASUAL FOOD

Aurora Market and Pizza (Rte. 90, Aurora, NY 13021) This is more like a general store, offering more than pizza—things like rental videos, groceries, and gifts.

Avicolli's (315-568-2233; 170 Fall St., Seneca Falls, NY 13148) This is a neat, clean, no-nonsense Italian restaurant, serving everything from sandwiches and pizza to full dinner. Very popular with locals.

Bailey's "It's a Wonderful . . ." Ice Cream Shop (315-568-0929; 95 Fall St., Seneca Falls, NY 13148) Cones, shakes, sundaes, and flurries in the "Bedford Falls" style from the movie *It's a Wonderful Life.*

Baker's Acres (607-533-3650; Rte. 34, North Lansing, NY 14882) The Lodge at Baker's Acres, once a feed store, has been converted into a tearoom and antiques and gift shop. Pleasantly decorated with hanging quilts, regional artwork, and a mixture of chairs and tables, the tearoom's menu has a number of creative dishes made with homegrown herbs and garnished with edible flowers. Open seasonally. For more information, see the entry in "Recreation."

Bubba's Dog House (315-568-8355; 2040 Rtes. 5 and 20, Seneca Falls, NY 13148) If you're craving a quarter-pound hot dog, ice cream, burger, salt potatoes, chicken, or curly fries, Bubba's is the place to come. I was hot and tired the day I stopped at the cheerful stand; the root beer float with a huge scoop of vanilla ice cream really hit the spot. Get a peek of the canal from the porch. Open Memorial Day weekend–Sept., Mon.–Thurs. and Sun. 11–8, Fri. and Sat. 11–9.

Cream at the Top (315-364-7504; Rte. 90, Ledyard, King Ferry, NY 13081) This is a good bet for a quick meal. Run by the Wilcox family, who also own a local grocery store, the place sells good ice cream and sandwiches. Open seasonally.

Dorie's (315-364-8818; 283 Main St., Aurora, NY 13026) A restored old-fashioned coffee shop and ice cream parlor. Service lunch, fresh baked breads, pastries and desserts. Also delightful selection of children's toys and books. Eat inside or on the open deck overlooking Cayuga Lake. Open daily Sun.–Thurs. 7am–8pm; Fri. and Sat. till 9.

The Lighthouse at Kidders (607-532-3446; County Road 153, Interlaken, NY 14847) On the western side of the lake; you can arrive by boat, then enjoy a well-priced menu with sandwiches, , and other typically American fare.

Mac's Drive-Inn (Rte. 20, Waterloo, NY 13165) A cheery red-and-white place selling light food and ice cream. There is a glass-enclosed eating area. Open seasonally.

Micawber's Tavern (607-273-9243; 118 N. Aurora St., Ithaca, NY 14850) Lots of good Irish pub-style nibbles and a good selection of beer and ale are enjoyed by locals usually early on and then college students after 8.

The Nines (607-272-1888; 311 College Ave., Ithaca, NY 14850) With music every night, this place is buzzing with the young and hip. A casual place with food staples like burgers and beer. Open Mon.–Sat. 11:30am–1am, Sun. 3:30pm–1am.

Pete's Treats (315-889-7636; Rte. 90, Union Springs, NY 13160) Open seasonally, Pete's is popular with locals and sells hard and soft ice cream, sundaes, and other ice cream treats plus barbecued duck, chicken tenders, and hamburgers. Take out or sit at one of the picnic tables.

The Restaurant at Knapp Vineyards (607-869-9481; 2770 Ernsberger Rd./128 County Rd., Romulus, NY 14541) Open April–December, this is a good place to stop for a bite to eat while touring the vineyards. Eat indoors or on the patio.

Pizzaurora (315-364-8804; 382 Main St., Aurora, 13026) A former garage, this new hot spot in the center of town serves freshly baked subs, homemade thin-crust pizza, calzones, and an assortment of salads. Eat indoors or, in warmer months, outside in the sidewalk café.

Rongovian Embassy (607-387-3334; 1 W. Main St., Trumansburg, NY 14886) Eclectic and casual in appointments, this place has a lot of brick and wood along with mismatched furniture and memorabilia. It also has one of the best beer lists around. Owner Eric Ott says, "If you can't find anything you like at our bar, you don't like drinking." Live music on most evenings. Open Tuesday through Sunday. (Author's note: As of publication, this restaurant was in transition to new management; plans call to start serving dinner.)

CULTURE

Ithaca

ARCHITECTURE

Ithaca has many outstanding buildings, spanning more than 200 years. The **Clinton House** (circa 1830), at 120 North Cayuga Street, was once a grand hotel with more than 150 rooms and several elegant public areas. Over the years the three-story structure has seen good times and bad, surviving several remodelings and a fire. Now this landmark building has been restored and is the headquarters for the Community Arts Project on the first floor; offices are on the top two.

The **State Theatre** is in the center of Ithaca's business district. This historic brick building, once a venue for theatrical performances, was built in 1915 as the Ithaca Security Company Garage, with a showroom on the first floor and copper-clad windows along the facade, many of which still exist. When the building was purchased by the Berinstein family in 1928, the interior was extensively remodeled to serve as a theater. Gargoyles, tapestries, stained glass, ornate columns, faux painted stone, and an illuminated celestial ceiling turned the building into a fantasy movie palace with a glitzy marquee. Movies continued to be shown into the early 1990s, but the building had deteriorated and was badly in need of repair. In 1998 Historic Ithaca acquired the building, and plans are in the works to restore it and put it back in use.

EDUCATION

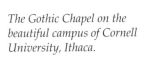

The Gothic Chapel on the beautiful campus of Cornell University, Ithaca.

Cornell University (607-255-2000; www.cornell.edu; Ithaca, NY 14850) Cornell has seven undergraduate colleges, and the liberal arts quad is one of the oldest and loveliest in the state. **The Herbert F. Johnson Museum of Art** is a major asset. Other key sites on the campus include the **Plantation,** with its many gardens, and the **Gothic Chapel**, with its rose window, painted ceiling, and brass chandelier. When you walk across the center of the older campus, you may notice messages written on the sidewalks in chalk: it's a student tradition. Guided tours are given daily.

Ithaca College (607-274-3124, 800-429-4274; www.ithaca.edu; 100 Job Hall, Ithaca College, Ithaca, NY 14850) This is a private residential college, offering 1,900 courses in more than 100 programs of study in five schools including the School of Music, School of Humanities and Sciences, School of Business, Roy H. Park School of Communications, and School of Health, Sciences, and Human Performance. More than 5,800 students attend.

MUSEUMS, EXHIBITS, AND HISTORIC SITES

Cornell Plantations (607-255-3020; www.plantations.cornell.edu; One Plantations Rd., Cornell University, Ithaca, NY 14850) A 3,000-acre area of great
beauty, this museum of living plants encompasses an arboretum, botanical
garden, and natural areas. There are woodlands, gorges, and lakeside trails
that go along the central campus. Orchids are displayed in a solarium. An educational program offers noncredit lectures, tours, and special events. The
herb garden is next to a gift shop. Grounds are free and open daily from sunrise to sunset.

Herbert F. Johnson Museum of Art (607-255-6464; www.museum.cornell.edu;
University Ave., Cornell University, Ithaca, NY 14850) Designed by I. M. Pei,
this dramatic modern structure—with 360-degree views of the countryside
from galleries and patios—has a permanent collection as well as revolving
exhibits. European, American, and Asian art collections span 40 centuries and
six continents. A sculpture garden offers a quiet place to contemplate what
you have seen. Open Tues.–Sun. 10–5.

Paleontological Research Institution (607-273-6623, ext. 10; www.englib.cornell
.edu/pri or www.priweb.org; 1259 Trumansburg Rd., Ithaca, NY 14850; on
Rte. 96) If you are interested in fossils or curious about how the glaciers
formed the gorges or what kind of animals and plant life existed on this land
long ago, come to this museum for the answers. Recently this facility has
tripled in size and is the largest of its type in the northeast. A member of the
Discovery Trail (the eight-member partnership of the Tompkins Country educational museums), the institute was established in 1932. The museum is a
combination of exhibits that change often and contain an enormous number
of fossils, shells, and other natural history specimens; photographs and paintings by regional artists; and many permanent displays such as a Tyran-
nosaurus rex skull more than four feet long. There are lectures in the winter
months, field trips and fossil hunting trips in the summer. Open Memorial
Day–Labor Day, Mon.–Sat. 11–4; Wed.–Sat. 11–4 the rest of year.

On the Trail of Art

More than 45 regional artists participate in a self-guided tour to their studios, organized in the **Greater Ithaca Art Trail.** You can watch the artists working and see
their finished work. Just about every media field is represented: painting, sculpture,
printing, ceramics, woodworking, jewelry making, stained glass, furniture making,
and more. The trail is in full operation during October but functions as an ongoing
activity throughout the year; call individual artists for an appointment. For information, check the website (www.arttrail.com), or obtain a brochure and map from a
participating gallery or the **Tompkins County Convention and Visitors Bureau.**

The Seneca Museum of Waterways and Industry, Seneca Falls.

Sagan Planet Walk (607-272-0600; www.sciencenter.org/saganpw; 601 First St., Ithaca, NY 14850) This walking tour, built in memory of astronomer Carl Sagan, starts with the sun at the Ithaca Commons downtown and continues to visit all nine planets along a three-quarter-mile route to the Sciencenter Museum. Get a "Passport to the Solar System" at locations around town ($2), get it stamped along the way, and earn a free visit to the museum at the end of the walk.

Sciencenter (607-272-0600; www.sciencenter.org; 601 First St., Ithaca, NY 14850) It's a great place to spend a day, with more than 100 exhibits, many hands-on. See a boa constrictor, water flume, two-story kinetic ball, and explore the workings of a walk-in camera. Whisper into a giant dish and navigate through the outdoor science park. Open Tues.–Sat. 10–5, Sun. noon–5. Admission $4.50, children 3–12 $3.50, under 3 free.

Tompkins County Museum (607-273-8284; www.LAKENET.org/dewitt; 401 E. State St., Ithaca, NY 14850) This is a vibrant museum, with changing exhibits and ongoing programs: lectures, poetry readings, musical performances, workshops, storytelling, and film. The focus of the museum and its programs is Tompkins County, its people, history, and culture. Typical exhibits include *Land of Clear Water: The Early Days* and *Celebrating the Towns of Tompkins County.* During the past 65 years, the museum has collected more than 18,000 interesting objects. Open Tues.–Sat. 11–5; Reference Room open Tues., Thurs., and Sat. 11–5.

PERFORMING ARTS

Cayuga Chamber Orchestra (607-273-8981; 116 N. Cayuga St., Ithaca, NY 14850) A fall-winter chamber music series held in various locations in Ithaca. Other performances such as "Caroling by Candlelight" and *Messiah* are also offered.

Cornell Center for Theatre Arts (607-254-2700; www.arts.cornell.edu/theatre arts; 430 College Ave., Ithaca, NY 14850) The Center is home to Cornell's Department of Theatre, Film, and Dance. Each year, a number of excellent concerts and dance and theatrical performances are held in the Proscenium Theatre. Lectures take place in the David L. Call Auditorium and Kennedy Hall, and outdoor concerts are staged in the Arts Quad.

Hangar Theatre (607-273-4497; www.hangartheatre.org; PO Box 205, Ithaca, NY 14850; on Rte. 89) This is one of the most respected theaters in the Finger Lakes. In operation since 1975, it continues to produce five main-stage productions each season. Recent productions have included *The Glass Menagerie*, *The Fantasticks*, and *Blithe Spirit*. The series KIDDSTUFF, for children, runs June through mid-August.

Ithaca College Theatre (607-274-3920; www.ithaca.edu/theatre; 201 Dillingham Center, Ithaca College, Ithaca, NY 14850) The Department of Theatre Arts presents drama, comedy, musicals, opera, and dance performances at the George R. Hoerner and Richard M. Clark theaters from September to May. The School of Music features concerts throughout the year.

The Kitchen Theatre Company (607-273-4497; www.kitchentheatre.com; 116 N. Cayuga St., Ithaca, NY 14850; corner Seneca and Cayuga Sts.) For performances up close and personal, try this year-round theater in the historic Clinton House, a renovated 170-year-old hotel. The intimate auditorium seats just 73 people on three sides of the stage so that no one is farther than 10 feet from the actors. The theater company focuses on imaginative, daring new work in a variety of theatrical styles. Talent is drawn from the local colleges and regional artists, and some productions are devoted to the work of area playwrights.

Summer Concert Series (607-277-8679; The Commons, Ithaca, NY 14850) Afternoon and evening concerts are held on Sundays, Tuesdays, Thursdays, and Fridays in pavilions in the Commons throughout the summer. Listen to everything from classic jazz to '50s rock and swing and blues. All concerts are free.

Seneca Falls

MUSEUMS, EXHIBITS, AND HISTORIC SITES

Elizabeth Cady Stanton House (315-568-2991; Washington St., Seneca Falls, NY 13148) Elizabeth Cady Stanton (1815–1902), a leader in the women's rights movement, organized the first Women's Rights Convention in Seneca Falls in 1848. She often worked with Susan B. Anthony, co-authoring *A History of Woman Suffrage*. Her simple white-frame home is now a museum containing memorabilia from her life and work. Open spring through fall.

National Women's Hall of Fame (315-568-2936; www.greatwomen.org; 76 Fall St., Seneca Falls, NY 13148) Displays and exhibits focus on important women in history who have been inducted into the National Women's Hall of Fame. Women honored include Eleanor Roosevelt, Pearl Buck, Rosa Parks, and Eileen Collins. Learn how they contributed to a variety of fields such as arts, education, business, government, humanities, philanthropy, government, and science. Open May–Oct., daily 9:30–5; Nov.–Apr., Wed.–Sat. 10–4, Sun. 12–4; closed Jan. except by appointment.

Seneca Falls Heritage Area Visitor Center (315-568-2703; www.senecafallsher itage.com; 115 Falls St., Seneca Falls, NY 13148) A good place to come first to get oriented to Seneca Falls and its important sites, buildings, and waterways. Open Mon.–Sat 10–4, Sun. 12–4.

Seneca Falls Historical Society (315-568-8412; fax 315-568-8426; www.wel come.to/sfhs/; 55 Cayuga St., Seneca Falls, NY 13148) This three-story, 23-room Queen Anne mansion grew from an early 1800s 1-room house. It was expanded in 1855 and remodeled in the 1880s to its present style. Many of the furnishings are from the Becker family, who lived in the house for more than 50 years. Custom-designed wallpapers, carpets from France, paintings, original lighting fixtures, stained-glass windows, carved golden oak woodwork, oak table and chairs, glass-globe lamps and other period lighting, and antique kitchen utensils and gadgets give visitors a good sense of what life was like during the Victorian era. Mannequins dressed in period clothing stand throughout the house. There is a research library on the premises as well as an 1895 Seth Thomas Town Clock and a charming Victorian outbuilding called the Beehive, now used as a gift shop. Open year-round Mon.–Fri. 8:30–4, Sat. and Sun. in the summer 1–4.

Seneca Museum of Waterways and Industry (315-568-1510; www.senecamuseum .com; 89 Fall St., Seneca Falls, NY 13148) This marvelous museum, housed in an early 1900s masonry-and-brick structure right on the Cayuga-Seneca Canal, just continues to grow and get better, with new exhibits, hands-on presentations, and an ongoing series of art and craft displays. A 35-foot mural depicts this canal, along with original drawings, engineers' plans, and photographs. Highly recommended for families: You can see how a pump works, see how the Erie Canal was built, and see the first fire engines and two-hose, people-driven carts. Children get a thrill working on an old-time loom and printing on an antique press. They can record their thoughts on the "Voices of the 20th Century," and observe how canals function by operating a working lock model. Often the site of regional arts and crafts exhibits, the museum offers periodic weaving demonstrations. A new three-part exhibit shows the development of Seneca Falls with lights that, with the push of a button, pinpoint the location of important buildings and sites. Open Tues.–Sat. 10–5, Sun. 1–5 in summer.

"This is Woman's Hour . . ." The Life of Mary Baker Eddy (315-568-6488; www.marybakereddy.org; 118 Fall St., Seneca Falls, NY 13148) Interactive displays tell how this woman challenged the conventional thinking of her time in theology, science, and medicine. A healer, author, and teacher, she spoke out about equal rights for women. Open May–Oct. Mon.–Sat. 9–5, Sun. 12–5; Nov.–Apr., Wed.–Sat. 9–5, Sun. 12–5.

Women's Rights National Historical Park (315-568-2991; www.nps.gov/wori; 136 Fall St., Seneca Falls, NY 13148) Near the northwestern tip of the lake, this park commemorates the first Women's Rights Convention held here in 1848. See exhibits relating to women's rights and Elizabeth Cady Stanton's house. A 25-minute film, *Dreams of Equality,* gives a good overview of the women's rights movement. A display of bronze figures honors those prominent in the efforts. Open daily 9–5.

Other Areas

MUSEUMS

Interlaken Historical Society Museum (Main St., Interlaken, NY 14847) See 18th- and 19th-century farm tools in both the Farmer's Museum and across the street on the second floor of the library, and browse exhibits of period clothing, pictures, and artifacts.

Rural Life Museum (315-364-8202; www.cayuganet.org/genoa.rural.life.museum/gha.html; Rte. 34B, King Ferry, NY 13081) Exhibits describe local agricultural life and traditions. Annual events include the Old Time Wheat Harvest Festival, with wagon rides, wheat cutting, a parade, and demonstrations of harvesting.

PERFORMING ARTS

Concert in the Park Series (607-387-6739; Taughannock Falls State Park, Trumansburg, NY 14886) Bring your blankets, lawn chairs, picnics, and appreciation to enjoy concerts under the stars on Cayuga Lake, held July and August in Taughannock State Park. Most of the concerts take place Saturday nights and occasionally on Thursday or Friday. Recent concerts included Rock 'n' Roll Oldies, Kansas City Jump, Afro-World Beat, the U.S. Air Force Band, folk music from the Burns Sisters, and Spiegle Willcox & his All Stars.

Morgan Opera House (315-364-5437; www.auroranewyork.com/moh/; Aurora, NY 13026) Housed in a century-old Tudor-style building, the opera house hosts a variety of productions, such as puppet shows, concerts, theater productions, variety shows, children's theater, and readings.

EDUCATION

Trumansburg Conservatory of Fine Arts (607-387-5939; www.trumansburg .ny.us/tcfa/; Congress at McLallen Sts., Trumansburg, NY 14886) Located in the heart of town, this is a not-for-profit learning and performing school of the arts for people of all ages.

Wells College (315-364-3264; www.wells.edu/; Main Street, Aurora, NY 13026) Founded in 1868 by Henry Wells, pioneer of Wells Fargo Stagecoach and American Express, Wells College is one of the oldest private liberal arts educational institutions for women in the country. The tree-shaded campus contains many redbrick historic buildings.

Photo Ops

Covered Bridge: (Rte. 13, 8 miles southwest of Ithaca Newfield) The only covered bridge in the Finger Lakes on a public road.

Top of Cornell Stadium: (Ithaca) Great views of the countryside.

Sunset Park: (Ithaca) Spectacular views of the valley from the south end of the lake.

The suspension bridge between Cayuga Heights and the Cornell campus (Ithaca) spans the river that cut through rocks, and, just below, a trail winds down to the water—a great place for a picnic or to catch some sun on a ledge.

Cayuga-Seneca Canal (Seneca Falls): Behind the main business block on Rte. 5 & 20, with the canal boats tied up along the pier.

RECREATION

BIKING

Cayuga Lake Loop: The grade is gently rolling; views are of the lake, fields, and farms. The total round trip is 90 miles. Parking is available in Cayuga Lake State Park, Rte. 89, about 3 miles south of Rte. 5 & 20. Several B&Bs as well as hotels and inns are along the way. Key areas to overnight include Ithaca, Seneca Falls, Aurora, and Trumansburg. There are also campsites in lakeside parks.

Gorge Trail: This 30.6-mile trail starts at the Ithaca Commons and takes you by Buttermilk Falls State Park, Robert Treman State Park, and Taughannock Falls State Park. All roads are paved, and there are some rolling hills. Starting on Elmira Road in Ithaca, take Rte. 13 south to Buttermilk Falls. You can spend the day here and return (a round-trip of about 8 miles). To continue, go right

Biking is popular along the lakes.

on Rte. 327 north to Halseyville Road, and go straight to Rte. 96 (about 16.9 miles at the turn). Take Taughannock Park Road, and follow it through the state park. At the intersection turn right onto Rte. 89, and go south, returning to Ithaca.

Eastern Route: Starting in Union Springs, this 36.2-mile trail goes on mostly paved roads with several rolling hills and a few steep inclines. Attractions along the way include the Frontenac Museum, McKenzie-Child, Wells College, Long Point State Park, King Ferry Winery, and the Rural Life Museum. Head south on Rte. 90 through Aurora and on to King Ferry. Stay right to go into Long Point, and at the stoplight, turn left onto Rte. 34B, and go north to Scipioville. At the turn veer left onto Ridge Road, and follow it straight to Rte. 326. Turn left onto Rte. 326 west, and follow signs to return to Union Springs.

BOATING

CRUISES

Alcyone Charters (607-272-7963; www.publiccom.com/web/alcyone/; 907 Taughannock Blvd., Ithaca NY 14850) Sail on a 1994 Hunter 35.5-foot sloop from Ithaca to Aurora. Half- and full-day charter packages are available. The four-hour cruise leaves from either Treman State Park or Johnson Boat Yard and is priced at $40 per person ($70 for full day). Overnight on board in one of the vessel's cabins, or bunk in at the Aurora Inn. The overnight trip is priced from $600 for two or four guests; $950 for six.

Erie Canal Cruise Line (800-962-1771; www.canalcruises.com) See the entry in Chapter Two, *Transportation,* for more information.

MARINAS AND LAUNCHES

Allan H. Treman State Marine Park (607-272-1460 summer, 607-273-3440 winter; Rte. 89, Ithaca, NY 14850) One of the largest inland marinas in the state, Allan H. Treman State Marine Park provides mooring and boating access to the southern end of Cayuga Lake. There are six piers with 370 seasonal boat slips, 30 transient boat slips, 30 dry slips, and a boat-launch area. Seasonal slips are assigned annually by lottery. Also on marina grounds are picnic areas, ball fields, electrical hookups, showers, and toilets.

Barrett's Marine (315-789-6605; Cayuga-Seneca Canal, Waterloo, NY 13165) Barrett's offers a variety of launches, overnight slips, showers, rest rooms, gasoline, and repair services as well as a hydraulic hoist.

Beacon Bay Marine (315-252-2849; 6223 Lake St., Cayuga, NY 13034) This facility has 25 slips.

Castelli's Marine (315-889-5532; Union Springs, NY 13160) This full-service marina has 160 boat slips, repair services, a supply store, and fuel.

Finger Lakes Marine Service (607-533-4422; 44 Marina Rd., Lansing NY 14882) Storage, outboard ramp, and a mobile hoist are available.

Oak Orchard Marina and Campground (315-365-3000 summer, 609-965-4647 winter; www.oakorchard.com; PO Box 148, Seneca Falls, NY 13148; Rte. 89N at May's Point) Camp on this 3,000-foot riverfront site that contains rental cottages overlooking the Erie Canal, tent and trailer sites, pool, playground, boat rentals, hiking, hayrides, boat launch, and hookup facilities.

Trade-A-Yacht (also known as Hibiscus) (315-889-5008; www.tradeayacht .com/hibiscus.html; Union Springs, NY 13160) On a protected inlet on the east side of Cayuga Lake, the marina has 205 slips, a marine store, restaurant, outside deck, bathrooms, showers, pool, tenting area ($25 per night), and boat rentals. At the Wheel House Restaurant you can eat inside or head outside and dine on a pleasant wood deck on the banks of the inlet. Live music on Sundays in-season.

Troy's Marina (315-889-5560; Backus Rd., Cayuga NY 13034) The marina offers 100 slips, a store, and services.

Boat launches are also at Long Point State Park (off Rte. 90, Aurora) and Deans Cove (Rte. 89, west side of Cayuga Lake).

FISHING

Judged by *Sports Afield* magazine as one of the top 10 bass lakes in the United States, Cayuga Lake is a fisherman's dream come true. In addition to the great bass fishing, anglers pull in lake trout, land-locked salmon, brown trout, and rainbow trout. Fly fishermen have more than 102 miles of trout streams and 28 miles of warm water streams to enjoy.

Cayuga Lake's AA rating means the water is fit for drinking and holds a healthy population of game fish. The fishing season runs from April to November on the lake and September to April on the Salmon River.

For the following charters, you'll need to bring a valid New York State fishing license, seasonal clothing, soft-soled shoes, a cooler to transport your catch home, snacks and beverages, and rain gear.

Eagle Rock Charters (315-889-5925; www.ctbw.com/eaglerock/; 5591 Rte. 90, Cayuga, NY 13034) Half, full, and evening light-tackle fishing charters with Capt. Glenn, a full-time guide for close to twenty years. You'll fish aboard *Eagle Rock II*, a 27-foot Baha cruiser. Eagle Rock Charters also has a 100-year-old five-bedroom rental house overlooking Cayuga Lake, 3.5 miles from the boat.

Release Tyme Charters (315-889-5395; Union Springs NY 13160) The company offers full and half day sport noodle rods and lite line fishing charters for trout and salmon using a 30-foot Penn Yan boat. Fish for lake trout, rainbow trout, brown trout, and landlocked salmon. Price for a full day is $275.

GOLF

Cayuga Links Golf Course (315-568-6597; Rte. 89 at New York Chiropractic College, Seneca Falls, NY 13148) This course has nine holes, several elevated greens, a small clubhouse, driving range, pro shop, and carts. Greens fees: $7–$8.

Cedar View Golf Course (315-364-7598; 125 Cedar View Rd., Lansing, NY 14882) Enjoy nine holes with views of Cayuga Lake. Greens fees: $11.75–$14.75; carts $11.

Indian Head Golf Course (315-253-6812; Rtes. 5 and 20 between Auburn and Seneca Falls) This rather flat nine-hole course is popular with locals. Facilities include carts, rental clubs, and snack bar. Greens fees from $9.

Hillendale Golf Course (607-273-2363; 218 N. Applegate Rd., Ithaca, NY 14850) An 18-hole public golf facility with a restaurant, bar, putting green, and practice area. Front nine is hilly; back nine considered harder. Greens fees (18 holes): $16–$18; cart $20; specials with greens fees, cart plus breakfast or hot dog and soda.

Silver Creek Golf Club (See Chapter Five, *Seneca Lake.*)

Trumansburg Golf Course (607-387-8844; 23 Halsey Rd., Trumansburg, NY 14886) This well-maintained course has18 holes, pro shop, bar, and restaurant. Greens fees (18 holes): $18–$20; cart $24 (for two)

Wells College Golf Course (315-364-8024; Wells College Campus, Aurora, NY 13026) This beautiful nine-hole course designed by Robert Trent Jones provides a pleasant round of golf. Club and cart rentals are available, and a pro shop and snack bar are on the premises. Greens fees: $11–$14.

HIKING

Cayuga Trail (from Rte. 366 off the southwestern tip of Cayuga Lake, go north on Monkey Run Rd.; park at the end) This 6.5-mile loop is difficult. Follow orange blazes along an abandoned railbed, up steep hills, through thickly planted woods, and along a creek.

Cornell Campus (Ithaca, NY 14850) Pick up a map at one of the gates, and walk around the campus on a self-guided tour. Cornell Plantations has a network of trails.

Esker Brook Nature Trail (315-568-5987; Montezuma National Wildlife Refuge, Rtes. 5 and 20 west of Auburn) This moderately easy 1.5-mile loop along dirt paths passes through woods, wetlands rich with wildlife and waterfowl, through old apple orchards, and around ponds.

Sapsucker Woods (607-254-BIRD; from Rte. 13 near the south end of Cayuga Lake, turn south on Brown Rd. Ext., then right on Sapsucker Woods Dr.) A wonderful area for bird lovers, this 2.5-mile loop along mulched trails and boardwalks makes for easy, soft walking. Press the voice boxes near the visitors center to learn about the wildlife in the area. Visit the Cornell Lab of Ornithology and the Lyman K. Stuart Observatory, where you can watch birds through a large window overlooking the pond. Wander past ponds and through woods.

Sweedler Preserve (607-275-9487; from Ithaca, go south on Rte. 13, left on Sand Bank Rd., and right at the Y on Town Line Rd.; park on the right side) White blazes mark the dirt and mulch trails of this 1.6-mile loop. Short but difficult, this part of the Finger Lakes Trail takes you down a steep hill and then back up the hill. Enjoy good views of the waterfalls in the Lick Brook gorge.

PARKS, NATURE PRESERVES, AND CAMPING

Black Rock Campgrounds (315-364-7262; Ledyard Rd., King Ferry NY 13081) This campgrounds has 100 rustic campsites, 2 cabins, 50 transient sites, fishing, and hiking.

Buttermilk Falls State Park (607-273-5761 summer, 607-273-3440 winter; www.

nysparks.state.ny.us/parks/; Rte. 13, Ithaca, NY 14850) Just a short drive from Ithaca, this 751-acre park contains several creeks and streams that converge to form 10 waterfalls that wind through a stunning series of gorges. There are two glens and a gorge trail that climbs more than 500 vertical feet in a mile; the grade is gentler in the upper part of the park. Swim in the pool at the foot of the waterfalls. Larch Meadows behind the ball fields is a refuge to many species of animals and birds. Facilities include 46 campsites, 7 cabins, swimming in the natural pool, picnic areas, playground, ball fields, toilets, and nature programs. Segments of the early 1900s movie *Perils of Pauline* were filmed in Buttermilk Glen.

Cayuga Lake State Park (315-568-5163; http://nysparks.state.ny.us/cgi-bin/cgiwrap/nysparks/parks.cgi?p+29; 2678 Lower Lake Rd., Seneca Falls, NY 13148) Level lawns, lots of trees, campsites, and a playground. Rte. 89, north end of the lake, western shore.

Frontenac Park (315-889-7341; Union Springs, NY 13160) On the eastern shore of the lake, Frontenac has a public boat launch, swimming, and picnic facilities.

Long Point State Park (315-497-1030; www.nysparks.state.ny.us/parks/; 1686 State Rte. 38, Moravia, NY 13118; on Lake Rd. off Rte. 90 4 miles south of Aurora) This park has two boat launches, pavilion, picnic area, swimming, dock, and fishing.

Montezuma National Wildlife Refuge (315-568-5987; www.fws.gov/r5mnwr/; 3395 Rtes. 5 and 20E, Seneca Falls, NY 13148) Dr. Peter Clark, a well-traveled physician from New York, named this refuge after the last Aztec emperor in honor of the large marshes surrounding Mexico City. This area is rich with wildlife and plant life. Each spring and fall, ducks, geese, herons, and other shorebirds are seen at this major resting and breeding area. The refuge includes a visitors center, a viewing platform from which you may be able to spot a nesting eagle or osprey, an easy-to-follow 1.5-mile walking loop, and a 3.5-mile wildlife drive.

Robert H. Treman State Park (607-273-3440; http://nysparks.state.ny.us/cgi-bin/cgiwrap/nysparks/parks.cgi?p+49; RD 10, off Rte. 327, Ithaca, NY 14850) This 1,070-acre park runs through rustic Enfield Glen—actually two glens interwoven. It has 4 hiking trails, 72 campsites, 14 cabins, swimming, 2 pavilions, a picnic area, and a camper recreation program. Twelve waterfalls can be viewed along a 3-mile trail. Tours are offered to the old gristmill in the upper park. The upper and lower falls are connected by hiking trails; a stream-fed pond beneath a waterfall provides a natural swimming hole. The most dramatic part is the upper half mile, where the scenery was often used as a backdrop for early Western movies before the industry moved to California. A beautiful stone path and steps lead to 115-foot Lucifer Falls. Just past this point you can look through the deep, wooded, interglacial gorge as it snakes its way to the lower park.

Ridgewood Campgrounds (607-869-9787; 6590 S. Cayuga Lake Rd., Ovid, NY 14521) You get lovely views of the water from this campground on the west

Recently-rolled hay bales sit on fields above Cayuga Lake.

side of the lake about 25 miles north of Ithaca. Facilities include tent and
trailer sites, utility hookups, picnic tables, grills, rest rooms, showers, camp
store, playground, arcade, pavilion, fishing pond, miniature golf, horseshoe
pits, volleyball, basketball, tether ball, and on-site trailer rentals.

Spruce Row Campsite and RV Resort (607-387-9225; www.campgrounds
.com/sprucerow; 2271 Kraft Rd., Ithaca, NY 14850; 7 miles north of Ithaca between Rtes. 89 and 96) Large open and shaded RV and tent sites on 125 acres.
Other facilities include a pool, hayrides, playgrounds, miniature golf, recreation building, paddleboat, store, and full hookups.

Stewart Park (607-273-8364; www.ci.ithaca.ny.us/; corner Rtes. 13 and 34;
Ithaca, NY 14850) This park is a major gathering place for year-round fun.
There are playing fields, playground, picnic area, concession stand, tennis
courts—even a restored carousel.

Taughannock Falls State Park (607-387-6739; www.taughannock.com; Rte. 89, Trumansburg, NY 14886) Towering Taughannock Falls, the highest vertical falls east of the Mississippi River, plunges 215 feet straight down through a rock amphitheater surrounded by rock walls, some as high as 400 feet. One gorge trail runs along the rim of the gorge; another winds from the base of the falls to Taughannock Creek Outlet on Cayuga Lake. Even in winter the frozen and flowing ice create a visual feast, and you can go whizzing down the sledding slope, skate on the rink, and hike the gorge trail. (The rim trail closes in winter.) Also on the park's 783 acres are 16 cabins and 76 campsites, picnic areas, toilets, fishing in the creek, swimming, and lake and boat rentals.

Waterloo Harbor Campground (315-539-8848; www.gocampingamerica.com/ waterloo/; 607-785-7891 off-season; right on Rte. 414W to Rtes. 5 & 20, Waterloo, NY 13165) Facilities include a boat ramp, utility hookups, and fishing areas.

SKIING

Downhill and cross-country ski at **Greek Peak** (607-835-6111, www.greek peak.net; Rte. 392, Virgil, NY 13045). Cross-country skiing is popular in **Robert H. Treman State Park, Taughannock Falls State Park, Upper Buttermilk Falls State Park,** and on some golf courses.

SWIMMING

The waters of Cayuga Lake are cool and clean. Several points of entry include the **Wells College dock, Aurora, off Myers Point**; **Long Point State Park**; and **Frontenac Park.** Also try the pools at the bottom of the falls at **Buttermilk Falls State Park** and **Robert Treman Park** and at the public area in the lake at **Taughannock Falls State Park.**

OTHER ATTRACTIONS

Bakers' Acres (607-533-3650; www.bakersacres.net; Mail: 1104 Auburn Rd., Groton, NY 13073; on Rte. 34, North Lansing) What started out as in 1980 as an easy retirement business for the Baker family has evolved into a very big deal. The 75-acre property contains several display gardens, like shade and sun perennial beds, rock gardens, an English rose garden, and vegetable gardens. There are 6 greenhouses, more than 100 sales frames, 600 apple trees, a cider press, and 3 barns for drying flowers—plus a woodland path leading to a pond. Have lunch in the Tea Room, enjoy great barbecued chicken, and check out the antiques upstairs in the Lodge. Plus you'll find a gift shop and fruit and vegetables for sale. Classes and workshops in gardening, cooking, and herbs are offered. So much for retirement.

Cayuga Nature Center (607-273-6260; www.fcinet.com/cnc/; 1420 Taughannock Blvd., Ithaca, NY 14850) This is a 241-acre fun place filled with things for kids of all ages to do and see. There is a visitors center, exhibits of live animals, a nature store, a working farm, and a number of special programs including summer camp and teen adventure. Get up close to farm animals and little creatures like snakes, turtles, and creepy-crawlers; explore the 5 miles of nature trails and life in the ponds; and learn about flowers.

Fallow Hollow Deer Farm (607-659-4635; www.fallowhollow.com; 125 William Rd., Candor NY 13743) New York's largest deer farm also has exotic and traditional farm animals. You can go on a narrated hayride and check out the information center. Open May–Oct.

Iron Kettle Farm (607-659-7707; www.ironkettlefarm.com; Rte. 96, Candor, NY 13743) More than a farm market, kids will love coming here in the fall for hayrides, farm animals, a spook barn, and pumpkins. There is also a craft shop on the property. Open spring–Oct., Mon.–Sat. 9–7.

Ithaca Farmers' Market (607-273-7109; www.ithacamarket.com; Third St. off Rte. 13, Ithaca, NY 14850) On Ithaca's waterfront where there is a pavilion, picnic area, docking facilities, and plenty of parking, the Ithaca Farmers Market sells local produce, plants, baked goods, meats and cheeses, crafts, clothing, and furniture. Everything is made or grown within a 30-mile radius. There is also a variety of special events throughout the season such as dancing, a strawberry festival, chili contest, a bee-day, Ping-Pong tournament, and live performances. Open Apr.–Christmas, Sat. 9–2 and mid-June–late Oct., Sun. 10–2; also open Tues. 9–1 mid-May–late Oct. at Dewitt Park, Buffalo and Cayuga Streets.

Lively Run Goat Dairy (607-532-4647; 8978 County Road 142, Interlaken, NY 14847) The Messmer family invites visitors to see and learn about dairy goats and cheese making, sample a variety of cheeses and perhaps even milk a goat. A pastoral setting, gourmet foods, local handcrafts and gifts, a hay jump, and an assortment of barnyard animals to admire, cuddle and pet (including 100 goats) make a visit here a memorable event. Cheeses made on the farm (sold at the farm and in gourmet shops) include fresh and aged cheeses in the classic style with and without herbs, tasty crumbly feta, Cayuga blue and caper, a Dutch-style hard cheese. Bring along a bottle of wine, purchase some cheese, and enjoy a picnic on the umbrella-shaded table. Open Saturdays May 31–mid-June and mid-Sept.–Oct. 31; open Mon–Wed., Fri. & Sat. from late June – mid-Sept.; tours given. Admission $4.50 adults; $2.50 children 5–16; under 5 free.

Wind Rider Balloon Co. (607-564-1009; Newfield, NY 14867) Scenic hot-air balloon rides over the Finger Lakes region last about an hour and depart at sunrise and late afternoon. Cost is $175 per person. Reservations required.

SHOPPING

Ithaca

ART GALLERIES AND STUDIOS

Etchings & Watercolors (607-277-2649; 222 The Commons, Ithaca, NY 14850; in the Ithaca Commons) Lovely watercolors and other artwork as well as a nice collection of amber jewelry are sold here.

Rock Stream Studios (607-272-0116; www.georgerhoads.com/RockStream Studios.html; 233 Cherry St., Ithaca, NY 14850) This shop contains an intriguing collection of items, including audiokinetic and wind sculptures and gurgling fountains.

Solá Gallery (607-272-6552; www.solagallery.com; 215 N. Cayuga St., Ithaca, NY 14850; in the Dewitt Mall) Japanese prints.

BOOKS AND MUSIC

Bookery and **Bookery II** (607-273-5055; www.thebookery.com; 215 N. Cayuga St., Ithaca, NY 14850; in the Dewitt Mall) The original Bookery specializes in selling and obtaining old out-of-print books. If they don't have it, they try to locate it for you. Bookery II offers a large selection of new books in all major categories. Open Mon.–Sat. 9:30–9:30; Sun. 11–6.

The Cornell Store (607-255-4111; www.store.cornell.edu; Cornell University, Ithaca, NY 14853) Browse through two floors of merchandise, where you'll find everything from Cornell shirts, gifts, and logo items to an excellent selection of books and magazines, including best-sellers, regional publications, fiction, and nonfiction. Also sells used books. Open Mon.–Fri. 8:30–6, Sat. 10–5.

Ithaca College Bookstore (607-274-3210; 140 Phillips Hall, Ithaca College, Ithaca, NY 14853) Find new and used books as well as college-related items. Open summer Mon.–Fri. 8:30–4:30; academic year Mon.–Fri. 9–4, Sat. 10–4.

CAMPING SUPPLIES

Eastern Mountain Sports (607-272-1935; 722 S. Meadow St., Ithaca NY 14850) Features a full array of clothing and equipment for skiers, hikers, tennis, and other sports.

Mountain Edge Outfitters (607-273-5158; The Commons, Ithaca, NY 14850; in the Ithaca Commons) Find everything you'll need for camping, such as sleeping bags, as well as fishing and hunting equipment, outdoor clothing, and work clothes.

CRAFTS AND GIFTS

Handblock (607-277-5525; 154 The Commons, Ithaca, NY 14850; in the Ithaca Commons) Beautiful linens star in this wonderful little shop. Also find children's clothes and lovely white nightwear and other clothing.

Handwork (607-273-9400; www.handwork.coop; 102–106 W. State St., Ithaca, NY 14850) More than 40 designers and artists display and sell their work in this exceptional cooperative of working artisans, who launched operations in 1976. There is artwork, baskets, clothing and accessories, glass, metals, home decor, jewelry, pottery, paper, and wood. Open Mon.–Sat. 10–6, Thurs. and Fri. until 9, Sun. 12–5.

Toko Imports (215 N. Cayuga St., Ithaca, NY 14850; in the Dewitt Mall) This specialty store has a huge collection of drums from Africa, Asia, and elsewhere, along with other ethnic items.

FARM MARKETS

Ithaca Farmers' Market (607-273-7109; www.ithacamarket.com; Mail: PO Box 6575, Ithaca, NY 14851; Third St. off Rte. 13) See listing under "Other Attractions" above.

Ludgate Farms (607-257-1765; www.ludgatefarms.com; 1552 Hanshaw Rd., Ithaca, NY 14850) This market offers local and imported fruits, vegetables, maple syrup, honey, preserves, salsa, fresh baked goods, flowers, and cider. Open daily 9–9.

FURNITURE

Contemporary Trends (607-273-5142; 121 N. Aurora St., Ithaca, NY 14850) This store sells high-quality Scandinavian and contemporary domestic furniture and accessories.

JEWELRY AND ACCESSORIES

House of Shalimar (607-273-7939; 142 The Commons, Ithaca, NY 14850; in the Ithaca Commons) Find ethnic and contemporary jewelry, clothing, and accessories from around the world.

Seneca Falls

ANTIQUES

Country Reflections (315-568-4176; 83 Cayuga St., Seneca, Falls NY 13148) We're told this store is "almost always open" and sells antiques and country gifts.

Jean's Antiques & Collectibles (315-568-4444; 2146 Rte. 5 & 20, Seneca Falls, NY 13148) Antiques, pine furniture, glass, china, and Victorian-era items.

FARM MARKETS

Bodine Farms (315-568-9529; E. Bayard St., Seneca Falls NY 13148; corner Rte. 89) Bodine's specializes in sweet corn but it also sells other fruits and vegetables as well as ice cream.

Sauder's Market and Store (315-568-2673; 2168 River Rd., Seneca Falls, NY 13148) Run by Amish, one building is a market, with lots of bulk goods, homemade buns and breads, and fresh produce. Another building sells such homemade crafts as candles, quilts, and toys, including a wooden contraption that routes a marble down chutes and around a little waterwheel-like gear. Well-made stuff; worth a visit. Open year-round Thurs. 8–5, Fri. 8–9.

GIFTS

Christina's Gift Shop (315-568-8826; 51 Fall St., Seneca Falls, NY 13148) Find wonderful silver jewelry, ceramics, cards and other unique gift items.

Crickets Gift Boutique (315-568-2921; 102–106 Fall St., Seneca Falls, NY 13148) Find a wide assortment of gifts such as Yankee Candles, silk and fresh flowers, toys, and cards.

Aurora

(Please note: At the time of publication, **Aurora Place,** a historic building housing small shops and businesses on Main Street, was undergoing extensive restoration.)

ANTIQUES

Cleavelands' Antiques (315-364-7266; corner Sherwood Rd. and Rte. 34B, Aurora, NY 13026) This store has an assortment of antiques, memorabilia, and just plain good old junk. Open Thurs.–Sun 1–5 or by appointment.

Vintage Lighting (315-364-8182; Main St., Aurora, NY 13026) The company both purchases and sells antique lamps and lighting fixtures as well as repairs and restores them. Tues.–Fri. 10–5, Sat. and Sun. 1–4:30.

CLOTHES

Jane Morgan's Little House (315-364-7715; Main St., Aurora, NY 13026) Fine women's fashions and accessories, including Austin Reed, Carol Anderson, Barry Bricken, and Sigrid Olsen.

FOOD

Village Market (315-364-8803, Main Street, Aurora, NY 13026) An attractive new market selling fresh breads, fresh fruits and vegetables, jams and jellies and other food items including picnic items. Presentation is great, perfect for gift baskets.

GIFTS

Aurora Lake Designs (315-364-7875; www.waterhousegallery.com; PO Box 88, Aurora, NY 13026) Anna Emma's oils, silks, and design services and consultation by 2nd Opinion.

Debbie's Corner Gift Shop (315-364-8085; Main St., Aurora, NY 13026; in The Aurora Place) All kinds of gifts, including Fenton Glass, jewelry, English bone china teapots, candles, paperweights, linens, "Aurora" shirts, and crafts.

Destiny Designs (315-364-9577; 2 Dublin Hill Rd., Aurora, NY 13026; corner Main St.) Custom-designed clothing items, paper goods, and promotional pieces as well as photo restoration.

Kron Lume Scandinavian Gift Outlet (315-364-7908; 800-447-6011; www.kron lume.com; 1891 Rte. 90, King Ferry, NY 13081) Lovely pine candlesticks, candelabra, wooden stars, Christmas decorations, lights, clogs, and other items from Sweden, Norway, Denmark, and Finland. Excellent prices. Open 10–5. Closed Mon.

A twig house sits amidst a garden at MacKenzie-Childs, Aurora.

MacKenzie-Childs (315-364-7123, 800-640-0546; www.mackenzie-childs.com; 3260 Rte. 90, Aurora NY 13026) If you happen to whiz by, turn around and go back. This place is worth seeing. Set on a hilltop overlooking the lake just north of Aurora, MacKenzie-Childs is a fantasy world of pottery, hand-painted wooden furniture, glass, ceramic vanity bowls, lamps, and other objects that are now sold in exclusive stores in the company's major cities. And this is where is all happens. Visit a sprawling workshop, a full-service restaurant, outlet store, and bird aviary. Whimsical, colorful, captivating. You'll probably leave with a few packages of loot, but beware: Even in the "factory outlet," nothing is inexpensive, though bargains can be found on the seconds tables. Two major sales bring lots of bargain hunters in spring and fall.

Posies (315-364-8817; 283 Main St., Aurora NY 13026) Fresh flowers, plants, and unique gift items.

Shakelton's Hardware (315-364-8211; Main St., Aurora NY 13026) An old-fashioned hardware store with wonderful wood floors. Open Mon.–Fri. 8–5, Sat. 9–4.

Other Areas

ANTIQUES

Barzilla's Barn Antiques (607-387-6820; 9402 Rte. 89, Trumansburg, NY 14886) A wide assortment of antiques and memorabilia is available. Open seasonally.

The Collection (607-387-6579; 9–11 W. Main St., Trumansburg, NY 14886; on Rte. 96,) Chris and Pat Whittle's shops sell antique furniture and accessories. Open Tues.–Sat. 11–5, Sun. 1–5

Turn of the Century (607-532-8822; 8406 Main St., Interlaken, NY 14847; on Rte. 96) A large shop with three showrooms of furniture mingled with accessories, collectibles, and other things. Open Tues.–Sat. 12–5, Sun. and Mon. by chance or appointment.

Turo's Treasures (315-364-8644; corner Rte. 34B & Rte. 90, King Ferry, NY 13081) This shop buys and sells antiques and sells collectibles, gifts, and reproductions.

ART GALLERIES AND STUDIOS

Blue Heron Gallery (607-387-9476; 63B Main St., Trumansburg, NY 14886) Arts and crafts by regional artisans are on sale along with antiques and books. A small shop crammed with good things.

Sherry's Bear and Frame Shop (315-568-5541; 67 Fall Street, Seneca Falls, NY 13148) Unique handmade Teddy bears, old and new artwork, and antiques, plus custom framing.

GIFTS AND TOYS

Black Sheep Designs (607-387-7078; www.fingerlakes.net/blacksheep; 63 Main St., Trumansburg, NY 14886) Local artists display their craft in an 1865 Italianate brick house. Find pottery, wooden pieces, baskets, candles, jewelry, toys, handmade soaps, bath gels, and lotions as well as gourmet coffees, teas, and chocolates. Open Tues.–Sat. 10–6.

T-Burg Toys (607-387-7891; 5301 Rte. 228, Trumansburg, NY 14886) Handmade wooden toys and other quality things for children are offered.

For More Information

Finger Lakes Tourism: 315-536-7488; www.fingerlakes.org; 309 Lake St., Penn Yan, NY 14527.

Ithaca/Tompkins County Convention & Visitors Bureau: 607-272-1313; 800-28 ITHACA; www.ithacaevents.com; www.visitithaca.com; 904 E. Shore Dr., Ithaca, NY 14850.

Seneca County Tourism:; 800-732-1848; www.visitsenecany.net; 1 DiPronio Dr., Waterloo. NY 13165.

Trumansburg Area Chamber of Commerce: 607-387-9254; http://trumansburg chamber.com/; PO Box 478, Trumansburg, NY 14886.

CHAPTER FIVE
Deep Waters and Gorges
SENECA LAKE

View over the vineyards to Seneca Lake.

The Native American translation for *Seneca*—"a Place of Stone"—hardly does the lake justice. About 40 vineyards covering hundreds of acres are planted on the hillsides that gently slope to the water's edge. They are, quite simply, a stunning sight. More than 600,000 visitors come here each year to visit these vineyards and wineries along the Seneca Wine Trail. Many participate in special events such as December's "Deck the Halls" and June's "Pasta and Wine."

In the parks, hikers and bikers explore the vast network of trails, and campers pitch their tents. Race enthusiasts flock to Watkins Glen for motor races, and residents and visitors alike attend theatrical performances and concerts, including weekly outdoor band concerts.

At 35 miles long and estimated to be more than 630 feet deep in some places, Seneca Lake is a coveted water playground for boaters, sailors, anglers, and swimmers. (As the second-deepest lake in the country, Seneca is a testing site

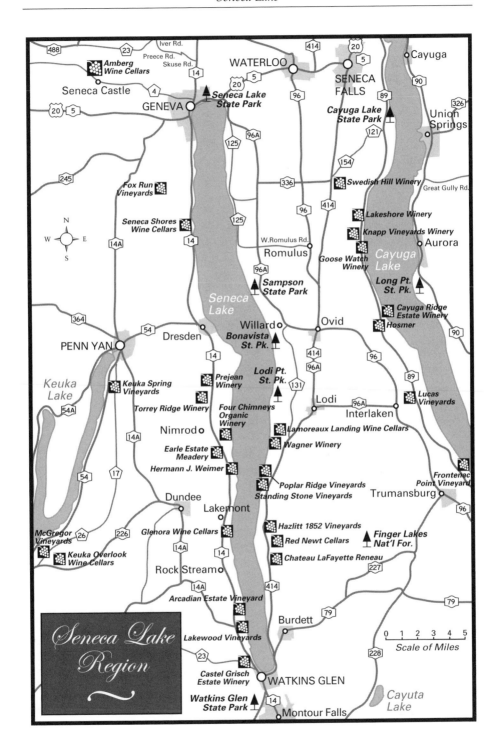

Seneca Lake Region

for sonar equipment; a station is set about midlake.) The Seneca-Cayuga Canal, which connects Seneca Lake with Cayuga Lake, the state barge canal, and waterways beyond, gives boaters a large cruising ground—the entire world, in fact. From Seneca Lake through the New York State canal system, you can actually reach the Atlantic Ocean, then circumnavigate the globe if you so choose.

Seneca Lake was once a stronghold of the Seneca nation. Many Native American artifacts have been recovered around the lake, including on the grounds of Belhurst Castle. The site of Kanadesaga, the capital of the nation destroyed in General Sullivan's campaign, is about where the New York State Agricultural Experiment Station now stands. In the 18th century, Kanadesaga (which means "dog town") was changed to Geneva.

The land opened up to settlers at the time of the Phelps-Gorham purchase in 1783. In 1794 Geneva was officially laid out by Charles Williamson, with Water Street (now Exchange Street) as the heart of the business district. At that time the northern shores of the lake were close to the rear of the stores, but in 1919 a portion of the lake was filled in to create a park.

In the early 1800s steamboats plied Seneca's waters, transporting agricultural products and livestock as well as passengers from one end to another. These steamboats were very important to the lake people, who relied on them to get from place to place.

Prominent companies in the early days were the Geneva Waterworks (1776), J. W. Smith Dry Goods (1847), Geneva Optical Company (1873), the Geneva Carriage Company (1891), and the Nester Malt House (1890). At the turn of the 20th century, railroads became an important means of transportation to the region. The Rochester and Eastern Rapid Roadway carried passengers and goods between Rochester and Geneva, with stops all along the way.

With the advent of the automobile, the steamboat and to some extent the railroad became obsolete in the people-moving business. Highways were paved, and the main route (now Routes 5 and 20) ran close to the shoreline. In the 1950s this bypass highway was relocated farther inland so that the lakefront property could be reclaimed as a park and recreational area.

The lake is now ringed by small villages, summer houses, camps, and parks. Geneva hovers at the northern end; Watkins Glen anchors the southern end. Other towns worth noting near or around the lake include Waterloo, just west of Geneva; Dresden, a small quiet village on the lake where residents enjoy a nice beach and superb fishing; and Dundee, 3 miles west of Seneca Lake. Almost midway between Seneca and Keuka Lakes, around Lamoka and Waneta Lakes, sites of ancient Native American villages are found.

A few miles south of Watkins Glen, Montour Falls is home to the beautiful SheQuaGa Falls, plunging 165 feet into a rocky pool. At the foot of Main Street, the falls are illuminated at night, a spectacular sight. Clustered around the falls are the historic "T buildings" built in the mid 19-th century, including the Memorial Library and museum with its lovely Tiffany glass windows. Also architecturally interesting is the Greek-Revival Village Hall.

Can You Hear the Lake Drums?

The Seneca believed they heard the low distant booms of the drums of their ancestors, thought to be manifestations of evil spirits or divine messages from the God of Thunder. Today these booms can sometimes be heard on very still evenings, but no one is sure just what causes them. Some think it's a result of gases building up from the lake bottom that create the noises as they escape.

GENEVA

With a population of more than 14,000, Geneva is one of the larger cities in the region. As you drive west into the city along Route 5 & 20, there is the expansive Seneca Lake State Park dotted with trees, picnic tables, and grills, a place you can swim, sunbathe, cycle along the trails, and laze away an afternoon. Next to this is Lakeside Park and the Chamber of Commerce Center, a good place to stop for information.

Geneva is home to several important events, including the National Lake Trout Derby, held each Memorial Day, and the Seneca Lake Whale Watch Festival, held in August, a fun-filled weekend of crafts, food, music, and special events. (You may not glimpse a spouting whale, but you are guaranteed to have a whale of a good time.)

Recently a number of piers and mooring slips have been built near the Ramada Inn, making it possible for boaters to tie up and walk into Geneva about two blocks away. Also new is a wide stone pier that protects the harbor. A tunnel walkway goes under Route 5 & 20 and the rail tracks, but it's just as easy to cross the road. Traffic is usually light: We're not talking about Manhattan here.

Over the years, Geneva has retained its quiet village ambiance. Large lovely turn-of-the-20th-century houses, the mini-mansions of their day with pillars, leaded windows, round towers, and generous lawns and gardens, reign along South Main Street. Rows of exquisite three-story brick Federal townhouses (circa 1820) ring tree-lined Pulteney Square, the original center of town, which sits on a hill above the lake. From the terraces and windows of the houses on the south side of the street, residents enjoy superb views of the water.

Noteworthy buildings in town include Belhurst Castle, a baronial-looking Romanesque structure; Geneva-on-the-Lake, a lakeside Italian-style villa; and Rose Hill, an 1839 Greek-Revival mansion that commands a prominent hillside position overlooking the lake.

Exchange Street, the "main drag," and the adjoining streets contain a mixture of trendy shops, restaurants, and local stores as well as old establishments that have been in the same location for decades. No chain stores are as yet evident in the center of town. The original movie house is still operating, although it now contains four smaller theaters where once there was one.

Handsome new period-style lighting, brick sidewalks, and bricklike crosswalks—along with vast renovations of the turn-of-the-century buildings—are transforming this area into one of the better small towns in the state.

The redbrick buildings of the in-town campus of Hobart and William Smith Colleges settle comfortably into the landscape. A liberal arts education is offered at Hobart for men, the oldest college (founded 1822) in western New York, and William Smith (founded 1908) for women, which are next to each other and share some facilities.

WATKINS GLEN

The Watkins Glen International Racing Circuit track roars with the sounds of auto racing.

In 1948 the green flag waved the start of world-class motor racing in Watkins Glen. In those days, the cars raced along village streets and hillsides. Now the thunder of Grand Prix auto racing has moved to its own course, but you can use a self-guided tour map to trace the route the racers used to follow.

The village's narrow main street is lined with several midrise buildings, housing stores and restaurants. There is a white-brick hotel open seasonally, and an attractive wide-board pier runs off the harbor.

WATERLOO

Two blocks of redbrick buildings define the business section of Waterloo. Neighborhoods are quiet and pleasant. It's the kind of place that typifies home-town America—so it's appropriate that Waterloo is the birthplace of Memorial Day, first observed on May 5, 1866. Many Memorial Day traditions stem from this day, when flags flew at half mast, wreaths were placed on war veteran's graves, and a parade of veterans and community leaders marched to the cemeteries and participated in ceremonial gun salutes and speeches. A museum on Main Street is dedicated to this holiday.

Waterloo is home to other museums, including the restored Peter Whitmer Farm, where the Church of Jesus Christ of Latter-Day Saints was formed in 1830.

LODGING

Seneca Lake is fortunate to have some exceptional lakefront hotels, such as Geneva on the Lake and Belhurst Castle. The contemporary Ramada Inn on the north shore is within walking distance of the business area and next to the new public docking facilities. There are also a number of good bed & breakfasts in the area.

LODGING RATES
$: Up to $75 per couple
$$: $76–$150 per couple
$$$: $151–$250 per couple
$$$$: More than $250 per couple

Geneva

HOTELS AND RESORTS

BELHURST CASTLE
Innkeepers: Duane Reeder family.
315-781-0201.
www.belhurstcastle.com.
4069 Rte. 14S, Geneva, NY 14456.
Rooms: 13, including 2 guest cottages.
Open: Year-round.
Price: $–$$$$.
Credit Cards: Most major.

An imposing 1890s Romanesque castle on 30 lakeshore acres is graced by tall trees and gardens. At first you may think that you have arrived at a private estate in the European Alps. Built by Carrie Harron Collins, who brought many of the building materials and furnishings from Europe, the rich oak doors and woodwork, stained-glass windows, and towers and turrets are indeed impressive. Over the years, Belhurst—which means "beautiful forest"—has served as a private home, a speakeasy, and a gambling casino. It is rumored that the castle even has secret tunnels and sliding panels to hidden rooms. Today Belhurst operates as an inn and restaurant. Many rooms have high ceilings with deep moldings; some have working fireplaces. The Tower Suite, often requested by honeymooners, has beamed ceilings, a large Jacuzzi, a spiral stairway leading up to a lookout, and a king-sized bed. The Billiards Room has a private balcony overlooking the lake and a king-sized bed. Enjoy lunch and dinner in the Library, Parlor Center Room, Conservatory, or on the Veranda. The Garden Room next to the main building provides space for functions of up to 300 people. If you're up for a glass of wine, simply head to the large wine cask in the lounge and help yourself. Editor's note: As of publication, an expansion of Belhurst Castle was in the works, which will add 20 more guest rooms, a wine shop, new lounge, and a new catering facility.

GENEVA ON THE LAKE RESORT
Innkeeper: William Schickel.
315-789-7190,
  800-3-GENEVA;
  fax 315-789-0322.
www.genevaonthelake.com.
1001 Lochland Rd., Geneva,
  NY 14456.
On Rte. 14.
Rooms: 30 suites and
  studios, 10 with 2
  bedrooms.
Open: Year-round.
Price: $$–$$$$.
Credit Cards: Most major.

Inspired by the Villa Lancellotti in Frascati outside of Rome, Mrs. Samuel Nester, a wealthy resident of Geneva, built this grand white mansion on a hillside above the lake in 1910. The Italian Renaissance architecture is unusual for this part of the world, a reminder of a period when European opulence was highly prized by the well-to-do. A small outdoor shrine recalls when the villa was once used as a seminary and monastery. Today Geneva on the Lake welcomes guests from around the world, including many famous artists, performers, and sports people. Beautifully renovated by Norbert and William Schickel in 1979, it continues to be refurbished. In 1995 the property was purchased by Mr. and Mrs. Alfred Audi, owners of L. & J. G. Stickley, a well-known area furniture maker. It is not surprising, therefore, to find Stickley pieces used throughout the villa in both private and public rooms. The Classic Suite, which features a fireplace in the living room and bedroom, is furnished in Stickley Chippendale with a four-poster rice-carved bed; the Loft Suite is furnished in Stickley Mission cherry and has a 16-foot ceiling, king-sized bed, and six windows overlooking the gardens; and the former chapel has been converted into the Whirlpool Suite with a very large tomato-red Jacuzzi—a bit out of sync with the rest of the room but still great fun. Most suites come with parlors and kitchens. Whether you're relaxing in your room—appointed with rich fabrics, Oriental rugs, tapestries, and interesting artwork—strolling in the formal gardens accented by classical sculpture, or lounging by the 70-foot pool at the end of the gardens, your surroundings will be peaceful. The rope swing hanging from the branch of a big old tree is a particularly nice touch. Brides having their receptions here like to stroll down the lawns and have their picture taken in the swing. At the end of a day, the resort's pontoon boat is ready to take you on a sunset cruise at a moment's notice. Then it's time to dine either on the Colonnade Pavilion or in one of the intimate dining rooms, where tables are set with linens, crystal, and, of course, candles. When it comes to romance, Geneva on the Lake gets a high five.

RAMADA GENEVA
Innkeeper: Victor Nelson.
315-789-0400, 800-990-0907;
  fax 315-789-4351.
www.genevany.com/biz/
  ramada.
41 Lakefront Dr., Geneva
  NY 14456.
Rooms: 148.
Open: Year-round.

With a decidedly nautical look, this four-year-old modern lakeside hotel, with its cobalt-blue roof and 148 comfortable, attractively decorated rooms, appeals to business and leisure travelers alike. Rooms come with all modern amenities, and most have lake views. The lobby is spacious and opens up to marvelous lake views through large windows. Three suites have Jacuzzis, and there is a gym and cool-down pool. The Pier House restaurant

Price: $$–$$$$.
Credit Cards: Most major.

is considered one of the better places to eat in town. The large open-air patio is a particularly good place on a pleasant summer's day. Meeting rooms can accommodate up to 220 people. The hotel is within easy walking distance of the main part of town, and a tunnel running under the highway provides safe, easy passage to the shopping district. New docking facilities on the shorefront invite people to come by boat.

BED & BREAKFASTS

WHITE SPRINGS MANOR
Innkeepers: The Reeder family.
315-781-0201.
PO Box 609, Geneva, NY 14456.
On Rte. 14S.
Rooms: 13.
Open: Year-round.
Price: $$–$$$$.
Credit Cards: Most major.

Once the site of a Native American village and later an important dairy farm and a fruit farm, this Georgian-Revival home was built in the early 1900s. The house sits on the top of a breezy hill, with magnificent views of the countryside and lake in the distance. Its pillared terraces, large sweeping grounds, and gazebo create a serene setting. High-ceilinged rooms are spacious and come with television/VCR, honor bar, and period furnishings. The Lewis Suite has beamed ceilings, a king-sized bed, sitting room, and fireplace. The Living Room (now a bedroom) has a fireplace, canopy bed, and sitting area. There's not much going on here: Even the free continental breakfast is served off the property at Belhurst Castle, the sister property nearby. So if it's solitude and good country air you're looking for, this is it.

Watkins Glen

HOTELS AND RESORTS

GLEN MOTOR INN AND MONTAGE RESTAURANT
Innkeeper: Victor Franzese.
607-535-2706;
fax 607-535-7635.
www.glenmotorinn.com.
3380 Rte. 14, Watkins Glen, NY 14891.
Rooms: 40.
Open: Year-round.
Price: $–$$.
Credit Cards: AE, MC, V.

This is your basic motel setup with all ground-floor rooms, some with balconies overlooking the lake. Rooms are simply furnished and come with two double beds. There is a pool and the Montage Restaurant, where you can eat inside or out on the deck. Those seeking an inexpensive, no-nonsense kind of place to use as a base to explore the region will find this a reasonable solution.

Grapevines line the walkway to the pier at Watkins Glen.

BED & BREAKFASTS

ANNA ROSE B&B
Innkeepers: Ken and Sharon
Miller.
607-243-5898.
www.annarose.com.
524 Rock Stream Rd., Rock
Stream, NY 14878
Rooms: 5 with private baths
including a suite,
Open: Year-round,
Price: $$–$$$,
Credit Cards: Most major,

This five-acre estate, formerly known as Peelle Farms of Rock Stream, was built in 1926 by John W. Peelle. The three-story brick house on a breezy hilltop contains spacious, well-appointed rooms decorated with designer fabrics, damask quilts, lots of pillows, pictures, and a mix of antiques and period reproductions. Some rooms have canopy beds; others king beds. One is a hand-carved mahogany Rococo-style bed. Rooms come with robes, lots of towels, and hair dryers; some have TVs. There is a guest television room, gazebo, grass tennis court, sunroom, gift shop, and a formal living room that has a lovely fireplace. A four-course breakfast is served with fruits, juices, hot casseroles, breakfast meats, baked goods, and coffee. Round-the-clock snacks and beverages are available in the butler's pantry, and the Millers offer goodies like homemade cookies, popcorn, rum cake, and cheese and crackers. This B&B with its three fireplaces is very romantic.

CASTEL GRISCH MANOR
Innkeepers: Chris and Erin
Schiavone.

A special hideaway with lots of charm, Castel Grisch is tucked into an enclave of gardens on an estate. A former private home, it has an octago-

607-535-7711; 607-535-5437
www.themanorbandb.org.
3390 County Rte. 28,
   Watkins Glen, NY 14891.
Rooms: 4 with private baths.
Open: Year-round.
Price: $$–$$$.
Credit Cards: Most major.

nal tower entrance hall and a brick-and-timber exterior—very European in style and very private, with unending views of vineyards and countryside. Castel Grisch has four rooms and suites, an enclosed spa garden room with a hot tub and treadmill, and a sitting room with a large fireplace, satellite television, and an honor bar. Decor is upbeat in roses and red. The Champagne Room has a king-sized bed, airy off-white fabrics and carpets, and a large tub and shower; the Riesling Room has a large whirlpool tub and is decorated in red toile. All rooms have private baths; three have balconies. Amenities include air-conditioning, ceiling fans, robes, toiletries, and full breakfast, perhaps with Belgian waffles.

CHERRY ORCHARD
Innkeeper: Vera Giasi.
607-535-7785, 607-535-9330.
www.cherryorchard.com.
Mail: PO Box 145, Watkins
   Glen NY 14891.
4194 State Rte. 14, Rock
   Stream, NY 14878.
Rooms: 5 with private baths.
Open: Year-round.
Price: $$.
Credit Cards: Most major.

This B&B comes by its name honestly: It's set in a cherry orchard and vineyard on the west side of the lake, with views of the east-side hills and the lake in the winter when the trees have lost their leaves. Fox Run golf course is across the street, and the Arcadian Estate Winery is next door. Although the house dates back more than 100 years, extensive modernizing and additions make it more of a contemporary. Two guest rooms have cathedral ceilings, and there is a very large great room/kitchen. Rooms are decorated mostly in soft neutrals and whites; beds are all different. For example, one is furnished with a 1940s pecan bed set, another pine. Three rooms have private entrances. There is an attractive stone spa accommodating nine people and an exercise room with a treadmill, weights, and other equipment. A full breakfast is served, including something hot like eggs or quiche, muffins, waffles, and apple crisp.

**FARM SANCTUARY AND
   B&B**
Managers: Lorri and Gene
   Bauston.
607-583-2225/4021;
   fax 607-583-2041.
www.farmsanctuary.org.
3100 Aikens Rd., PO Box
   150, Watkins Glen, NY
   14891.
Rooms: 3 cabins.
Open: May 1–Oct. 31.
Price: $–$$.
Credit Cards: Most major.

Stay on a farm filled with animals. Each of three cabins here can sleep up to six people, with two double beds and sleeping mats for children. The cabins have wicker furniture and a porch. For more information, see the description in the "Recreation" section below.

GENTLE GIANTS BED AND BREAKFAST
Innkeepers: Bill and Glenda Nash.
866-894-3821, 315-781-2723.
www.gentlegiants.pair.com.
1826 County Rd. 4, PO Box 723, Geneva NY 14456.
Rooms: 2 with private baths.
Open: Year-round.
Price: $–$$.
Credit Cards: Most major.

Located on the edge of a large vegetable crop farm, the house—a recently restored 1856 Italianate Victorian—has a nice parlor with a piano, books, and games. Out back is a large barn, home to registered Belgian horses—the "gentle giants." Guests are always welcome to visit with Mr. Boston and his ladies. Two friendly dogs, Bear and Dover, are also on hand to greet you—gently. Rooms are centrally air-conditioned and very comfortable. A full country breakfast is served, with fresh eggs from the farm's chickens and produce from the farm such as asparagus, onions, peppers, apples, and raspberries—it depends on the season. You can eat in the formal dining room or the large sunny kitchen. Catch up on your reading under a tree in the backyard or in the swing on the porch.

An old stove becomes a breakfast bar for those staying at Lake House B&B in Rock Stream.

LAKE HOUSE B&B
Innkeeper: Susan Lewis.
607-243-5637.
www.linkny.com/lakehouse bandb.
46 Hunt Rd., Rock Stream, NY 14878.
Rooms: 4, 2 with private baths.
Open: Year-round.
Price: $$.
Credit Cards: Cash or check.

Few of the more remote B&Bs stay open during the winter months, but this one 6 miles north of Watkins Glen is an exception. After all, says Susan Lewis, "I love the winter." Her guests come here to cross-country ski, snowshoe, and get away and unwind. And what a good place to do it! This restored late 19th-century farmhouse overlooking the lake features eclectically furnished and very spacious rooms, modern baths, and a large sitting room with a good collection of books. Oriental carpets, a few Victorian pieces, and polished hardwood floors create a casual but gracious ambiance. There is beach access just a quarter-mile walk away plus a big old front porch where you can start the day with a cup of coffee or tea and home-baked breads before digging into Susan's sumptuous breakfast.

READING HOUSE
Innkeepers: Rita and Bill
  Newell.
607-535-9785.
www.bbhost.com/reading
  house.
4610 Rte. 14, Rock Stream,
  NY 14878.
Mail: PO Box 321, Watkins
  Glen NY 14891.
Rooms: 4 with private baths.
Open: Year-round.
Price: $$.
Credit Cards: Most major.

You get superb views of the lake from this large 1820s house on the east side of the lake about 5 miles north of Watkins Glen. Over the years the house evolved from a Federal farmhouse to a Greek-Revival with Victorian flourishes. Today it is restored to its original 19th-century character and contains a number of nice antiques. The grounds cover several acres with ponds, gardens, and lawns. An ample supply of reading matter includes old and new books, which you can read in your room or in one of the two parlors. Guests enjoy a full breakfast with juice, fruit, cereal, fresh baked muffins, and a main course—perhaps French toast, buttermilk pancakes with local sausage, or omelets. Reading House is ideal for exploring the area. It's within 5 miles of the International Auto raceway at Watkins Glen and close to wineries, Corning, Cornell, and other local attractions. It's quiet place surrounded by wonderful wildlife.

**SENECA LAKE WATCH
  B&B**
Innkeepers: George and
  Julie Conway.
607-535-4490.
www.bbhost.com/seneca
  lakewatchbb.
104 Seneca St., Watkins
  Glen, NY 14891.
Rooms: 5 with private baths.
Price: $$.
Credit Cards: Most major.
Open: Year-round.

Built in 1820, the Seneca Lake Watch B&B is the oldest house in town, a grand Victorian home in a quiet lakeview setting. It has wide pumpkin-pine floors, vintage furniture (many antique pieces), a sitting room with fireplace, a wonderful Chickering piano circa 1880, and a comfortable lived-in feeling. A 65-foot wraparound porch, a large deck, gazebo, and extensive gardens promise lots of ways to enjoy the outdoors. The five guest rooms offer queen and king beds. King rooms have private decks and views of the water. All have private baths and air-conditioning. George cooks the lavish breakfast; Julie does the baking. You can stay here for two weeks and never have the same thing twice. Unless you want to: George says he keeps a computerized account of what is served to whom so that when guests return, he knows what they like. The B&B is just a quarter-mile walk from town.

Other Area Lodging

HOTELS AND RESORTS

**ABBEY FARM AT SPRING
  HILL B&B**
585-526-5420.
www.abbeyhistoricalfarm.org.
1862 Rte. 5 & 20, Stanley, NY.

See listing under "Other Attractions."

THE INN AT GLENORA WINE CELLARS
General Manager: Melissa Cady.
607-243-9500, 800-243-5513.
www.glenora.com.
5435 Rte. 14, Dundee, NY 14837.
Rooms: 30.
Open: Year-round.
Price: $$–$$$, packages available.
Credit Cards: Most major.

Enormous barrels announce the entrance to this new inn set into a hillside overlooking the lake and surrounded by vineyards. Built in a Napa, California, redwood style with lots of windows, high ceilings, and generous spaces, this inn is a departure from the B&Bs and country inns typically found in the region. There is a light, open feeling throughout. All rooms have private balconies or patios and feature cherry and pine molding, flowers, local artwork, traditional Stickley Mission-style furniture, and Waverly-style quilts and fabrics. Adirondack-style chairs made of wood from wine barrels are on the decks. Some rooms are furnished with two queen beds, others with a king, fireplace, and Jacuzzi. All rooms have a table, clock radio, television, minifridge, hair dryer, and coffee and tea facilities. At one end of the inn, the restaurant, like all of the guest rooms, offer sweeping views of the lake. The main building of the visitors center and winery operations is farther up the hill.

The waterfront at Rainbow Cove Resort Motel and Restaurant in Nimrod.

RAINBOW COVE RESORT MOTEL AND RESTAURANT
Innkeepers: Jeff and Helen Ripley.
607-243-7535.
3482 Plum Point Rd., Himrod, NY 14842.
Rooms: 24.
Open: Mid-May–late Oct.
Price: $–$$.
Credit Cards: Most major.

If you remember '50s-style motels, you'll get the picture. Still, the rooms have been upgraded and modernized, and they're neat and clean. Some even have lake views: the top units in the two-story building and rooms 1 to 6 in the one-story buildings. There is a pool and recreation room, as well, and the beachfront is quite nice, with a gazebo, a private pier, and boat slips.

**SHOWBOAT MOTEL
AND RESTAURANT**
Innkeeper: John Socha.
607-243-7434;
fax 607-243-8050.
3434 N. Plum Point Rd.,
Himrod, NY 14842.
Rooms: 43 plus a cottage.
Open: May 1–Oct. 31.
Price: $–$$.
Credit Cards: Visa, MC.

This rustic old motel is "moored" on the lake just off Route 14 between Geneva and Watkins Glen. Lakeside rooms have water views; others overlook the pool. Another building is across the street. The restaurant is open daily for breakfast, lunch, and dinner in-season (off-season on weekends only), and you can eat inside or out on the deck. Water toys include canoes and other boats, and there is a private pier.

BED & BREAKFASTS

**THE COTTAGE
LAKEMONT ON
SENECA**
Innkeepers: Carol and
Bernie Kline.
607-243-7194.
www.bedandbreakfast
.com/property/ppf/id/
613653/mainphoto.aspx.
4964 Apple Rd., PO Box 63,
Lakemont, NY 14857.
On Rte. 14.
Rooms: 3 with private baths.
Open: Year-round.
Price: $$.
Credit Cards: Most major.

There's no sign on Route 14 for the road that winds a long way down the hillside right to the lakeshore where the Cottage Lakemont sits on a beautiful piece of waterfront. The house has been in Carol's family since the 1950s, when it was built by her father. Since then, Carol and Bernie have remodeled and added new furniture that blends with some antique family pieces to create a comfortable retreat on the lake. The two suites on the second floor open onto a balcony overlooking the lake; the first-floor room opens onto a patio. Baths are modern, and queen beds have down comforters. There is a television and phone in each room and central air-conditioning throughout house. The green-painted cedar-sided cottage has two sitting rooms with a fireplace. Guests can swim or explore the lake using the canoe or paddleboat. A full breakfast is served. A four-wheel drive vehicle is recommended for winter visitors. No pets, please.

COUNTRY GARDENS
Innkeeper: Lori Percival.
607-546-2272;
fax 607-546-2288.
www.bbhost.com/country
gardens.
5116 Rte. 414, Burdett, NY
14814
Rooms: 3; 1 with private
bath, 2 shared.
Open: Year-round.
Price: $–$$.
Credit Cards: MC, Visa.

This white 19th-century farmhouse is perched on a hillside with super views of the lake. Rooms are large, air-conditioned, and comfortably furnished in a country style, using print fabrics, paintings, and quilts. There is a phone and television in the sitting room, along with books and games. The property features lovely perennial gardens, a gazebo, and swing seat. A full breakfast is served, and a refrigerator is available for guests' use.

THE INN AT CHATEAU LAFAYETTE RENEAU
Innkeepers: Dick and Betty Reno.
607-546-2062;
  fax 607-546-2069.
www.clrwine.com.
PO Box 238, Hector, NY 14841.
On Rte. 414.
Rooms: 5 with private baths.
Open: Year-round.
Price: $$.
Credit Cards: Most major.

This beautifully restored 1911 rustic farmhouse is next to the Chateau LaFayette Reneau Winery. The view of the countryside and lake is spectacular. Each room is different and furnished with family antiques, double beds, and country accents. Three rooms have double Jacuzzis. One sitting room has a television; the other does not and can be shut off with a pocket door. There is a front porch and a large wraparound deck—perfect for viewing the lake. A full breakfast is served.

LAKE COUNTRY ESTATES
Innkeepers: Eva and Charlie Bennett.
607-869-5182.
www.lakecountryestates
  .com.
Timber Lake Terrace, Ovid, NY 14521.
Off Rte. 89.
Rooms: Suites, apartment, and townhouses.
Open: Year-round.
Price: $$–$$$.
Credit Cards: Most major.

Rent a suite, an apartment, or an entire brick townhouse in an attractive private community situated along an 800-foot private beach. One, two, and three-bedroom units come with modern and pleasant fully equipped kitchens. Suites include bedroom, private bath, common living room, dining room, and balcony. The three-bedroom townhouse has a living room with fireplace, television, dining room, kitchen, powder room, and balcony overlooking the lake. The townhouses are on over 10 acres of lawns, woods, and nature trails. There is a dock, a barbecue, and tables for picnicking. There are also plenty of lawn tables and chairs beneath the towering oak and maple trees.

MAGNOLIA PLACE B&B
Innkeepers: Theresa Kelly Remmers and Ted Palevsky.
607-546-5338.
www.magnoliaplace414
  .com.
5240 Rte. 414, Hector, NY 14841.
Rooms: 8 with private baths.
Open: Year-round.
Price: $$–$$$.
Credit Cards: Most major.

This 1830s pink farmhouse with icy-white shutters sits on 7 country acres that guests can look out over from the wraparound veranda and deck. Air-conditioned guest rooms are on the first and second floors, and the second-story rooms open onto a lovely porch with great lake vistas. Three rooms have Jacuzzis, two have fireplaces, and the suite features a double Jacuzzi and a fireplace. Breakfast is served on the porch or in the dining room and is always bounteous. It might be blueberry-stuffed French toast with cinnamon syrup, special omelets, smoked pork chops, and honey-dipped muffins. Coffee is available in the living room, a great place to unwind especially on a brisk day when you can sit in front of a fire after antiques hunting, wine tasting or biking. "Most people come here to disconnect" says innkeeper Ted Palevsky.

RED HOUSE COUNTRY INN
Innkeepers: Joan Martin and Sandy Schmanke.
607-546-8566;
fax 607-546-4105.
www.fingerlakes.net/redhouse.
4586 Picnic Area Rd., Burdett, NY 14818.
Rooms: 5 rooms share 4 baths.
Open: Year-round.
Price: $$.
Credit Cards: Most major.

Nestled on 5 acres in the Finger Lake National Forest next to 30 miles of hiking and cross-country ski trails, this is one of the region's loveliest restored farmsteads. The house is red, of course, with a white-painted veranda accented by lattice-work. Rooms are decorated in soft colors and attractively appointed with period wallpapers and fabrics, handmade quilts, four-poster full and queen beds, wicker furniture, old china, and paintings and antiques. One of the rooms has a fireplace; the Blue Room is the largest with a queen bed and two twins. There is a fully equipped guest kitchen, two dining rooms, an in-ground pool with a cabana and barbecue grill, a country store, and gardens. A full country breakfast, served in the large kitchen in front of the brick fireplace, includes homemade breads, pastries, jams, eggs, meat, juices, and fresh fruit. No children under 12, please.

SOUTH GLENORA TREE FARM
Innkeepers: Steve and Judy Ebert.
607-243-7414.
546 S. Glenora Rd., Dundee, NY 14837.
www.fingerlakes.net/treefarm.
Rooms: 5 with private baths.
Open: Year-round.
Price: $$.
Credit Cards: Most major.

Set on a 68-acre tree farm, this barn-style home with a gambrel roof is surrounded by pines, meadows, and brooks. There is a private suite as well as one king- and three queen-sized rooms. All are centrally air-conditioned, and the suite and king room have fireplaces. Relax in the Great Room in front of the large fireplace with cocktails or a good book. In warmer weather, head to the wraparound porch or picnic pavilion, where there is a gas grill for casual cooking. A full breakfast is served in the dining room, and the kitchen facilities can be rented for a special gathering.

THROUGH THE GRAPEVINE
Innkeepers: Mike and Joan Smith.
315-539-8620, 866-272-1270.
www.throughthegrapevine.us.
108 Virginia Street, Waterloo, NY 13165.
Rooms: 2 with private baths.
Open: Year-round Fri.–Mon. plus holidays and special event weeks.
Price: $$.
Credit Cards: Most major.

This charming 1870 brick Italianate home with a full front porch was built by Col. Frederick Manning of the Union Army's 148th regiment. Rooms—which are decorated in the Victorian mode—have queen-sized beds with pillow-top mattresses, cable TV, and air-conditioning. One room features an ornate white-and-brass scroll bed, antique trunk, and bath with a pedestal sink; another has an iron bed and a separate sitting area. A new hot tub is located on the porch. A full breakfast is served, including fresh fruit, a hot dish, and breads accompanied with coffee made from freshly ground beans. Children are welcome.

Tillinghast Manor in Ovid takes you back in time.

TILLINGHAST MANOR
Innkeepers: The Tillinghast
  Family.
607-869-3584.
www.bnbfinder.com/bed
  andbreakfast/level2/3132.
7246 S. Main St., Ovid, NY
  14521.
Rooms: 5 rooms, some with
  shared bath.
Open: Year-round.
Price: $–$$.
Credit Cards: Most major.

Ovid, a small sleepy town in the heart of the wine region, provides a perfect respite after a day of touring. When you stay at Tillinghast Manor, you take a step back in time. Much of the lumber used in the mansion's construction was personally sawed and worked by George Jones, the man who built this elegant Victorian house in 1873 with a cupola, lovely long windows, and high ceilings. Although the rooms don't have closets, they are spacious and comfortable. The furnishings are an eclectic mix of antiques and period furniture—decor that, although not in the currently fashionable highly honed decorator mode, is as you might expect were you visiting a grandparent or an aunt who had lived in the same place for years. Breakfasts are hearty, with things like eggs, homemade jams, and home fries. Out on the back lawn is a nice patio, a perfect place to read a book or sip an iced tea. Children and pets are welcome; one bedroom can accommodate three beds.

RESTAURANTS

Aside from a handful of restaurants in elegant mansions like Geneva on the Lake and Belhurst Castle, most of the places to eat are more on the casual side. Few are right on the lake, but many have lake views.

Prices are estimated per person for appetizer and dinner entrée without tax, tip, or alcoholic beverages.

$: Up to $10.
$$: $11–$25.
$$$: $26–$40.
$$$$: More than $40.

Geneva and Waterloo

ABIGAIL'S RESTAURANT
315-539-9300.
1978 Rte. 5 & 20, Waterloo, NY 13165.
Open: Mon.–Thurs. 11–2, 5–9; Fri. until 10; Sat. 5–10; Sun. 1–9:30.
Price: $–$$.
Cuisine: American.
Serving: L, D.
Credit Cards: Most major.

A modern, casual restaurant, offering a large menu for lunch and dinner. In the warmer months you can dine on the deck overlooking the Seneca-Cayuga Canal. Typical lunch items include a veggie burger, stir-fry chicken with rice, and a variety of salads, wraps, and pasta dishes. An all-you-can-eat luncheon buffet is nicely priced at $5.25. Dinner choices include several Italian specialties such as shrimp scampi, chicken parmigiana, and mussels marinara as well as staples like steak au poivre and baby-back ribs. Some diners arrive by boat via the canal.

BELHURST CASTLE
315-781-0201.
www.belhurstcastle.com.
Rte. 14S, Geneva, NY 14456.
Open: L Mon.–Sat. 11–2; D Mon.–Sat. 5–9:30, Sun. 3:30–9:30; SB 11–2.
Price: $$–$$$.
Cuisine: Continental.
Serving: L, D, SB.
Credit Cards: Most major.

Dine like a baron in this 1890s Romanesque castle by the lake. The Golden Pheasant, a prized possession of Carrie Harron Collins, who built Belhurst, is the motif on the fine china that contributes to the Old-World ambiance of the lakeside dining room. Leaded-glass French doors, carved aged cherry, chestnut, and mahogany, mosaic-tiled fireplaces, and beamed cathedral ceilings further establish the mood. Descriptions of the dishes read like a romantic poet's work. For example: "Fallow deer rack chops roasted on cedar planks served on root vegetables, pan-cast and finished with forest mushrooms, pesto, and toasted pignoli." Fortunately, the food also tastes good. You can dine in one of the six inside rooms or outside on the veranda in warmer weather. The Garden Room next to the main building provides space for functions of up to 300 people. (Also see the description of Belhurst Castle in "Lodging.")

FLOUR PETAL CAFÉ
315-781-2233.
34 Linden St., Geneva, NY 14456.

A tiny bit of perfection serving baked goods made from scratch. A wide selection of teas, sandwiches, wraps, soups, pastries, bagels, pie, rice or bread pudding, and other tempting items make

Open: Mon.–Tues.
 8am–6pm; Wed. and
 Thurs. 8am–8pm; Fri.
 8am–9pm; Sat. 8am–5pm.
Price: $.
Cuisine: Light meals and
 snacks.
Serving: B, L, D.
Credit Cards: Cash, local
 checks.

this a good place to stop for a light bite to eat. Try their Ninja Turtle or smoothie drinks: just $1.50 each.

**GENEVA ON THE LAKE
 RESORT**
315-789-7190,
 800-3-GENEVA;
 fax 315-789-0322.
www.genevaonthelake
 .com.
1001 Lochland Rd., Geneva,
 NY 14456.
On Rte. 14.
Open: Daily.
Price: $$–$$$$.
Cuisine: Continental.
Serving: B, L, D, SB.
Credit Cards: Most major.

This is elegant dining at its best. Tables are beautifully set with linens, crystal, candles, silver, and fine china. Dinner is served each evening, with a choice of dining in the gracious Lancellotti Room or the more intimate smaller room next to it. Lunch is available on the Colonnade Pavilion patio in warm weather; breakfast is served daily in the Lancellotti Dining Room or in the Pavilion. Each Friday there is a wine and cheese party followed by gourmet dining. And no matter where you dine, you overlook the gardens with their neatly trimmed hedges and borders of flowers and the lake beyond. Lunch might be fresh seafood salad served in a phyllo pastry shell or perhaps a mesquite-grilled tenderloin sandwich. Dinner may be fresh fish or lobster or perhaps rack of lamb or prime rib, always served with the freshest of vegetables and herbs. (Also see the description in the "Lodging" section.)

HAMILTON 258
315-781-5323.
258 Hamilton St., Geneva,
 NY 14456.
Open: Daily 5–9, weekends
 until 10.
Price: $–$$.
Cuisine: Eclectic.
Serving: D.
Credit Cards: Most major.

It has the same owner and chef, but the name and location of the former Spinnakers has been changed. Now the restaurant is housed in a renovated colonial home across from Hobart College. It has four dining rooms, a bar, and a fireplace. Menu items continue to be creative: goat cheese-crusted salmon with pesto-cream drizzle, seared tuna with coconut-steamed rice, or pork tenderloin with five-spice apple chutney served with maple-whipped yams.

**NONNA COSENTINO'S
 TRATTORIA**
315-789-1638.
1 Railroad Place, Geneva,
 NY 14456.
Open: Closed Tues.

Dine inside at a table or booth or outside on the deck; while you're waiting, check out the bar. Nonna's is known for homemade Italian sauces and dishes like lasagna, manicotti, braciola, and other pasta specialties as well as steak, veal, and seafood.

Price: $$.
Cuisine: Italian-American.
Serving: L, D.
Credit Cards: Most major.

**PARKERS GRILLE AND
TAP HOUSE**
315-789-4656.
100 Seneca St., Geneva, NY
    14456.
Open: Daily 11am–1am.
Price: $–$$.
Cuisine: American pub.
Serving: L, D.
Credit Cards: Most major.

**PATTI'S LAKEVIEW
DINER**
315-789-6433.
43 Lake St., Geneva, NY
    14456.
Open: Mon.–Wed.
    5:30am–3pm, Thurs.
    and Fri. 5:30am–8pm,
    Sat. 6:30am–2:30pm,
    Sun. 5:30am–12:30pm.
Price: $.
Cuisine: Diner food.
Serving: B, L, D.
Credit Cards: Cash, checks.

PIER HOUSE
315-789-0400.
Ramada Geneva, 41
    Lakefront Dr., Geneva,
    NY 14456.
Open: Year-round.
Price: $–$$.
Cuisine: American.
Serving: B, L, D.
Credit Cards: Most major.

PINKY'S RESTAURANT
315-789-9753.
14 Castle St., Geneva, NY
    14456.
Open: Mon.–Fri. 11:30–2,
    Wed. and Fri. 5–9.

One of the most popular items is seafood pasta. The restaurant is near the waterfront.

Next to the Smith Opera House and a popular lunch spot for local business people, with its green-painted walls, woodwork, booths, bar, and high-top tables, Parkers has the look and feel of an old-time traditional bistro. Hot sellers on the menu include burgers, Philly steak, and homemade soups. The veggie basket is also very good. Parkers offers a very large selection of beers and ales. In the warmer weather, enjoy eating on the outside sidewalk patio.

One of the last of its kind, this diner could be used in a 1950s movie set. It has a counter, booths, a few tables, and a location in the middle of everything. Try the "Quickie"—liver with bacon and onions—or burgers. The "Big Frank" gives you three eggs, two links, two bacon strips, home fries, and toast, all for about $5.

The popular Pier House is definitely into fish and seafood. Lunchtime they serve a "whale of a sandwich," along with haddock, trout, steamed clams, and other fish and seafood dishes. Try the Pier House crab cakes or the fried calamari. For dinner there are tasty traditional items like veal marsala and captain's cut prime rib of beef. And while you're eating, enjoy the views of the lake through large windows, or head to the patio and sit at one of the umbrella tables.

The former mayor of Geneva wears many hats, including that of chef in his long-time restaurant. In fact, Pinky may just pop out from the kitchen to take or deliver an order and say hello to friends. It's not fancy or trendy—just a favorite

Price: $.
Cuisine: Italian.
Serving: L, D.
Credit Cards: Most major.

PORTS CAFÉ & GRILL
315-789-2020.
4432 West Lake Rd, Geneva,
    NY 14456.
Open: Tues.–Sat. 5–9.
Price: $–$$.
Cuisine: American.
Serving: D.
Credit Cards: Most major.

Watkins Glen Area

**CURLY'S FAMILY
    RESTAURANT**
607-535-4383.
2780 Rte. 14, Watkins Glen,
    NY 14891.
Between Watkins Glen and
    Montour Falls.
Open: Daily 6am–8pm.
Price: $–$$.
Cuisine: American.
Serving: B, L, D.
Credit Cards: Most major.

THE DECOY
607-535-2607.
4576 Rte. 14, Rock Stream,
    NY 14878.
Open: Wed.–Sat. 5–10.
Price: $–$$.
Cuisine: American.
Serving: D.
Credit Cards: Most major.

**SENECA HARBOR
    STATION**
607-535-6101.
3 North Franklin St.,
    Watkins Glen, NY 14891.
Open: Daily April–Nov.
    Sun.–Thurs. 11:30–9;
    Fri. and Sat. 11:30–10.
Price: $–$$.
Cuisine: American.

among locals, with a jukebox in the corner. The menu includes everything from soup to nuts, along with great onion rings and homemade pasta sauces and wine by the glass for about $3.25.

Casual, popular, this little place is often recommended as a good place to eat by area B&Bs. Located by the lake, the dining room is oriented so you can see the water. Ports specializes in cooked-to-order food, fresh seafood, grilled meats, and local produce and cheese as well as Finger Lakes micro beers and wines by the glass.

The Connelly family treats you to some down-home cooking in a casual atmosphere with counter and table service as well as takeout. Try their fish dinners, Italian specialties, Texas hot sandwiches, and homemade soups. This is a good place to bring Mom, Dad, and the kids.

A casual, friendly family-run business, with a full bar and daily and weekly specials. Some have called it a "cow on a plate"—we're talking about the prime ribs, which are a Saturday night tradition. Many diners call ahead to reserve them. Rock Stream is 5 miles north of Watkins Glen.

This beautifully restored 19th-century train station, with its 16-foot fanned ceilings, mahogany bar, spiral staircase, and original hardwood floors, is now the Seneca Harbor Station restaurant. Located right on the water next to Captain Bill's Seneca Lake Cruises, the restaurant has a dining deck, large bar, and inside dining rooms with expansive windows looking out to the lake and the

The Seneca Harbor station restaurant offers dining overlooking Seneca Lake.

Serving: L, D.
Credit Cards: Most major.

public fishing pier. The food, like the decor, is quietly themed with a nautical flavor. Items on the menu include clam chowder, crab cakes, fisherman's salad, lobster pasta, "boatman's grilled meats," rainbow trout Florentine, burgers, "sailor sides," and "sweetwater desserts." Special fun drinks are also on the menu.

Other Areas

PASTA ONLY'S COBBLESTONE RESTAURANT
315-789-8498.
www.pastaonlyscobblestone
.com.
3610 Pre-Emption Rd.,
Geneva, NY 14456.
Corner Rte. 5 & 20.
Open: Open L Tues.–Fri.
11:30–2; D Fri. and Sat.
5–10, Tues.–Thurs. and
Sun. 5–9.
Price: $–$$$.

Combine an historic 1825 farmhouse, classic Italian cooking, and a wood-fired grill, and you come up with an exceptional dining experience. When the owners of the successful Pasta Only restaurant decided they needed more space, they discovered this lovely old building with porches, fireplaces, and cozy rooms. They bought it and changed the name a bit but not the quality of the food. It has a lovely garden patio, verandas, and several dining rooms. Seafood comes from Boston, produce from local farmers as much as possible, and pasta is made fresh daily. Chicken pesto,

Cuisine: Northern Italian.
Serving: L, D.
Credit Cards: Most major.

boscaida Verona, crab cakes, veal cobblestone, and sea bass are just some of the tempting selections.

**VERAISONS AT
  GLENORA INN AND
  VINEYARD**
607-243-9500.
www.glenora.com.
5435 Rte. 14, Dundee, NY
  14837.
Open: Daily.
Price: $–$$$.
Cuisine: Regional fusion
  with classic influences.
Serving: B, L, D.
Credit Cards: Most major.

Midway up the hill from the lake, smack in the middle of the Glenora vineyards, this restaurant invites you to sit for hours and just enjoy the view through the large windows over the vineyards and out to the lake. Veraisons is a departure from the country-style restaurants usually found in the region. They call their cuisine "regional fusion," which translates to using the freshest of local produce combined with flavors and textures from around the world, along with wines. Breakfast might be buckwheat pancakes or Texas-stuffed French toast filled with homemade strawberry marmalade and New York State maple syrup. On the lunch menu is the Caesar cannoli salad (with real anchovies) and the southwestern chicken salad made of cold spiced chicken with roasted Mexican vegetables and blue corn chips, served with a corn-and-salsa ranch dressing. The Baton Rouge catfish sandwich is also tempting. Dinner selections include grilled medallions of Chilean sea bass, coriander crusted ahi tuna, shredded soba duck, even barbecued bison ribs—and so many other things that are hard to resist. A good idea is to go with a few friends, each order something different, and share. Jazz concerts, weddings, and other events are welcome. The restaurant is adjacent to the hotel, also heartily recommended (see the listing in "Lodging").

CASUAL FOOD

Cams (315-789-6297; 476 Exchange St., Geneva, NY 14456) Creative pizzas and hand-stretched fresh dough, super subs, Buffalo wings, calzones, and sausage rolls: It's a winner. Open Mon.–Sat. 11–closing, Sun. 1pm–closing.

Chef's Diner (607-535-9975; Montour-Watkins Highway, Montour Falls, NY 14865) Good old diner food from short orders to complete dinner served in an area institution owned and operated by Anthony Pulos. Open daily for breakfast, lunch, dinner.

Cleo's (315-781-1960; Lakeside Park, Geneva, NY 14456) A weathered old sandwich board on the street announces the entrance. A couple of picnic tables, a peek of the lake across the highway, and a spot under the trees just off the main drag add up to a neat location for one of Geneva's old-time snack stands. There is a huge choice of Cleo's Hots, Hoffman German Hots, red and white, served on a large roll so you can pile on your favorite topping. Other items include BBQ chicken (just $3.85), Italian sausage sandwich ($3.75), and a Big Daddy burger with everything ($3.35). This is the place to get real frozen custards and great sundaes. Open daily 11–9.

Geneva Downtown Deli (315-789-4617; 30 Castle St., Geneva, NY 14456) A full-service deli and small restaurant selling over-the-counter and custom-catering services offering giant subs, combo trays, veggie and dip trays, and hot dishes.

Riverside Inn (315-781-0600; 415 Booty Hill Rd., Geneva, NY 14456) Seafood and fish, along with burgers and other sandwiches, are served on a waterfront deck. Next to the Seneca Marina, it's very casual. Open April–December.

Seneca Lodge (607-535-2014; PO Box 272, Watkins Glen, NY 14891; on Rte. 329, by the south entrance to the Watkins Glen State Park) Homemade breads, soups, and other freshly made dishes as well as a nice salad bar keep locals happy here. It's the place to come for lunch and dinner when looking for a casual meal. The Bench & Bar Tavern Room is always fun. Open May–October 31.

Skyland Farm features flowers, animals, wonderful gifts, crafts as well as a gem of a little snack bar.

Skyland Farm (607-546-5050; 4966 Rte. 414, Burdett, NY 14818) A wonderful farm, garden, and barn. You can spend a long time looking through the unique crafts, many locally produced, and outside there are a few goats and other farm animals kids love to see. Order a sandwich, soup, or special lunch, and eat it outside on the porch on one of the handful of tables. I had the best ever grilled tuna with cheese, dill, and apples on homemade bread. Just about everything is produced on the farm or locally—the eggs are fresh from the chickens just outside. Also try the yummy gelato (like raspberry and hibiscus) imported from New York—it's great, trust me. Open mid-May–December 23; Wed.–Sun. 11–5 (summer); Fri.–Sun 11–5 (fall)

CULTURE

ARCHITECTURE

Geneva

The Geneva Historical Society has a self-guided walking tour of South Main Street. It starts at **380 South Main,** an 1832 Greek-Revival originally built as a church. Each house of interest is described in the brochure, including those of Pulteney Park, the original village green. Notable historic buildings in the area include a Victorian Gothic Revival house at **112 Jay Street,** built in 1862; the Smith Opera House, circa 1894, at **82 Seneca Street,** a four-story Romanesque building with arched windows and an ornate facade; and the Williamson House, an elegant Federal home built in 1827 at **839 South Main Street.** Geneva's South Main Historic District, often compared to Charleston, South Carolina, contains several stately Federal-style row houses. The Durfee House, circa 1787, at **639 South Main** was the first frame structure to be built west of Rome, New York. Over the years it went through several alterations and was moved from its original location on Main Street to its present site.

Flint

Noteworthy is a saltbox-style structure on Route 5 & 20 that in 1800 was the **Ball Tavern,** a stop on the stagecoach route.

Richmond

The **Reed Homestead,** circa 1803, is a gracious central-entrance colonial brick house at 4357 Reed Street.

MUSEUMS AND HISTORIC HOUSES

Geneva and Waterloo

Lee School Museum (607-535-9741; 108 N. Catherine, Montour Falls, NY 14865; on Rte. 14, just south of Geneva) See exhibits of what life was life in the 1830s. Open by appointment only.

First Woman Doctor

In 1849,when Hobart was Geneva College, Elizabeth Blackwell graduated from Geneva Medical College, becoming the first female physician in this hemisphere.

Mike Weaver Drain Tile Museum (315-789-3848; E. Hill Rd., Geneva, NY 14456) Adjacent to the Rose Hill Mansion, this museum is contained inside the restored 1821 John Johnston farmhouse. (Johnston introduced tile drainage to America.) More than 350 tiles are on exhibit, dating from 100 BCE.

Peter Whitmer Log Home (315-539-2552; www.hillcumorah.com/whitmer .htm; 1451 Aunkst Rd., Waterloo, NY 13165; on Rte. 96,) A reconstructed 1810 log home, site of the Church of Jesus Christ of Latter-Day Saints who organized here in 1830. Period furnishings, colonial-style chapel, and visitors center. Open daily Mon.–Sat. 9–6, Sun. 12–6.

Prouty-Chew Museum (315-789-5151; www.genevahistoricalsociety.com/PC _House.htm543; S. Main St., Geneva, NY 14456) The Geneva Historical Society is located in this 1829 Federal-style house, which contains four period rooms and regularly changing exhibitions as well as collections of furniture, decorative arts, and period clothing. The society collects, preserves, and interprets the historic and cultural heritage of the area. Special events are held throughout the year, and the society's archives are available for research. The museum shop sells local history publications and gift items and offers a self-guided walking tour of Geneva's Historical District along South Main Street and a driving tour of noteworthy homes. Open Tues.–Fri. 9:30–4:30; Sat. (Sun. in July and Aug.) 1:30–4:30. Archives open Tues.–Fri. 1:30–4:30 or by appointment. Free.

Rose Hill Mansion (315-789-3848; www.genevahistoricalsociety.com/Rose _Hill.htm; Rte. 96A, Geneva, NY 14456; 1 mile south of Rte. 5 & 20) If you happen to be boating on the lake, you'll quickly notice the impressive white-pillared mansion on the eastern shore. Built in 1839, this stately Greek-Revival mansion commands a prominent site overlooking Seneca Lake. The property was purchased in 1850 by Robert Swan, who is famous for developing and implementing revolutionary agricultural technology in tile drainage during the mid-1800s. Furnished in the Empire style, this 24-room house is considered one of America's most distinguished examples of the period. Many pieces were originally owned by the Swan family. Next door is the Mike Weaver Drain Tile Museum in the John Johnston House. Open May 1–Oct. 31, 10–4, Sun. 1–5. Admission: adults $3, seniors and students $2, under 10 free.

Other Areas

Memorial Day Museum (315-539-9611, 315-539-0533; www.waterloony.com/ MdayMus.html; 35 E. Main St., Waterloo, NY 13165) Waterloo is recognized as the birthplace of Memorial Day because of its observance on May 5, 1866, and Waterloo's museum is dedicated to this occasion, containing items pertaining to the day and the Civil War era, as well. Open July 5–Sept. 15 Tues.–Sat. 1–4.

Robert Ingersoll Museum (315-536-1074; www.secularhumanism.org/ingersoll/museum.html; 61 Main St., Dresden, NY 14441) This is the birthplace of the famous 19th-century orator, writer, and a founder of the Stanford & Woodstock Art Communities. See local history, exhibits, and artifacts. Memorial Day–Halloween, Sat. and Sun. noon–5.

Sampson World War II Navy Museum (315-585-6203, 800-357-1814; www.rpadden.com/samtoday/museum.htm; Rte. 96A, Romulus, NY 14541) Established as a naval training station in 1942, it was here that more than 411,429 young men were taught to be sailors and then sent overseas to participate in World War II. This museum, created by the thousands of members of the Sampson WW II Navy Veterans organization, is dedicated to these men. It contains artifacts from the veterans, photos, porthole displays, the ship's bell from FDR's presidential yacht *Potomac,* guns, and other memorabilia. Open May 30–Labor Day, Wed.–Sun. 10–4; Labor Day–Oct. 12, weekends only.

Schuyler County Historical Museum (607-535-9741; 108 N. Catharine St., Montour Falls, NY 14865; on Rte. 14) Historical museum in an early 19th-century building. Open Mon.–Thurs., Sat. 10–4; research hours 10–3.

THEATER

Smith Opera House (315-781-LIVE, 866-355-LIVE; www.thesmith.org; 82 Seneca St., Geneva, NY 14456) This elegant theater with its ornate facade was built in 1894 and still operates today as a performing arts venue, featuring dance, theater, music, and films. The interior was renovated in 1931 in the Baroque style, and most recently the entire theater has been refurbished. Many famous musicians have performed here, including Itzhak Perlman, who praised its magnificent acoustics.

EDUCATION

Hobart and William Smith Colleges (315-781-3000; www.hws.edu; 300 Pulteney St., Geneva, NY 14456) These two four-year institutions provide programs in the liberal arts and sciences, enrolling approximately 1,900 students. The two colleges share a common curriculum and some facilities, but each awards its own degree and has its own dean, admissions office, student government, and athletic programs. Hobart for men was founded in 1822; William Smith for women, in 1908. The focal point for the campus, Coxe Hall, a grand Jacobean-style building, houses the administration and Bartlett Theatre.

RECREATION

BIKING

A bicycle path runs along both shores of the lake. The grade is gently rolling, and views are of the lake, fields, and farms.

Dresden/Dundee/Dresden Route (800-868-9283; start on Main St., Dresden NY 14837) This 38.7-mile ride takes you along paved roads with some rolling hills. Highlights are the Robert Ingersoll Museum, the wineries along the Seneca Wine Trail, Wixon's Honey Stand, Dundee Historical Society, and the Windmill Farm & Craft Market (open Saturday). Cycle south on Route 14 for 14.9 miles, turn right at Dundee-Glenora Road, then right again onto Route 14A in Dundee. Stay on Route 14A north until you have traveled a total of 27.6 miles; then go right onto Milo Center Road, and when you reach the T, turn left, and then make a quick right onto Leach Road, and follow it to the end. Turn left at the stop sign and follow Route 14A north back into Dresden.

Geneva Skyline Loop (877-FUN-IN-NY; start in Geneva) This 35.7-mile route is mostly paved, with some dirt roads. Highlights include Seneca Lake State Park, Smith Opera House, South Main Street Historic District, Prouty-Chew Museum, Hobart and William Smith Colleges, and the NYS Agricultural Experiment Station Grounds. From Main Street (Route 14), turn left onto South Main Street, and ride to Jay Street. Turn right onto Jay to the end, then left on White Springs Road; at the stop sign, go right onto Snell Road all the way to Slate Rock Road (3.1 miles to this point). Turn left onto Slate Rock, right on Billsboro Road, left onto Wabash Road, and follow to Alexander Road, where you turn right. Go left on North Flat Road. Make a quick right onto Curtis Road, cross Route 14A, and then go right onto Wilson Road (14.5 miles at this point). Follow 14A north to #9 Road; then turn left. Cross Route 5 & 20, following Whitney Road to County Road 4, and turn left. Make a quick right onto Tileyard Road, then another right onto McIvor Road. Turn right onto Johnson Road, left onto County Road 4, and right onto Castle Road back into town.

BOATING

CRUISES

Captain Bill's Seneca Lake Cruises (607-535-4541; www.senecaharborstation .com/cruise; 1 N. Franklin St., Watkins Glen, NY 14891) The white double-decker *Columbia*, a 150-passenger boat with a bright-blue awning, is a picturesque sight as it cruises up and down Seneca Lake. Enjoy a full-course lunch

Captain Bill's Seneca Lake cruises depart from Watkins Glen Dock.

or dinner aboard this vessel or a sightseeing cruise on the *Stroller IV* as well as miniature golf located right outside Captain Bill's gift shop.

Malabar X/**Seneca Lake Day Sails** (607-535-LAKE; www.cayugawoodenboat works.com/malabar24.htm; Watkins Glen Waterfront, Watkins Glen, NY 14891) Cruise the lake aboard the vintage schooner *Malabar X*. Raced success-fully in the 1930 and 1932 Bermuda Race, this sleek wooden racing yacht is a great way to see Seneca Lake. Try the helm, help with the sails, or simply sit back and bask in a pleasant summer's day cruise while the captain does the work. Two- and three-hour cruises, private charters with rates from $27 to $37.

MARINAS

A&B Marina (315-781-1755; albimarine@aol.com; 634 Waterloo-Geneva Rd., Waterloo, NY 13165) A full-service marina and campground, offering boat rentals, hoist, and dock installations, skies, kneeboards, and sales.

Barrett's Marine (315-789-6605, Cayuga-Seneca Canal, Waterloo, NY 13165) Barrett's offers a variety of launches, overnight slips, showers, rest rooms, and repair services as well as a hydraulic hoist.

Roy's Marina (315-789-3094; 4398 Clark's Pt., Geneva, NY 14456; on Rte. 14 on Seneca Lake, 3 miles south of Geneva) A full-service facility, with rentals, fish-ing boats, pontoon boats, hoists, launch, dockages, and storage.

Stivers Seneca Marina (315-789-5520, 401 Booty Hill Rd., Waterloo, NY 13165) On the Seneca-Cayuga Canal, off Route 96A, this marina has a travel lift service, boat sales and repairs, and marine supplies.

FISHING

Seneca Lake provides excellent fishing grounds. For the latest fishing report, check with one of the local bait shops (such as Barry's Bait and Tackle, Route 5 & 20, Waterloo; 315-539-5341). For example, one account stated that "smallmouth bass are active over rock piles at the north end of the lake and off Hi Banks in 15 to 30 feet of water. Crabs, minnows, and worms are all catching fish. A few nice perch and pike have also been taken by bass fishermen. If you want to target the perch, use softshell crabs. If you want pike, use minnows. For lakers, drag copper at the north end in water 90 to 150 feet deep. Farther south, lakers have been hot around the barge off Dresden. Look for them 100 feet down over a 400 to 500 foot bottom." The report goes on to tell where browns, rainbows, and landlocked salmon can be found. Catharine Creek (at the head of Seneca Lake in Watkins Glen) offers anglers fishing in a thriving trout stream.

Great White Charters (315-781-1038; www.flare.net/greatwhitecharters/great .htm; 301 White Springs Rd., Geneva, NY 14456) Charter a boat for sport fishing on Seneca Lake or Lake Ontario and fish for salmon, steelhead, trout, bass, or perch. Boats include 26-foot and 31-foot fully equipped Penn Yan Hardtops. Ask for Capt. Jack Prutzman.

GOLF

Big Oak Public Golf Course (315-789-9419; www.silvercreekgc.com/bo-golf.php; 33 Packwood Rd., Geneva, NY 14456; off Rte. 14) This is a "Jekyll and Hyde" course, with two completely different nines. The front is wide open and fairly straightforward. The more dramatic new back is cut through trees and wetlands with water on six holes requiring some skillful target shooting. This par-70 course plays 5,755 from the tips. There is a clubhouse, snack bar, golf carts, club rentals, and pro shop. Greens fees on weekdays are $9 for 9 holes, $15 for 18 holes, $13 and $20 for a cart; weekend greens fees are $10 and $17; $14 and $25 for a cart.

Fox Run Golf Course (607-535-4413; http://thegolfcourses.net/golfcourses/ NY/10560.htm; 4195 Rte. 14, Rock Stream, NY 14878) A pretty nine-hole course providing rental clubs, pull carts, and gas carts. Restaurant and lounge.

Geneva Country Club (315-789-8786; Rte. 14S, Geneva, NY 14456) A nine-hole, par-71 course playing 6,214 from the tips. Enjoy good views of the lake with your round of golf.

Seneca Lake Country Club (315-789-4681; Rte. 14S, Geneva NY 14456) An 18-hole, par-72 course playing 6,259 from the tips.

A miniature golf course is adjacent to Captain Bill's at Watkins Glen.

Silver Creek (315-539-8076; www.silvercreekgc.com/bo-golf.php; 1790 East River Rd., Waterloo NY 13165) This is a scenic 18-hole public course with watered fairways, tees, and greens. There is a driving range, putting green, gas carts, lounge, and pro shop. They specialize in golf tournaments and outings. The restaurant facility can seat up to 300 people.

HIKING

Finger Lakes National Forest (607-546-4470; 5218 State Rte. 414, Hector, NY 14841) This park offers a variety of hiking trails as well as primitive camping sites. The 12-mile **Interlaken Trail** runs along Parmenter Road, crosses the Finger Lakes National Forest from north to south, and passes through varied terrain and vegetation. Southern portions are steeper and more wooded. On the way, stop at the Foster and Teeter Pond areas.

In the **Montour Falls** area, hiking trails are in **Queen Catharine Marsh, Havana Glen,** the **Montour Falls Historic District,** and **Queen Catharine's Grave.**

PARKS, NATURE PRESERVES, & CAMPING

Cheerful Valley Campground (315-781-1222; Rte. 14, Phelps, NY 14532) Located in a 110-acre private river valley midway between Rochester and Syracuse just north of the Thruway, this campground has 100 sites, all necessary hookups, convenience store, rest rooms, pool, party pavilion, picnic tables, fire rings, disposal station, and propane.

Finger Lakes National Forest (607-546-4470; www.fs.fed.us/r9/gmfl/finger lakes/index.htm; 5218 State Rte. 414, Hector, NY 14841) A 15,000-acre woodland offering hiking, cross-country skiing, snowmobiling, horse trails, camping, fishing, hunting, berry picking, and bird-watching.

Havana Glen Park and Campground (607-535-9476; 135 Havana Glen Rd., PO Box 579, Montour Falls, NY 14865) This park offers tent and trailer sites, hiking trails, shower and toilet facilities, playgrounds, and ball fields plus three pavilions for outings. A magnificent gorge is perfect for picnics and soaking up the beauty of the falls and surrounding countryside. Open May 15–Oct. 15

Hector Land Use Area: Operated by the U.S. Forest Service, this area contains 25 miles of marked trails, water and toilet facilities, three picnic spots, and nine camping sites. Motorized sports are not allowed.

Lakeshore Park (at the north end of the lake adjacent to the state park, Geneva, NY 14456) This is a pleasant, grassy park where you can stroll along the water and stop by the Chamber of Commerce to get area information. There are new boat slips and a dock.

Municipal Campground and Marina (607-535-9397; Rte. 14, Montour Falls, NY 14865) Ninety camp sites in this park, along with 190 boat slips. On the Old Barge Canal, boats have access to Seneca Lake. Public boat launch, cable television, store, picnic pavilions, playground, and ball fields.

Sampson State Park (315-585-6392; 6096 Rte. 96A, Romulus, NY 14541; 12 miles south of Geneva on east side of Seneca Lake) This park on the lake offers tent, trailer, and camping facilities as well as a marina, biking, and hiking. The Sampson World War II Navy Museum is also on the grounds.

Seneca Lake State Park (315-789-2331, Rte. 5 & 20, Geneva, NY 14456) One of the hottest things here is the new Spray Park, with fountains kids of all ages can run through—it's cool, wet, and fun. On the lake's north shore, this wide, pleasant park also offers bike and walking paths, picnic areas, and swimming facilities. There is also a boat launch, marina, and beach. A modest fee is charged.

Smith Park and Campground (607-546-9911, 607-546-5286 off-season; PO Box 73, Hector, NY 14841; off Rte. 414,) Available on this 92-acre site along 2,000 feet of Seneca Lake shoreline are boat launching facilities, swimming, hiking trails, and more than 56 campsites. Some of the campsites have water views, most are wooded. Open May 1–Sept. 30.

Warren W. Clute Memorial Park and Campground (607-535-4438, 521 E. Forth St., Watkins Glen, NY 14891) Campsites, tennis, playground, swimming, ball field, picnic facilities, boat launch, and a lakeside pavilion.

Watkins Glen State Park and Gorge (607-535-4511; nysparks.state.ny.us/cgi-bin /cgiwrap/nysparks/parks.cgi?p+50; Watkins Glen, NY 14891) One of the most beautiful parks in the Finger Lakes, Watkins Glen is a deep rock-walled canyon with 19 waterfalls, many cascades, grottoes, and amphitheaters. There is an Olympic-size swimming pool, picnic facilities, camping, and non-stop views. As the sun sets, enjoy Timespell, a sound and light laser show depicting the birth of the gorge.

OTHER ATTRACTIONS

Abbey Farm at Spring Hill (585-526-5420; www.abbeyhistoricalfarm.org; 1862 Rte. 5 & 20, Stanley, NY 14561) Experience what life was like on a farm in Victorian days. A costumed interpreter takes you through the farmyard and barn, where you'll hear how a man walked 300 miles of Indian trails to find and establish a home for his family on this site. Pet and feed the animals, ride in a horse-drawn buggy, enjoy a special home-cooked dinner served in period style, and gather in the parlor for fun and games. Victorian teas, rope making, goat milking, butter churning, candle dipping, woodworking, tinsmithing, spinning, wheat plaiting, stitchery, bread making, and other skills are taught in hands-on workshops. There is a gift shop and bed & breakfast with three guest rooms on the property.

Community Playground Complex (S. Exchange St., Geneva, NY 14456) In addition to ice skating offered in the winter, there are ball fields, playgrounds, and shuffleboard.

Farm Sanctuary and B&B (607-583-2225; fax 607-583-2041; www.farmsanctuary .org; 3100 Aikens Rd., PO Box 150, Watkins Glen, NY 14891; on County Rte. 23) Lorri and Gene Bauston's barns and 175 acres bordering a state forest are sanctuary for animals of all kinds. There are cows, pigs, sheep, turkeys, chickens, rabbits, and other animals and birds. Animals that have been abandoned or injured are housed in the Refuge Barn. Children can get close to a wide variety of animals here and can learn about the importance of humane care of animals at the visitors center's exhibits; guided tours are also given. To experience the farm fully, you can overnight in one of three cabins that accommodate up to six people. The cabins contain two double beds, a sitting area, wicker furnishings, and porch. Sleeping mats for children are available. Rates are from $55 per night.

New York State Agricultural Experiment Station (a division of Cornell University's College of Agriculture and Life Sciences, 630 W. North St., Geneva, NY 14456) Group tours arranged through the Publications Office.

Seneca Grand Prix (607-535-7981; Rte. 414 S., Watkins Glen, NY 14891) Take the family on a day's outing to drive the go-carts and bumper boats, play arcade games, and go for par on the miniature golf course. Hours vary; call ahead.

Skyland Farm (607-546-5050; 4966 Rte. 414, Burdett, NY 14818) If you stop nowhere else on a trip around the lake, make this a must. There's something to delight everyone in the family, from the dinosaur house and farm animals for the kids to the barn crammed with unusual handcrafted items and food products like jams, jellies, and candies. The garden is filled with flowers, and you can pick what you need at very reasonable prices. Hungry? The sandwiches and soups are delicious—a whole meal. Open mid-May–Dec. 23; Wed.–Sun. 11–5 (summer); Fri.–Sun 11–5 (fall)

Sugar Hill Recreation Area (Tower Hill Road, 7 miles west of Watkins Glen) National and international archery tournaments are held here. There is also a wheelchair course designed for tournament competition. Other facilities include horse trails, campsites and shelters, picnic grounds, fishing areas, and wildflower fields.

Watkins Glen International Racing Circuit (607-535-2481; www.theglen.com; 2790 County Rte. 16, Watkins Glen, NY 14891) On the hills overlooking the town, the facility is the site of eight major racing weekends a year including NASCAR events and the U.S. Vintage Grand Prix.

SHOPPING

From Waterloo Premium Outlets to small boutiques and gift stores in downtown Geneva, plenty of shopping options are available for the regular as well as casual shopper. There are also a number of farm markets and pick-your-own fruit places.

ANTIQUES/ART

One Man's Junk (716-526-6862; 4539 Rte. 14A, Geneva, NY 14456) This place has lots of Victorian pieces, lighting fixtures, glass shades, and accessories. Lamp restoration and repair, too.

Rose Hill Antique Consignment Shop (315-789-5915; Rte. 96A, Geneva, NY 14456) Fine antiques and collectibles are sold in this shop on the grounds of Rose Hill Mansion. Open daily July and Aug. 11–4, Sun. 1–5; June and Sept. Wed.–Sun.; May and Oct. weekends.

Seneca Gallery Arts & Antiques (607-546-4393; 4393 Rte. 414, Burdett, NY 14818) Artist/owner RJ Kneeland not only sells more than 300 of his paintings, which are hung on walls in an old barn, he also sells an enormous vari-

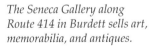

The Seneca Gallery along Route 414 in Burdett sells art, memorabilia, and antiques.

ety of other things, from antiques and farm implements to memorabilia. The place and grounds are packed.

BOOKS

J. W. Brace Books (607-535-2728; www.jwbrace.com; 211 N. Franklin St., Watkins Glen, NY 14891) All kinds of books and free out-of-print searches are available in this independently owned store right in the center of town.

Long & Brace (315-719-0337; 551 Exchange St., Geneva, NY 14456) New and used books, special orders, and same services as J. W. Books.

FACTORY OUTLETS

Famous Brands (607-535-4952; 412 Franklin St., Watkins Glen, NY 14891) Three floors of merchandise offer close to 20 stores selling discounted items. Find famous names such as Timberland, Northern Isles, Dexter, Levi's, Woolrich, Duofold, and other brands. Open daily.

Waterloo Premium Outlets (315-539-1100; Rte. 318 between exits 41 & 42 off the NY State Thruway, Waterloo, NY 13165) A huge complex of factory outlets for just about everything, including clothes, cosmetics, entertainment, food, home furnishings, housewares, jewelry, luggage, shoes, and specialty items.

FOOD

Geneva Area Farmers Market (315-789-5005; 666 S. Exchange St., Geneva, NY 14456) Every Thursday from mid-June through mid-October, farmers come here to sell their produce including fruits and vegetables, breads, and flowers.

Minn's Farms (716-526-6502; Rte. 14A, between Geneva and Hall) Seasonal fruits and vegetables with sweet corn, cabbage, cauliflower, broccoli, and brussels sprouts.

Rasta Ranch Vineyard & Nursery (607-546-2974; 5882 Rte. 414, Hector, NY 14841) An eclectic farmhouse experience selling all sorts of things. Greenhouses, lawns, specialty perennials and herbs, organic grapes, wine, gift shop, handcrafted jewelry, and much more. Open daily Apr.–Nov. noon–5.

Red Jacket Orchards (315-781-2749, 800-828-9410; www.redjacketorchards .com; 957 Rte. 5 & 20, Geneva, NY 14456; 1 mile west of town) This big operation has been owned for three generations by the Nicholson family. More than 450 acres are in fruit production with several varieties of apples, strawberries, sweet cherries, prunes, plums, and apricots. Products sold in the farm store include cider, fruit butters, relishes, chili sauces, honey, cheeses, jams and jellies. In the Fruit Cellar you can select your own fruit and often taste the different kinds, as well. You can pick your own strawberries and cherries in season. Red Jacket also prepares fruit gift baskets.

GIFTS AND TOYS

The Attique (315-781-0529; 266 Hamilton St., NY 14456) This store is packed with interesting items: antique reproductions, garden decor, door stops, American Chestnut Collection, candles, clocks, lamps, pottery, lace, aromatherapy products, Boyd's Bears, wrought-iron items, and, of course, a lot more. Open Mon.–Thurs. 10–6, Fri. 10–8, Sat. 10–5, Sun. noon–4.

Earthly Possessions (315-781-1078; 70 Seneca St., Geneva, NY 14456) This small store carries lots of unique gifts, such as scented candles, handcrafted jewelry, bath products, and other items. Open Tues.–Thurs. 10–6, Fri. 10–8, Sat. 10–6 (until 3 during the summer).

Guards Cards (315-789-6919; 60 Seneca St., Geneva, NY 14456) Right on a corner in the heart of downtown Geneva, it has the ambiance of a 1920s drugstore and is a wonderful place to shop. It's the only store in the state that carries Failte dolls from Ireland. Also find other popular products such as wind kites, Seagull pewter, jewelry, and greeting cards. Collectibles include Nao by Lladro, Swarovski, Lang & Wise, Hallmark, Gund animals, Anheuser-Busch steins, and Folkstones & Dollstones. Open Mon.–Thurs. and Sat. 8:30–5:30; Fri. 8:30–8; Sun. noon–4.

Mary Ann's Treasures (315-539-3889; sut@rochester.rr.com; 209 W. Main St., Waterloo, NY 13165) Find all kinds of "treasures," from Boyd's Bears, dolls, and handmade quilts to candles, crafts, and seasonal gifts.

Seneca Hillside (607-243-9090; Rte. 14, Dundee, NY 14837) Miniatures, produce, handcrafted items, and dollhouses.

Seneca Lake Jewelry & Pottery (607-535-6799; 22 North Franklin St., Watkins Glen, NY 14891) A beautiful shop, with handcrafted jewelry, pottery and works of art from top artisans. Open daily.

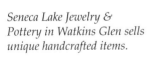

Seneca Lake Jewelry & Pottery in Watkins Glen sells unique handcrafted items.

Skyland Farm (607-546-5050; 4966 Rte. 414, Burdett, NY 14818) This two-story barn is chock-full of exceptional craft items from more than 150 regional craftspeople, plus there's a working pottery, small food bar, and farm. Don't plan on making a quick stop: You'll want to spend at least an hour exploring all the things there are to see and buy here . . . it's a real turn-on to anyone with an iota of creativity in their bones. Open mid-May–Dec. 23; Wed.–Sun. 11–5 (summer), Fri.–Sun 11–5 (fall).

Waterfalls of the Fingerlakes (607-535-9709; 20 North Franklin St., Watkins Glen, NY 14891) Exotic water fountains, walls of water, sphere fountains, handmade tabletop fountains, candleholders, stained-glass lamps, mirror fountains, and other unusual items are found here, from small to wall-sized.

Weaver-View Farms Amish Country Store (315-781-2571; www.weaverview farms.com; 1190 Earls Hill Rd., Penn Yan, NY 14527; off Rte. 14, 7 miles south of Geneva) Amish/Mennonite quilts and country gifts in a turn-of-the-20th-century farmhouse. Also find Amish dolls, books, furniture, toys, gingham dresses and bonnets, pottery and kitchen decor. Open year-round; closed Sun. (See listing in Chapter Six, *Keuka Lake*.)

For More Information

Finger Lakes Tourism: 315-536-7488; www.fingerlakes.org. 309 Lake St., Penn Yan, NY 14527.

Geneva Area Chamber of Commerce, Information Center: 315-789-1776; fax 315-789-3993; www.genevany.com; 35 Lakefront Dr., PO Box 587, Geneva, NY 14456.

Ontario County Tourism: 585-394-3915, 877-386-4669; www.visitfingerlakes .com; 25 Gorham St., Canandaigua, NY 14424.

Schuyler County Chamber of Commerce: 607-535-4300; www.schuylerny.com; 100 North Franklin St., Watkins Glen, NY 14891.

CHAPTER SIX
Split Personality
KEUKA LAKE

A view of Keuka Lake from the veranda of Esperanza Mansion.

To the Senecas who lived in the region long before the white man came, *Keuka* meant "canoe landing"—a name that ultimately prevailed even after settlers tried to change the name to Crooked Lake. Over the years, this 22-mile Y-shaped lake, which forks about midway to the north, has been the epicenter of first a thriving steamship transportation company and later an important wine-producing area. The largest town, Penn Yan, lies at the tip of the northeastern branch; Branchport is nestled around the northwestern branch, and Hammondsport lies at the southern end. Keuka is on the eastern shore just where the eastern branch of the lake forks up.

The lake is one of the warmest of the Finger Lakes as it is shallower in comparison, so swimming is comfortable the entire summer season. And of all the Finger Lakes, Keuka's 70 miles of shoreline harbors the most lake-hugging restaurants. Many have decks literally over the water and several boat slips so that diners can arrive by water.

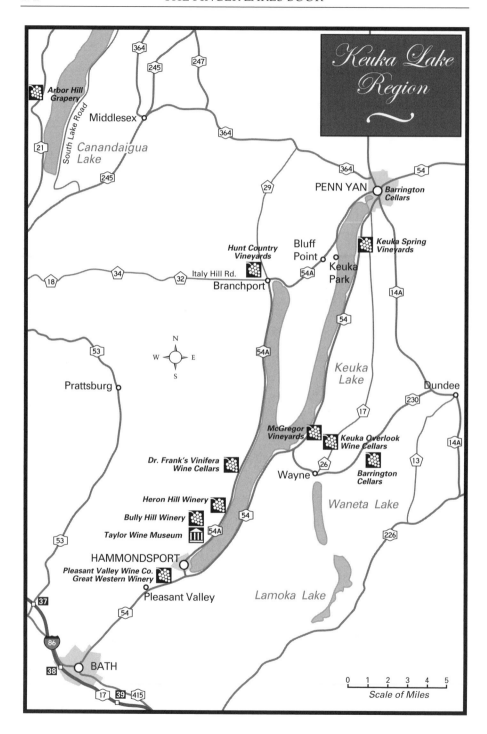

Keuka Lake
Region

364
245
247

Arbor Hill
Grapery

Middlesex

21

South Lake Road

Canandaigua
Lake

245

364

364   54

29   PENN YAN   Barrington
Cellars

Keuka Spring
Vineyards

Hunt Country   Bluff
Vineyards   Point   Keuka
Park

18   34   32   Italy Hill Rd.   54A
Branchport   14A

54

54A

N

53   W   E   Keuka
Lake   Dundee

S

Prattsburg   230

17

McGregor   14A
Vineyards   Keuka Overlook
Wine Cellars   13

Dr. Frank's Vinifera   26
Wine Cellars   Wayne   Barrington
Cellars

Waneta Lake

Heron Hill Winery

Bully Hill Winery   54

Taylor Wine Museum   54A   226

53

HAMMONDSPORT   Lamoka Lake

Pleasant Valley Wine Co.
Great Western Winery

37   Pleasant Valley

54

86

38   BATH   0   1   2   3   4   5

Scale of Miles

17   39   415

Although most visitors come here for the wineries, there are several superb museums and other attractions. The Glenn H. Curtiss Museum explores the early days of aviation; the Greyton H. Taylor Wine Museum is at the Bully Hill Winery. For a pleasant summer's day activity, climb aboard the *Keuka Maid*, which leaves from its pier in Hammondsport and offers a variety of cruises around the lake. Keuka College, a four-year co-ed liberal arts school founded in 1890, has a beautiful 1,300 foot lakeshore site on the west side of the lake, four miles southwest of Penn Yan. Area residents enjoy programs and events offered by the college throughout the year.

Pleasure craft now cruise Keuka's waters, but early in the 19th century, the lake was the scene of a bustling commercial shipping business. The schooner *Sally* used to transport grain to Hammondsport, where it was loaded on wagons and hauled 10 miles to Bath, then shipped by river to Philadelphia and Baltimore. The opening of the Erie Canal in 1825 resulted in traffic being diverted to northern ports.

For about 40 years (1830–1870) the "Crooked Lake Canal" linked Penn Yan to Dresden on Seneca Lake; however, the coming of the railroad made the canal obsolete. All that remains today are traces of some of the 28 locks, mill foundations, and towpath. The canal's path is now defined by the Keuka Outlet Trail, popular with hikers and bikers.

By the late 1800s the emphasis on transporting grains had shifted to grapes, bringing new prosperity to the region. And thanks to a spirited rivalry between steamboat companies, extensive publicity spread the word about the leisure assets of Keuka Lake, attracting affluent visitors who built lovely summer homes along the shores.

One of the best-known boats, the 600-passenger *Mary Bell* steamboat launched in 1892, plied the lake for 30 years, carrying both passengers and grapes. The steamboat age recalls a time of romance: dances in lakeside pavilions, booming resorts at Grove Springs, Gibson's Landing and Urbana; and big-name entertainers like Fred Waring and Hoagy Carmichael.

Since that time, grapes have been the most important industry around the lake. Considered the center of the champagne industry in New York State, the hills around Hammondsport are covered with vineyards, including the well-known Bully Hill Vineyards, Dr. Konstantin Frank's Vinifera Wine Cellars, and the Pleasant Valley Wine Company.

It all started in an Episcopal rector's garden around 1840. Planted by the Reverend William Bostwick of Hammondsport, his Isabella and Catawba grapes flourished. Others took notice and planted their own vines. Seven years later local entrepreneurs sent 50 pounds of grapes to the New York market. By 1860 some 200 acres of vineyards were planted around the lake, and at the turn of the 20th century more than 23,000 acres were dedicated to growing grapes. Today the wine industry here is still alive, well, and expanding.

Route 54A from Penn Yan to Hammondsport along the western shore of Keuka's western branch meanders along the shoreline, providing one of the most scenic drives in the world. Middle Road, above it, gives you superb hillside views of vineyards and the lake below.

Red Jacket

On Route 54A just south of Branchport, a granite monument marks the burial spot for the mother of the Seneca chief Red Jacket. This famous Native American orator of the Seneca tribe—whose Seneca name was Sagoyewatha—is believed to have been given his Anglican name because of a British army jacket he was given and wore constantly. His longhouse was believed to have been at this site in 1752.

PENN YAN

O n the tip of the northeastern branch of the lake, Penn Yan is a pretty peaceful place, considering it was once nicknamed "Pandemonium" by its neighbors because of its rowdy reputation. About 1808, looking for a real name for the town, the leaders settled on Penn Yan, satisfying two factions who were having trouble agreeing: immigrants from Pennsylvania and Yankees from New England.

One of the first founders of the town, David Wagener, a follower of cult leader Jemima Wilkinson, came here from Pennsylvania. He built a gristmill on the site where the Birkett Mills now stand on the south end of Main Street, along the Keuka Lake Outlet. Wagener's son Abraham, who is considered to be the father of the town, built the first frame house and first inn, the Mansion House, and constructed the grand manor house above Bluff Point.

In addition to gristmills, shops and taverns were gradually built both at the north end of Main Street and around the mills. The construction of the county buildings midway between the two areas tied these two commercial centers together. Since then the heart of the business district has drifted more toward the former mill areas, where the Crooked Canal was built.

This National Register Historic District includes several historic buildings. A comprehensive Historic Main Street Walking Tour describes the Holowell House, a late-19th-century Queen-Anne home at 219 Main Street, the Victorian King-Post House at 215 Main Street, the Bordwell House, a brick Italianate residence build in 1868 on the site of Abraham Wagener's first house, and others. The guide is available at the Oliver House Museum and other key sites.

HAMMONDSPORT

H ammondsport centers on a lovely compact square with shops and restaurants arranged around a park of trees, gardens, and a gazebo. Walk a couple of blocks to the lakeshore, where there is a public park and the old Hammondsport Depot, now the Keuka Moon art gallery; a vintage rail car is parked alongside. During the summer months, band concerts are held in the square at 7pm on Thursday evenings.

Considered the wine capital of the state, Hammondsport has several vineyards within its boundaries, including the Great Western and Pleasant Valley Wineries.

Hammondsport is also the site of the oldest running county fair, and for history buffs, the buildings along Pulteney Square and Liberty Street, as well as the Erie Freight House, are especially interesting. Several private homes are on the National Register of Historic Places. Walking tours reveal buildings in several styles: Greek-Revival, Queen-Anne, Italianate, and Tuscan. For a dose of the 1950s, take in a movie at one of the few drive-in theaters still left in the country (open spring through fall).

BATH

South of Hammondsport, the town of Bath—site of the oldest-running county fair—was named after Lady Bath of England, by founder Colonel Charles Williamson, whose dream was to create the state's first planned community. Believing that Bath's pivotal location at the junction of the Susquehanna, Conhocton, and Chemung Rivers would be a surefire combination to creating a highway to the West, "The Baron of the Backwoods"—as his peers anointed him—acting as the agent for some wealthy Englishmen, including Sir William Pulteney, promoted the site as the next great metropolitan area.

In 1793 when 15 families moved into the village, Williamson did not foresee that the Erie Canal and the coming of the railroad would negate the importance of the rivers. But his dynamic personality and boundless energy prevailed to some extent, despite continual setbacks. Eventually Bath was developed with a gristmill, sawmill, several residences, and even a theater and race course.

Today Bath is hardly the great city Williamson imagined, but it *is* a nice town with a most interesting history. Cemetery buffs will find the white headstones

---

The Friend

One of the area's most interesting personalities, Jemima Wilkinson (1752–1819), an imposing figure in flowing robes with long raven hair, believed she had been reincarnated by the Divine Spirit as a Universal Friend to save sinners. Relocating from Rhode Island, she founded a community of faithful followers, first settling near Dresden at one end of the Keuka Outlet. Her group built the first gristmill in the area, harvested the first wheat sown west of Seneca Lake, and soon became the largest community in the region. Ruling with an iron hand, she forbade her subjects to marry, controlled the finances, and scorned attending such entertainments as dances, theater, and horse races. Her creed was simple: Be good, go to heaven; sin, and burn in hell. Eventually the settlement relocated to Branchport, where the Friend built a three-story house with nine fireplaces.

in the Bath National Cemetery adjacent to the V.A. Medical Center complex a stunning sight.

LAMOKA AND WANETA LAKES

The comparatively tiny lakes of Lamoka and Waneta, just east of the southern end of Keuka Lake, are hardly on some of the area maps. Less than 4 miles long and 1,000 feet above sea level, Lamoka is the site of a prehistoric Indian settlement, one of the oldest such sites in the state. Peaceful places.

LODGING

There are no major hotels in the area. Places to stay include bed & breakfasts and small inns or 1960s-style motels. There are also cottage rentals available through reservation services. Some of the B&Bs are right on the lake and come with access to canoes and rowboats. They range from elegant estate homes with pillars and formal gardens to cozy, homey places with lots of fluff and knick-knacks.

LODGING RATES
$: Up to $75 per couple $$$: $151–$250 per couple
$$: $76–$150 per couple $$$$: More than $250 per couple

Branchport

ESPERANZA MANSION
315-536-4400;
   fax 315-536-4900
www.esperanzamansion
   .com
3456 Rtes. 54A
Bluff Point, NY 14478
Innkeeper: Rene Bloom
Rooms: 21 in the inn plus 9
   suites in the mansion
Open: Year-round.
Price: $$$–$$$$
Credit Cards: Most major.

The view from the terrace sitting high above Keuka Lake doesn't get much better. This elegant yellow Greek Revival house with pillars and verandas was originally built by John Nicholas Rose, who in 1838 had traveled here from his plantation in Virginia. Listed as a national landmark, the mansion, once a stop of the Underground Railroad, has been totally renovated. Additions include a full service banquet facility and new guest rooms and suites, many contained in the new inn adjacent to the main house. Mansion house suites are based on the original sleeping quarters of the Rose family. Some have canopy beds, some sleigh beds, and feature period decorative fireplaces. A private entrance leads upstairs to the honeymoon suite, which features a king bed and antique furniture. Quilts from Belgium are quite beautiful and reassemble a large petit point work of art. There are modern amenities such as in-room telecommunica-

The beautiful bedrooms in Esperanza Mansion, Branchport, feature Belgian quilts

tions connections and tumbled marble baths. An 88-seat restaurant is located in the front two rooms of the house, both restored and furnished in 19th-century manner. The library is also available for a more intimate dining experience and casual fare is available in the tavern. Dinner choices include items like lobster ravioli Fra Diavolo, Provençal rack of lamb, and chicken apple frangelico.

OLDE TAVERN INN
President/Manager: Brian
    Zerges.
888-414-5253;
    fax 315-595-2825.
www.rentalplus.com.
Rental Plus, 3858 County
    House Rd., Branchport
    NY 14418.
Rooms: 5 bedrooms,
    2 baths.
Open: Year-round.
Price: $$$–$$$$ for the
    entire house.
Credit Cards: Most major.

A good place for families and small groups, this circa-1823 restored National Historic Landmark can accommodate 10 people. Once a major stop on the stagecoach line from Penn Yan, the colonial-style house is in a rural setting about 2 miles north of Keuka Lake. Throughout the area are hiking trails. History buffs will find the Native American connection fascinating: The building sits in the Gu-ya-no-ga Valley, named for the Seneca tribal chief who once lived on this land. The house is self-catering and completely furnished with linens and kitchenware; decor is attractive country-style with area rugs, quilts, and spreads. Check out the website for more than 100 other house, condo, cottage, and luxury-home rentals on Keuka, Seneca, and Canandaigua Lakes.

10,000 DELIGHTS B&B
Innkeeper: Vera Van Atta.
607-868-3731.
1170 West Lake, Rte. 54A,
    Branchport, NY 14418.
Rooms: 10, some shared
    baths.
Open: Year-round.

You have a delicious choice: Stay in the Lake House, the apartment, or in one of the six rooms in the Greek-Revival-style home. With 50 acres of woods and waterfalls, a private beach, canoe, paddleboat, canoe, gardens, a Japanese teahouse, and a new tree house with stained-glass windows, there is plenty to discover outside, as well. Rooms feature stenciling,

Price: $–$$.
Credit Cards: None.

wide-plank floors, wood paneling, and 18th-century beams; furnishings include antiques, quilts, vintage dolls, and original artwork. Gourmet breakfasts.

Hammondsport

MOTELS AND HOTELS

**HAMMONDSPORT
  MOTEL**
Innkeepers: Ralph and
  Maxine Brown.
607-569-2600.
PO Box 311,
  Hammondsport, NY
  14840.
Corner Williams and Water
  Sts.
Rooms: 17 with baths.
Open: Apr. 1–mid-Nov.
Price: $.
Credit Cards: Visa, MC.

Don't let the neon sign on the end of the building turn you off. If you're a no-frills kind of person and care mostly about being right on the shore at an economical price, this motel might be a good bet. It sits on a little piece of land jutting into the water and is simply furnished in a '60s-type style. Rooms are clean, and half of them have views of the lake. There are smoking and nonsmoking rooms, all with televisions, air-conditioning, radios, and phones; coffee is available mornings in the office. A pretty gazebo sits on the end of the property near the water. Boat launch and dock space are on site; a public beach and main shopping area are within easy walking distance.

VINEHURST INN
Innkeeper: Jim Heil.
607-569-2300.
www.vinehurstinn.com.
Rte. 54, Hammondsport, NY
  14840.
Rooms: 25 with private
  baths.
Open: Year-round.
Price: $–$$.
Credit Cards: All major.

Ever since Jim Heil bought this place two years ago, he has been in the middle of a major renovation program to bring this circa mid-1960s hotel/motel up to par. Near the southern tip of Keuka Lake, the property has a multitude of room styles, including efficiencies, apartments, and suites. All baths have been updated, the exercise room is new, and a new patio out front sports tables and trellis. Also new are the themed suites: One is based on a winery, another on an Adirondack cabin. Some suites come with cathedral ceilings, a king or queen bed, and sitting room with a double whirlpool. Rooms are furnished in a homey style, each one a bit different. A family activity area offers volleyball, croquet, and other games plus a new conference room. Included in the rates is a continental breakfast.

BED & BREAKFASTS

AMITY ROSE B&B
Innkeepers: Ellen and Frank
  Laufersweiler.
607-569-3408, 800-982-8818.
www.amityroseinn.com.

This simple frame house is a homey, comfortable B&B. Rooms are named after the Laufersweiler daughters: Emma, Ellen, Dawn, and Hannah. Floral wallpaper, lace, and Waverly-style fabrics are used

8264 Main St.,
  Hammondsport, NY
  14840.
Rooms: 4 with private baths.
Open: Closed mid-
  Dec.–mid-Apr.
Price: $$.
Credit Cards: Cash or
  personal and travelers
  checks only.

BLUSHING ROSE B&B
Innkeepers: Pat and Dick
  Leonberger.
607-569-2687, 866-569-2687.
www.blushingroseinn.com.
11 William St., PO Box 153,
  Hammondsport, NY
  14840.
Rooms: 4 with private baths.
Open: Closed mid-
  Dec.–mid-Apr.
Price: $$
Credit Cards: Cash or
  personal and travelers
  checks only

**FEATHER TICK'N THYME
  B&B**
Innkeepers: Ruth, Deb, and
  Greg Cody.
607-522-4113
www.bbnyfingerlakes.com.
7661 Tuttle Rd., Prattsburgh,
  NY 14873.
Off Italy Hill Rd.
Rooms: 4 private and shared
  baths.
Open: Year-round.
Price: $$.
Credit Cards: Most major.

**GONE WITH THE WIND
  ON KEUKA LAKE B&B**
Innkeepers: Linda and
  Robert Lewis.
607-868-4603.
www.gonewiththewindon
  keukalake.com.
14905 W. Lake Rd.,
  Branchport, NY 14418.

throughout. Dawn's Delight has a queen bed, sitting area, and balcony. Ellen's Retreat, on the ground floor, features a four-poster queen bed, whirlpool tub, and a private entrance. Full breakfasts are served in the simple but pleasant dining room.

An 1843 Italianate home with period-furnished rooms on the lacey, flowery side. This B&B features brass, four-poster, and antique queen and king beds, deep New England colors like reds and greens, quilts, wainscoting, stenciling, wicker chairs with plump cushions, dried flower arrangements, area rugs, and lots of small knick-knacks. The Burgundy Room has a king-sized bed and sitting area; the magnificent Walnut Room has a walnut (what else?) queen bed with ruffles. Relax in one of the chairs lining the large porch that runs across the front of the house. Just a block from the public beach and the main shopping square, this is a pleasant, well-maintained home. Nonsmoking, air-conditioned; no pets, please.

Located in the Hammondsport area, this 1890s Victorian country home sits in the middle of 80 acres surrounded by open fields and trees. The rooms are furnished with a mix of antiques, quilts, and period reproductions. Sit on the wraparound porch, and sip an early-morning cup of coffee. Freshly baked muffins, breads, and a full-course breakfast are provided. This B&B is nonsmoking; no pets.

Relax with a cup of coffee, a good book, or a cocktail on the porch of this 1887 pillared county Victorian. Or simply sit back and enjoy the lovely views of the lake and countryside. Rooms are in the main house and in a log lodge on the edge of the woods; all are different. For example, one has a Southwestern theme, another a rustic feeling (with a headboard made by a local Amish craftsman). The

On Rte. 54A, Pulteney.
Rooms: 10, some shared
   baths, some private.
Open: Year-round.
Price: $$.
Credit Cards: Cash or check.

Rhett and Scarlet Hideaway on the second floor of the main house has a private veranda and a king-sized bed. Rooms are tastefully uncluttered. There are some antiques and period reproductions, but the furnishings complement the theme of the room. Mattresses are new and mostly queen sized; bathrooms may be accented by oak, brass, and marble. There is a solarium hot tub, three fireplaces, a private cove with a gazebo and dock, and a rowboat. It's a peaceful setting, with several hiking trails fanning out from the 14-acre property and no televisions or phones to distract.

**J. S. HUBBS B&B and
   STONEHEDGE GUEST
   HOUSE**
Innkeepers: Walter Carl and
   Linda Elias-Carl.
607-569-2440;
   fax 607-868-4355.
www.jshubbs.com.
17 Shethar St., PO Box 428,
   Hammondsport, NY
   14840.
Rooms: 4 with private baths,
   plus lakeside cottage.
Open: Year-round.
Price: $$.
Credit Cards: Visa, MC.

Surrounded by a wrought-iron fence and gardens, this historic 1840 Greek-Revival in the middle of town is in the exact place where Judge Hammond had his original log cabin. The house features period furniture, antiques, a fireplace in the sitting room, high ceilings with deep moldings, and even original wallpaper on some walls. The four air-conditioned guestrooms are all different. The Captain John Shethar Room has a queen-sized bed and a nice free-standing mirror. The Judge Lazarus Hammond Room, named after the founder of Hammondsport, has a canopy queen-sized bed and the largest bathroom in the house. The largest room in the house, the Adsit-Pierce Suite, has a queen-sized bed and sitting room with a sofa bed, television/VCR, and desk. From the bright, airy cupola, you get great views of the lake and town. Breakfast includes fruit and special dishes such as cheese strata or cottage cheese pancakes, along with something fresh from the oven like rolls or coffee cake.

Stonehedge Cottage: The Carls also have a cottage, sleeping five or six, on the lake 2 miles from Hammondsport. It sits on a private beach with its own swimming area, and its three floors have a spiral staircase connecting each level. The living room on the top floor has a large deck; the kitchen is fully equipped. Cost is $875/week, which includes all utilities and taxes, plus a $500 security deposit; cost can be pro-rated for shorter or longer stays (607-868-4358).

**PLEASANT VALLEY INN
   AND RESTAURANT**
Innkeepers: Marianne and
   Tom Simons.
607-569-2282.
www.pleasantvalleyinn.com.
7979 Rte. 54, Hammondsport,
   NY 14840.

This grand 1848 Victorian is 2 miles out of town on a property surrounded by large trees and vineyards. Air-conditioned rooms, recently renovated, are furnished in a Victorian style, some with queen-size four-poster beds. A continental breakfast is served on the porches overlooking the vineyards.

Rooms: 4 with private baths.
Open: May–Nov.
Price: $$.
Credit Cards: Most major.

There is a restaurant in the house serving candle-light dinners Thursday through Sunday. Rack of lamb is recommended by the owner/chef; steak is also a good choice. The Simonses supply their kitchens with herbs grown from their garden and like to use local fruits and vegetables.

COTTAGE RENTALS

WRIGHT'S COTTAGES ON WANETA LAKE

Owners/Managers: James and Mary Ann Wright.
607-292-6786.
www.wrightscottages.com.
9472 Lakeshore Dr., Hammondsport, NY 14840.
Rooms: 6 cottages.
Open: Apr.–Nov.
Price: 2 nights $$–$$$.
Credit Cards: Check or cash.

Located between Seneca and Keuka Lakes, this cottage complex is popular with families and groups. There are six furnished board-and-batten cottages with fireplaces and 250 feet of lakefront. Kitchens have a stove, refrigerator, microwave, and gas grill plus all basic appliances. There is a television/VCR in each cottage (but only two cabins have cable). Each cottage has its own lot and campfire pit; a large common area of lawns and trees leads down to the water, where there is a long dock and a raft. Kids of all ages will find plenty of water toys: row-boats, paddleboats, kayaks, and canoes. A scenic trail runs along the lake for 2.5 miles, and there are a lot of country roads perfect for walking. This is a quiet place—if you crave nightlife, you should go somewhere else. The hot entertainment here is singing around the campfire. Wood is provided for your fireplace and for campfires; bring your own towels and bedding. Wayne Market is within walking distance for ice cream, hot dogs, hamburgers, and anything else you might need from movie rentals to steak. The nearest launderette is in Penn Yan.

Penn Yan

MOTELS AND HOTELS

COLONIAL MOTEL AND RESORT CENTER

Innkeepers: Nancy and Dan Brooks.
315-536-3056, 800-724-3008.
175 W. Lake Rd., Penn Yan, NY 14527.
Rooms: 17.
Open: Year-round.
Price: $$.
Credit Cards: Most major.

This family-owned-and-operated hotel—just across the road from the lake—is a combination of a colonial house and two-story motel. All but three of the air-conditioned accommodations are ef-ficiencies—neat, clean, cottage-style but not elabo-rate. The appliances have been updated, and there are coffeemakers and toasters. Many visitors like to sit on the patio in front of the motel, where a fire is lit in a fire pit each evening. If you're visiting Keuka College, this one is just a mile away. Year-round and weekly rates available.

VIKING RESORT
Innkeeper: Ken Christensen.
315-536-7061;
   fax 315-536-0737.
www.vikingresort.com.
680 E. Lake Road, Rte. 54,
   Penn Yan, NY 14527.
Rooms: 39, plus a 6- and
   a 3-bedroom cottage.
Open: Mid-May–mid-Oct.
Price: $–$$$$.
Credit Cards: Most major.

This no-frills cabin and motel resort has efficiencies, apartments, suites, and rooms furnished in a 1950s knotty-pine mode. The whole complex is spotless: Owner Ken Christensen credits his Norwegian ancestry for this. There is more than 1,000 feet of lakeshore, perfect for swimming and boating. There's also a hot tub and outdoor pool, fishing, free rowboats, and pontoon and power boat rentals. Guests often look forward to a late-afternoon lake cruise aboard *The Viking Spirit* party boat or perhaps a sail with Ken on his 38-foot A-Scow. Docking facilities are available for privately owned boats. This is a family-oriented place, with plenty of water sports and a nightly bonfire.

BED & BREAKFASTS

**FINTON'S LANDING
   B&B**
Innkeepers: Doug and
   Arianne Tepper.
315-536-3146;
   fax 315-536-3791.
http://home.eznet.net/
   ~tepperd.
661 E. Lake Rd., Penn Yan,
   NY 14527.
Rooms: 4 with private
   baths.
Open: Please call.
Price: $$.
Credit Cards: MC, Visa,
   checks.

Sitting in the restored gazebo on the lake, you can almost imagine steamboats plying the waters as they did at the turn of the 20th century. Actually, they would have pulled into the dock here: In the 1860s, Finton's was a steamboat landing. It's the only B&B right on Keuka Lake between Penn Yan and Hammondsport. Enjoy breakfast on the spacious wraparound porch of this pretty Victorian, or simply relax in one of the rocking chairs. There are 165 feet of private beach and a marvelous redwood dock with a bench on the end, a perfect perch for romantic interludes—so perfect, in fact, that owner Doug Tepper says couples often get engaged there. There is also a hammock for two by the beach. Furnished in a comfortable Adirondacks style, all rooms are air-conditioned. The Garden Room with a queen bed looks out onto a wildflower garden filled with special plantings that attract birds and butterflies; many plants date from Victorian times. The Wisteria Room has a double bed and is directly on the lake. The Cherub Room, with a queen mahogany four-poster, is also on the lake and has a larger bath. Acorn and Oak Leaves has both a brass double bed and Victorian metal twin bed. You can see the lake from the room, but the better view is of a stream and a row of grape vines. Of interest in this historic home are the many photos, maps, and artifacts dating from the days of the steamboats. Finton's Landing appeals to those who love nature; many bikers and hikers stay here. At night you can roast marshmallows over a fire in the firepit on the beach as you count stars overhead. Breakfasts are not only hearty, they feature a lot of fresh produce from local farms, perhaps strawberries, peaches, or pears. Starting with fresh fruit and often sorbet, you may move on to buttermilk waffles, buckwheat pancakes, or Havarti baked eggs. Along with your French batards, you are offered homemade jams made from plums, raspberries, and other regional fruits. This is a no-smoking, no-pets place. Children more than 10 years of age are welcome, and feel free to bring your own kayak or canoe.

THE FOX INN B&B
Innkeepers: Cliff and Michele Orr.
315-536-3101, 800-901-7997.
www.foxinnbandb.com.
158 Main St., Penn Yan, NY 14527.
Rooms: 6 with private baths.
Open: Year-round.
Price: $$.
Credit Cards: Most major.

Right on Main Street just a block from the center of town, the yellow brick Fox Inn is surrounded by wide lawns with huge trees; rose gardens bloom profusely from May through October. Built in 1820 by William Morris Oliver, the first judge of Yates County and a New York State senator, lieutenant governor, and U.S. congressman, this property should appeal to those who love traditional elegance. The new owners have furnished this gracious 1820s pillared Greek-Revival house with an exceptional collection of antiques, artwork, and reproductions. Some rooms have a fireplace and whirlpool bath; all have television/VCR. The William Fox Suite has two bedrooms and a large country bathroom. There is a large billiard room, a living room with a marble fireplace, a sun porch with flowers and plants, and a formal dining room. Gourmet breakfasts include fresh fruit, muffins, several types of pancakes, French toast, and eggs. The inn has rooms for small receptions and meetings. For business travelers, word-processing, copy, and e-mail services are available.

MERRITT HILL MANOR B&B
Innkeepers: Susan and Marc Hyser.
315-536-7682.
www.merritthillmanor.com.
2756 Coates Rd., Penn Yan, NY 14527.
Rooms: 5 with private baths.
Open: Year-round.
Price: $$.
Credit Cards: MC, Visa.

Once thought to be one of the havens on the Underground Railroad, Merritt Hill is one of the grander B&Bs in the area. This 1822 Federal-style country home on the crest of a hill offers spectacular views of Keuka and Seneca Lakes and the hills leading to Canandaigua. On 12 acres, the house is surrounded by open pasture land and gardens; a stream runs through the property. The guestrooms are exceptionally large; rooms #1 and #5 are the ones to ask for if you want nonstop vistas of this lovely countryside. You can also relax and soak it all up in the Adirondack chairs on the lawn. Once thought to be one of the havens long the Underground Railroad, this is one of the grander B&Bs in the area. Each of the rooms is tastefully furnished with antiques and period reproductions. Full breakfasts may include German apple pancakes or blueberry French toast, along with a large selection of fresh fruit and homemade bread or muffins.

TRIMMER HOUSE B&B
Innkeeper: Gary Smith.
315-536-8304, 800-968-8735.
www.trimmerhouse.com.
145 E. Main St., Penn Yan,
  NY 14527.
Rooms: 5 with private baths
  (1 with 2 bedrooms).
Open: Year-round.
Price: $$.
Credit Cards: Visa, MC.

Once the home of wine merchant David Orville Trimmer, this lovely restored 1891 Victorian house is now owned by Gary Smith, a professor of hospitality management at Keuka College. His Queen Anne–style home is furnished with period wall coverings and fabrics, with such special features as hand-oiled oak, cypress and mahogany woodwork, marble and oak floors, painted ceilings, and chandeliers. All rooms have air-conditioning and television/VCR. There are two parlors, a library with fireplace, a formal dining room and music room as well as an outdoor hot tub. Guests enjoy a full breakfast plus complimentary snacks and beverages. Trimmer House is within walking distance of restaurants and shops.

TUDOR HALL B&B
Innkeepers: Priscilla and
  Don Erickson.
315-536-9962.
www.trimmerhouse.com.
762 E. Bluff Dr., Penn Yan,
  NY 14527.
Rooms: 3 suites with private
  baths.
Open: Apr.–Thanksgiving;
  check for off-season.
Price: $$.
Credit Cards: Visa, MC.

This Tudor-style house has a decidedly English feel both inside and out. It's right on the lake at the site of a former steamboat landing—in fact, one of the suites is sited where grapes were kept in cold storage until the steamboat could transport them to market. This suite comes with a kitchen and private entrance. All suites have great views of the lake and sitting areas; the 400-square-foot Royal Suite has a four-poster canopy bed and a private balcony overlooking the lake. And all come with television, phone, refrigerator, and coffeemaker. There are terraced gardens, a private beach, and three boats: a rowboat, canoe, and paddleboat. There is also a power boat that the Ericksons use to take their guests on lake cruises and a 20-foot pontoon boat that can be rented. Gourmet breakfasts are served by candlelight using crystal and china—the whole works.

THE WAGENER ESTATE
Innkeeper: Lisa Akers and
  Ken Greenwood.
315-536-4591;
  fax 315-531-8142.
www.wagenerestate.com.
351 Elm St., Penn Yan NY
  14527.
Rooms: 5 with private baths.
Open: Year-round.
Price: $$.
Credit Cards: Most major.

Built in 1794, this gracious old Colonial farmhouse is set on a magnificent 4-acre property, with sweeping lawns, trees, and flowering shrubs. It once contained an extensive orchard, and many of these trees are still here: pear, apple, and cherry along with maples, sycamores, and pines—a virtual arboretum. A large porch furnished with many chairs overlooks the lawns with a peek of the lake through the trees; a hammock invites a late-afternoon snooze. Furnishings include country antiques; rooms come with televisions. The Delaware Room, with its own bathroom and private deck and entrance, is a good choice. In the morning find a breakfast ranging from a country spread to a three-course gourmet deal. Fresh fruit and such entrées as banana-stuffed French toast with blueberry compote or buckwheat pancakes with apple cider syrup are offered; on Sundays you get dessert.

CABINS

FINGER LAKES GUIDE CABIN
607-868-7800.
www.flguideservice.com.
Near Keuka Lake State Park.
Open: Apr.–Oct.
Price: $–$$.

The cabin is surrounded by 60 acres of private land. There is a large open living room and dining area with cathedral ceiling, full kitchen, bathroom, mudroom, large loft bedroom, and wraparound deck. On the grounds are three ponds stocked with fish, 20 acres of pine, and lots of trails to explore. Rentals from $25 per person, per night. In-season (July and August) $950 per week (no nightly rates).

Vacation Rentals and Services

Lakespell Vacation Rentals (315-536-9234; www.yatesny.com/lakespell; 158 Main St., Penn Yan, NY 14527) Manager Cliff Orr offers accommodations on the lake for 6 to 26 people, from cottages to a private villa and manor. Private lake frontage, boat rentals. Open year-round, summer for weekly rentals only; off-season weekends only. Check or cash only; no credit cards.

Rental Plus (315-536-2201, 888-414-5253; fax 315-595-2825; www.rentalplus.com) President/manager Brian Zerges has more than 100 house, condo, cottage, and luxury-home rentals on Keuka, Seneca, and Canandaigua Lakes. Rent weekly, monthly, seasonally, or for a few days. Off-season discounts and vacation packages available. Visa, MC.

RESTAURANTS

Keuka is the star when it comes to restaurants right on the lake. Several provide docks and tie-up facilities so that you can arrive by boat. Many of the wineries have restaurants, as well, with local wines prominently featured on the menu. Regional specialties include fresh fish from the lakes and produce from the regional markets. Some restaurants offer Amish and Mennonite food.

Prices are estimated per person for appetizer and dinner entrée without tax, tip, or alcoholic beverages.

$: Up to $10
$$: $11–$25

$$$: $26–$40
$$$$: More than $40

Branchport

ESPERANZA MANSION
315-536-4400;
    fax 315-536-4900
www.esperanzamansion
    .com
3456 Rtes. 54A
Bluff Point, NY 14478
Open: Open L 11–2:30;
    D 5–10; tavern until
    midnight.
Price: $$–$$$; tavern $
Serving: L, D
Credit Cards: Most major.

(See listing under Lodging.)

KNOTTY PINE INN
607-868-4664.
293 W. Lake Rd.,
    Branchport, NY 14418.
Open: Wed.–Sun.
Price: $–$$$.
Cuisine: Continental,
    American.
Serving: D.
Credit Cards: Most major.

A cozy log cabin on the water, this place is well-known for serving great prime rib. Also good are the steaks, crab legs, fried fish, chicken Parmesan, and stuffed mushrooms. The decor is casual, with snappy hunter-green table linens. Eat outdoors on the deck overlooking the lake or inside in the dining room where a fire warms you up in the winter.

Hammondsport

**BULLY HILL
RESTAURANT**
607-868-3490.
www.bullyhill.com.
8834 Greyton H. Taylor
    Memorial Dr.,
    Hammondsport, NY
    14840.
At the Wine Museum of
    Greyton H. Taylor.
Open: Apr.–Nov.
Price: $–$$.
Cuisine: American,
    California bistro.
Serving: L 11:30–4, D Fri.
    and Sat. 5–9.
Credit Cards: Most major.

B esides good food and good portions, this restaurant offers a wonderful hilltop view of the vineyards, gardens, and the lake. There are two dining rooms with copper-topped tables as well as a large deck with umbrella tables. The Maryland blue crab cakes, grilled chicken salad with honey-Dijon mustard dressing, garlic-laced puréed eggplant with shrimp, and grilled chicken with applewood-smoked bacon and smoked mozzarella cheese are excellent. Vegetarian dishes include pizza, a garden-medley vegetable burger topped with a portabella mushroom, and grilled veggies. Cuisine is prepared from fresh ingredients and local produce. Before or after dining, be sure to stop at the Greyton H. Taylor Wine Museum and the new visitors center and sample some of their wines. My favorite: Chardonnay Elise, a simple, clean, dry wine.

LAKESIDE RESTAURANT
607-868-3636.
www.lakeside-restaurant.com.
800 W. Lake Rd.,
Hammondsport, NY
14840.
Open: Seasonally; 5–10
daily; 11–4:30 Thurs.–Sun.
Price: $$.
Cuisine: Continental,
American.
Serving: L, D.
Credit Cards: Most major.

Come by car or boat, and dine overlooking the west side of the lake from this restored Victorian home. You can sit on the outdoor patios or inside in the attractive dining room. Owners John Loehnert and Deb Laros say they like using fresh, not frozen, ingredients. The lunch menu includes such items as a warm steak salad and mache greens with peppercorn chèvre and frizzled leeks or pan-seared scallops with a chipotle pepper and tomato compote. For dinner try prime rib served with garlic mashed potatoes, catfish oreganata served in a lemon-artichoke butter sauce over herbed long grain rice, or eggplant and portobello stacks. The restaurant has been upgraded, with renovations to the bar area and new decks. There are 17 boat slips and a dining room for private parties on the second floor. The Bates family also caters parties on the *Viking Spirit* cruise boat.

**THREE BIRDS
RESTAURANT**
607-868-SNUG (7684),
607-868-7684.
144 W. Lake Rd.,
Hammondsport, NY
14840.
Open: Daily D 5–9; 5–10 Fri.
and Sat.
Price: $–$$.
Cuisine: American,
Continental.
Serving: L, D; check for off-season hours.
Credit Cards: Most major.

Being right on the shores of Keuka Lake, Three Birds lets you arrive here by either car or boat. The three-story building, dating from 1889, was once a private lakeside cottage, and later a small hotel—guests were ferried here by steamboat from the village landing. It has open decks plus indoor dining rooms; tables are attractively appointed with linen tablecloths and napkins and candles. Just about everything (except ice cream and French fries) is prepared from fresh, not frozen, ingredients. New owner/chef de cuisine John Loehnert (CIA trained) features such items as prime aged beef, beer-battered cod, medallions of veal sautéed and served with a peppercorn demi-glace and fresh mushrooms, and chocolate obsession cake. Everything is made from scratch including cakes, breads, pies, and dressings. An excellent selection of international wines complements the menu. Banquet facilities are available for private parties.

A two-bedroom efficiency apartment on third floor rents for $175 per night. Not luxurious, but roomy with great views of the water from the big old private deck. There are 24 boat slips for those coming by water.

THE VILLAGE TAVERN
607-569-2528;
fax 607-569-3560.
www.villagetaverninn.com.

On a corner of the village square in Hammondsport, this one pulls in the crowds—especially for their Friday fish fries. You can eat at tables outside in good weather as well as inside in the restaurant

On the Square, Hammonds-
   port, NY 14840.
Open: Daily.
Price: $$.
Cuisine: American,
   International.
Serving: L, D.
Credit Cards: Most major.

next to the bar area. In addition to fish and seafood dishes, the extensive menu includes specialty items such as tournedos Rossini with truffles, Thai chicken, and roasted New Zealand lamb. The tavern is known for its extensive wine list and more than 130 different beers on tap, 18 on draft. A bistro menu is also available with simpler fare. Most prefer to sit in the bar area. The inn also has four guestrooms.

**THE WATERFRONT
   RESTAURANT**
607-868-3455.
648 W. Lake Rd.,
   Hammondsport, NY
   14840.
On Rte. 54A, 6.5 miles north
   of Hammondsport.
Open: Noon–10 Sat. and
   Sun.; 5–10 Mon.–Fri. July
   and Aug.; check for other
   months.
Price: $–$$.
Cuisine: Ribs, seafood.
Serving: L, D.
Credit Cards: Most major.

Come by boat or car for food and drink at this casual waterside restaurant that almost hangs over the water. Eleven boat slips are often full, especially on Sundays in July and August when the popular clambake is held along with a live music concert, Jimmy Buffett–style. Many visitors anchor just offshore to listen to the concert. When all the slips are taken, people have been known to jump into the water and swim in to pick up their clams. Sit on one of the multiple open-air decks, some right over the water, or the air-conditioned dining room. Grilled meats, fish, and pasta are popular fare as well as fish and chips; crab legs and clams a specialty. Very lively in the summer.

Penn Yan

ANTIQUE INN
315-536-6576.
2940 Rte. 54A, Penn Yan, NY
   14527.
Open: Year-round;
   Mon.–Sat. 11–9; Sun.
   noon–8pm; call for
   seasonal hours.
Price: $–$$.
Cuisine: American.
Serving: L, D.
Credit Cards: Most major.

A casual, rustic, family-style place with reasonably priced good food. Specialties include haddock, pasta dishes, and seafood. Try the spaghetti sauce: They make it themselves. The fried fish, fried oysters, and liver and onions are local favorites. Some prefer to eat in the bar; same menu.

**LLOYDS LIMITED "A
   PUB"**
315-536-9029.
3 Main St., Penn Yan, NY
   14527.
Open: Daily after 4.
Price: $.
Cuisine: English pub,
   American.

Pure Finger Lakes vintage: tin ceiling, historic photos of area on walls, beer and wine memorabilia, old copies of *Reader's Digest*, blow-up beer bottles, 1910 skates, old keg taps—you name it. Starting life as a bar, Lloyds has added booths and casual pub dinners serving things like pizza, chicken wings, potato skins, and other finger foods. Loyal to

Serving: D, late-night service.
Credit Cards: Check or cash only.

the Finger Lakes, Lloyds serves wines only from area vineyards. At this community hangout, you can order a beer and some Buffalo wings, and linger in a booth reading a newspaper. Walls and booths are dark-stained wood. Very cozy.

Miller's Essenhaus, Penn Yan.

MILLER'S ESSENHAUS
315-531-8260.
1300 Rte. 14A, Penn Yan, NY 14527.
Open: Year-round Tues.–Sun.
Price: $–$$.
Cuisine: Home-baked Amish-style foods.
Serving: B, L, D.
Credit Cards: Most major.

When it comes to fresh and homemade, it does-n't get much better with things like chicken and biscuits, real mashed potatoes, french fries, peanut butter fudge pie, and apple crisp. There's a bakery that turns out mouthwatering sticky buns, rolls, pies, apple crisp, cheesecake, and other good-ies. Local fresh produce is used whenever possible. In a new building, the decor is fresh with a contem-porary flair. Handmade quilts hang on the walls, brass lanterns provide light, and hand-painted chairs are arranged around linen-covered tables. On Saturday mornings they roll out a super buffet with lots of pastries, sticky buns, fresh fruits, breakfast casserole, French toast, and oatmeal. There is a retail bakery and nice gift shop on the premises.

RED ROOSTER
315-536-9800.
12 Maiden Ln., Penn Yan NY 14527.
Open: Mon.–Fri. 11–closing, Sat. from 4.
Price: $.
Cuisine: Family favorites.
Serving: L, D.
Credit Cards: Cash or check.

Casual dining here is especially popular with families. Tables are set around a central bar. Prime rib is great here, as well as steaks, pasta, ham-burgers, onion rings, and finger foods. Walls are decorated with early 1900s pictures from Penn Yan. Plus there's a good selection of wines and beer on tap.

CASUAL FOOD

Chat-a-Whyle (607-776-8040; 28 Liberty St., Bath, NY 14810) Family owned, family operated for years, this cozy casual place is known for its sticky buns. Great buffets on weekends.

Crooked Lake Ice Cream Parlor (607-569-2751; 35 Shethar St., Hammondsport, NY 14840; on the Square) Old-fashioned ice-cream parlor with original tin ceiling and soda fountain dating from 1948. Counter and booths look like the originals, too. The hot fudge sundaes, topped with mounds of whipped cream and a cherry, cost $2.95 to $3.95; cones are $1.48 and $2.50. Also ice-cream floats, old fashioned phosphates, sodas, shakes, and other temptations. Open Mon.–Sat. 7–7, Sun. 8–5.

Grapevine Florist and Gifts (607-569-2105; 68 Shether St., Hammondsport, NY 14840) The only ice-cream parlor I know of that's in a florist shop. Take out cones, milkshakes, sundaes, and floats, or eat at one of the tables just outside on the garden patio. It's really very pleasant. Open seasonally for ice cream 11–10 daily; gift and flower shop open year-round.

Maloney's Pub (607-569-2264; 57 Pulteney St., Hammondsport, NY 14840) The closest thing you'll come to an Irish pub in town with a great variety of beer and local wines.

CULTURE

At the turn of the 20th century, Hammondsport was buzzing with activity around the work of aviation pioneer Glenn H. Curtiss. Recognized as the father of naval aviation, Curtiss co-created the first powered aircraft, trained the first American woman pilot, built the first transatlantic aircraft, and attained a number of world speed records. And that was just the beginning. People came from all over the world to the Curtiss Motor Company in Hammondsport, where engines and aircraft were being manufactured and developed, including the famous Jenny JN-4s World War I plane. The **Glenn Curtiss Museum** on Route 54 is filled with actual planes and memorabilia from the life and achievements of this innovative hometown hero.

In 1860 the **Pleasant Valley Wine Company**, producer of Great Western Champagne, was founded south of Hammondsport. A comprehensive visitors center tells the story of the winery and the growth of the industry in the area. Over the years more than a dozen wineries have been established around the lake. An important museum at **Bully Hill Vineyards** explores the growth of the wine industry.

Annual festivals here celebrate the grape harvest and Native American customs and history.

Bath

Bath Drive-In (607-776-3191; Lake Rd., Rte. 415S, Bath, NY 14810) One of the few drive-in movie theaters left in the country, this one is open seasonally.

Bath Veterans Administration Medical Center Historical Museum and National Cemetery (607-664-4772; Veterans Ave., Bath, NY 14810) Redbrick buildings and a large landscaped campus make the center seems more like a college than a medical center. Established in 1878, a museum on the grounds contains artifacts dating from the Civil War to the present. The cemetery holds the graves of five Medal of Honor recipients and 29 unknown soldiers from the War of 1812, along with thousands of other veterans. Open Apr.–Oct. Tues., Thurs., and Fri. 10–3.

Magee House (607-776-3582; W. Morris and Cameron Sts., Bath, NY 14810) This house contains early-American artifacts, such as an original mail carrier's bike. Mon.–Fri. 10–3. Sun. by appointment.

Hammondsport

Glenn H. Curtiss Museum (607-569-2160; www.linkny.com/CurtissMuseum; 8419 Rte. 54, Hammondsport, NY 14840) Inspired by Hammondsport's Glenn Curtiss, whose daring adventures with early motorcycles, dirigibles, and airplanes thrilled the country. His *June Bug* was the first aircraft to fly more than 1 kilometer, and he organized a Flying Circus, bringing colorful barnstormers to Hammondsport. The museum, housed in a huge warehouselike building, contains memorabilia from the early days of aviation. See *June Bug II*, a Curtiss "Jenny," a tractor biplane 1913 flying boat, vintage autos, motorcycles, bicycles, antique toys, and even winemaking memorabilia. More than 17 aircraft, early motorcycles, and even the first "mobile home" are here. In the workshop see how airplanes are constructed and restored. A new Children's Innovation Arcade offers interactive exhibits that demonstrate the physics of flight. Open May 1–Oct. 31 Mon.–Sat. 9–5, Sun. 11–5; Nov.–Apr. 30 Mon.–Sat. 10–4, Sun. noon–5; Jan.–Mar. Thurs–Sat. 10–4, Sun. noon–5.

Greyton H. Taylor Wine Museum (607-868-3610; www.bullyhill.com; 8843 Greyton H. Taylor Memorial Dr., Hammondsport, NY 14840; Bully Hill Vineyards, off Rte. 54A,) Impressive collection of 18th-century vineyard equipment, winemaking supplies, and brandy and cooper production in a rustic barnlike building. Also lots of memorabilia relating to the history of the area. This is the first wine museum in America. Open daily May–Nov.: Mon.–Sat. 9–5, Sun. noon–5.

Pleasant Valley Visitor Center and Great Western Winery (607-569-6111; 8260 Pleasant Valley Rd., Hammondsport, NY 14840; County Rte. 88) It's not just that this is the winery that started it all in 1860 and is the home of Great Western champagnes, but the fabulous stone buildings and Great Western Winery Visitor Center that makes this a must-see. The eight stone buildings are listed on the National Register of Historic Places, and the visitors center provides a comprehensive history of wine with exhibits, displays, and wine tastings. Don't miss the Wine Cask Theater. Open Jan.–May, Tues.–Sat. 10–4; Apr.–Dec. daily 10–5. (See the listing in Chapter Eight, *Wineries,* for more information.)

Penn Yan

Agricultural Memories Museum (315-536-1206; 1100 Townline Rd., Penn Yan, NY 14527) See John Deere tractors, horse-drawn carriages from the 1800s, engines, toys, and other farm-related items. Open June–Nov., Sun. 1–4 or by appointment.

The Birkett Mills (315-536-3311; 1 Main St., Penn Yan, NY 14527) This imposing yellow-brick building displaying a giant griddle is at the end of Main Street. Although it was constructed in 1824, the original mill operation dates back to 1796. The mill still grinds flour, including its highly prized buckwheat flour, and sells a variety of food products.

Garrett Memorial Chapel (end of Skyline Drive, Bluff Point, between Branchport and Penn Yan) A lovely Gothic stone Episcopal chapel built in memory of Charles William Garrett, the son of a wealthy wine merchant. William died at 26 of tuberculosis. Poems the young man had loved are represented on the stained-glass windows of the crypt. Known as the Chapel on the Mount, it is set in one of the most scenic areas of the Finger Lakes.

Norton Chapel (Keuka College, W. Lake Rd., Penn Yan, NY 14527) Catch the light streaming through the magnificent stained-glass windows designed by Gabriel Loire of Chartres Cathedral fame.

Oliver House Museum (315-536-7318; ycghs@linkny.com; 200 Main St., Penn Yan, NY 14527) The 19th-century brick home of the Oliver family is now filled with local history and genealogical information. Most of the rooms on the first floor are furnished with pieces from the Victorian period, including a large array of china. The second floor contains a good collection of historical materials from Yates County, often used for research by students and genealogists. Changing exhibits. Open all year Mon.–Fri. 9:30–4:30.

Photo Ops

Bluff Point (off Rte. 54A to Skyline Dr.; between Branchport and Penn Yan) At one end of an 11-mile bluff separating the two branches of Keuka Lake. Across the top of the bluff, Skyline Drive, a scenic road, takes you to the crook of the two prongs. The Wagener Mansion is at the top of the bluff; the Garrett Memorial Chapel is barely visible in the trees on the east side of the hill. From here you can look out to the east side of the lake to Marlena Point. Some say you can see several counties and a dozen lakes on a clear day.

Hammondsport's Village Square: With its Tudor-style gazebo, it's classic early Americana.

Old Railroad Station and Vintage Rail Car: On the waterfront (on Water Street) next to the public beach in Hammondsport.

RECREATION

Nature plays a big role in the recreational pursuits of those who come to Keuka Lake. Swimming, waterskiing, sailing, kayaking, canoeing, and fishing are all pursued on and in Keuka's clean, beautiful water. Sometimes the lake freezes over, and it becomes a giant ice-skating rink.

The gentle hills, good roads, and densely forested parklands that surround the lake provide wonderful opportunities for bikers, hikers, campers, and horseback riders. Golf courses, some winding through old vineyards, treat players to spectacular views of lake and hills.

BIKING

The bike trip around the outer perimeter of the lake is 46 miles. Grades are moderate, so it's a pretty easy ride.

Hammondsport-Area Winery Route: From the center of Hammondsport, it's about a 3-mile round-trip to the Great Western Winery and Pleasant Valley Visitor Center. In another direction from town, going up Middle Road to Bully Hill Winery, it's a 4.5-mile round-trip.

Bike Route 17: A stretch of a 435-mile route that goes from the Hudson River to Lake Erie. Travel through small villages along rural roads with paved shoulders. Signed with green ovals and "17."

Bluff Point: Skyline Drive, a 7.5-mile road that runs along the crest of the gently mounded peninsula between the two branches of Keuka Lake, is one way to reach the area at the fork known as Bluff Point—well worth a stop for the views and a visit to Garrett Chapel. You can also take West Bluff and East Bluff Drives to make a loop along the shorelines. A good place to push off on this 14.3-mile trip is Keuka College in Keuka Lake State Park. The trip can take all day if you visit vineyards along the way.

BOATING

CRUISES

Keuka Maid **Cruises** (607-569-2628, fax 607-962-9589; www.keukamaid.com; south end of lake off Rte. 54, Hammondsport; off-season: 94 Cedar St., Corning, NY 14830) Up to 450 people can be accommodated on lunch, dinner, and Sunday-brunch cruises aboard this 107-foot three-deck, air-conditioned, and heated boat. The *Keuka Maid*, the dream of area entrepreneur Stanley M. Clark, was built in Hammondsport using area labor. Live entertainment is featured on Saturdays for dinner and moonlight cruises. After the boat docks at 9pm, the music continues, and the bars remain open. Most Saturdays the boat goes out for a one-hour moonlight cruise around 11, free to those on board. The company offers two-hour lunch cruises, Sunday brunches, dinner cruises, and charters for parties and meetings. Runs May 1–Oct. 31.

Viking Spirit **Tour and Party Boat** (315-536-7061; viking@vikingresort.com; Rte. 54 just south of Penn Yan at the Viking Resort) Cruise Keuka Lake aboard a two-deck boat with climate-controlled lounge area with 4-foot windows and open decks. Daily cruises at 5pm and group charters. Bring your own picnic.

MARINAS AND LAUNCHES

Basin Park Marina (315-595-8808; 46 W. Lake Rd., Branchport, NY 14418) Boat rentals, dockage, pontoons, winter storage, and ski boat rentals. Also three-bedroom cottage rental.

East Bluff Harbor Marina (315-536-8236; www.keukaonline.com; 654 E. Bluff Dr., Penn Yan, NY 14527) A full-service marina with 20 slips, boat rentals, Four Winns sales, shop, and boats on consignment of all kinds.

Hammondsport Motel (607-569-2600) At the corner of Water and William Sts.

Harbor Club Boat Storage (315-595-6669; 42 W. Lake Rd., Branchport, NY 14418) This facility offers docking with 84 slips, repairs, and storage only: no gas sales.

H. L. Watersports in Harbor Lights Marina (607-868-4848; 797 W. Lake Rd., Hammondsport, NY 14840) A full-service marina affiliated with West Branch Marina, H. L. sells gas, bait, used boats, and kayaks; it also rents boats. Convenience store and boat launch as well as 30 slips.

Keuka Bay Marine Park (607-569-2777; www.keukaonline.com; 55 W. Lake Rd., Hammondsport, NY 14840) The same owners as East Bluff; this marina has more than 130 slips as well as gas sales, snack stand, and boat rentals.

Keuka Lake State Park (3370 Pepper Rd., Bluff Point, NY 14478) Boat-launch facilities.

Morgan Marine (315-536-8166; 100 E. Lake Rd, Penn Yan, NY 14527; Rte. 54) Motor-, paddle-, and sailboat rentals and sales; ski sales. Full-service repairs, dockage, storage.

North End Landings and Marina (315-595-2853; 3553 Rte. 54A, PO Box 322, Branchport, NY 14418) Full-service marina, boat rentals, moorings, clubhouse, bait and tackle shop, and year-round cottage rentals.

Penn Yan Boat Launch (315-536-3015; corner of Water and Keuka Sts., Penn Yan, NY 14527)

West Branch Marina (607-868-4677; 803 W. Lake Rd., Hammondsport, NY 14840) Primarily storage, service, and boat rentals.

FISHING

Seth Green, a world-class fisherman, proclaimed that Keuka Lake has the finest fishing grounds in the world. Although other Finger Lakes might make the same claim, there is no doubt that these waters are mighty good for catching rainbow trout, yellow perch, black bass, pickerel, and other lake fish.

GOLF

Bath Country Club (607-776-5043; May St., Bath, NY 14810) This 18-hole, 6,400- yard, par-72 course is hilly and scenic with water coming into play on six holes. Greens fees are $24, $37 with a cart. Restaurant is open to public.
Lakeside Country Club (315-536-6251; 200 E. Lake Rd./Rte. 54, Penn Yan, NY 14527) At the top of Keuka Lake in Penn Yan, the course runs right through a vineyard. Older push-up-style greens tend to fall toward the lake; greens rebuilt in 1995 are more level, some two-tiered. Fairways climb up and down the slopes, revealing wonderful views of the lake and Keuka College. The 16th par-five dogleg, which plays 416 yards into the wind, can be wicked. Once you make the bend you're in a gully and have to hit up to the green. Holes 11 and 14 follow rows of grapes; 15 is carved through them. On your way out, stop at the clubhouse, and pick up some homemade grape jam and preserves. Greens fees are $35 plus $10 for a cart. On the property are a driving range, pro shop, and restaurant.

HIKING

Outlet Trail: The Keuka Lake Outlet, a 6-mile ribbon of water connecting Keuka Lake with Seneca Lake, is now banked by a linear park, a pleasant place to hike and bike. The 7.5-mile trail takes you past mill ruins, through Lock 17 and remains of other locks, and by waterfalls and bridges. It runs from Penn Yan to Dresden, with entrance points at either end and along the way.
Urbana State Forest (607-776-2165) Between Prattsburg and Hammondsport west of the southern end of the lake, this trail gives you two ways to go: the long route (7.1 miles) and the shorter loop (4.8 miles). Both take you along dirt trails, up a hill to a plateau (where it's easier), through woods, and by Huckleberry Bog (no huckleberries but plenty of high- and low-bush blueberries). The well-marked trails go over streams and follow country lanes. From Route 17, go north on Route 53, then east on Bean Station Road. Look for FLT signs (Finger Lakes Trail) after you pass Colegrove Road.

PARKS, NATURE PRESERVES, CAMPING, GUIDE SERVICES & OUTFITTERS

Birdseye Hollow Park and State Forest (607-776-2165; Birdseye Hollow Rd., Bradford, NY 14815) Self-guided trails for viewing animals and birds in the forest. You can fish here from a 200-foot pier. Pavilion, picnic tables, grill.

Camp Good Days and Special Times Recreational Facility (315-595-2779; www.campgooddays.org; 58 W. Lake Rd., Branchport, NY 14418) A summer camp for children with cancer.

Eagle Eye Outfitters (315-536-9768; c/o Dale Lane, 1675 Oakleaf Lane, Penn Yan, NY 14527 Guides for deer hunts with shotgun and bow and arrow as well as turkey hunts, duck hunts, and fishing trips. Lodging, transportation, stands, ground blinds, and dressing of deer are included. All hunts include home-cooked meals, and meat processing is available.

Finger Lakes Guide Services (607-868-7800; 797 West Lake Rd, Hammondsport, NY 14840 (operating out of Harbour Lights Marina) Find out where the fish and game are located and how to get them with a guide with more than 30 years of experience. The company offers cabin rentals, adult fishing charters, children's charters, Keuka Lake boat tours, stream fishing, and guided hunts.

Flint Creek Campground (800-914-3550; 716-554-3567 season; 716-323-2406 winter; www.flintcreekcampground.com; 1455 Phelps Rd., Middlesex, NY 14507; on Rte. 364) Midway between Canandaigua and Penn Yan, this campground has 120 sites with fire rings and picnic tables. Playground, pool, mini golf, showers, laundry, electric, hook-ups, pavilion.

Hickory Hill Family Camping Resort (607-776-4345, 800-760-0947; www.hickory hillcampresort.com; 7531 Mitchellsville Rd., Bath, NY 14810) Several camping sites, two pools, playground, hiking trails, full hook-ups, miniature golf, rec room, hayrides, basketball court, plus cottage and cabin rentals.

Indian Pines Park (315-536-3015; Rte. 54A, Penn Yan, NY 14527) On the west side of Keuka Lake. Swimming, pavilion, picnic area with grills, playground, and volleyball.

Keuka Lake State Park (315-536-3666; 3370 Pepper Rd., Bluff Point, NY 14478) A 621-acre park with pavilion, boat launch, hiking trails, bathhouses, fishing, and 150 campsites for tents and trailers.

Outlet Trail Park (315-536-3111; Lake St., Penn Yan NY, 14527) Pavilion, picnic area with grills, playground, access to Keuka Outlet Trail.

Penn Yan Boat Launch (315-536-3015; Keuka and Water Sts., Penn Yan, NY 14527) Basketball court, tennis, and boat launch.

Red Jacket Park (315-536-3015; Lake St., Penn Yan NY, 14527) On the east shore of Keuka Lake's eastern branch. Pavilion for rent, swimming, picnic area with grills, playground.

Wagon Wheel Campground (607-522-3270; 10378 Presler Rd., Prattsburgh, NY 14873) Close to vineyards and Keuka Lake, with 95 sites. Pool, fishing ponds, recreation hall, entertainment, showers, laundry, LP gas. Exit 37N off Rte. 17; take Rte. 53 N., right on County Rd. 74.

Wigwam Keuka Lake Campground (315-536-6352; www.wigwamkeukalake campground.com; 3324 Esperanza Rd., Bluff Point, NY 14478; off Rte. 54A, then up James Rd.) If you're looking for great lake views, camp here. Sixty quiet, secluded sites, family-oriented, playground, fishing pond, pool, rental cabins, tents, and trailer and seasonal sites. Open mid-May–mid-Oct.

OTHER ATTRACTIONS

Keuka Karts Go-Kart Track (315-536-4833; kkarts@eznet.net; 98 W. Lake Rd., Penn Yan, NY 14527, on Rte. 54A) Good family fun. Take a spin on a go-cart. Single and double carts. Open Apr.–Oct. varying days and hours.

NY State Fish Hatchery (607-776-7087; 7169 Fish Hatchery Rd., Bath, NY 14810) See lake, brown, and rainbow trout in various stages of growth from eggs to full size. Open daily Mon.–Fri. 8–3:45.

SHOPPING

Penn Yan's shopping is mostly along Main Street, anchored by Birkett Mills. Hammondsport's stores are arranged around the village square and down a couple of side streets. Just outside town is Mehlenbacher's Taffy, an old-fashioned candy store with hand-pulled candy. For airplane models and other transportation-related items, try the gift shop at the Glenn Curtiss Museum. Many of the wineries have nice shops selling everything from corkscrews to books on wines.

Hammondsport

ANTIQUES

Antiques at the Warehouse (607-569-3655; 8091 County Rte. 88, Hammondsport, NY 14840) Open daily Apr.–Oct. 10–4; Nov.–Mar. by chance or appointment.

Opera House Antiques (607-569-3525; 61–63 Shethar St., Hammondsport, NY 14840) Showcases merchandise of several dealers selling furniture, silver, paintings, prints, glass, collectibles, and much more. Open Memorial Day–Dec. daily 10–5; Jan.–Memorial Day, Sat. and Sun. only.

Over the Bridge Antiques (607-569-2708; 54 Pulteney St., Hammondsport, NY 14840) Featuring enamel and graniteware, prints and paintings, Depression glass, toys, and more. Open May–Nov. daily 10–5; Jan–Apr. Sat. and Sun. only.

Note Those Mailbox Numbers

You can tell how far you are from major towns simply by looking at the numbers on the mailboxes. Mileage is measured from Penn Yan, Branchport, and Hammondsport. For example, the address 661 E. Lake Rd., Penn Yan (Finton's Landing), shows that you are 6.61 miles from the village of Penn Yan. Use this information to see how far you are from town.

Wild Goose Chase Antiques II (607-868-3946; 10060 County Rte. 76, Hammondsport, NY 14840) Housed in an old vineyard barn, with lots of goodies; open by chance or appointment Apr.–Nov.

ART GALLERIES

Keuka Moon Gallery (607-734-9780; Historic Train Depot, Hammondsport, NY 14840) Historic artwork and other art by William F. Hopkins.

CRAFTS AND GIFTS

Browsers (607-569-2497; 33 Shethar St., Hammondsport, NY 14840) A variety of items not unlike a small department store: clothing, gifts, wind chimes, flags, wooden bowls, glassware, and much more.
The Cinnamon Stick (607-569-2277; www.cinnamonstick.com; 26 Mechanic St., Hammondsport, NY 14840) An attractive shop with two levels of gifts such as dolls, candles, teddy bears, glassware, and a whole room filled with Christmas items, including limited edition pieces.
Lake Country Patchwork (607-569-3530; 67 Shethar St., Hammondsport, NY 14840) A good selection of everything a stitcher needs to make a quilt.

FOOD

Mehlenbacher's Taffy (607-569-3538; www.mehlenbacherstaffy.com; 8428 Rte. 54, Hammondsport, NY 14840) Twenty years ago the owners found an old hook hanging in their small building: It was a hook for pulling taffy. Today the company makes old-fashioned, hand-pulled taffy that is sold through local stores, mail-order (plus Internet or phone orders), and even Disney. It's really good and so, so fresh.

Penn Yan

The Quilt Room (315-536-5964; 1870 Hoyt Rd., Penn Yan, NY 14527; just off Rte. 14A) Mennonite handmade quilts, wall hangings, and craft items. Open May–Dec., Mon.–Sat.; Jan.–Apr., Thurs.–Sat.
Weaver-View Farms (315-781-2571; www.weaverviewfarms.com; 1190 Earls Hill Rd., Penn Yan, NY 14527; off Rte. 14 on the west side of Seneca Lake) A neat 14-room farmhouse on the top of a hill houses an Amish-Mennonite store crammed with exceptional handcrafted items and gifts. Owner Pauline Weaver said she started out with just one room; now the store sprawls through several rooms up- and downstairs. There are dozens of quilts designed and handmade by friends and family of the Amish-Mennonite community. Also find homespun aprons, table runners, pillows, furniture, art, wrought iron, pierced tin lampshades, toys, gingham dresses and bonnets,

kitchen decor, pottery, and beautiful one-of-a-kind handmade dolls and miniature toy carriages. Prices are very fair. The Weavers' black carriage is parked just outside next to the red barns. Horses and cows graze in the field nearby. Don't miss this one. Open year-round; closed Sun.

The Windmill Farm and Craft Market (315-536-3032; Rte. 14A, Penn Yan, NY 14527) It started with just a dozen people selling Amish and Mennonite quilts, food, crafts, and other items. It has been so successful, the Windmill is now regarded as a model for a running a successful co-operative. More than 250 vendors now sell crafts, farm produce, plants, antiques, quilts, cheeses, baked goods, and furniture. Open every Saturday late April–December plus Memorial Day Monday, July 4, and Labor Day Monday.

For More Information

Greater Bath Area Chamber of Commerce: 607-776-7122; www.bathnychamber .com; 10 Pulteney Square, West Bath, NY 14810.

Finger Lakes Tourism: 315-536-7488; www.fingerlakes.org; 309 Lake St., Penn Yan NY 14527.

Hammondsport Chamber of Commerce: 607-569-2989; www.hammondsport.org; 47 Sheather St., Hammondsport, NY 14840; open 11–3.

Steuben County Conference and Visitors Bureau: 607-974-2066, 800-284-3352; 866-WINEFUN (866-946-3386) or 607-936-6544; www.corningfingerlakes.com; One Baron Steuben Place, Second Floor, Corning, NY 14830.

Yates County Tourism: 800-868-9283; www.yatesny.com; 2375 Rte. 14A, Penn Yan, NY 14527.

CHAPTER SEVEN

Scenic Vistas and Small Town Charm

CANANDAIGUA LAKE

Canadice, Conesus, Hemlock, and Honeoye Lakes

Canandaigua Lake.

The western frontier of the region is home to 16-mile Canandaigua Lake, along with the smallest Finger Lakes: Canadice, Honeoye, Hemlock, and Conesus, ranging from 3 miles to 8 miles in length. The area is rich in natural beauty, with many undeveloped areas of woodlands and meadows. The largest town, Canandaigua, sits at the northern end of Canandaigua Lake; Naples at the southern end is considered the heart of the wine industry.

"People of the Great Hill," the Senecas, populated the western Finger Lakes long before Columbus found his way to the New World. One of the Seneca's largest communities was on a breezy hilltop site known as Ganondagan, now a

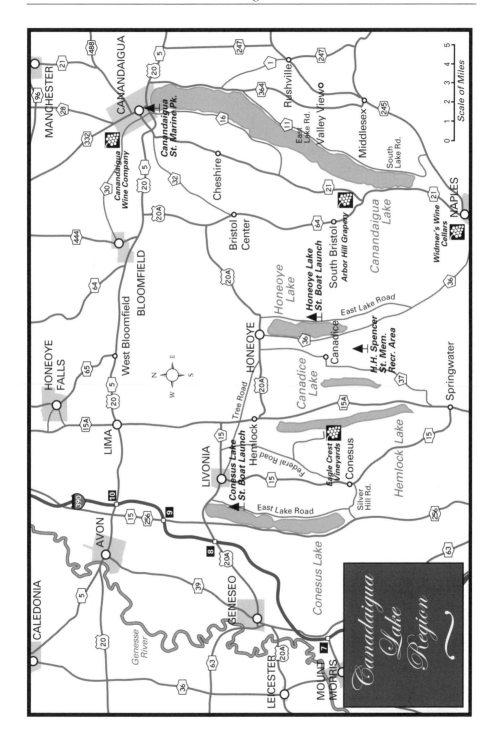

New York State Historic Site, in Victor. Here were more than 150 bark long-houses, 4 tall storehouses for corn, and an estimated population of 4,500. In the 17th century the people of this "Town of Peace" were at the center of a thriving beaver fur trade, a vital and profitable industry. The fur was sent to such places as Holland and France to use in making beaver hats, a hot fashion item of the times. To eliminate the Seneca's competition in the fur trade, in the 1660s the Marquis de Denonville and his French troops invaded Ganondagan and destroyed it.

One hundred years later, during the Revolutionary War, Native Americans and Loyalist rangers staged raids against the colonists until General John Sullivan, acting on orders from George Washington, retaliated and wiped out most of the other Seneca towns in the region.

At one time, this region belonged to Massachusetts; later New York State claimed sovereignty. Then Congressmen Oliver Phelps and Nathaniel Gorham put together a syndicate and negotiated to purchase the land, which they then marketed and sold to settlers. Phelps and Gorham could thus be called some of our country's earliest land developers. The settlers came and built, towns were established, and communities like Canandaigua and Clifton Springs grew.

CANANDAIGUA

Just a 10-minute drive from Exits 43 and 44 off the New York Thruway and within easy commuting distance of Rochester, the city of Canandaigua supports a substantial variety of residential services—yet with just 10,000 people, it maintains a small-town environment. The main part of town is just north of the lake.

The wide Main Street, divided by a landscaped grassy strip, is lined by stores, banks, restaurants, and service companies. Along with businesses that cater to local trade, there are an increasing number of art galleries and specialty shops, such as Nadal Glass and Renaissance Goody II Shoppe.

The revitalized waterfront park, the weathered old boathouses that stand side by side on wooden stilts in the water, and the postage-stamp-size Squaw Island—the smallest New York State Park and the place where Seneca women and children sought refuge from Sullivan's rampage—are major assets. The Granger Homestead and Sonnenberg Gardens are important historical museums; tree-lined streets like Gibson and Howell display many gracious turn-of-the-20th-century homes fronted by deep lawns.

Canandaigua's notable citizens include Mary Clark Thompson, who gave the town a children's playground, hospital, home for the elderly, a library, historical society, and land for a post office. Her husband built Sonnenberg Gardens. And many famous visitors have come to Canandaigua for one reason or another. In 1824 the Marquis de Lafayette visited the city. In 1872 Susan B. Anthony was found guilty of violating a federal statute by voting in Rochester and was fined $100 at a hearing in the Ontario County Courthouse. Helen Keller was a guest of Antoinette Granger, a member of a prominent local family; Stephen Douglas,

Lincoln's main rival, was educated at the Canandaigua Academy, and Humphrey Bogart spent summers on the lake.

Canandaigua residents and visitors alike enjoy the Finger Lakes Race Track, Captain Gray's Boat Tours, and the *Canandaigua Lady*; and performances in the Finger Lakes Performing Arts Center and band concerts in Atwater Park. Willow Pond Aqua Farm and Ganondagan, the site of the 17th-century Seneca village, are also important attractions.

New in town is the handsome Inn at Bristol Harbour, an Adirondacks-style lodge on the golf course; Roseland Water Park with its giant wave pool; and Steamboat Landing restaurant. To get around to all of Canandaigua's attractions without stress, take the free Spot-Hop bus service that runs July and August to all major sites of interest from Steamboat Landing to Kershaw Park Beach House (585-394-4400).

CANANDAIGUA LAKE

Cottages, camps, and homes ring Canandaigua Lake. *Canandaigua* is a Native American word meaning "the chosen spot," and the definition is most apt. It's a beautiful drive all the way around, especially on West Lake Road (County Road 16) and East Lake Road, which generally go along the shoreline. Route 21, the middle road, called the "High Road to Naples" by the locals, is a quicker way to get from one end to another. It runs along the top of the hills on the west side, revealing some lovely scenic vistas. The farther south you go, the better the views.

Between the northern end of the lake, anchored by the town of Canandaigua, and the southern end, inhabited by Naples, you pass through small villages, some merely a gas station, a few houses, and a general store or two. Cheshire is worth noting for its wonderful Company Store and, above it, an antique and gift shop housed in a former schoolhouse. The newly formed Canandaigua Wine Trail promotes vineyards and allied businesses around the lake.

NAPLES

When you notice the purple fire hydrants, you're reminded that in Naples, grapes are big. Most of the year it's business as usual for this quiet place at the southern end of the lake, nestled in a valley of the Bristol Hills. But come September some 75,000 people pour into town for the annual Grape Festival. The main street is lined with booths of more than 250 artists and food vendors; jazz, country, blues, and other musical groups entertain; and, of course, everyone enjoys "The World's Greatest Grape Pie Contest."

Naples stands on the site of the original Seneca village of Nundawao and is the burial place of Conesque, the chief of the Senecas, who died in 1794. A plaque notes that it is here that Washington first took command of the American army on July 3, 1775.

Original landmarks include the Ephraim Cleveland House (1794) and Memorial Town Hall. There is also the Cumming Nature Center, Bristol Valley Theatre, and several area vineyards, including Widmers.

Naples has a new golf course, Reservoir Creek Golf Club; the second largest wine company in the United States, the Canandaigua Wine Company (which includes Widmers); and at Sutton Company, you can buy fishing lures and gear and even learn to make your own flies.

The town's eclectic nature also appeals to artists who come here to live and work.

MIDDLESEX

On the east side of Canandaigua Lake, where Routes 364, 245, and 247 meet, you'll find Middlesex, the birthplace of the Seneca Nation. This is celebrated the Saturday before Labor Day, when Seneca Heritage Day is held at Overackers Corners Schoolhouse, culminating with a thanksgiving and bonfire on Bare Hill. This kicks off the spectacular Festival of Lights on the lake, beginning around dusk as flares are lit around the shoreline.

CANADICE, CONESUS, HEMLOCK, AND HONEOYE LAKES

There is little or no commercial development on lakes Canadice and Hemlock, which serve as water reservoirs for Rochester. Only nonmotorized craft are allowed on these lakes, making these attractive waters to those who want to paddle their canoes and not fight the wakes of powerboats.

On Honeoye Lake, the size of the motors is restricted, and this Finger Lake is small enough—5 miles long, compared to Seneca's 35-mile length—that you can hike around it in a day. Heading south on West Lake Road, you pass the Savoy Sandy Bottom Nature Trail, a few camps, and some lovely shoreline scenery. Nearing the south end of the lake, the terrain gets dramatically hillier. As you round the southern part of the lake, a dirt road to the left will take you to the paved road that runs along the east side of the lake. This is a good stretch of road, but there's not much going on except an occasional house here and there and a marina—which makes it a fantastic place to bike. At the north end of the lake is the one-light village of Honeoye.

There are some cottages on Honeoye as well as on Conesus, but certainly not the density you find on Canandaigua. These smaller lakes attract those who have the attitude, "I'm on vacation; leave me alone."

HONEOYE

About 17 miles west of Canandaigua Lake, the town of Honeoye, set on its tree-fringed namesake lake, has more than 150 historic homes and buildings, one grocery store, and one rental house. It's close to Bristol Mountain Ski Center and Harriet Hollister Spencer Park.

Folks in this pleasant residential town go about their business in a friendly yet unobtrusive manner. When their Richmond Memorial bandstand gazebo in front of the town hall was destroyed last year by arson, donations to rebuild the structure poured in totaling $18,000—without a fundraising committee. The new gazebo, which is larger and has a Memorial Wall made out of granite and brick, is where a community band gives concerts on a regular basis. A new museum has opened on Main Street, a one-room schoolhouse that contains exhibits about the area's agricultural history.

CLIFTON SPRINGS

Clifton Springs, north of Canandaigua, developed as wealthy people came here to take in the natural sulphur springs that were believed to have curative powers. The spa building built at the turn of the 20th century, site of Dr. Henry Foster's Clifton Springs Water Cure, is still an impressive landmark on Main Street as is Dr. Foster's gingerbread cottage, now home of the town's mayor. (The Foster Block has been renovated and contains a number of retail establishments, many still sporting their original tin ceilings.) The Peirce Pavilion houses a sulphur spring and is surrounded by ball fields and picnic areas; a sulphur spring runs through 15-acre Village Park. The history of the Sulphur Cure and the town is told in the Foster Cottage Museum on Main Street.

Festival of Lights

In the days of the Senecas, the start of the annual harvest was signaled by a huge council fire on top of Bare Hill on Canandaigua Lake. Smaller fires blazed along the shores. To commemorate this tradition, on the Saturday of Labor Day weekend, residents around the lake light flares at dusk.

CONESUS LAKE

Quiet and pretty Conesus Lake, the most western of the Finger Lakes, is ringed by private homes and many camps, along with a few bed & breakfasts and a strip of fast-food places at the northern end. Route 256 along the western side of the lake runs less than 20 feet from the water's edge in some places. The hills at the northern end are low and gentle; at the southern end, they're higher.

LODGING

Canandaigua offers the most places to stay by far. There are large hotels such as the Inn on the Lake, chain hotels such as the EconoLodge, and many B&Bs. Naples is short on lodging, but the Naples Hotel recently opened with six guest rooms, and its restaurant continues to draw a local crowd: Lakeside condominiums and the new Bristol Harbour Inn (part of the Bristol Harbour Resort golf complex), as well as several new B&Bs, are welcome additions to the lodging scene.

LODGING RATES

$: Up to $75 per couple $$$: $151–$250 per couple
$$: $76–$150 per couple $$$$: More than $250 per couple

Canandaigua

HOTELS AND MOTELS

Bristol Harbour Resort's new inn offers balconies looking out onto Canandaigua Lake.

BRISTOL HARBOUR RESORT
Manager: Dale Styoker.

This lakeside resort community with a lovely rolling Robert Trent Jones golf course occupies 454 acres along the lake. A new Adirondacks-style

585-396-2200, 800-288-8248; fax 585-394-9254.
www.bristolharbour.com.
5410 Seneca Point Rd., Canandaigua, NY 14424.
Rooms: 31 rooms in the inn, 240 condominiums (35 in rental pool).
Open: Year-round.
Price: $$–$$$$.
Credit Cards: Most major.

inn has 31 rooms with views of the lake, fireplaces, heated tile floors in bathrooms, and all modern amenities. The resort also rents tastefully furnished midrise condominiums, town homes, and patio homes that hang close to the water's edge, the roadway cut into the shale banks. Most have balconies looking out to the lake. Other homes are along the golf course fairways. There is a marina, private beach, pool, spa, restaurant, tennis courts, boat slips, and ball course. Cross-country skiing is on site and downhill skiing is just 7 miles away. Golf and stay packages are available.

ECONOLODGE
Manager: Cindy Gardner.
585-394-9000, 800-797-1222.
www.hudsonhotels.com.
170 Eastern Blvd., Canandaigua, NY 14424.
On Rte. 5 & 20.
Rooms: 65.
Open: Year-round.
Price: $–$$.
Credit Cards: Most major.

A clean, efficient small chain hotel along a commercial strip, where you can find all the major fast-food places, including Burger King, McDonalds, and Arby's. Continental breakfast is included in the rates.

CANANDAIGUA INN ON THE LAKE
Manager: Barbara Natale.
585-394-7800, 800-228-2801.
www.hudsonhotels.com.
770 S. Main St., Canandaigua, NY 14424.
Rooms: 134.
Open: Year-round.
Price: $$–$$$$.
Credit Cards: Most major.

A modern resort and conference center on the shores of Canandaigua Lake. You can pull up by boat, tie up at the new docks just outside, and come in for the night or for lunch or dinner. Many rooms as well as the large dining room overlook the water. Facilities include Jacuzzis, indoor and outdoor pools with spa, fitness center, restaurant, wine bar, and meeting and conference rooms. A nice deck waterside offers dining or cocktails. Ask for the lake view rooms.

KELLOGG'S PAN-TREE INN
Innkeepers: Nancy and John Kellogg.
585-394-3909.
www.stegalls.com/kelloggs.
130 Lakeshore Dr., Canandaigua, NY 14424.
Rooms: 15.
Open: End April–Oct.
Price: $.
Credit Cards: Most major.

Fifteen motel rooms are just behind the restaurant and within walking distance to the lakefront. Rooms are on the small side, clean and basic but no phones, and very reasonably priced. (See the listing under "Restaurants" for more information.)

BED & BREAKFASTS AND INNS

1795 ACORN INN B&B
Innkeepers: Joan and Louis
  Clark.
585-229-2834;
  fax 585-229-5046.
http://acorninnbb.com.
4508 St. Rd. 64 S., Bristol
  Center, Canandaigua, NY
  14424.
Rooms: 4 with baths.
Open: Year-round.
Price: $$–$$$.
Credit Cards: Most major.

One of the most romantic B&Bs I have come across. Walled gardens, private brick patios, outdoor Jacuzzi, a hammock tucked into a hidden corner, and stone walls provide an intimate setting for this stagecoach inn built in 1795 by Ephraim Wilder. Tastefully furnished with a mix of antiques and period reproductions, rooms are filled with interesting collections and accessories without the clutter. Oriental rugs, original paintings, shelves of books, a fireplace, and floor-to-ceiling windows make the living room a most comfortable place to linger. All guest rooms have private baths, queen-sized beds, luxury bedding, sitting area, central air-conditioning, bathrobes, slippers, reading lights, a selection of books, television/VCR, radio/CD player, clock, beverage cabinets, and duvets and electric blankets in the winter. The Hotchkiss Room, perfect for honeymooners, has its own fireplace, canopy bed, French doors leading to a private garden terrace, whirlpool tub, and sitting area. The largest room, the Bristol, also has a fireplace, canopy bed, chaise longue, and huge shower as well as a window seat overlooking the flowers and lawns. In the Wilder Room the bathroom is large enough for a wicker lounge chair. A large candlelit country breakfast is served on antique English china. The Clarks have thought of everything, even complimentary beverages and snacks. Although the entire inn has been soundproofed, this is not a place for young children or smokers. It's the closest B&B to Bristol Mountain.

**BED & BREAKFAST at
  OLIVER PHELPS**
585-396-1650.
www.oliverphelps.com.
252 N. Main St.,
  Canandaigua, NY 14424.
Innkeeper: John and Joanne
  Button.
Rooms: 4 with private baths.
Open: Year-round.
Price: $$.
Credit Cards: Most major.

On Main Street, across from the Granger Homestead, this historic inn is a perfect location if you want to be in the heart of town. New owners John and Joanne Button have refreshed the guest rooms with new decor. Because it has a large open common room, it is often used for large parties. Breakfasts are sumptuous.

CHAMBERY COTTAGE
Innkeepers: Terence and
  Zora Molkenthin.
585-393-1505.
www.chamberycottage.com.
6104 Monks Rd.,
  Canandaigua, NY 14424.

You have room to stretch out on this beautiful 30-acre property in the Bristol Hills, where you can explore pine forests and open meadowland. Relax and take in the scenery on the back patio, picnic in the meadow, hike down a path to a gorge, and sit by

Rooms: 4 with private baths.
Open: Year-round.
Price: $$–$$$.
Credit Cards: Most major.

a clear stream rambling through a grove of hemlock trees . . . we're talking *unwinding*. At the end of the day you can look forward to retiring to one of Chambery's well appointed rooms. The Chambery Suite has a private covered porch, king-sized bed, and a fireplace; the Viennese Retreat has a king-sized canopy bed and fireplace; the Bohemian Rhapsody also has a king bed and a sunken whirlpool tub; and the Provence, decorated in elegant toile, has a queen bed and a shower big enough for two—and wait until you see the views. All rooms come with TV/VCRs and CD players. There is a guest fridge in the drawing room.

HABERSHAM COUNTRY INN

Innkeepers: Raymond and Sharon Lesio.
585-394-1510, 800-240-0644.
www.HabershamInn.com.
6124 Rtes. 5 & 20, Canandaigua., NY 14424.
Rooms: 5, some private, some shared baths.
Open: Year-round.
Price: $$.
Credit Cards: Most major.

You'll get a warm welcome from Sharon and Raymond, who obviously love helping their guests feel at home. Set on 11 acres with a pond and gardens, this restored 1840 Federal-style home is simply but tastefully furnished with a mix of reproductions and antiques. The suite has a canopy bed, fireplace, and Jacuzzi and country-style furnishings. Rooms are air-conditioned, and a gourmet breakfast is served. A porch and deck provide a good place to cool off on a hot summer's day; the tavern and dining room evokes Williamsburg.

MORGAN SAMUELS INN

Innkeepers: John and Julie Sullivan.
585-394-9232.
www.morgansamuelsinn.com.
2920 Smith Rd., Canandaigua, NY 14424.
Rooms: 6 with private baths, including 1 suite.
Open: Year-round.
Price: $$–$$$.
Credit Cards: Most major.

You approach this beautifully maintained 1810 stone mansion by two 2,000-foot tree-lined drives. Once home to Judson Morgan of the Morgan Department Stores of Canada, and also Howard Samuels, an industrialist (he invented the plastic bag), the property features exquisite gardens with roses, other perennials, and fountains: Three gardeners work full time just to maintain them. Furnishings in the house include museum-quality antiques, carpets, and oil paintings; 11 fireplaces are throughout. Guests have a choice of several common rooms, including a parlor and a glassed-in Victorian porch overlooking the gardens. Comfortable and elegant, the extremely well appointed guest rooms all have fireplaces and antiques. The suite contains French inlaid wood pieces from the 1800s; another room has hand-painted furniture. Some rooms have Jacuzzis, three have balconies. There is a tennis court. Full breakfasts are served, and the food comes highly recommended. Arrangements can be made for a five-course gourmet dinner for eight or more people. The inn is about 2 miles outside of town.

**1885 SUTHERLAND
    HOUSE B&B**
Innkeepers: Bonnie and
    Gary Ross.
585-396-0375, 800-396-0375.
www.sutherlandhouse.com.
3179 State Rte. 21S,
    Canandaigua, NY 14424.
Rooms: 5 with private baths.
Open: Year-round.
Price: $$–$$$.
Credit Cards: Most major.

This gracious Victorian home just a mile and a half from Main Street features five rooms with private baths, television/VCR, and CD players; three rooms have king-sized beds. The Parkerhouse Suite has a two-person whirlpool, rice-carved four-poster king bed, its own sitting room, and fireplace. The Rose Fever room has a super-sized bath with large shower, expansive windows, queen brass bed, and is decorated in romantic pinks and roses. Furnishings are in keeping with the period of the house, with lots of interesting memorabilia, paintings, and stenciling. The back garden features a lovely Victorian trellis. Try to be there when they serve afternoon refreshments: You'll love the homemade cookies.

**THENDARA INN AND
    RESTAURANT**
Innkeeper: Laurie Leonard.
585-394-4868.
www.thendarainn.com.
4356 E. Lake Rd.,
    Canandaigua, NY 14424.
Rooms: 4 with private baths.
Price: $$–$$$
Credit Cards: Most major.

In this wonderful setting on the east side of Canandaigua Lake, you can enjoy a meal by the water either in the casual boathouse restaurant or in the more formal dining room in the house. Then you can settle in for the night in one of the comfortable rooms in this turn-of-the-century restored Victorian "cottage." The place has a decidedly homey, country feeling. Guest rooms are air-conditioned and have phones. If you want to arrive by boat, go for it. The main-house restaurant is open year-round; the Boathouse is open seasonally. (For more information on dining here, see the entry in the "Restaurant" section.)

VILLA BIANCA
Innkeeper: Lisa Herrick.
800-724-6379; 585-396-1947.
www.villablancabandb.com.
4272 County Rd. 18,
    Canandaigua., NY 14424.
Rooms: 3 with private baths.
Open: Year-round.
Price: $–$$.
Credit Cards: Most major.

Set on 133 acres, this 110-year-old Greek-Revival country home features spacious rooms, full country breakfasts, and lovely lawns and gardens. One of the rooms is air-conditioned; others have fans and atrium doors opening onto a second-story veranda. Rooms are furnished with queen, twin, or king beds, comforters, and televisions. There is a guest kitchen, sitting room, and above-ground pool. Villa Bianca is just five minutes from downtown Canandaigua.

Naples

**INN AT RESERVOIR
    CREEK**
Innkeeper: Tim Trojian.
585-374-6828.

New in 2002, the inn is a good accompaniment to the Reservoir Creek Golf Course. The rooms are located in a 100 year-old farmhouse and are

www.rcgolf.com/inn.
8613 Cohocton St., Rte. 21,
   Naples, NY 14512.
Rooms: 6 with private baths.
Open: Seasonally.
Price: $.
Credit Cards: Most major.

pleasantly furnished with period reproductions, quilts and homey accessories. The rooms have cable TV and a hearty continental breakfast is served, which includes homemade muffins, jams, and jellies. The Creek Café is located on the property, and generous golf-and-stay packages are available.

MAXFIELD INN
Innkeeper: Russ Cochran.
585-374-2510.
105 N. Main St., Naples, NY
   14512.
Rooms: 7 with private baths.
Open: Year-round.
Price: $$.
Credit Cards: Visa, MC.

Right on Main Street and one of the few good places to stay in town, this B&B occupies a large Greek-Revival estate house, circa 1841. The home comes with a lot of history: It was once a stop on the Underground Railroad.

MONIER MANOR
Innkeepers: Mary and
   Chuck Hewitt.
585-374-6719.
154 North Main St., Naples,
   NY 14512.
Rooms: 4 with private baths.
Open: Year-round.
Price: $$.
Credit Cards: Most major.

This 1850 Italianate Victorian home is located on 2 lovely acres. There is a deck with a hot tub, and the oversized guest rooms—all with queen-sized four-poster beds—are furnished in period decor with antiques and reproductions. A full breakfast, as well as afternoon tea, is included.

THE VAGABOND INN
Innkeeper: Celeste
   Stanhope-Wiley.
585-554-6271.
www.thevagabondinn.com.
3300 Slitor Rd., Naples, NY
   14512.
Rooms: 5 with private baths.
Open: Year-round.
Price: $–$$.
Credit Cards: Visa, MC.

Those looking for quiet seclusion will find it at the Vagabond. This 7,000-foot rustic inn on a mountain features an enormous 1,800-square-foot great room, made mostly of local woods. The fireplace is constructed of native stone and black walnut. The formal dining room looks out to the Bristol Mountains, with a drop of 1,000 feet to the valley: a four-season masterpiece. The Lodge Suite features a massive river-stone fireplace and a king-sized bed, along with a TV/VCR. A dining area, hot tub, and bar complete the space. The Bristol Suite has two decks and a private porch as well as a king-sized canopy bed, two armoires, sitting areas, fireplace, TV/VCR. The bathroom has a two-person Jacuzzi and 14-foot vanity with two sinks. The Kimberly is large and airy with wraparound windows. The Shannon, a large room with a queen-sized bed, has a sitting area in front of a large glass door opening onto a patio with a mountain view. The Mahogany has a tall carved mahogany double bed and TV/VCR. A full breakfast is served, and a kitchen is available for guests to use. There's an in-ground pool, too.

Honeoye, Hemlock, Canadice, and Conesus

**EASTLAKE BED &
  BREAKFAST**
Innkeepers: Dennis and
  Charlotte Witte.
585-346-3350, 866-222-1544.
www.eastlakeBB.com.
5305 E. Lake Rd., Conesus,
  NY 14435.
Rooms: 4 with private baths.
Open: Year-round.
Price: $$.
Credit Cards: Most major.

When the Wittes set out to build their new home, they designed it to be one of the best bed & breakfasts in the area. Their "prairie cottage," as they call it, is set on a hill with views of the lake from the large windows and the wraparound porch. Each guest room is very spacious and extremely well decorated, some with Laura Ashley fabrics. Rooms come with central air-conditioning and television/VCR. The white-carpeted Romance Suite has a canopy queen bed, a sitting area with a see-through fireplace, a fireside whirlpool bath for two, and a large private deck. The Garden Room has a canopy queen bed; French doors lead out onto a private deck with lake views. The Garrett, another roomy suite, is furnished with antique family treasures and has a king canopy bed, a double bed, and a full bath with double sinks. The Study is on the main floor and features French doors opening onto the porch. Enjoy the 430-foot waterfront, with a pedal boat and picnic facilities. Rates include a full breakfast, complimentary refreshments, and an evening dessert tray.

**GREENWOODS BED &
  BREAKFAST INN**
Innkeepers: Mike and Lisa
  Ligon.
585-229-2111, 800-914-3559.
www.greenwoodsinn.com.
8136 Quayle Rd., Honeoye,
  NY 14471.
Rooms: 5 with private baths.
Open: Year-round.
Price: $$.
Credit Cards: Most major.

You drive just off Route 5 & 20 to reach this spacious two-story log inn, which has the ambiance of an Adirondack great camp with all the comforts of a fine country house. It's a quiet, peaceful place on three acres on the top of a hill with plenty of trails to explore and three ponds just outside. Public and guest rooms are large and well appointed. The Timberlake Suite has a canopy bed, fireplace, and outside entrance leading onto a wide deck overlooking gardens and a fish pond. Great views on the top floor are a highlight of the Comstock Room, decorated in Bob Timberlake wall coverings in black-and-white checks and scenic calligraphy wall borders. Rooms on the back have views of the hills; those on the front get a peek out over the hills to the lake. All rooms are air-conditioned and come with queen-sized feather beds and television/VCR. Public rooms include a well-stocked library, game room, and media room with a 40-inch television. There is an outdoor spa, deck, and trails cut into the hills behind the house. A full breakfast is served in the dining room. This one is a winner.

Vacation Rentals and Services

Rental Plus (315-536-3032, 888-414-5253; fax 315-595-2825; www.rentalplus.com; 22 Lakeshore Dr., Canandaigua, NY 14424) President/manager Brian Zerges has more than 100 house, condo, cottage, and luxury home rentals in and around Keuka, Seneca, and Canandaigua Lakes. Rent weekly, monthly, seasonally or for a few days. Off-season discounts and vacation packages available. Visa, MC.

RESTAURANTS

Most of the restaurants are in the Canandaigua area, some near the lake. Teens love places like Koozinas, where they chow down on pizza and pasta; the older set prefers such places as the more formal Inn on the Lake and the casual Kellogg's Pan-Tree Inn, a town institution. Popular Thendara on the Lake and Lincoln Hill Inn are in historic houses in beautiful country settings. New on the scene is the nautically themed Steamboat Landing. There is Harlee's Grill on Honeoye but few other restaurants on that or the other three smaller lakes.

Prices are estimated per person for appetizer and dinner entrée without tax, tip, or alcoholic beverages.

$: Up to $10
$$: $11–$25
$$$: $26–$40
$$$$: More than $40

Canandaigua

CASA DE PASTA
585-394-3710.
125 Bemis St., Canandaigua, NY 14424.
Open: Year-round
  Sun.–Thurs. 5–9, Fri. and Sat. 5–10.
Price: $$.
Cuisine: Italian American.
Serving: D.
Credit Cards: Most major.

One of those places the locals know about, with just a few tables, a bar, and little fuss in decor. Favorite dishes include veal parmigiana, spaghetti, and other Italian specialties. If you like Northern Italian food, you'll be pleased with the menu, which features white sauces along with the usual tomato-based fare. Produce is obtained from local farmers whenever possible. The bar area fills up fast but is not for kids.

ELIZABETH'S
585-394-8060.
76 S. Main St., Canandaigua,
  NY 14424.
Open: Mon.–Sat. 7–3; Sun.
  8–12 breakfast only.
Price: $.
Cuisine: American bistro.
Serving: B, L.
Credit Cards: Cash only.

In a historic building next to the bank in the business area, this place is a bit different—the menu includes trendy items like wraps and specialty coffees. Though the menu is new, the ambiance is old, with tin ceilings and an old-style ice-cream and soda shop. It's fun and a very good deal all around.

**KELLOGG'S PAN-TREE
  INN**
585-394-3909.
130 Lakeshore Dr.,
  Canandaigua, NY 14424.
Open: Daily
  7:30am–7:30pm.
Price: $–$$.
Cuisine: American.
Serving: B, L, D.
Credit Cards: Visa, MC.

It's been around since 1924, right across the street from the newly renovated Kershaw Park on the lake. Eat on the open deck or in the main dining room with windows overlooking the lake. Each day offers a new special. People will drive from Rochester just to have the creamed codfish on Wednesdays or the beef stew on Thursday. Pancakes are served all day. Rolls, breads, and cookies are homemade. The cinnamon buns are yummy. Some of the featured entrées include chicken pie, ham steak, French fried shrimp, and chicken Parmesan, along with a large selection of homemade soups, salads, and hamburgers. You get can get beer and wine here, but they don't go out of their way to promote it. Diners tend to be more on the seasoned side. There are a few motel-style rooms behind the restaurant (see the section on "Lodging" above).

KOOZINA'S
585-396-0360.
699 S. Main St.,
  Canandaigua, NY 14424.
Open: Daily.
Price: $–$$.
Cuisine: Italian.
Serving: L, D.
Credit Cards: Most major.

Contemporary and fun. Try their great nachos, wood-fired pizza, and pasta specials such as fettuccine with broccoli. In addition to the dining area, there is a full-service bar and takeout is available. The wild colors and noise level say "yes" to young adults, who love it.

LINCOLN HILL INN
585-394-8254;
  fax 585-394-2244.
www.lincolnhill.com.
3365 E. Lake Rd.,
  Canandaigua, NY 14424.
Open: Daily in-season; call
  for other times.
Price: $$–$$$.
Cuisine: American.
Serving: D.
Credit Cards: Most major.

Bill and Cheryl Ward welcome their guests to this casual, friendly 1804 farmhouse. In the warmer weather, dine on the covered decks and porches. A new garden patio is perched above the old-fashioned gardens and lawns. Inside, the rooms are wonderfully inviting—there's even a little room set up with a table just for two. The menu features tempting items such as mandarin orange and walnut salad, shrimp martini, escargot cornucopia, sesame-crusted salmon filet, pan-roasted sea bass,

---

Grape Pie

The area around Naples is famous for grape pie. It tastes and looks much like blueberry pie, but it definitely tastes like, well, grapes. Grape pies can be purchased from local bakeries and at the Grapery. In the past, this delicious treat was available only at grape harvest time. Now the pulp is frozen for use throughout the year.
Want to make your own? Here's a recipe, courtesy Ontario County Tourism.

Pastry for two-crust, 9-inch pie (your own recipe or ready-made)
4 cups Concord grapes
3/4 cup sugar
2 tablespoons quick-cooking tapioca
1-1/2 tablespoons lemon juice
1/2 tablespoon grated lemon rind

Prepare the pastry for the pie.
Stem and wash grapes. Squeeze grapes between thumb and forefinger, popping pulp and skins into separate bowls. Cook pulp in covered pan, stirring occasionally until seeds are loosened. Press through a sieve to remove seeds. Pour hot pulp over skins, and let set until cool. Mix cooled mixture with sugar, tapioca, and lemon juice and rind. Line pie plate with pastry. Fill with grape mixture. Cover with top crust (or lattice). Bake at 450 degrees for 20 minutes. Reduce to 350 degrees for 20 minutes longer. Add ice cream and enjoy.

---

lake trout, and herb-crusted New Zealand lamb chops. The Wards use herbs and edible flowers from their gardens in the preparation and presentation of their meals. From here you can walk to the Finger Lakes Performing Arts Center. The 4-acre site is ideal for a tented garden wedding.

THE LODGE AT BRISTOL HARBOUR RESORT
800-288-8248.
www.bristolharbour.com.
5410 Seneca Point Rd.,
   Canandaigua, NY 14424.
Open: Daily.
Price: $–$$.
Cuisine: American.
Serving: B (in-season), L, D.
Credit Cards: Most major.

There's hardly a better place to appreciate the beauty of the lake than from a perch on Bristol Harbour's terrace high above the water, with the rolling golf course and vineyards all around. Although the food quality and service has not yet quite caught up to the quality of the scenery, this is by far one of the nicest places to wine and dine in the area. And latest reports are that things are getting better, thanks to an enthusiastic young staff. Inside the lofty dining room and bar, both made of heavy timbers and other wood, the views through the large windows are almost as good as those from the terrace. Chairs fit the rustic theme: They're made of bent twigs and branches.

**MACGREGOR'S GRILL &
  TAP ROOM**
585-394-8080.
759 S. Main St.,
  Canandaigua, NY 14424.
Open: Daily 11am–1am.
Price: $.
Cuisine: Pub food.
Serving: L, D.
Credit Cards: Most major.

Facing the waterfront and looking very colonial in its white-frame building and red, white, and blue bunting, this old landmark restaurant offers sports, pub food, wine, and beer. This is a good place to get a brew and simple meal like finger foods, burgers, and sandwiches. Popular with the younger set.

**NICOLE'S AT THE INN
  ON THE LAKE**
585-394-7800, 800-228-2801.
770 S. Main St.,
  Canandaigua, NY 14424.
Open: Daily.
Price: $–$$$.
Cuisine: New American.
Serving: B, L, D.
Credit Cards: Most major.

The views are great, either unobstructed from the patio or through the huge windows that overlook Canandaigua Lake. Several of the dishes have a Mediterranean flair, such as the ahi tuna; Thai grilled chicken breast stuffed with cilantro and mascarpone cheese, drizzled with mango coulis, and served with couscous; or their mint-pesto-rubbed lamb chop. I also like the bruschetta with roasted peppers and roma tomatoes. Service is excellent, and table setting is on the elegant side, with linens, candles, crystal, and charger plates. Entertainment is provided weekends. There is a wine bar.

**SCHOONER'S
  RESTAURANT**
585-396-3360.
407 Lake Shore Dr.,
  Canandaigua, NY 14424.
Open: Mon.–Thurs. 11–9; Fri.
  and Sat. 11–10; closed Sun.
Price: $–$$.
Cuisine: American.
Serving: L, D.
Credit Cards: Most major

Family owned and run by the Hollys, this is a good down-home restaurant, offering generous portions of pasta, steak, soups, salads, and seafood in a yachtlike setting. Wednesday is chicken 'n' biscuit night; Friday is fish and chips. A favorite with the older crowd.

STEAMBOAT LANDING
585-394-5365,
  866-9-ANCHOR.
www.steamboatlanding
  online.com.
205 Lakeshore Dr.,
  Canandaigua, NY 14424.
Open: L Mon.–Sat. 11:30–3,
  Sun. 11:30–4;
  D Mon.–Thurs. 5–9,
  Fri.–Sat. 5–10, Sun. 4–9.
Price: $$.
Cuisine: American.
Serving: L, D.
Credit Cards: Most major.

On the waterfront near the Canandaigua Lady pier, this new restaurant on the northern end of Canandaigua Lake has been designed in the style of the steamboat era and has outdoor dining on lakeside decks.

THENDARA INN RESTAURANT & BOATHOUSE RESTAURANT
585-394-4868.
www.thendarainn.com.
4356 E. Lake Rd,
Canandaigua, NY 14424.
Open: Thendara, in the inn, dinner year-round; Boathouse, seasonally.
Price: $$–$$$.
Cuisine: American.
Serving: L, D (Boathouse only); D (Boathouse and Thendara dining room).
Credit Cards: Most major.

There are two restaurants on this site: Thendara, in a 1903 Victorian house that is perched on a hill over looking the lake, and the Boathouse, which sits over the water. Once the Canandaigua Yacht Club, this is one of the only places on the lake where you can arrive by boat and then eat either casually in the converted boathouse inside or on the deck, or more elegantly in the main dining room, where you can enjoy views of the water from the large dining room windows. The menu includes grilled salmon, beef filet, pasta and other American-style specialties and changes with the seasons. Thendara Inn also offers overnight accommodations (see "Lodging" section).

CASUAL FOOD

Catskill Bagel and Deli (585-394-5830; 103 S. Main St., Canandaigua, NY 14424) Generous-sized sandwiches, fresh warm bagels with flavored cream cheese, and freshly ground gourmet coffees. For lunch try hot and cold soups, deli salads, and ice cream. Eat inside, or on a nice day, try their "Catskill Gardens," a small but pleasant outdoor patio.

Clement's Country Store (585-229-4201; 4503 Rte. 64, Canandaigua, NY 14424) At Clement's you can eat downstairs and do your gift shopping upstairs in an antiques cooperative filled with merchandise from a variety of dealers. Have your doughnuts, pizza, and deli fare at one of the oil-cloth covered tables. The crab salad is particularly good. You can also help yourself to ice cream from the frozen custard machine, and pick a peanut butter or molasses cookie or perhaps a Rice Krispie square from the basket of baked goods. Open daily. ATM machine and video rentals also in the store.

Naples

BOB 'N' RUTH'S IN THE VINEYARD
585-374-5122.
Corner Rtes. 245 & 21,
Naples, NY 14512.
Open: Daily 6am–8pm.
Price: $–$$.
Cuisine: American.
Serving: B, L, D.
Credit Cards: MC, Visa.

Casual down-home cooking here offers soups, desserts, baked goods, and all the usual suspects. Dine in the front area of counters and booths similar to Friendly's, or go to the Vineyard Room in the back, where tables are set with linens and crystal. On a recent visit, a pot-roast special with potatoes and vegetables was just $8.95. There is also the outdoor deck just off the Vineyard—especially pretty in the fall when the hill is ablaze with color. In a hurry? Go to the outside pick-up window for sim-

Bob 'N' Ruth's in the Vineyard has been popular for years in Naples

ple sandwiches and ice cream, and take them to one of the picnic tables in the grove of trees adjacent to the restaurant.

Honeoye, Hemlock, Canadice, and Conesus

CONESUS INN
585-346-6100.
5654 E. Lake Rd., Conesus, NY 14435.
Open: Daily July and Aug.; closed Mon. off-season.
Price: $$–$$$.
Cuisine: American.
Serving: D.
Credit Cards: Most major.

You can arrive by car or by boat and tie up at the dock. There is a big bar, two main dining rooms, and a deck overlooking the lake. People have been raving over the prime rib for many years. Also good are the lobster, tuna, swordfish, chicken Mediterranean, and king crab. It's a pretty casual place, and shorts are fine—but, please, no cutoffs or tank tops.

Clifton Springs

WARFIELD'S
315-462-7184.
7 West Main St., Clifton Springs, NY 14432.
Open: Daily.
Price: $–$$.
Cuisine: International and pub food.
Serving: L, D.
Credit Cards: Most major.

Located in an historic three-story brick building in the center of town, Warfield's combines the ambiance of the 1800s with an authentic English Pub Bar, colonial paneling, and fireplace and tapestries, with an extensive menu featuring dishes from all parts of the world. There is a main restaurant, lounge, piano bar, bakery, and banquet rooms as well as the pub.

CASUAL FOOD

Beachcomber Inn (585-245-9850; 5909 W. Lake Rd, Conesus, NY 14435) It's right on the lake and appears to have been around for a long time, with its weathered gray siding and deck. You'll know you're there when you see the post with hand-painted signs pointing to fun places like Cancun and Nice. The deck is popular with locals who come for a casual bite to eat and a beer. Open daily in-season.

Other Area Restaurants

Minnehans Restaurant and Custard (585-346-6167; corner Rtes. 20A and 256, Lakeville NY 14480) You can't miss it: It's at a major crossroads, and the parking lot is usually busy with cars coming and going. Minnehans serves breakfast, lunch, and dinner, and it's hard to spend more than $10. Order at the long counter, and eat at tables or booths or take it out. Weekly specials include stuffed peppers, Spanish rice, meat loaf (my favorite here), goulash, chicken and biscuits, and fish fry. Burgers, battered fries, onion rings, sandwiches, breaded fried shrimp, hot roast-pork sandwich, and a whole column of other items give you plenty of choices for that quick meal. There is a good selection of frozen custard and yogurt along with milkshakes, sundaes, and floats. There is a mini-golf course open seasonally as well as batter cages and laser tag. Open 8am–8pm in-season.

Victor Grilling Company (585-924-1760; 75 Coville St., Whistlestop Arcade, Victor, NY 14564) Sue and Mark Cupolo cook up a storm on their grill, offering beef, poultry, pork, lamb, and seafood. They try to use local cuisine whenever possible. The menu includes grilled Black Angus rib-eye with mashed potatoes and onion rings, and sweet corn chowder. There are three dining rooms, two fireplaces. Very cozy and casual. Open Tues.–Sat. from 5:30, Sun. from 4.

CULTURE

ARCHITECTURE

In the early 1800s, Federal and Greek-Revival homes were built here by the wealthy, showplaces made of wood, brick, cut stone, and local cobblestone. By the mid-1800s, many homes in a "Romantic" style emerged, reflecting Asian, Swiss, and Egyptian influences. The Stick style and mansard roofs were popular. From about 1845 to 1880, Gothic-Revival and Italianate styles came on the scene, followed by Queen Anne, Shingle, and Richardsonian Romanesque.

The early 20th century ushered in Colonial-Revival and Neoclassical styles for important public buildings, such as the courthouse, and gracious residences; Tudor and modern were also popular.

In Canandaigua, notable houses and buildings in the area include those along North Main Street, Gibson Street, and Howell Street; in Clifton Springs; the **Foster Cottage** (circa 1854), with its triple dormers and fancy fretwork; and **St. John's Episcopal Church** (circa 1879), made of Medina sandstone in the Gothic style and featuring windows by Tiffany; in Gorham, two houses made of Lake Ontario cobblestones, the **Mapes House** and the **Whitman-Fox House**; and in Victor, on Maple Street, the **Emily Harris House** (circa 1850) in the Italianate style. In Honeoye the **Pennell House** is a colonial (circa 1795) at 79 East Main. In East Bloomfield, the Greek-Revival **Giaconia House** (circa 1840) and the Holloway House (circa 1808), a Federal style, are on Routes 5 & 20. The **Reed Homestead** (circa 1803) at 4357 Reed Street is a fine brick colonial. The **Morgan Fire House**, Naples, a three-story frame structure, served as a firehouse from 1890 to 1916.

Canandaigua

MUSEUMS AND HISTORIC SITES

Ganondagan State Historic Site (585-924-5848; www.ggw.org/ganondagan; County Rd. 41 at Boughton Hill, Victor, NY 14564) In the 17th century, the largest village of the Seneca nation occupied this hilltop mesa. When you stand on the wide meadows, you understand why they chose this site. There are magnificent sweeping views of the hills and lake all around. A bark longhouse has been recreated and depicts how the Seneca lived. Tools, clothing, cooking utensils, weapons, ornaments, and accessories have all been made by Native American craftsmen selected because of their exceptional skills. At one time more than 75 longhouses were on the land here. There are interpretative trails and a small museum. Each summer, the Music and Dance Festival brings skilled artists to perform and demonstrate crafts, such as bow making, cornhusk doll making, wood, bone and antler carving, and other arts. A visitors center and Native American gift shop are also part of the site. Peter Jemison, a descendant of Mary Jemison, a white woman captured and adopted by Native Americans, is the director of the site. Open mid-May–first week of Nov.

Granger Homestead and Carriage Museum (585-394-1472; www.granger homestead.org; 295 N. Main St., Canandaigua, NY 14424) A fine example of Federal architecture built in 1816 by Gideon Granger, who was postmaster general for Jefferson and Madison. Inside is a collection of period furnishings, some original to the house, along with lovely hand-carved woodwork.

The Granger Homestead Carriage Museum collection includes more than 50 vehicles, including pleasure, sporting, and commercial conveyances. Most have been fully restored. Of special interest are two hearses, one for summer on wheels, one for winter on runners; *The Eagle,* Canandaigua's first fire engine built in 1816; a private Road Coach used by the Vanderbilts; a tinker's

The Granger Homestead and Carriage Museum in Canandaigua dates back to 1816.

wagon, several sleighs, and a rare Coachee (1790s), one of only five known in the country. Carriage rides are given seasonally. The house and museum are open mid-May–mid-Oct., Tues.–Fri. 1–5; June 1–Aug. 31, Sat. and Sun. 1–5.

Ontario County Courthouse (585-396-4239; 27 N. Main St., Canandaigua, NY 14424) The venue of a number of hotly contested trials over the years, including many that challenged the Fugitive Slave Law, the courthouse has gone through several transformations. In 1794 it was a square wooden structure; in 1824, a new brick building was built (now the city hall); in 1857 a more substantial building with pillars and a dome was built, then enlarged in 1909; and in 1988 two new wings were added.

Ontario County Historical Society Museum (585-394-4975; www.ochs.org; 55 N. Main St., Canandaigua, NY 14424) See hundreds of original deeds for area lands and maps. Of particular interest is the Native American copy of the 1794 Pickering treaty between the six nations of the Haudenosaunee (Iroquois) Confederacy and the U.S. government, which is on display on Treaty Day, November 11. The museum contains a valuable collection of Native American signatures along with artifacts and early farm and home implements. There is a huge library of family histories, photographs, and other materials. Open Tues.–Sat. 10–4:30, Wed. until 9.

Sonnenberg Mansion and Gardens (585-394-4922; www.sonnenberg.org; 151 Charlotte St., Canandaigua, NY 14424) Built in 1887 as the summer home of bank magnate Frederick Ferris Thompson and his wife Mary Clark, who

The Sonnenberg Gardens in Canandaigua features nine formal theme gardens created between 1902 and 1919.

would become one of Canandaigua's most generous benefactors, the Victorian mansion features turrets, towers, stone, and heavily carved wood details. On the 50-acre grounds are nine formal theme gardens created between 1902 and 1919, along with many unique specimen trees and a large greenhouse complex. The 40-room mansion contains several period pieces. The house and grounds are open daily mid-May–mid-Oct.; seasonal events are offered through December, including a fabulous Holiday Festival of Lights. There is a small café on the property in one of the greenhouses.

Photo Ops

Canandaigua City Pier's boathouses form a Rockport-like line of stilted buildings in the water.

Bristol Harbour: View from the restaurant's patio looking over the lake.

Harriet Hollister Spencer Memorial State Recreation Area: Stop just past the guardrails after you enter for a stunning view of Honeoye Lake. From Route 15A, go south on Canadice Hill Road, and turn left into the park.

Overlook on Route 21, South Bristol: The town of South Bristol bought the land to preserve this great scenic spot on the lake. Look to the left and see Bare Hill (the second mound), the rise where fires announced the start of the American Indian harvest.

South Bristol Cultural Center (585-396-9504; www.members.aol.com/sulind; 5323 Seneca Point Rd, Canandaigua, NY 14424) Practical and visual arts are the core of this unique center's focus. You can take classes in many different areas, such as cooking and gardening as well as canoe building and acting. The Gallery features works of local artists and artisans.

PERFORMING ARTS

Concerts in the Park (585-396-0300; Atwater Park Gazebo, Canandaigua, NY 14424) Every Friday evening during July and August, concerts are held from 6:30–8:30. Free.

Finger Lakes Performing Arts Center (585-222-5000; www.fingerlakes.edu/flpac; Lincoln Hill Rd., Canandaigua NY 14424) Summer home of the Rochester Philharmonic Orchestra and Rochester Performing Theatre League, performances take place inside a 65-foot amphitheater at the base of a grassy hill. Choose seating inside the shell or bring lawn chairs and blankets, and picnic on the lawn while listening to great music, including classical, pop, rock, jazz, and blues. A large video screen makes the performances more accessible to those sitting on the grass. Located on the campus of Finger Lakes Community College, the pavilion seats 2,600; the hillside can accommodate 10,000 more.

Naples

Bristol Valley Theater (585-374-6318; www.bvtnaples.org; 151 S. Main St., Naples, NY 14512) Super summer-stock productions as well as children's theater held in a former church. Enjoy musicals, comedy, and mystery thrillers.

Willow Pond Aqua Farm

Is it a farm, a retail outlet, or an educational experience? Actually it's all three. If you're into ponds and water life, Willow Pond has everything you could ever ask for, from fish, tadpoles, and crayfish to fountains. Jim Kennedy, owner of one of the newest niche businesses that have recently started up in the area, is continually coming up with creative ideas for products and facilities in this water-oriented world of exotic aquatic plants and artistic water sculptures. There are more than 40 ponds stocked with eight species of fish such as Japanese koi, golden orfe, and rainbow trout. Kennedy offers an ever-expanding program to teach fishing skills and gives lectures on aquaculture. The farm also sells pond and pool-related items such as hand-blown glass candle globes that float in the water and aerators, air and water pumps, and other accessories. Tours are offered through rough-cut trails to the ponds, where you can get a close-up view of some of the more than 75 kinds of water lilies in all colors. (585-394-5890, 888-854-8945; www.willow pondaquafarms.com; 3581 Swamp Rd., Hopewell NY 14424; open Mon.–Fri. 10–5, Sat. 9–5, Sun. 10–3.)

The Gell Center (585-473-2590; www.wab.org/gell; County Rd. 33, Naples, NY 14512) Here at the southern end of Canandaigua Lake, writers and poets come to reflect, write, and learn. Surrounded by fields and woods, the Gleason Lodge, with its large stone fireplace, is used for meetings and special programs; the Gell House accommodates overnight guests.

Mees Observatory (585-374-2433; 6486 Gannett Hill Rd., Naples, NY 14512) Operated by the Rochester Museum and Science Center. Planet gazing and special programs, using a 24-inch telescope. Tours Fri. and Sat. evenings, June–Aug. by appointment.

Honeoye Falls

Peacock Oriental Antiques Museum (585-624-6058; 61 N. Main St., Honeoye Falls, NY 14472) More than 700 peacocks; Chinese and Japanese artifacts from 206 BC to World War II. Extensive library is available for research. Tues.–Sun. 10am–5pm, closed Mon.

RECREATION

BIKING

Canandaigua Loop, Bristol Hills: With steep inclines and winding roads, this 35-mile ride is for the experienced, fit cyclist. Start at the City Pier on Lakeshore Drive in Canandaigua on Route 5 & 20. Heading west, turn left on Parrish Street. Go up the hill to Route 21S and south toward Bristol Springs. Here at almost the halfway point, you can take a break and check out the Arbor Hill Grapery and Winery. Turn right onto Route 64N, and continue to the intersection of Route 5 & 20. On the way up Route 64, you'll pass the Wizard of Clay Pottery. Head east (right) to Canandaigua, and turn right onto Pearl Street, following signs for the hospital. Turn left on Parrish Street, and take that road until you reach the intersection of Main Street. At the stoplight turn right onto Main, and follow to starting point.

BOATING AND CRUISES

Canandaigua Lady (585-394-5365, 877-771-LADY; 215 Lakeshore Dr., PO Box 856, Canandaigua, NY 14424) Lunch, dinner, and brunch cruises as well as annual fall foliage cruises aboard a fanciful two-deck 150-passenger paddle wheel/steamboat. Special events include New Orleans Night, Italian Fest, and a Hawaiian luau. Fall foliage cruises ($28 per person) combine great scenery, with a brief history of the area, and lunch with wine and grape pie. Indoor and outdoor seating for cruises that operate May–October.

Canandaigua Lake State Marine Park offers a boat launch site.

Captain Gray's Boat Tours (585-394-5270; www.captgrays.com; 770 S. Main St., Canandaigua, NY 14424) Cruise around the lake, charter one of the two boats for a party, or climb on board for a morning coffee cruise. The *Jennifer Mac* has been piloted by Captain Gray Hoffman for more than 30 years. His son, Jadon, bought the operation from his father a couple of years ago. The cruises' commentary on the local sites and history is especially informative: Learn about General Sullivan's campaign, the glory days of the steamboat era, and area facts. Departs from the Inn on the Lake. End of May through Labor Day weekend; daily departures also available September and October, weather permitting. Ask about the fall foliage tours.

MARINAS AND LAUNCHES

Canandaigua Lake State Marine Park (S. Main St. at northern end of lake near Rte. 5 & 20 and Rte. 332, Canandaigua) $4 launch fee.
German Brothers Marina (585-394-4000; www.germanbrothers.com; 3907 W. Lake Rd., Canandaigua, NY 14424) Full services, dockage, and winter storage. Boat rentals and sales.

Jansen Marina, Conesus (585-346-2060; www.jansenmarina.com; 5750 E. Lake Rd., Conesus, NY 14435) This facility has 22 slips, gas, winter storage, boat sales, and service.

Jansen Marina, Naples (585-374-2384; www.jansenmarina.com; 7099 Rte. 21, Naples, NY 14512) A full-service marina with sales, service, bait, gas, and convenience store. Fish, ski, pontoon and wave runners for rent, and 75 slips.

Sutter's Canandaigua Marina (585-394-0918; www.suttersmarina.com; City Pier, Canandaigua, NY 14424) On the north end of the lake. Recreational boat rentals for cruising, fishing, tubing, and sightseeing. Slip rentals, storage, store and picnic area. Not a public launching area.

Woodville Boat Launch (Rte. 21 south end of Canandaigua Lake)

FISHING

Canandaigua Lake: Lake trout, brown trout, and rainbow trout are well stocked in Canandaigua Lake. Naples Creek has six fishing access points; three additional fishing sites are maintained on the lake, two for ice fishing at Woodville and Onanda Park. You can fish in the lake or from the City Pier, but you must have a license. Fishing licenses can be purchased at City Hall, 2 N. Main Street or at Wal-Mart on Route 5 & 20 East.

Candice, Conesus, Hemlock, and Honeoye Lakes: Smaller and quieter, these lakes provide excellent fishing. Honeoye has an abundance of smallmouth bass, and its shallow waters make it ideal for ice fishing. Limitations on boat and motor size exist for Canadice and Hemlock, which are natural and undeveloped and serve as the water supply for the City of Rochester. Hemlock is stocked with many kinds of fish; Canadice is best for smallmouth bass.

GOLF

Bristol Harbour Golf Course (800-288-8248; 585-396-2460; www.bristolharbour .com; 5410 Seneca Point Rd., Canandaigua, NY 14424) When Robert Trent Jones came to this site more than 25 years ago, he said, "In all the world and of all the properties I've seen, this one has just been waiting for a golf course." The front nine plays like a links course, with large bunkers, nasty rough, and fickle winds. The hilly back nine winds through woods. Many holes reveal splendid views of the lake. There is a driving range, inn, and restaurant on site. Course: 6,700 yards, par 70. Greens fees, including cart: $46 to $55.

CenterPointe Country Club (585-394-0346; www.hws.edu/athletics/center-pointe.asp; 2231 Brickyard Rd., Canandaigua, NY 14424; off Rte. 332) This semiprivate course features a blend of open fairways and tighter tree-lined fairways. Course: 6,478 yards, par 71. Green fees including cart: $25–$35.

Ravenwood Golf Club (585-924-5100; www.ravenwoodgolf.com; 929 Lynaugh Rd., Victor, NY 14564) Home of the 2003 New York State Amateur tournament, this course combines traditional and links features with water carries, bunkers, and angled greens. Course: 7,056 yards, par 72.

The Bristol Harbour Golf Course features spectacular views of Canandaigua Lake.

Reservoir Creek (585-374-6828; www.rcgolf.com; 8613 Rte. 21, Naples, NY 14512) This hilly course is characterized by berms and moguls that separate the fairways. There is a pro shop and restaurant with outside deck as well as a B&B. A recently planted vineyard adds interest. Course: 5,750 yards, par 71. Greens fees including cart: $39–$43.

Victor Hills Golf Club (585-924-3480; 1450 Brace Rd., Victor, NY 14564) A nice 45-hole course; restaurant and pro shop. Course: 6,143 yards, par 72. Greens fees including cart: $32–$36.

Winged Pleasant Golf Links (585-289-8846; 1475 Sand Hill Rd., exit 43 off NYS Thruway, Shortsville, NY 14548) 18 holes, pro shop, carts, lessons, golf outings. Course: 6,500 yards, par 70. Greens fees including cart: $25–$34.

HIKING

Bare Hill Unique Area (607-776-2165, ext. 10) Going south from Canandaigua on Route 364, turn right (west) on Town Line Road, left (south) on Bare Hill Road, and right (west) on Van Epps Road, where it stops. This moderately difficult 3.1-mile loop goes along cut grass and stone trails, through woods, by a pond, and up to the top of Bare Hill. The view of the lake and valley from here is worth the trip. It is here the Senecas used to light a huge fire in celebration of a successful harvest. Today this tradition is carried out in the Genundowa Festival of Lights, held on the lake each year.

Big Oak Trail and Sidewinder Trail (585-335-8111; Harriet Hollister Spencer Memorial State Recreation Area, Honeoye, NY 14471) From Route 15A, go south on Canadice Hill Road, and turn left into the park. The trail is marked by cross-country ski trail signs and leads north from the parking lot. Big Oak Trail, a 1-mile loop through woods, over a stream, to the top of a hill, is moderately difficult on wide dirt trails with some steep climbs. Sidewinder Trail snakes 3.3 miles through the trees with some ups and downs. It's also moderately difficult.

Conesus Inlet Path (Park on the south side of Silker Hill Rd. near the intersection of Rte. 256, Conesus) An easy 1-mile walk along a mowed grass path just south of the lake. The trail starts from the parking area and is marked with round plastic discs. Walk through woods along the wetlands; stop to see wildlife from viewing platforms. You can picnic along the way. It's managed by the NYS Department of Environmental Conservation.

Cumming Nature Center (585-374-6160; 6472 Gulick Rd., Naples, NY 14512) Six miles of walking trails are laced throughout the 900-acre park.

Hi Tor Wildlife Management Area (585-226-2466; www.dec.state.ny.us/website/reg8/wma/hitor.html; from Naples take Rte. 245, cross Naples Creek Bridge, park near the Dept. of Environmental Conservation building) Several trails wind through this 6,100-acre area of steep hills, craggy outcroppings, ponds, and old logging roads. Trails can be steep and strenuous. Depending on how far you want to go, you can hike the Conklin Gully Trail, a 1.6-mile loop; the main trail, a 4.5-mile loop; or tie into several other trails along the way and backpack for several days. In the Hi Tor area of hills, forests, and wetlands, you'll be rewarded for your more strenuous climbs by some great views of gullies, lake, and cliffs. Most of the trails are marked.

Onanda Park (585-394-0315; the Upland Hiking Trail is a 1.2-mile loop from the park on W. Lake Rd. about 7 miles south of Canandaigua) Easy-to-follow dirt paths go through woods to observation platforms overlooking gorges and waterfalls. Some uphill climbing makes it moderately difficult. Cabins and pavilion are available for rent; picnic, beach, tennis, and playgrounds also on site.

Ontario County Park at Gannett Hill (585-374-6250; 6475 Gannett Hill Rd., Naples, NY 14512) Several self-guided tours, as well as playgrounds, fishing pond, picnic site, and shelters. The Jump Off trail area is the highest point in Ontario County.

Quinn Oak Openings (607-776-2165, ext. 10; Honeoye Falls, NY 14472; from Rte. 15, turn east on Five Points Rd., and watch for Quinn Oak Openings parking) A 1.5-mile loop, moderately challenging along mowed and sometimes scruffy trails through fields of grasses surrounded by oak forests. This highly diverse area has more than 400 species of wildlife, rare prickly ash trees, and tall grasses. The trail is unmarked, so get a map from the Department of Environmental Conservation, or take your chances.

Seneca Trail (585-234-8226) From Route 96, turn west on Broughton Hill Road (County Route 41), and look for the parking area near the corner of Victor-Bloomfield Road (Route 444); the trail is marked by red blazes and diamond-shaped red metal markers. You can also start at the northern end of the trail at Fishers Firehall. This 5.8-mile (one way) trail recalls the time when the Senecas dominated this part of the world. Start at the Ganondagan State Historic Site, and head out on several trails that loop through the region. The trail through wooded hills, meadows, and wetlands and along abandoned rail beds is moderately difficult. Maps are available at the center.

Resources:

Finger Lakes Trail Conference (585-288-7191) Provides hiking information throughout the Finger Lakes.

Ontario Pathways (585-394-7968; www.ontariopathways.com; 200 Ontario St., Canandaigua, NY 14424) A 23-mile rails-to-trails recreational trail is open for walkers, bikers, cross-country skiers, snowshoers, and horseback riders. Seasonal events include the Great Pumpkin Walk.

Victor Hiking Trails (585-724-7028; www.ggw.org/vht; 85 E. Main St., Victor, NY 14564) Maintains more than 18 miles of foot trails in Victor with open fields, wooded wetlands, hills and valleys.

HORSEBACK RIDING

Copper Creek Farm (585-289-4441; 5041 Shortsville Rd., Shortsville, NY 14548) Offers horseback riding, lessons, sleigh and wagon rides. Indoor and outdoor facilities.

PARKS, NATURE PRESERVES, AND CAMPING

Bristol Woodlands Campgrounds (585-229-2290; 4835 S. Hill Rd., Bristol, NY 14424; mail: 3300 E. Lake Rd. #4C, Canandaigua, NY 14424; from Rte. 64S, turn right at Bristol Center, go 1.5 miles, then left on S. Hill Rd. to campground) Facilities include campgrounds, trails, and fishing pond on 100 acres with views of the hills. The area is often used as a camping ground for artists during the summer.

Cumming Nature Center (585-374-6160; www.rmsc.org/cnc; 6472 Gulick Rd., Naples, NY 14512) A vast natural environment of 900 acres with hiking and cross-country ski trails, tall red pines, and meadowland. There is an informative visitors center, gift shop, and interpretative programs with animals and birds. The nature center is an extension of the Rochester Museum and Science Center. Open end of Dec.–mid-Nov., Wed.–Sun. 9–5. Adults $4, children K–Grade 12 $1.50, seniors and college students $3.

Harriet Hollister Spencer Park (585-335-8111; Canadice Hill Rd., Honeoye; mail: c/o Stony Brook State Park, 10820 Rte. 36S, Dansville, NY 14437) There are several undeveloped trails and great views of the lake north toward the Rochester skyline.

Honeoye Lake State Park (585-335-8111; off Rte. 20A, 4 miles south of Honeoye; mail: c/o Stony Brook State Park, address above) This is a boat-launch area with minimal facilities and undeveloped trails.

Kershaw Park (585-396-5080; Lakeshore Dr., Canandaigua, NY 14424) At the foot of the north end of the lake, this newly renovated 8-acre park has a walkway along the beach, bathhouses, picnic shelters, and gazebo. There is a sailboard and canoe launch. Beach open Memorial Day–Labor Day 9am–9pm; park open year-round.

Letchworth State Park (585-493-3600; www.letchworthpark.com/index.htm; entrances at Mount Morris, Perry, Castile, Portageville, and the Parade Grounds from Rte. 436) Often called the "Grand Canyon of the East," Letchworth runs through a narrow, winding 17-mile bedrock canyon punctuated by three falls, including the 107-foot drop of the Middle Falls. Lights illuminate the falls after dark from May through October. The William Pryor Letchworth Museum contains a collection of Native American and pioneer history items of the Genesee Valley as well as archeological and natural history displays. The statue of Mary Jemison stands on the Council Grounds in the park, along with the Seneca Council House. Jemison's gravesite is on a bluff behind the museum. Cabins and campsites are on the grounds, but those who prefer not to rough it can stay at Pinewood Lodge and the Glen Iris Inn within the park. Swimming pools, fishing areas, hiking trails, hot air ballooning, whitewater rafting, and canoeing by permit are also available.

Onanda Park (585-394-0315; W. Lake Rd., Canandaigua, NY 14424) Eight miles south of the northern end of Canandaigua Lake, this park covers more than 80 acres of land, 7 by the water. Activities include swimming, sledding, crosscountry skiing, fishing, playground, and picnic area, along with cabins, pavilions, lodge, and tennis and ball courts. Cabin rentals are $30–$50 per night; $175–$400 (non-residents) and $100–$350 (residents) weekly. Open all year 9–9; cabins open from last frost to October.

Ontario County Park at Gannett Hill (585-374-6250; off Rt. 64, Naples, NY 14512) The highest point in Canandaigua, this rolling grassy park with groves of very tall pines offers hiking trails, tent sites, a playground, pavilion, and great views, especially from "Jump Off" point, which looks over the Bristol hills. This is one of the best places to view the "Ring of Fire" on Labor Day weekend.

SKIING

Bristol Mountain Ski Resort (585-374-6000; www.bristolmountain.com; 5662 Rte. 64, Canandaigua, NY 14424) It's not long as ski hills go, but the 1,200-foot vertical rise is impressive. There are 30 slopes and trails, snowmaking, night skiing, ski school, rentals, baby-sitting, and a restaurant. It's the tallest ski area between the Adirondack/Catskill region and the Rockies and has the only Olympic-style pipe in Western New York.

OTHER ATTRACTIONS

Balloons Over Letchworth (585-493-3340; www.balloonsoverletchworth.com; 6645 Denton Corners Rd., Castile, NY 14427) Fly over the vast natural wonderland of Letchworth State Park—14,350 acres with 20 waterfalls and cliffs up to 600 feet high. The launch site is at the Middle/Upper Falls picnic area, 1,000 feet south of the Glen Iris Inn. Prices are $189 per person; $178 per person for three or more in party.

Canandaigua Speedway (315-834-6606; www.dirtmotorsports.com; Ontario County Fairgrounds, Townline Rd,. Canandaigua, NY 14424) DIRT motorsport stock racing held Sat. evenings from mid-April–Labor Day. The grandstand opens at 5pm; racing begins at 7.

Copper Creek Farms (585-289-4441; 5041 Shortsville Rd., Shortsville, NY 14548) You can ride horseback or in a carriage along the trails on the property. Riding and lessons for all ages; pony rides for kids. They have a surrey for use in weddings and other special occasions and sleigh rides are given in-season. In the fall ride their hay wagons into the fields and pick your own pumpkin. Open year-round. Call in advance for reservations.

The Finger Lakes Race Track (585-924-3232; www.fingerlakesracetrack.com; 5857 Rte. 96, Farmington, NY 14425) Thoroughbred racing runs from early April through the first week in December. There are about 10 races a day. One mile south of NY State Thruway Exit 44 just east of junction for Routes 96 and 332.

Roseland Waterpark (585-396-2000; www.roselandwaterpark.com; 250 Eastern Blvd., Rte. 5 & 20, Canandaigua, NY 14424) A 58-acre playground for family fun with water slides, giant wave pool, Adventure River, two body flumes, Splash Factory, three tube rides, a 30-acre private lake, river rafts, and playground. Open Memorial Day–Labor Day.

The South Bristol Cultural Center (585-396-9504; www.members.aol.com/sulind; 5323 Seneca Point Rd., Canandaigua, NY 14224) Located midway between Canandaigua and Naples, the South Bristol Cultural Center is a place to come for classes and special events in a wide spectrum of the arts, from canoe building to acting for kids to cooking and gardening to crafts. Galley features work of local artists.

SHOPPING

This area is known for its grape-related products such as wines, jellies, pies, and salad dressings. Farm markets sell a variety of local produce, including fruits and vegetables, maple syrup, apples and cider, and sauerkraut. Local crafts include pottery, handblown glass, paintings, wooden duck decoys, fishing lures, kites, and teddy bears. Furniture and other items made by the Mennonites and Amish are beautifully crafted. There are many antique shops where you can find good buys.

ANTIQUES

More than 50 antique shops can be found in and around Canandaigua. One of the biggest concentrations of shops is located in Bloomfield west of Canandaigua.

Bloomfield Antique Country Mile (585-394-5530; 4244 Rte. 21S, South Cheshire, Canandaigua, NY 14424) A mecca for antique buffs, this stretch along Route 5 & 20 in a charming 200-year-old village features more than 175 dealers in nine shops. Find furniture, memorabilia, primitive tools, toys, vintage books, stoneware, glassware, dolls, collectibles, tools, period firearms, and much more. Also in Bloomfield is the Quail Run Studio, an art studio. The unusual Vintage Tracks Museum features more than 100 Crawler tractors and memorabilia from the early 1900s (585-657-6608).

The Cheshire Union Gift Shop and Antique Center (585-394-5530; 4244 Rte. 21S, South Cheshire, Canandaigua, NY 14424) Filled with an assortment of antiques and gift items, the Cheshire Union is above the Company Store. The old blackboard is still on the wall and the embossed tin ceiling is still in place, reminders that this space was once a school room, circa 1915. Tucked into nooks and crannies are collections of bears, a pair of old snowshoes, baskets, candles, an antique sled, a wooden box that once held boneless salt cod, and hand-knit sweaters for the stuffed bears for $4.

Ontario Mall Antiques (585-398-0240; 1740 Rte. 332, Farmington, NY 14425) Contains a fascinating and extensive collection of antiques and memorabilia.

Peirce's Antiques and Gifts (585-526-6970; 2 West Main, Clifton Springs, NY 14432) Housed in a lovely 19th-century building. Here you'll find a large selection of antiques along with Christmas gifts.

CLOTHING

The Country Ewe (585-396-9580; 79 S. Main St., Canandaigua, NY 14424) In downtown Canandaigua, this store features classic clothing including hand-knit sweaters from Ireland, Iceland, Norway, and other parts of the world. Also find fleece outerwear, oilskin dusters, Finger Lakes shirts and jewelry. Open Mon.–Fri. 9:30–8, Sat. 9:30–5:30, Sun. 11–4.

CRAFTS

East Hill Gallery (585-554-3539; www.rfag.org/crafts.htm; 1445 Upper Hill Rd., Middlesex, NY 14507) Pottery, handblown glass, handicrafts, furniture, weaving, custom clothing. Open May–Oct. Fri.–Mon.

Gallery on Main Street (585-394-2780; www.members.aol.com/aquarellel; 131 South Main Street, Canandaigua, NY 14424) This not-for-profit cooperative represents more than 25 local artists and craftspeople.

Nadal Glass Art Studios (585-394-7850; www.nadalglass.com; 20 Phoenix St., Canandaigua, NY 14424) Handblown glass in bright primary colors, Nadal's designs are sold in more than 200 galleries and shops around the country. Tues.–Sat. 11–5.

Timberwood (585-374-5660; 197 N. Main St., Naples, NY 14512) Handcrafted Amish and Mennonite gifts, crafts, outdoor windmills, flags, wooden garden accessories, lights, and furniture. Open daily Apr.–Dec. 31.

The Wizard of Clay Pottery (585-229-2980; www.wizardofclay.com; 7851 Rte. 20A, Bloomfield, NY 14469; 3 miles east of Honeoye Lake) Housed in geodesic domes designed and built by master potter Jim Kozlowski, the complex includes workshops with potter's wheels and kilns where every piece is individually crafted and fired. The store's shelves are filled with dinnerware, casseroles, oil-burning lamps, pie plates, pitchers, planters, bells, mugs, bowls, and more. The Bristoleaf designs are especially interesting: actual leaves gathered from the area are pressed into the soft clay before firing. When the piece is fired, the leaf burns away, leaving the impression behind. There is also a good selection of earthy red, white, and blue pottery. Workshop and store are open 9–5 daily. The pieces are reasonably priced when compared to similar pottery elsewhere; for example, a handmade ceramic fluted pie plate with an American flag motif was less than $25.

For More Information

Canandaigua Chamber of Commerce Tourist Center Information: 585-394-4400; www.canandaigua.com/chamber; 113 S. Main St., Canandaigua, NY 14424.

Finger Lakes Tourism: 800-548-4386; www.fingerlakes.org; 309 Lake St., Penn Yan, NY 14527.

Honeoye Chamber of Commerce: Call the Ontario County Tourism as phone number changes each year.

Ontario County Tourism: 585-394-3915; www.visitfingerlakes.com; 25 Gorham St., Canandaigua, NY 14424.

Types of Carriages

Coach: Private vehicle of the wealthy; mostly used in urban areas. Passengers traveled in an enclosed cabin with windows and doors.

Phaeton: Light, four-wheeled vehicle used for personal and commercial needs. Some had roofs, some did not. Most were owner rather than coachman driven.

Surrey: Convenient two-seated family vehicles; many were outfitted with a top decorated with fringe.

Runabout: A one-seat, two-passenger utility vehicle, usually topless.

Buckboard: Simple, single-seated vehicles mounted on a board.

Game Cart: Sporting vehicles used for sightseeing and hunting excursions.

Private Drag: Resembled a commercial coach but was used privately for outings such as picnics. Under the back seat were a zinc-lined box for food and often a drawer for cutlery. It could seat 14 people and needed four or six horses to pull.

Break: Used for recreational purposes. The seats are "on the roof."

Cutter and Sleigh: Vehicles on runners.

Speciality Vehicle: Carriage adapted for specific uses, including fire wagons, hearses, traveling stores, and delivery wagons.

FARM MARKETS

Barrons Pratt Farm (585-394-9344; 4990 Rte. 21S, Palmyra, NY 14522) This vineyard produces grapes primarily for people to buy by the bushel and use for pies, jellies, and other things. A tiny gift shop sells items crafted by the owner, such as hand-painted saws and slates.

Gentner's Valley View (585-374-5417; Cty. Rd. 12, Naples, NY 14512) Great jellies, grape pies, tarts, table grapes, honey and cheese. Also a super photo op.

Hanna Junction (585-394-7740; 4375 Rte. 21N Canandaigua, NY 14522; just north of town) More than 100 vendors under one roof selling fresh vegetables, fruits, meats, baked goods, relishes, plants, furniture, crafts, antiques. Open Apr.–Dec. Thurs. 10–8.

Jerome's U-Pick (800-UPICKIT; 8936 Rte. 53, Naples, NY 14512) Pick-your-own strawberries, peas, raspberries, grapes, pumpkins, and other fruits and vegetables in-season.

Joseph's Wayside Market (585-374-2380; 201 S. Main St., Rte. 21, Naples, NY 14512) Every (regional) imaginable fruit is here in-season, along with maple syrup, honey, cheddar cheese, baked goods, jams, jellies, and locally made crafts and gifts. The market is especially known for grapes, grape pies, and juice. They also sell flowers: Their hanging baskets are beautiful.

Monica's Pies (585-374-2139; www.monicaspies.com; 7599 Rte. 21, Naples, NY 14512) Selling homemade grape pies as well as blueberry, strawberry, rhubarb, raspberry, peach, apple, and other fruit pies, jellies, jams, conserves, relish, and other items. No preservatives are used in any of Monica's products.

FOOD

Arbor Hill Grapery and Winery (585-374-2870, 800-554-7553; fax 585-374-9198; www.thegrapery.com; 6461 Rte. 64, Naples NY 14512; 3 miles south of Bristol Mt.) Grape everything: jelly, grape pies, taffy, cookbooks, salad dressings, wines (the Traminette at $11.95 a bottle is a good buy), corkscrews, pottery—you name it. John Brahm III, the founder and owner of the company, now has more than 50 products that he makes, packages, and sells from his modest-sized production area next to the store. His Black Raspberry Celery Seed Dressing is one of the 14-year-old company's hottest items. While I was there, he invited me to sample one of his newest products, fortified teas: Strawberry Iced Tea, Peach Breezes, Lemon Delight, and Raspberry Wisp. Open daily May to Dec. Mon.–Sat. 10–5; Sun 11–5; winter weekends only.

Conesus Lake Trading Co. (585-346-2514; 5975 E. Lake Rd., Conesus, NY 14435) In the spirit of an old-time general store, this store sells everything from groceries, gas, and subs to candy, "fry cakes," jellies, jams, cards, teddy bears, and seasonal gifts. Open daily 7–7.

Finger Lakes Wine Center at Sonnenberg Gardens (585-394-9016; www.fingerlakeswinecenter.com; 151 Charlotte St., Canandaigua, NY 14424) Your one-stop shopping center for wines and gourmet foods from more than 40 Finger Lakes wineries.

GIFTS

Canandaigua Nature Co. (585-396-9807; www.cnature.com; 13 Niagara St., Canandaigua, NY 14424) Wild-bird supplies, nature gifts, wind chimes, lawn art, weathervanes, and other items that celebrate nature and the outdoors.

Cheshire Union Antique Shop and Gift Center (585-394-5530; Rte. 21, South Cheshire, Canandaigua NY 14424) Filled with an assortment of antiques and gift items, the Cheshire Union is above the Company Store. (See the listing in the "Antiques" section above.)

Classics (585-374-5650; 199 N. Main St., Village Corner, Naples, NY 14512) As the name implies, the gift items in this store tend to be timeless in appeal: Jewelry, leather goods, glassware, pottery, books, cards, porcelain dolls, kalei-

Judge Cribb's Passion for Carriages Creates a Collection

Today's teens may dream of owning a red Mustang convertible, but back in 1927, when the late Honorable Joseph W. Cribb was but 13, his heart's desire was a nifty runabout for summer driving and a cutter for getting around in winter. "I think I paid about $25 for both," he once recalled, pinpointing the onset of his passion.

Growing up in Canandaigua, New York, he had been able to nurture this obsession. "After school, I used to hang around the stables at the old Granger place. I especially enjoyed Lafayette Cooper, Antoinette Granger's coachman, and liked to ride with him in Miss Granger's carriage: It was pulled by her old horse, Nero. Whenever I could, I went with Mr. Cooper when he took letters to the post office and did other errands."

When Joe was 16, he purchased a two-seated surrey, stripped off the body, and converted the vehicle into a buckboard. As he had told the tale: "This was my pickup truck. After school, I'd drive to the edge of town, pick carrots and beets for 5 cents a bushel, load them onto the wagon, and take them into town to sell. I could make 70 or 80 cents that way. I also earned money taking care of horses that were boarded in a barn on the Granger property."

Young Joe went on to study law at Cornell, becoming an attorney and a highly respected Ontario County surrogate judge, but he diligently continued to collect and restore one carriage after another. Whenever anyone had an old wagon or carriage for sale, no matter what state it was in, someone would say, "Call Judge Joe. He'll take it." He soon had close to 50 vehicles stored in sheds and barns all over town.

In the late '50s, about the time he'd just about run out of empty barns, Judge Joe ended up full circle back at the Granger Homestead. The property—once the home of Gideon Granger, postmaster general under presidents Jefferson and Madison—had been purchased in 1945 (at the urging of Judge Joe) by the Granger Homestead Society and was being maintained by a dedicated group of volunteers as a historic home and venue for social functions.

Since some of Judge Joe's vehicles were already stored amid the corn cobs, moldy hay, and flotsam of the old Granger barn, an idea started to germinate: Why not create a carriage museum, using the judge's carriages as the nucleus for the display? What a wonderful addition it would make to the property. Judge Joe was all for it.

So, spearheaded by Stephen Hamlin (now director of Sonnenberg Estate and Gardens), funds were raised through a series of plays and benefits, as well as contributions from Mr. Hamlin's family and other local benefactors, to construct a substantial steel building to augment the smaller, wooden barn. The barn raising was a gala affair, with a chicken barbecue, children's carriage rides, and a horde of volunteer workers, including Arthur Hamlin, the local bank president, and Granger board member Byron Delavan, who provided hours of physical labor as well as executive expertise by suggesting that a crane might be useful to raise the heavy rafters. Thus the Granger Carriage Museum became a reality, opening its doors to the public in 1961 and showcasing 30 of Judge Joe's carriages that he had either donated or loaned to the new museum.

Since that time, the Granger carriage collection has almost doubled, with donations not only from Judge Joe but also from other benefactors, as well. Additional horse-drawn vehicles are displayed in the Carriage House at Sonnenberg, a turn-of-the-century "Tudor-Victorian" 40-room stone mansion, once the summer home of Mary Clark Thompson and her husband, Frederick, a banking magnate.

I had the pleasure of getting a firsthand peek at some of Judge Joe's favorite carriages by visiting his private stables at the back of his Main Street property. The stables and surrounding paddocks were also home to five Morgan carriage horses: Lucy, Green Meads Emily, Pete, and J. C. Stormwatch. As we walked along the corridors between more than 15 carriages, Judge Joe put his hand on the red-painted wheel of a smart runabout. "My parents gave me this for Christmas in 1930," he noted. Then he moved past a wall of sleigh bells to a Kimbal Brothers' Coach and pointed out a cleverly hidden footman's seat (some wags refer to these as "mother-in-law" seats).

Moving to another carriage, a game cart, he showed me where hunting dogs could be contained in a specially built compartment. He then pointed out a handsome Victoria carriage from England, a two-wheeled gig built by Studebaker (forerunner of their automobiles), and an Ointment Peddler's Wagon with advertising on the side panels.

His enthusiasm for an Essex Trap been boundless. "You're driving along with your pal and you see a couple of pretty girls. Now watch this," he said, walking to the back of the carriage to demonstrate how the back folds out to make an additional ("rumble") seat. "Now you can invite the girls to come aboard."

Almost until his death (in late November 2003), Judge Joe often traveled with his driver, Dale Vidler, to carriage shows around the country. It was not unusual for his stable to take top honors, as shown by the impressive display of ribbons and awards on the walls and an ornate silver bowl bestowed for a "Best of Show" win at Walnut Hill, New York.

doscopes, educational toys, Christmas things, garden statuary, and birdfeeders are just a sample of what you can find.

1812 Country Store (585-367-2802; 4270 Rte. 15A, Hemlock, NY 14466) The merchandise lives up to its name. The store is filled with country gifts, quilts, Christmas things, baskets, jams, jellies, cookie cutters, lamps, cards, and antiques. Open Tues.–Sat. 10–5:30; Sun. 12–5; in Dec. also open on Mon. 10–5:30.

Loomis Barn and Country Shops (585-554-3154; www.loomisbarn.com; 4942 Loomis Rd., Rushville, NY 14544; Rte. 5 & 20 to Rte. 247 between Geneva and Canandaigua, south 7 miles to Rushville, then right on Loomis Rd.) A large country complex with a barn filled with home furnishings as well as the Colonial Bouquets flower shop and Corn House Café.

Patch of Country (585-398-2913; 1734 Rte. 332, Farmington, NY 14425) Historical items, the Cat's Meow collection, and other unique gifts.

Renaissance—The Goodie II Shoppe (585-394-6528; 86 S. Main St., Canandaigua, NY 14424) In a fanciful landmark building, this store is well worth a visit, especially if you're looking for a very special gift.

HARDWARE

Turner's Hemlock Farm & Home (585-367-2315; Rte. 15A, 4638 Main St., Hemlock, NY 14466) A real oldie, this store sells everything you can think of: feed sacks, pet supplies, tools, burlap bags, a rabbit cage for $39.99, seeds. It's worth a stop just to get a flavor of what stores used to be like before packaged nails.

CHAPTER EIGHT
Gold Medal Grapes
WINERIES

Grapes ripen in the sun in a Finger Lakes vineyard.

This is an exciting time for the wine industry in the Finger Lakes. Where just a handful of vineyards existed in the Finger Lakes in the early 1960s, today there are close to 80 vineyards and wineries sprawled on the hillsides of three lakes: Seneca, Cayuga, and Keuka. A few more are huddled around the southern end of Canandaigua, and within the past two years, several acres of land on the west shores of Skaneateles have been planted with grapes. Three new vineyards are under construction on Seneca Lake, and Belhurst Castle is adding a vineyard.

Yet it's not just the number of vineyards but the quality of the wines being produced in the region that give cause to celebrate. After many years of ho-hum acceptance, where regional wines were generally considered inferior to those from France and California, Finger Lakes wines are finally being recognized as standing with the best in the world.

As early as 1873, Great Western was the first champagne from the United States to win a gold prize at the Vienna Exposition. Glenora Wine Cellar's 1987 Chardonnay was featured at George Bush's inaugural dinner in 1989, and wines from the Hermann J. Wiemer Vineyard are served at New York City's famed Lutèce restaurant. In 1998 this winery was recognized by *Food and Wine* magazine for producing an outstanding Riesling. Dr. Frank's Vinifera Wine Cellars won a double gold in a recent California wine tasting, and their semidry Riesling came away with a gold medal in a wine tasting in Alsace. Dr. Frank's wines have been served at the White House and continue to beat French wines in blind tastings.

Unlike many winemaking regions in the world, where the majority of the wineries are owned by outsiders, the Finger Lakes vineyards are usually owned and run by families whose roots are sunk deep here. Often their families and ancestors were farmers who sent their children to college to study marketing, business, agriculture, and viniculture. After obtaining their degrees, these sons and daughters returned, armed with new knowledge of how to use the land to build a first-class winemaking business.

Jerry and Elaine Hazlitt, who opened their winery in 1985 (Hazlitt 1852 Vineyards Winery), are the sixth generation in a family that has been growing grapes in the Finger Lakes since the mid-1800s; Art Hunt (Hunt Country Vineyard) is also the sixth generation to live on his farm; Bill Wagner (Wagner Vineyards) started in 1947 as a vegetable and dairy farmer before concentrating on growing grapes and making wine; and the grandfather of Walter S. Taylor (Bully Hill Vineyards) arrived in Hammondsport in the late 19th century and established Taylor Winery. Eventually Walter left the family fold and founded his own vineyard, going on to make superb wines and marketing them with great flair and humor. His wines have names like Le Goat Blush, Thunder Road, and Happy Hen White.

Finger Lakes wines, although slow to appear on the wine lists of New York City's top restaurants, are finally making inroads into what used to be almost exclusively California and European territory. Restaurants like Gramercy Tavern (where 30 percent of their wines come from such regional wineries as Fox Run), Union Square Café (which sells Dr. Frank's Vinifera Wine Cellars Riesling, Silver Thread Riesling, and Hunt Country Ice Wine), and the famous Oyster Bar at Grand Central Station (which offers Finger Lakes Riesling and Fleur de Pinot Noir) are helping to spread the word that some high quality wine is coming from not very far away.

Whereas the Finger Lakes is best known for its white wines, in particular Rieslings, reds like Fox Run's Cabernet Sauvignon and Hazlitt's, Hosmer's, and Lakewood's Cabernet Franc are becoming prominent. In four recent international and national wine competitions, 25 Finger Lakes wineries took gold medals for close to 60 wines.

In 2003 Glenora's 1998 Brut, a complex sparkling wine made from the traditional blend of Pinot Noir and Chardonnay, was chosen by the Culinary Institute of America to be their official house champagne.

HISTORY

The Reverend William Bostwick is credited with planting the first grapevines in the Finger Lakes: In 1829 he planted Catawba and Isabella grapes in the rectory garden of St. James Episcopal Church in Hammondsport. But the good reverend was in another business, and it wouldn't be until 1865 when the first bonded Finger Lakes winery was founded, the Pleasant Valley Winery. The Urbana Wine Company was established in 1865 and renamed Gold Seal Winery in 1887, and Taylor Winery began operations in 1880. By this time there were more than 30 vineyards in the region.

The sale of wines was banned in the 1919 Volstead Act; by the time it was repealed in 1933, all but a few wineries had gone out of business. Some like Taylor and Widmer survived by selling grape juice and sacramental wine.

One of the greatest boosts to winemaking in the Finger Lakes occurred when Vitis vinifera grapes were introduced in the early 1940s. Up until this time, the region had primarily concentrated on growing Vitis labrusca grapes like Catawba, Concord, Delaware, Elvira, and Niagara—hardy varieties that grew very well in the cool climate on the protected lakeside hills. Wines produced from these grapes tended to be fruity, foxy, grapey in taste—certainly no match for the Chardonnays and Pinot Noirs from France and California. Most area winemakers were convinced that the European grapes like Chardonnay, Pinot Noir, and Cabernet Sauvignon could not survive the region's harsh winters.

In 1934 Gold Seal's president went to Rheims, France, and persuaded Charles Fournier, chief winemaker of Cliquot Ponsardin, to come to Hammondsport and rebuild the winery's Prohibition-devastated reputation. Fournier brought with him several French-American hybrid grapes that had been developed in France to withstand diseases. These new hybrids added another dimension to the quality of the grapes grown in the Finger Lakes.

In 1943 the winery's Charles Fournier Brut was introduced; the winery won a gold medal in 1950 for champagne at the California State Fair. In the following years no non-Californian wines were allowed in the competition.

By this time, interest was escalating in growing purely European grapes—going beyond the hybrids. Only by growing the Chardonnays, Pinots, and other prized varieties could the Finger Lakes produce better wines, some believed.

The industry received a major boost when Fournier brought Dr. Konstantin Frank, an immigrant from the Ukraine, to Gold Seal to establish a Vitis vinifera nursery. Before his arrival in the United States, Dr. Frank had studied agriculture at the Polytechnic Institute of Odessa, completing studies in enology and viticulture and going on to teach. After World War II, he came to the U.S. with his family in 1951. He had no money and could not speak English. After working at several menial jobs, he found his way to the New York State Agricultural Experiment Station in Geneva, a grape research facility. Here he was given jobs like picking blueberries and clearing fields.

It wasn't until Charles Fournier heard that that Dr. Frank had been talking about Vitis vinifera as an option for area grape growers that he approached the man from the Ukraine. Dr. Frank explained that he had seen these grapes grow in the Ukraine in temperatures 40 degrees below zero. His theory—graft the Vitis vinifera grapes to hardy root stock to make the vines winter-proof—was convincing. Dr. Frank was hired to establish a Vitis vinifera nursery at Gold Seal.

By proving that the finest grapes in the world could be grown in the Finger Lakes, Dr. Frank triggered enormous growth in the wine industry. He eventually founded his own vineyard, Dr. Frank's Vinifera Wine Cellars Ltd., in the hills above the west side of Keuka Lake. Dr. Frank died in 1985, but the legacy continues with his son Willy and grandson Fred.

Today Finger Lakes wineries and vineyards are producing award-winning wines from grafted, winter-hardy Chardonnays, Riesling, Pinot Noir, and other European grapes.

Wine Trails

Four of the lake areas, Cayuga, Seneca, Keuka, and Canandaigua, have established wine trails, with maps and listings of the participating wineries. All sponsor wine-related events.

Cayuga Wine Trail: 800-684-5217; www.cayugawinetrail.com.
Seneca Lake Wine Trail/Seneca Lake Winery Association: 877-536-2717; 607-535-8080; www.senecalakewine.com.
Keuka Lake Wine Trail: 800-440-4898; www.keukawinetrail.com.
Canandaigua Wine: 877-386-4669; www.canandaiguawinetrailonline.com.

Following is a sampling of the many Finger Lakes wineries. It is not meant as an all-inclusive listing—several excellent books do that job well, among them *Touring East Coast Wine Country* by Marguerite Thomas, another volume in the Great Destinations series. Rather, it is meant to whet your appetite for visiting the wineries and sampling their wines—and to come away with a greater appreciation for what is produced here. You will find everything from small family-run businesses to larger, sophisticated wineries with handsome facilities, including shops, restaurants, lodging, and tours. Many wineries offer wine tastings and participate in events throughout the year. Be sure to call for hours; some are open for visitors year-round; others, seasonally.

Special events incorporating several wineries along the wine trails invite you to sample wines and food at bargain prices of around $20 per person. For example, Cayuga Wine Trail's Wine and Herb Fest in the spring pairs wines with herbs and vegetables. Guests get a souvenir wine glass, 15 potted herbs, a garden plan to help them get started in their planting, a plant carrier, recipes, and wine and food tastings. Cayuga Lake wineries also feature their popular Mardi Gras event in February and Holiday Shopping Spree the first week in December.

At the end of the year, the Seneca Wine Trail's "Deck the Halls" features wine and food tastings along with a grapevine wreath that you can decorate with ornaments collected at each winery and recipes of the foods offered. The wineries also offer their "Pasta & Wine" weekend; Bargain Bash in January, Chocolate & Wine in February, Pasta & Wine in March, Spring Wine and Cheese in April, and the Finger Lakes Wine Festival in July. Seneca Lake has more than 25 vineyards, so to see each one, you might want to spend two or three days.

With six different themed events over eight weekends, the Keuka Lake Wine Association offers six major events each year: Be Mine with Wine in February, Scavenger Hunt in March, Murder Mystery Tour in April, Food Tour of Italy in May, Barbecue at the Wineries in June and Keuka Holidays in November. Each July, all the regions come together for the Finger Lakes Wine Festival in Watkins Glen.

WINERIES AND VINEYARDS

Cayuga Lake

Cayuga Ridge Estate Winery (607-869-5158, 800-598-WINE; www.cayugaridge .com; 6800 Rte. 89, Ovid, NY 14521; at Elm Beach) Owners Susie and Tom Challen feature Chardonnay, Riesling, Cayuga White, Chancellor (French-American hybrid), Pinot Noir, Vignoles, and Cabernet Franc; also Cranberry Essence and Cranberry Frost. Cayuga Ridge is set on 38 acres with wine-tasting facilities in a gigantic old barn with a deck. Picnic tables are also on the grounds. The winery sponsors special events and a vigneron, a "rent-a-grapevine" program. Learn how to grow, tend, and harvest rented vines, then take the grapes or sell them to the vineyard and pay to have them made into wine.

Frontenac Point Vineyard (607-387-9619; www.frontenacpoint.com; 9501 Rte. 89, Trumansburg, NY 14886; 12 miles north of Ithaca) Wine tastings and tours by appointment are offered by owners Jim and Carol Doolittle at their vineyard on the west side of the lake. Their wines include Vinifera varieties such as Chardonnay, Pinot Noir, and Riesling as well as French-American hybrids including Chambourcin, Chelois, and Vidal Blanc. Blends include Proprietor's Reserve Red, oak-aged Proprietor's Reserve White, and Chateau Doolittle made with Riesling and Chambourcin. Frontenac Red is a blend of four varieties. Brut champagne is produced in the *méthode champenoise,* where fermentation generating the bubbles takes place in the bottle.

Goose Watch Winery (315-549-2599; www.goosewatch.com; 5480 Rte. 89, Romulus, NY 14541; 15 minutes south of Seneca Falls) Owners Dick and Cindy Peterson feature classic premium European-style wines such as Merlot, Brut Rosé Champagne, Pinot Gris, Villard Blanc, Viognier, and Finale White Port. Traminette and Melody, from newer grape varieties developed by Cornell University, are also offered. A half mile north of Dean's Cove on the western shore of the lake, Goose Watch is accessible by boat. The winery is in a restored 100-year-old barn set in a grove of chestnut trees. Visitors can enjoy a picnic area, boat dock, and agriculture tram tours; the winery also sells a selection of cheeses, smoked trout, and other gourmet items. In addition to producing wines, Goose Watch has an aquaculture trout operation.

Hosmer Winery (607-869-3393, 888-HOSWINE; fax 607-869-9409; http://hosmer winery.com; 6999 Rte. 89, Ovid, NY 14521) Winners of the 2002 Governor's cup for their Riesling, Cameron and Maren Hosmer also offer Cayuga White, Seyval Blanc, Chardonnay, and Pinot Noir; visitors can enjoy wine tastings, picnic tables, a gift shop, and snack foods. The winery is set on 40 acres on the western shore of the lake. A new wine, Raspberry Rhapsody, is made from fresh raspberries and grape wine.

King Ferry Winery (315-364-5100, 800-439-5271; fax 315-364-8078; www.tre leavenwines.com; 658 Lake Rd., King Ferry, NY 13081; 16 miles north of Ithaca) Owners Peter and Tacie Saltonstall offer wine tastings and sell most of their production at the winery, which is on the eastern shore of Cayuga Lake. However, some of their wines are available in restaurants and New York City stores. King Ferry has a retail store at Prime Outlets in Waterloo. Featured wines are Cabernet Franc, Treleaven Chardonnays aged in French oak, Treleaven Rieslings, Pinot Noir, and Gewürztraminer. Three wines introduced in 2003 include Vintner's Cuvée, a late-harvest Vignole and a sweet red wine named Mystere.

Knapp Vineyards Winery and Restaurant (607-869-9271, 800-869-9271; fax 607-869-3212; www.knappwine.com; 2770 Ernsberger Rd., Romulus, NY 14541, on County Rte. 128) Featured are classic European wines such as Barrel Reserve Chardonnay, Cayuga Lake Chardonnay, Dutchman's Breeches (a combination of Vidal and Vignoles), Ruby Port, and Sangiovese, a red wine originating in Tuscany. The stylish modern winery is set on 99 acres and offers wine tastings, picnic facilities, and a harvest festival. The excellent restaurant on site features American cuisine and European dishes as well as winemaker's dinners. Guests can eat indoors or on the outdoor garden patio. Knapp also concocts brandy and grappa in a hand-hammered copper onion-dome distillery.

Helpful Terms

Barrel fermented: Wine is aged in oak barrels, which creates a more complex flavored, full-bodied wine.

Brut: A measure of the dryness of a champagne (extra dry, brut, or natural).

Enology: Winemaking.

Enophile: A lover of wine.

Estate bottled: Wine made from grapes grown on the property.

Finish: Indicates flavors that remain in the mouth after the wine is consumed.

French-American hybrid: A cross (hybrid) of American and European grape varieties.

Grafted Vitis vinifera: European grapes grafted to hardier root stock to help survive low temperatures.

Late harvest: Grapes picked very ripe at the end of the season. Used to produce sweet dessert wines.

Méthode champenoise: When making champagne, the second fermentation takes place in the bottle.

Nose: The smell of a wine.

Reserve: Wines marked as special by the producing vineyard.

Varietal wines: Wines of one grape variety.

Viniculture: Grape growing, winemaking, and marketing wine.

Vinification: The fermentation process by which juice is converted into wine.

Vitis labrusca: Hardy grapes like Catawba, Concord, Delaware, Elvira, and Niagara, known for their foxy/grapey taste. Because of their ability to survive harsh winters, these were the first grapes grown in the Finger Lakes region.

Vitis vinifera: Classic European varieties like Chardonnay, Pinot Noir, Gewürztraminer, Riesling, Sauvignon Blanc, Cabernet Sauvignon, Cabernet Franc, Merlot, and Meunier.

A vineyard carpets the hillside overlooking Seneca Lake.

Lakeshore Winery (315-549-7075; fax 315-549-7102; www.lakeshorewinery.com; 5132 Rte. 89; Romulus, NY 14541) On the west side of the lake with beautiful views, this is a friendly, relaxed place with a large stone fireplace and rocking chairs. Outside are picnic tables and a boat dock. Owners John and Annie Bachman feature Vinifera varieties such as Cabernet Sauvignon and Pinot Noir, and French-American hybrids including Baco Noir and Cayuga White. Aunt Clara and Uncle Charlie are blends of Labrusca grapes, based on the Catawba variety. Food is served with wine at the sit-down tastings; special activities include Lakeshore Nouveau Weekend in early November to celebrate the harvest.

Long Point Winery (315-364-6990; www.longpointwinery.com; 1485 Lake Rd., Aurora, NY 13026) Though the winery itself is relatively new to the region, Long Point winery owner and vintner Gary Barletta is no stranger to the wine business. As an amateur winemaker, he garnered more than 60 awards during the past two decades. Among the featured wines estate bottled from California grapes are dry Rieslings, Cabernet Sauvignon (2001 Bronze Medal in the NY State Fair wine competition), a barrel-fermented Chardonnay, Merlot (2001 Silver Medal in the NY State Fair), Syrah (double gold medal in the NY State Fair and gold medal in the 2001 Eastern International Wine Competition), and a Cambrie, a light red table wine similar in taste to beaujolais. A gift shop is on the premises.

Lucas Vineyards (607-532-4825, 800-682-WINE [NY only]; fax 607-532-8580; www.lucasvineyards.com; 3862 County Rd. 150, Interlaken, NY 14847; 18 miles north of Ithaca) The oldest winery on Cayuga Lake, Lucas Vineyards is set on 68 acres on the west side of the lake with beautiful views of the water from the tasting room. Owner Ruth Lucas features Vinifera, French-American varietals, and sparkling wines. The tugboat wines—Captain Belle Blush, a blend of five hybrids; Blues, a blend of Cayuga White and Seyval Blanc; and Harbor Moon, a blend of Cayuga White and Vidal Blanc—recall founder Bill Lucas's early years as a tugboat captain on the eastern seaboard. Visitors can enjoy wine tastings, gift shop, picnic facilities, special events.

Montezuma Winery (315-568-8190, fax 315-568-8607; www.montezumawinery .com; 2981 Auburn Rd., Seneca Falls, NY 13148) This new winery specializes in honey mead, grape and fruit wines such as Redwing, a semisweet red Catawba blend, a Rhubarb Wine and a Cranberry-Apple Wine. The gift shop sells beeswax candles, honey, wine accessories and gift baskets along with "mead," the first alcoholic beverage ever consumed. Picnic area on site.

Sheldrake Point Vineyard & Café (607-532-9401; fax: 607-532-8967; www.shel drakepoint.com; 7448 County Road 153, Ovid, NY 14521) Set on the edge of the lake, Sheldrake Point Vineyard's wines include Pinot Noir, Gamay, Merlot, Gewürztraminer, and other varietals. There is a wine-tasting room, gift shop, and café serving lunch and Sunday brunch. Specialties include herbed Tuscany bruschetta, smoked salmon, broiled stuffed trout, and duck Sheldrake as well as sandwiches and salads. Their function room and permanent tent is a popular place for weddings and other events.

Swedish Hill Winery (315-549-8326, 888-549-WINE; fax 315-549-8477; www .swedishhill.com; 4565 Rte. 414, Romulus, NY 14541; 8 miles south of Seneca Falls on the west side of the lake) Although owners Dick and Cindy Peterson make wine from European varieties, they have successfully produced excellent wines from Labrusca and French-American hybrids. Notable wines include Rieslings, Svenska White, Svenska Red, Late Harvest Vignoles, Optimus (a Bordeaux-style blend), Cynthia Marie Vintage Port, and Eaux-De-Vie grape brandy. Set on 35 acres, the winery has a rustic red barn with a deck overlooking a pond. An old still sits near the entrance. And be sure to walk over to the pasture near the picnic area and say hello to the miniature donkey. The large wine-tasting room has three separate tasting bars. Amish-baked breads and gift wine packs are also available at Swedish Hill. In addition to the gift shop, tours, and tastings, the winery hosts many annual events, including the Scandinavian Festival, a Wine and Art Festival, and a Champagne and Dessert Wine Festival.

Thirsty Owl Wine Company (866-869-5805; www.thirstyowl.com; 6799 Elm Beach Road, Ovid, NY 14521) This new winery, which debuted in spring 2003, produces Chardonnay, Dry Riesling, Vidal Blanc, Riesling, Blushing Moon, Red Moon, Pinot Noir, Lot 99, and Merlot. The winery has a gift shop and wine tastings. Ask about their new bistro.

Seneca Lake

Amberg Wine Cellars (585-526-6742; fax 315-462-6512; www.ambergwine.com; 2200 Rte. 5 & 20, Flint, NY 14561; 6 miles west of Geneva) The Amberg family has been growing grapes for more than 30 years. Eric Amberg, winemaker, offers Chardonnay, Pinot Noir, Riesling, and Chambourcin, a French-American hybrid. Blends include Blanc, Burgundy, Pearl, Gypsy, and Red Panda, a semisweet wine. Red Baron is a rich fruity wine. When the original barns of the family farm (circa 1795) burned down, a new winery was built. A huge wooden wine cask serves as a sign to announce the entrance. Wine tastings and a shop are offered to visitors.

Anthony Road Wine Company.

Anthony Road Wine Company (315-536-2182, 800-559-2182; fax 315-536-5851; www.anthonyroadwine.com; 1225 Anthony Rd., Penn Yan, NY 14527) Owners John and Ann Martini feature a premium veritas wine series; Chardonnay, Riesling, Cabernet Franc, Seyval Blanc, and late harvest Vignoles; blends include Poulet Rouge, Tony's Red, Vintner's Red, and Vintner's Select. Wine tastings are held in an attractive building with high ceilings, blue and tan early-American faux painted designs, and a good view of the lake. The spacious facility has become a popular place for weddings.

Arcadian Estate Vineyards (607-535-2068, 800-298-1346; fax 607-535-4692; www.arcadianwine.com; 4184 Rte. 14, Rock Stream, NY 14878) Wine tastings, an art gallery, a gourmet food court, and special events are offered in a 170-year-old knotty-pine barn set on 72 acres. Owners Mike and Joanne Hastrich feature Dechaunac (French-American hybrid), Pinot Noir, Chardonnay, Riesling, and Cabernet Sauvignon; blends include Sail Away (Chardonnay and Cayuga), Pinot Rougeon, and Flora de la Noche. They suggest trying their Simple Pleasures fruit wines like blackberry, black raspberry, cherry, and pear.

Castel Grisch Estate Winery (607-535-9614; fax 607-535-2994; www.fingerlakes-ny.com/CastelGrisch; 3380 County Rte. 28, Watkins Glen, NY 14891) The Malina family offers Chardonnay, Gewürztraminer, Johannesburg Riesling, Blanc Noir, Chablis Grand Cru, Baco Noir, Estate Reserve Burgundy, Cabernet Frank, Seneca Blush, Seneca Dream Red and White, Vidal Blanc Ice Wine, and Riesling Ice Wine. Their 138-acre vineyard has an Alps-style chalet winery, deli, bake shop, gift shop, and an open deck.

Chateau LaFayette Reneau (607-546-2062, 800-469-9463; fax 607-546-2069; www.clrwine.com; Box 238, Rte. 414, Hector, NY 14841) Owners Dick and Betty Reno offer hayrides through the vineyards here; the site encompasses 140 acres of grapevines, meadows, woodlands, and ponds on the east side of the lake. Featured wines are Chardonnay, Riesling, Cuvee Rouge, Pinot Noir,

Vidal Blanc, Blanc de Blanc, and Pinot Noir Blanc. Visitors can enjoy wine tastings, picnic tables, and a terrace overlooking the lake.

Earle Estate Meadery (607-243-9011; fax 607-243-9058; www.meadery.com; 3586 Rte. 14, Himrod, NY 14842) This large retail store and wine-tasting facility has its own beehives and honey. Owners John and Esther Earle are known for their honey and fruit-influenced wines such as Pear-Mead, Peach Perfection, Cherry Charisma, Raspberry Reflections, and Strawberry Shadows as well as a light fruity Chardonnay, Riesling, Cayuga White, and Seyval Blanc. The wine bottles alone are worth the price. The family also owns the new Torrey Ridge Winery down the road.

Four Chimneys Organic Winery (607-243-7502; fax 607-243-8156; www.four chimneysorganicwines.com; 211 Hall Rd., Himrod, NY 14842) At the first organic winery in the region, owner Scott R. Smith features Reserve White (mostly Chardonnay), Alsatian-style Dry Cayuga, Kingdom White and Red, Reserve Reds, Eye of the Bee (from Concord), Coronation, organic champagne, and specialty fruit wines. On the property is an Italianate villa with four chimneys, and a large Victorian barn. Wine tastings are offered.

Fox Run Vineyards (315-536-4616, 800-636-9786; www.foxrunvineyards.com; 670 Rte. 14, Penn Yan, NY 14527) Winner of the 1997 Governor's Cup for the Best New York State Wine, Fox Run features Riesling, Pinot Noir, Chardonnay, Cabernet Sauvignon, Cabernet Franc, Merlot; Reserve Chardonnay and Reserve Pinot Noir; also Ruby Vixon, a semidry blush, Arctic Fox, and Port. Owners Scott Osborn and Brooks Hale preside over a lovely barn with a deck overlooking the lake, a large wine-tasting area, gift shop, café, and wine tours.

Glenora Wine Cellars (607-243-5511, 800-243-5513; www.glenora.com; 5435 Rte. 14, Dundee, NY 14837) Owners Gene Pierce, Ed Dalrymple, and Scott Welliver feature Chardonnay, Chardonnay/Barrel Fermented, Pinot Noir, Riesling, Merlot, Cabernet Sauvignon, and Gewürztraminer; sparkling wines including Brut (blend of Pinot Noir, Pinot Blanc, and Chardonnay), Blanc de Blancs, and Brut Rosé; and French-American hybrid wines such as Cayuga White and Seyval Blanc. The magnificent lakeside setting includes a large wine-tasting room, gift shop, deck, restaurant, and inn; the winery often hosts special events.

Hazlitt 1852 Vineyards (607-546-9463; fax 607-546-5712; www.hazlitt1852.com; 5712 Rte. 414, PO Box 53, Hector, NY 14841) The Hazlitt family features Chardonnay, Riesling, Gewürztraminer, Schooner White, Cabernet, Merlot, Pinot Gris, and Red Cat, a blend of Catawba and Baco Noir. The winery is in a wonderful rustic barn filled with antiques and memorabilia. Tastings take place around two U-shaped bars. It's a lively, friendly place run by a fun group of people.

Hermann J. Wiemer (607-243-7971, 800-371-7971; fax 607-243-7983; www.wiemer .com; 3962 Rte. 14, PO Box 38, Dundee, NY 14837; halfway between Geneva and Dundee on the west side of the lake) Owner Hermann Wiemer features wines only from Vitis vinifera grapes: Chardonnay, Alsace-style Keuka Lake.

Lakewood Vineyards (607-535-9252; fax 607-535-6656; www.lakewoodvineyards .com; 4024 Rte. 14, Watkins Glen, NY 14891) Three generations of the Stamp family pour their souls into making this vineyard work. Featured are Labrusca wines such as Delaware, Niagara, and White Catawba; French-American hybrids Long Stem White and Long Stem Red; Chardonnay, Riesling, and Ice Wine. The winery and tasting room occupy a long, modern wood building on the east side of the lake near fields full of sunflowers. This is a kid-friendly place, with tours, picnic facilities, and a playground.

Lamoreaux Landing Wine Cellars, Lodi.

Lamoreaux Landing Wine Cellars (607-582-6011; fax 607-582-6010; www.lamo reauxwine.com; 9224 Rte. 414, Lodi, NY 14860) Owner Mark J. Wagner targets the ultrapremium market and produces a full-bodied Pinot Noir, as well as Chardonnay, Gewürztraminer, Riesling, Merlot, Cabernet Franc, and Brut; blends include Estate White and Estate Red. Lamoreaux's wines have recently received many awards, including gold medals for their 2001 Gewürztraminer, 99 Brut, 2002 Chardonnay Reserve, and the 2001 Cabernet Franc. The winery—and its tasting room, a striking tall, narrow building with four square columns, resembling a Greek temple—is set on 130 acres overlooking the east side of the lake. Picnic tables are available.

Miles Wine Cellars (607243-7742; fax 607-243-3827; www.mileswinecellars.com; 168 Randall Crossing Rd., Himrod, NY 14842) Located in a 200-year-old Greek-Revival home, the winery provides a special tasting experience. Sip estate-grown wines on the lake-view porch or under an enormous weeping willow. One of their newest wines, Ghost Wine, a Chardonnay-Cayuga blend, celebrates the Miles manse's resident spirit. Crackers and cheese can be purchased on site. There is a dock, so you can arrive by boat.

Nagy's New Land Vineyard (315-585-4432; fax 315-585-9881; www.nagyswines .com; 623 Lerch Rd., Geneva, NY 14456) From the starting gate, this new vineyard has delivered premium-quality varietals. Especially lauded is their 2001 Reserve Sauvignon Blanc

Prejean (315-536-7524, 800-548-2216; fax 315-536-7635; 2634; www.prejean winery.com; Rte. 14, Penn Yan, NY 14527; just south of Dresden) Owners Elizabeth and Tom Prejean feature Merlot, semidry Gewürztraminer, premium Chardonay, Riesling, Cayuga, Vignoles, and Port. Wine tastings and a gift shop are in a weathered old barn with a deck overlooking the west side of the lake. Prejean is one of the top producers of Gewürztraminer, a wine known to go well with Cajun food. (Prejean is a Cajun name).

Red Newt Cellar Winery and Bistro (607-546-4100; fax 607-546-4101; www.red newt.com; 3675 Tichenor Rd., Hector, NY 14841; 10 miles north of Watkins Glen) This new winery features Chardonnay, Riesling, Red Newt White, Cabernet Franc, Merlot, and Cabernet Sauvignon. Co-owner David Whiting is well known for his winemaking skills at other local vineyards, where he created award-winning wines. The winery, set on the east side of the lake with stunning views, also houses "The Bistro" run by co-owner Debra Whiting, who comes from the catering business. You can eat inside or out on the deck.

Seneca Shores Wine Cellars (315-536-0882; 929 Davy Rd., Penn Yan, NY 14527; on Rte. 14) Owner David DeMarco offers Cabernet Franc, Gewürztraminer, barrel-fermented Chardonnay, Riesling, White Castle blend, Cabernet Sauvignon, Merlot and Red Castle blend. A new modest-size blue building with rocking chairs and a covered deck overlooks the lake; tours and a picnic area are also available. The wine tasting room features a medieval theme complete with battle axes and shield to complement its "medieval wines."

Standing Stone Vineyards (607-582-6051, 800-803-7135; fax 607-582-6312; www .standingstonewines.com; 9934 Rte. 414, Hector NY 14841) In a nifty restored chicken coop with a spacious terrace, this winery features Chardonnay, Gewürztraminer, Riesling, Cabernet Franc, Merlot, Pinnacle blend, and Dry Vidal Blanc aged in oak. Owners Marti and Tom Macinski's Riesling and Gewürztraminer have won several awards; Cabarnet Franc was awarded the Governor's Cup at a recent New York Wine and Food Classic. Wine tastings and picnic tables are available.

Torrey Ridge Winery (315-536-1210; www.torreyridgewinery.com; 2770 Rte. 14, Penn Yan, NY 14527) Owners John and Esther Earle feature Chardonnay, Riesling, Cayuga White, Seyval Blanc, Baco Noir; native varieties such as Concord, Diamond, and Niagara; and Bandit Red, Virtue, Bandit Blush, and Summer Delight, a semisweet fruit wine. This new winery, owned by the Earle Estates Meadery family, is in a handsome white building with wine tasting rooms on both floors; don't miss views of the lake from the second floor balcony. Educational tours are offered.

Torrey Ridge Winery, Penn Yan.

Wagner Vineyards (607-582-6450; fax 607-582-6446; www.wagnervineyards.com; 9322 Rte. 414, Lodi NY 14860) Featured wines are Chardonnay, Gewürztraminer, Riesling, Cabernet Franc, Cabernet Sauvignon, Merlot, and Pinot Noir. Also Brut Champagne, Riesling Ice Wine, Vignoles Ice Wine, OCR (Octagon Cellars Reserve), and Reserve Red and White. Unique to the area are the fruity beer varieties like Captain Curry's Lager, Grace House Honey Wheat, Mill Street Pilsner, Seneca Trail Pale Ale, and Caywood Station Stout. One of the largest operations in the Finger Lakes, the winery is in a striking octagonal building set in the 250-acre vineyard, along with a 20-barrel German-style brewery. Owner Bill Wagner also presides over beer and wine tastings, a large gift shop, and café.

Keuka Lake

Barrington Cellars (315-536-9686; www.barringtoncellars.com; 2772 Gray Rd., Penn Yan, NY 14527) This small, family-owned winery features wines made from Vitis labrusca grapes (a native variety) and French hybrids. Owners Ken and Eileen Farnan offer Reislings, Pink Cat, Isabella Rosé, and dessert wines; Bliss, Isabella, and Niagara Ice Wines. Visitors can enjoy wine tastings, a wine shop, and the 100-year-old farmhouse. Recently a new winery building was built.

Bully Hill Vineyards (607-868-3610, 607-868-3210; fax 607-868-3205; www.bully hill.com; 8843 Greyton H. Taylor Memorial Dr., Hammondsport, NY 14840-1458) Owner Walter S. Taylor, a creative pioneer in winemaking and a grandson of the founder of the Taylor Wine Company, has produced many award-winning wines. Wines from French-American hybrids include Aurora, Baco Noir, Cayuga White, Ravat (Vignoles), Seyval Blanc, and Vidal Blanc. Blends carry often humorous names like Meat Market Red, Miss Love White, Space Shuttle Rosé, and Le Goat Blush. Flying Fortress pays tribute to the National Warplane Museum in Elmira. Champagnes include Mother Ship Over Paris champagne Rouge and Seyval Blanc Brut champagne. The winery's lovely weathered barns in hillside gardens look out over marvelous lake views; the Bully Hill Restaurant has both indoor and deck dining. Wine tastings, three gift shops and the Greyton H. Taylor Wine and Grape Museum also enhance the visit. Bully Hill's colorful and distinctive wine labels are worthy of collecting.

Chateau Renaissance Wine Cellars (866-4 CORKIE; fax 607-569-3758; www. chateaurenaissance.com; 7494 Fish Hatchery Rd., Bath, NY 14810) Just south of Hammondsport, this new winery offers wine tastings in an attractive facility. The winery makes table, fruit and *méthode champenoise* sparkling wines. Free tastings and tours are offered, and there is a gift shop and special events.

Dr. Frank's Vinifera Wine Cellars and Chateau Frank (607-868-4884, 800-320-0735; fax 607-868-4888; www.drfrankwines.com; 9749 Middle Rd., Hammondsport, NY 14840) The Frank family winery, set on 79 hillside acres overlooking Keuka Lake, features barrel-fermented Chardonnay Gewürztraminer, Riesling, Pinot Noir, Rkatskieli, Cabernet Sauvignon, and a sparkling Riesling, Ceiebre. Chateau Frank is a premium sparkling wine made in the *méthode champenoise* style. The winery was founded in 1962 by one of the Finger Lakes' most important winemakers, Dr. Konstantin Frank, who showed how the prized European grape varieties could be grown in the region and how world-class table wines could be produced. His Pinot Noir vines are the oldest in the Finger Lakes, producing a more complex, full-bodied wine not possible with younger vines. It is no wonder his wines have been critically acclaimed. After Dr. Frank's death in 1985, his son Willy took over the operations. Willy's son, Fred, is president of the company. Wine tastings are offered daily. Recently the vineyard acquired 13 more acres that have been planted with Riesling Clone 90, Rkatsiteli, and Pinot Gris.

Heron Hill Winery (607-868-4241, 800-441-4241; fax: 607-868-3435; www.heronhill.com; 9249 County Rte. 76, Hammondsport, NY14840) A handsome new building with a wine tasting room and other facilities showcases a breathtaking view of the lake. Owners John and Josephine Ingle feature Chardonnay, Johannisberg Riesling, Pinot Noir, Eclipse, Baco Noir, Seyval Blanc, Harmony Red and White, blends from hybrid and Vitis vinifera grapes. The Rockin' Robin series uses native grapes. The Game Bird series comes with recipes for preparing game. Visitors can enjoy wine tastings, a shop, restaurant, deli, conference room, banquet space, oak barrel room and patio.

Hunt Country Vineyards (315-595-2812, 800-946-3289; fax 315-595-2835; www.huntcountryvineyards.com; 4021 Italy Hill Rd., Branchport, NY 14418) Scenic trails here are open to hikers and cyclists, who are invited to bring their lunch for picnicking. The operating family farm, with horses grazing near the entrance road, includes a renovated 1820s barn with a wine tasting room, deck, and shop. Owners Art and Joyce Hunt focus on specialty wines and feature Riesling, Barrel Reserve Chardonnay, Foxy Lady (blush), Classic Red and White, Seyval, Cayuga, Vignoles, and Vidal Ice wine. Tours and wine tastings are offered.

Keuka Overlook Wine Cellars (607-292-6877; www.keukaoverlook.com; 5777 Old Bath Rd., Dundee NY 14837) Owners Bob and Terry Barrett feature barrel-fermented and aged Chardonnay, Gewürztraminer, Riesling, Cabernet Sauvignon, Cabernet Franc, Pinot Noir, and Merlot. Blends include Heritage and Triumph. The winery is set on one of the highest hillsides overlooking Keuka and Waneta Lakes; there are wine tastings, a large gift shop, picnic area, and the Keuka Overlook Bed & Breakfast Inn. Weekend getaway packages are offered with dinner and stay at the B&B.

Keuka Spring Winery (315-536-3147; 585-620-4850 off-season Nov.–May; www.keukaspringwinery.com; 273 E. Lake Rd., Penn Yan NY 14527; on Rte. 54,) Owners Judy and Len Wiltberger's gambrel-roofed barn houses the wine tasting room; also on the historic property overlooking the lake is an 1840s homestead, and a picnic area. Featured wines are Chardonnay, Riesling, Cayuga Whites, Seyval Blanc, Vignoles, Cabernet Franc, Cabernet Sauvignon, Merlot, Pinot Noir, and Crooked Lake Red.

McGregor Vineyard and Winery (800-272-0192; 607-292-3999; fax 607-292-6929; www.mcgregorwinery.com; 5503 Dutch St., Dundee, NY 14837) Set on a hill overlooking Bluff Point on the east side of the lake—one of the most scenic overviews in the state—the winery is located in a modest-sized barn. Owners Robert and Margaret McGregor feature Chardonnay, Pinot Noir aged in French oak, Alsatian-style Riesling, Gewürztraminer, Johannisberg Riesling, Blanc de Noir, Muscat Ottonel, Lake Harvest Vignoles, Black Russian Red, Highlands Red, Chardonnay Blanc de Blanc champagne, and Sunflower White, a blend of Vitis vinifera and French-American hybrid grapes. Verdelet and Muscat Ottonel are produced by only a few other vineyards in the Finger Lakes, and the winery is one of the few estate-growth producers of premium vinifera wines in the region. Visitors can enjoy wine tastings, picnic on the terrace, and purchase homemade gourmet foods, including Bob McGregor's smoked lake trout, brie, fruit and nut torte, and a chocolate Riesling fondue.

Pleasant Valley Wine Company/Great Western Winery (607-569-6111; fax 607-569-6112; GWWinery@InfoBlvd.net; 8260 Pleasant Valley Rd., Hammondsport, NY 14840) Owner Michael Doyle features Great Western Champagne, Chardonnay, Riesling, Verdelet, Port, Sherry, Marsala, Madeira, Brut Rosé, and Labrusca grape varieties. The eight stone buildings here, very European in feeling, are listed on the National Register of Historic Places. Their ornate interiors have elaborate carved-wood paneling and molding and period furniture. The storage areas house enormous wine vats and barrels. Caves are carved into the valley's hillside, and a working model of the Bath-Hammondsport

Railroad is on the grounds. Visitors can also enjoy wine tastings, tours, and the Great Western Winery visitors center, with a theater, memorabilia, and wine equipment spanning 140 years. Established in 1860, this was the first bonded United States winery. In 1873 Great Western became the first American champagne to win a gold medal in Europe at the Vienna exposition.

Rooster Hill Vineyards (315-536-4773; www.roosterhill.com; Penn Yan, NY 14527) One of the newest kids on the block, Rooster Hill Vineyards opened May 3, 2003, under the enthusiastic helm of Amy and David Hoffman, refugees from the corporate world. Their wines include Riesling, Seyval blanc, Cayuga White, Merlot, and Silver Pencil, a proprietary blend of Seyval White and Cayuga White. The Tuscan-style wine-tasting room and wraparound porch reveal stunning views of the lake.

Canandaigua

Arbor Hill Grapery (585-374-2406; www.thegrapery.com; 6459 Rte. 64, Bristol Springs, Naples, NY 14512) John and Katie Brahm preside over 18 acres and feature Chardonnay, Riesling, Pinot Noir, Cayuga White, Maréchal Foch, Traminette, Vidal Blanc, Catawba, Niagara, and Celebration sparkling wine. Wine tastings are offered, and the shop sells everything remotely connected to grapes. Try their homemade grape pies and other gourmet foods using wine and grapes.

Casa Larga (585-223-4210; www.casalarga.com; 2287 Turk Hill Rd, Fairport, NY 14450) The winery received a double golf for their 2001 Reserve Chardonnay at the Tasters Guild International Wine Competition and golf for both their nonvintage Cabernet-Merlot and 2002 Riesling. Its premium category includes limited-release, hand-selected, barrel-fermented and aged and unfiltered Oak Reserve Pinot Noir, French Oak Reserve Chardonnay, and American Oak Reserve Chardonnay. The winery has a wine and gift shop and sponsors special events.

Widmer's Wine Cellars (585-374-6311, 800-836-5253; fax 585-374-2028; www.widmerwine.com; 1 Lake Niagara Lane, Naples, NY 14512) On the hills overlooking the Naples valley, the Canandaigua Wine Company offers sherries, sparkling wines, Lake Niagara, Crackling Lake Niagara, and Port. Visitors can enjoy wine tastings, tours of underground cellars and the bottling facility, and the gift and wine shop. The Widmer Antique Museum displays a collection of old winemaking equipment. Manischewitz, a line of kosher premium varietals, is made here.

CHAPTER NINE
Host Cities
SYRACUSE, CORTLAND, ELMIRA, CORNING, AND ROCHESTER

Hillside near Cortland.

Five major cities anchor the Finger Lakes region. Starting in the northeast corner is Syracuse, a city on the move to rebuild and recharge the vitality of its downtown. Farther south on the eastern border of the region and just off Interstate 81 is Cortland, hub of downhill skiing for the eastern Finger Lakes.

Elmira, once the home of Samuel Clemens (Mark Twain), sits on the southern fringe just off Route 17. Corning, home of the extraordinary Museum of Glass, is just west of Elmira. At the northwestern corner is Rochester, a vibrant city of high-tech business, museums, and upscale suburbs.

I have lived in Rochester and grew up just a half hour from Syracuse. Still, it was only in revisiting these and other cities for the purpose of writing this book that I realized just how much these places have to offer. Although these cities do serve as gateways to the Finger Lakes region, it would be a pity simply to pass through to get where you're going—each one of these cities is worth a good, long linger. This is the reason I call them "Host Cities."

As of this writing, the Pyramid Company's proposed $2.2 billion Destiny USA megaplex venture, projected to be the biggest thing to happen in the region in decades and expected to bring between 12 million and 24 million visitors to the site each year, is in limbo. Plans called for a "Destiny wine train" to the Finger Lakes wine area, an outdoor replica of the old Erie Canal, a huge entertainment and retail complex, a 47-story 1,300- room Grand Destiny Hotel and megamall. However, the project appears to be derailed in a tangle of political maneuverings.

SYRACUSE

S yracuse is perhaps best known as the home of Syracuse University and the site of the New York State Fair, which brings close to a million visitors to the fairgrounds each year. Increasingly, however, the city has much more to offer.

At the crossroads of two interstate highway systems, the east-west New York State Thruway (Interstate 90) and the north-south Interstate 81, Syracuse is home to important businesses, such as New Process Gear, Carrier Corporation, Niagara Mohawk, and Lockheed Martin, three major newspapers, an international airport, and excellent hospitals, including SUNY Upstate Medical Center. Forty-four private and state colleges are in the Greater Syracuse region; in Onondaga County alone there are eight schools, including Syracuse University, with more than 18,000 students, and Le Moyne College.

On the cultural scene, Syracuse has its own symphony orchestra, opera company, and several museums and art galleries, including the **Everson Museum of Art**. The **Carrier Dome** (a venue for athletic and other events), the gigantic **New York State Fair**, **Oncenter** (a multipurpose facility), and the many parks and golf courses are further assets that both residents and visitors enjoy.

This past year the long-awaited **Delavan Art Gallery** opened in Delavan Center, a turn-of-the-20th-century four-story brick building, once a manufacturing facility for John Deere. The gallery represents the fulfillment of a dream of owner Bill Delavan, who sees the gallery as an exciting new way to meet the needs of area artists for sales and exhibits and the needs of the community for a good space to view art produced by those artists.

Syracuse has its own lake, Onondaga, but unfortunately it is not yet safe for swimming or drinking. In the past, companies on the lakeshores haphazardly allowed their industrial waste to run into the lake and pollute its waters. More than five years ago the courts put a stop to waste dumping, and a massive $380 million lake cleanup plan is underway, but experts predict it will take several years before the lake is back to where it should be. Recent reports, though, indicate that the cleanup process is going faster than was predicted. Good news for Syracuse residents.

Still, it is a pleasant visual asset with a recreational area, **Onondaga Lake Park,** which runs for 5 miles along the west shore of the lake. The park has three trails: one for walking and running, one for biking and in-line skating, and another for exploring. A new Visitors Center, Skateboard Park, and Boundless Playground opened late in 2003. The Onondaga Lake Parkway is closed to traffic in the summer months on Sunday for hikers, inline skaters, joggers, and the like.

At the Inner Harbor at the lake's southern tip, plans are progressing to complete a recreational trail looping the lake. The harbor has been dredged, and a nice little park has been completed, with volleyball courts at the water's edge just north of Spencer Street. Hopes are that the cleanup will be completed by 2008.

Fifty years ago **Salina Street** in downtown Syracuse was the place to come for fashionable shopping. Those looking for clothes and gifts shopped in department stores like W. E. Addis Co. (1916), E. W. Edward, and Dey Brothers; they stopped for hot-fudge sundaes at Schrafts and dined at the Hotel Syracuse. When the malls opened in the suburbs, shoppers left downtown. One after another the retailers either moved to the malls or closed their doors.

Now Syracuse's downtown is making a comeback. Armory Square, an area of buildings in the center of town, has been reclaimed and houses chic shops and restaurants. Several in-town hotels and buildings are being renovated; the striking Art Deco **Niagara Mohawk** building is illuminated by layers of color when the sun sets, and there are plans to light up the entire downtown area at night. **Clinton Square** is the site of concerts and other summer events and is transformed into a skating rink in the winter; automobile enthusiasts are being drawn into the city with such events as the Syracuse Nationals Classic Show, which bring up to 6,000 participants and more than 40,000 spectators to the **Empire Exposition Center.** The Carousel Center, already the largest mall in the region, may get even bigger if a major new project goes through to build a complex just across from the Center. The plans call for three hotels, an aquarium, entertainment facilities, and a sky bridge connecting it to the Carousel Center.

For information on the Onondaga Lake Cleanup project: **www.onlake partners.org.**

LODGING

Syracuse is represented by most major hotel chains. Several of the in-city hotels are undergoing restoration. The Syracuse Hotel, listed as one of the Historic Hotels of America and now a part of the Radisson group, has renovated its grand ballroom and its guest rooms. The following specialty hotels and B&Bs provide other options.

The Craftsman Inn (315-637-8000; www.craftsmaninn.com; 300 E. Genesee St., Fayetteville, NY 13066) The 93 rooms and suites are furnished in the simple Arts and Crafts mode, with clean lines, rich colors, wood moldings, and Stickley tables and chairs. Rooms are equipped with the latest in communications equipment.

Crest Hill Suites (315-463-0258, 888-723-1655; www.cresthillsuites.com; 6410 New Venture Gear Dr., E. Syracuse, NY 13057) At Carrier Circle near I-81, the NY State Thruway, and major area employers, this all-suites hotel is designed for extended-stay business travelers and frequent guests. Suites are spacious and come with work areas equipped with free high-speed Internet access, multiple telephone lines with speaker phones, and voice mail. There are studios and one- and two-bedroom suites.

Dickerson House on James (315-423-4777; 1504 James St., Syracuse, NY 13203) The five guest rooms in this B&B are on the top floor of this gracious old house on one of the best residential streets in the city.

Genesee Inn Hotel (800-365-HOME; 315-476-4212; 1060 East Genesee St., Syracuse, NY 13210) This new hotel, located in the heart of the city's historic University Hill section, is one of the most upscale places to stay in Syracuse. With 160 rooms, a world-class restaurant, and a casual bistro, the inn features amenities like pillow-top mattresses, marble vanities, and elegant fabrics and linens.

Giddings Garden B&B (315-492-8542, 800-377-3452; www.giddingsgarden .com; 290 E. Seneca Tpke., Syracuse, NY 13207) The three rooms in this historic 1810 house feature four-poster beds, down comforters, and marble baths. Guests also enjoy fireplaces, gardens, and a full breakfast.

Hotel Syracuse/Radisson Plaza (315-422-5121, 800-333-3333; www.hotelradis son.com or www.hotelsyracuse.com; 500 S. Warren St., Syracuse, NY 13202) There are 600 guestrooms in this historic hotel in the heart of Syracuse; an indoor pool, fitness facility, three ballrooms, and meeting rooms.

Sheraton University University Hotel and Conference Center (315-475-3000, 800-395-2105; www.syracusesheraton.com; 801 University Ave., Syracuse, NY 13210) This 231-room hotel with an indoor pool and fitness facility is on the campus of Syracuse University.

RESTAURANTS

Alto Cinco (315-422-6399; 526 Wescott St., Syracuse) Mexican cuisine: the real thing.

Arad Evans Inn (315-637-2020; 7206 E. Genesee St., Fayetteville) Serving French American food beautifully presented. Desserts are over the moon.

Aunt Josie's Restaurant (315-471-9082; 1110 N. Salina St., Syracuse) Tradition, tradition, tradition, Italian style. Red-and-white checkered tablecloths and a simple setting with excellent homemade pasta and sauces.

Brick Alley Grille House (315-472-3990; 317 Montgomery St., Syracuse) A café-style restaurant serving creative cuisine inside or out.

Coleman's Authentic Irish Pub (315-476-1933; 100 S. Lowell Ave., Syracuse) A super pub, with a long wooden bar and full-service restaurant housed in a wonderful old building on the west side of town. Great pub fare, ales, and beer.

The Craftsman House (315-637-9999; 7300 E. Genesee St., Fayetteville) The interior is furnished in the simple Arts and Crafts mode—clean lines with lots of wood and Stickley tables and chairs. Food is American traditional with items like steak, brook trout, and prime rib.

Dinosaur Bar-B-Q (315-476-4937; 246 Willow St., Syracuse) It's been called the best place to get barbecue in the east. One thing is for sure: Portions are huge, the ribs are finger-lickin' good, and the decor featuring biker memorabilia is fun. The place is full all the time. Outside, Harleys are parked next to BMWs and SUVs.

Empire Brewing Company (315-475-2337; 120 Walton St., Syracuse) Enjoy a casual meal and a glass of Stout or "Skinny Atlas Light" while watching beer being brewed behind the glass wall.

Glen Loch Restaurant (315-469-6969; 4626 North St., Jamesville) What a setting: an 1827 mill alongside a stream and waterfall. Food is hearty American traditional.

Hyde's of Liverpool (315-451-0786; 305 Oswego St., Corner of Old Liverpool Rd. and Onondaga Lake Parkway, Liverpool) It's been here for years, serving up Coneys, bratwurst, and all the fixin's.

The Inn Between Restaurant (315-672-3166; 2290 W. Genesee Turnpike, Rte. 5, Camillus) See Chapter Three, *Skaneateles.*

Kahunaville (315-422-4500; Carousel Center, Syracuse) There's a gushing waterfall with a periodic sound and light show, a dark jungly rainforest ambiance, and lots of plants and bird sounds. The menu includes exotic drinks garnished with flowers, tortilla wraps, burgers, nachos, stir fries, and other such fare. Kids get a kick out of it.

Lemon Grass Grille (315-475-1111; 238 W. Jefferson St., Syracuse) Pacific Rim cuisine, including Thai specialties. In the Armory Square.

The Mission Restaurant (315-475-7344; 304 E. Onondaga St., Syracuse) It looks like a tiny church with a steeple; inside, red brick, stained glass, and hand-painted walls add to the sense of mission. Food is south of the border and island Caribbean, with super margaritas and fajitas.

Pascale's Wine Bar and Restaurant (315-471-3040; 204 W. Fayette St., Syracuse) An elegant little place specializing in Continental cuisine. Fabulous bakery scones.

Pastabilities (315-474-1153; 311 S. Franklin St., Syracuse) The name says it all. Homemade bread, too, from their bread and bake shop across the street.

Spaghetti Warehouse (315-475-1807; 689 N. Clinton St., Syracuse) It's huge, with lots of brick and wood and lofty ceilings, but the booths make it more intimate. Serves spaghetti and much more.

ATTRACTIONS

Beaver Lake Nature Center (315-638-2519; 8477 E. Mud Lake Rd., Baldwinsville, NY 13027) Explore forest, meadows, and wetlands along miles of trails and boardwalks. Paddle a canoe across the lake, learn about maple sugaring, go snowshoeing, and tour the visitors center.

Clinton Square (in the center of downtown Syracuse near Armory Square) This is the venue for a variety of outdoor musical and theatrical events in the summer such as jazz nights and blues festivals. During the Blues Festival, every bar and restaurant in the area features entertainment. In the winter Clinton Square becomes an ice skating rink.

Delevan Art Gallery, an exciting new showcase for regional artists.

Delavan Art Gallery (dAG) (315-425-7500; 501 West Fayette St., Syracuse, NY 13204; two blocks from Armory Square) This exciting new gallery showcases the work of more than 50 area artists representing a wide spectrum of visual arts: ceramics, drawing, fiber design, glass, illustrations, multimedia painting, paper making, photography, sculpture and woodworking. Located in Delavan Center, a huge four-story former brick warehouse building near the center of town (before it was a warehouse, it was a John Deere factory) during the past 35 years, a virtual art community has developed in one part of the building as more and more artists have moved into generous-sized spaces with wood floors, high ceilings, and plenty of light. Each year these artists have opened their studios to the public for an art show and sale. Now 3,800 square feet of space on the first floor of Delavan Center's north wing has been renovated to create a stunning new art gallery. Hardwood floors, state-of-the-art lighting, and movable wall surfaces allow work to be shown off to the best advantage. Open Thurs. and Fri. 5pm–9pm; Sat. 10am–5pm.

Erie Canal Museum (315-471-0593; www.eriecanalmuseum.org; 318 Erie Blvd., E. Rte. 5 at Montgomery St., Syracuse, NY 13202) Find out about the history of the canal in the 19th-century Weighlock Building. You can view the story of Syracuse in the theater, take a historical walking tour, and explore the *Frank B. Thomson*, a 65-foot replica of an old canal boat. A reconstructed vintage tavern has a bar and a gift shop. The research library contains more than 40,000 prints. The museum is also available for private parties.

Erie Canal Park and Sims' Museum (315-488-3409; http://eriecanalcamill us.com/sims.htm; 5750 Devoe Rd., Camillus, NY 13031) Set on the banks of the old Erie Canal, this park has both a museum and boat tours. Cruises include a summer dinner cruise Wednesday, boat rides Sunday. Open weekends May–Oct.

Everson Museum of Art (315-474-6064; www.everson.org; 401 Harrison St., Syracuse, NY 13202) Designed by I. M. Pei, this museum contains a fabulous collection of ceramics as well as other arts and revolving exhibits. Ten galleries on three levels. Special exhibitions, tours, lectures, workshops, and film series. Open Tues.–Fri. and Sun. 12–5, Sat. 10–5.

MOST: Milton J. Rubenstein Museum of Science and Technology (315-425-9068; www.most.org; 500 S. Franklin St., Syracuse, NY 13202) Buzzing with activity, this handsome brick building is filled with exhibits, many interactive. Go through the giant maze, thrill to dinosaurs, climb the rock wall, see how your lungs work as you navigate your way through the human body, stand inside a gigantic bubble, and learn about the universe at the Silverman Planetarium. The only domed IMAX theater in the state, the Bristol Omnitheater, with its six-story screen, puts you in the middle of the action of sweeping films about climbing Mt. Everest or diving into the depths of the ocean.

Oncenter (315-435-8000; www.oncenter.org; 800 S. State St., Syracuse, NY 13202) This multi-purpose facility combines the Onondaga County Convention Center, Onondaga County War Memorial, and John H. Mulroy Civic Center. It's used as a convention center, sports arena, meeting place, banquet hall, ice rink, concert hall, showroom, and theater.

Onondaga Historical Association Museum (315-428-1864; www.cnyhistory .org; 321 Montgomery St., Syracuse, NY 13202) Filled with historical information, paintings, maps, and rare artifacts spanning 300 years of history. Of special interest are letters home from Civil War soldiers. The OHA's Research Center, next door at 311 Montgomery, contains thousands of photos, maps, and other documents.

Ontrack (800-424-1212; platforms at Carousel Center, Armory Square, Syracuse University) Originally established to get Syracuse University students around, its services have been expanded to include an extensive network of routes taking in historic areas, fall foliage tours, even cowboy holdups and a Santa's train.

P&C Stadium (315-474-7833; www.ongov.net/Parks/stadium.html; Hiawatha Blvd., Syracuse, NY 13208) Home of the Toronto Blue Jays–affiliated Syracuse SkyChiefs and a venue for many events.

Elephant exhibit at the Rosamond Gifford Zoo at Burnet Park.

Rosamond Gifford Zoo at Burnet Park (315-435-8511; www.rosamondgifford zoo.com; One Conservation Place, Syracuse, NY 13204) Recent improvements to the original Burnet Park facility have resulted in a first-class zoo. See Siberian tigers, penguins and seals, a rainforest with birds, and 600 other animals that live in spacious, natural-looking environments. And don't miss the monkey house. Open daily 10–4:30.

The Salt Museum (315-453-6715; www.ongov.net/Parks/salt.html; Rte. 370, Liverpool, NY 13088) Covers 150 years of the salt industry.

Syracuse Opera (315-476-7372; www.syracuseopera.com; 411 Montgomery St., PO Box 1223, Syracuse, NY 13201) This year-round opera company offers three productions each season in addition to ongoing educational programs.

Syracuse Stage (315-443-3275; www.syracusestage.org; 820 E. Genesee St., Syracuse, NY 13210) This professional theater produces seven or more mainstage plays during the season, which runs from September through May. It also features productions for young people.

Syracuse Symphony Orchestra (315-424-8222; www.syracusesymphony.org; 411 Montgomery St., Syracuse, NY 13202) The symphony offers concerts at various venues around the city.

RECREATION

Syracuse has several excellent 18-hole golf courses, including the following:

Lafayette Golf & Country Club: 315-469-3296; 4480 Lafayette Rd., Jamesville.

Links at Erie Village: 315-656-4653; 5900 N. Burdick St., E. Syracuse.

Liverpool Golf & Public Country Club: 315-457-7170; 7209 Morgan Rd., Liverpool.

Foxfire North Golf and Tennis: 315-638-2930; 1 Village Blvd., Baldwinsville.

Radisson Community Golf Course: 315-638-0092; Potter Rd., Baldwinsville.

West Hill Golf and Country Club: 315-672-8677; West Hill, Camillus.

SHOPPING

Armory Square (Headquarters: 500 S. Franklin St., Syracuse) Located in an area taking in Walton Street, South Clinton Street, West Jefferson Street, and South Franklin, Armory Square is highly recommended for more intimate specialty shopping where you can get away from the mall crowds. Browse small boutiques, crafts shops, and other specialty stores such as **Artifice Gallery, Dobbs Glassworks, Eureka Crafts,** and **I've Been Framed.** Gift shops include **The Added Touch, Enchanted Bazaar, Just for You Design, M.O.S.T. Gift Shop, P'Liptin's Something Special,** and **Suzie Q. Gift Shoppe.** There are also jewelry stores, clothing stores, and other specialty retailers as well as restaurants and pubs.

The Carousel Center (315-466-7000; www.carouselcenter.com; 9090 Carousel Center Dr., Syracuse, NY 13290) With close to 250 retail outlets and services as well as a working carousel and food court, this is the largest mall in the Northeast. It contains a 19-screen cinema complex, banquet and meeting facilities, and a 1909 antique carousel.

Muench-Kreuzer Candle Company (315-423-0319; 617 E. Hiawatha Blvd., Syracuse, NY 13208) It's small and hard to find (four blocks from the Carousel Center), but with prices from about 20 cents and up for tapers, votives, and novelty candles, it's worth the effort.

Pascale's Bake House & Café (315-471-3050; 304 Hawley Ave., Syracuse, NY 13230) A small café and bakery where the smell of freshly baked breads and pastries entices you to indulge.

Syracuse China Factory Outlet Store (315-455-4581; 2900 Court St., Syracuse, NY 13208) Syracuse China and Libbey Glass at 20 to 70 percent off. Open Mon.–Wed. 10–7, Thurs. and Fri. 10–9, Sat. 10–6, Sun. 11–5.

CORTLAND

On the southeastern corner of the Finger Lakes region, Cortland is home to the State University at Cortland and is close to three popular ski areas: **Greek Peak** at Virgil, **Song Mountain** at Preble, and **Labrador** at Truxton. Just north of Cortland around Preble are several natural lakes, including **Tully Lake,**

Song Lake, Goodale Lake, and Little Green Lake. Little York Lake is part of **Dwyer Memorial Park,** where you find Little York Pavilion, a National Historical Preservation site, and the Cortland Repertory Theatre.

Just west of Cortland, the historic district of **Homer Village** contains dozens of lovely 19th-century homes in the Greek-Revival and Queen Anne style. The village green is the scene of year-round activities: concerts, fairs, sporting events, ice skating. At **26 Clinton Street,** there is an excellent example of an octagonal house, a popular architectural style during the mid-1800s. The **Salisbury-Pratt Homestead,** on Route 281 between Homer and Little York, was part of the Underground Railroad.

First Baptist Church, Homer.

LODGING

Cortland Area Innkeepers Association (800-314-4667; 607-756-1968; www.us get aways.com/newyork/cortland) Find hotels/motels, condominiums, campgrounds, and B&Bs.

ATTRACTIONS

Cortland Country Music Park (607-753-0377; www.cortlandcountrymusic park.com; Rte. 13N, Cortland, NY 13045) Dance Hall, Hall of Fame Museum, campground, and outdoor performance center.

Cortland Repertory Theatre (607-756-2627; www.cortlandrep.org; Dwyer
   Memorial Park, Rte. 281, Pavilion Theatre, Little York Lake, Cortland, NY
   13045) Professionals have been performing comedies and musicals for more
   than 35 years from June through August.

1890 House Museum and Center for Victorian Arts (607-756-7551; 37 Tompkins St., Cortland, NY 13045) A castlelike stone manor with a round tower
   houses artifacts, furniture, and memorabilia from the Victorian era.

Suggett House Museum and Kellogg Memorial Research Library (607-756-
   6071; www.cortland.org/ent/museums/museum3.htm; 25 Homer Ave.,
   Cortland, NY 13045) Home of the Cortland County Historical Society.

RECREATION

GOLF

Elm Tree Golf Course (607-753-1341; State Rte. 13, Cortland, NY 13045) 18
   holes, weekday specials.

Maple Hill (607-849-3285; Conrad Rd., Marathon, NY 13803) Highest rated of
   18-hole area courses from the back tees with ponds and dog-legs. Pro shop,
   restaurant.

Walden Oaks Country Club (607-753-9452; www.waldenoakscc.com; 3369
   Walden Oaks Blvd., Cortland, NY 13045) Highest rated from the white and
   red tees for area 18-hole courses. Watered tees and fairways; ponds, restaurant, clubhouse, locker rooms, and showers.

*The signpost for the Homer
village green.*

Willow Brook Golf Club (607-756-7382; 3267 Rte. 215, Cortland, NY 13045) 18 holes, restaurant, pro shop, and weekday specials. A pleasant family-owned course.

HIKING

Lime Hollow Nature Center (607-758-5462; www.limehollow.org; Gracie Rd., Cortland, NY 13045) An interpretive center, hiking trails.

SKIING

Greek Peak Ski Resort (607-835-6111, 800-955-2754; www.greekpeak.net; 2000 Rte. 392, Cortland, NY 13045) Home of the Magic Carpet lift, Greek Peak has close to 30 trails, 7 ski lifts, a tubing center, more than 200 instructors, night skiing, cross-country trails, Children's Learning Center, slopeside accommodations, lodge, and restaurants.

Labrador Mountain (607-842-6204, 800-446-9559; www.labradormtn.com; Rte. 91, Truxton, NY 13158) Twenty-two slopes, downhill skiing, snowboarding, night skiing, three base lodges, instruction, babysitting, and ski rentals.

Song Mountain (315-696-5711; www.songmountain.com; 1 Song Mountain Rd., Tully, NY 13159) Song has 25 trails and 5 lifts.

Toggenburg Ski and Board Center (315-683-5842; Toggenburg Rd., Fabius, NY 13063) Trails and lodge.

SHOPPING

BOOKS

The College Store (607-753-4621; Neubig Hall, SUNY, Cortland, NY 13045) Lots of books, clothing, logo items, and gifts.

FOOD

Hollenbeck's Cider Mill (607-835-6455; 1265 Rt. 392, Virgil, NY 13045) Sells cider, apples, cheese, fudge, bakery goods, and much more.

Hollywood Restaurant (607-753-3242; 27 Groton Ave, Cortland, NY 13045) Good Italian food, pizza, steaks, and seafood. Open daily for lunch and dinner.

GIFTS AND CLOTHING

Bev & Co. (607-749-5567; 3 S. Main St., Homer, NY 13077) Gifts, clothes, and antiques.

ELMIRA

S amuel Clemens, better known as Mark Twain, spent several summers in this quiet town with his wife, Olivia Langdon, an Elmira native. Here he wrote much of such beloved novels as *The Adventures of Huckleberry Finn* and *Tom Sawyer*. He did much of his work in an octagonal study that's now on the Elmira College Campus.

Those interested in the life and work of this famous author can visit the Mark Twain Exhibit in **Hamilton Hall** and see his grave in **Woodlawn Cemetery.**

Elmira is also known as the "Soaring Capital of America." From 1930 to 1946, the city hosted national soaring contests. Today you can visit the National Soaring Museum and take a sailplane ride at Harris Hill Soaring Corp.

Other area attractions include the **Clemens Center**, a great venue for plays, concerts, and other cultural performances; Arnot Art Museum, exhibiting current work as well as old masters and 19th-century paintings; **Tanglewood Nature Center,** site of walking and hiking trails, and picnic areas; and the **Near Westside Historic District,** featuring guided and self-guided tours of historic houses.

LODGING

Holiday Inn (607-734-4211; www.ichotelsgroup.com/h/d/hi/1/en/hd/ELMDT; Elmira-Riverview, 760 E. Water St., No. 1 Holiday Plaza, Elmira, NY 14901) Convenient for business or leisure travelers.

Lindenwald Haus (607-733-8753; www.innsite.com/inns/B007550.html; 1526 Grand Central Ave., Elmira, NY 14901) Set on 5 acres with an outdoor pool, this 1875 Italianate mansion is conducive to relaxing in the huge living room or cooling off in the pool.

The Painted Lady (607-732-7515; www.thepaintedlady.net; 520 W. Water St., Elmira, NY 14901) A B&B with five rooms with private baths in an elegant Victorian house circa 1875. Original sift tufted and satin ceilings, 10 marble fireplaces, antique stained glass windows, lovely billiard parlor, and period wallpaper and wall coverings add to the experience. All guest rooms have fireplaces and Jacuzzis. Romance, fine dining, spa and wine country tour packages available.

Rufus Tanner House (607-732-0213; www.rufustanner.com; 60 Sagetown Rd., Pine City, NY 14871) A B&B with four rooms with private baths and moderate rates. Like many old houses in the area, this 1864 farmhouse sits in a grove of 100-year-old sugar maples that produce enough maple syrup for pancake breakfasts. Furnishings are mostly antiques; one room has a queen-sized bed and a fireplace. Another has a Jacuzzi. Rooms are air-conditioned.

RESTAURANTS

Beijing Garden (607-732-7464; 145 W. Gray St., Elmira, NY 14901) One of the most elegant Chinese restaurants around, with upholstered dining chairs, linens, and crystal. It's the place Asians like to eat.

Hill Top Inn (607-732-6728; www.hill-top-inn.com; 171 Jerusalem Hill Rd., Elmira, NY 14901) The oldest licensed restaurant in Elmira, Hill Top serves American cuisine indoors or outdoors, where diners enjoy beautiful views of the countryside.

Moretti's Restaurant (607-734, 1535; 800 Hatch St., Elmira, NY 14901) One of the city's most popular places to eat since 1917, Moretti's serves Italian food, steaks, and chops in a Rathskeller-style dining room.

Pierce's 1894 Restaurant (607-734-2022; www.pierces1894.com; 228 Oakwood Ave., Elmira Heights, NY 14903) Serving American and continental cuisine, Pierce's is on the elegant side with period furnishings.

ATTRACTIONS

Arnot Art Museum (607-734-3697; www.arnotartmuseum.org; 235 Lake St., Elmira, NY 14901) European and American art exhibits as well as contemporary traveling exhibits are housed in a neoclassical mansion.

Chemung Valley Living History Center (607-732-3944; Newtown Battlefield Reservation, 455 Oneida Rd., Elmira, NY 14901) Historic re-enactments and encampments in May, August, and October.

The Clemens Center (607-733-5639; www.clemenscenter.com; 207 Clemens Center Pkwy., PO Box 1046, Elmira, NY 14902) This is a major performing arts center offering international touring artists, Broadway musicals, concerts, jazz, rock 'n' roll, dance, stand-up comedy, and children's theater.

Harris Hill Soaring (607-796-2988, 607-734-0641; www.harrishillsoaring.org; Harris Hill, Rte. 17, Soaring Hill Dr., Elmira; mail: PO Box 544, Horseheads, NY 14845) Soar above the countryside with FAA-certified pilots.

Mark Twain Study and Exhibit (607-735-1941; www.elmira.edu/academics/MarkTwain/mt_study.shtml; Elmira College campus, 1 Park Pl., Elmira, NY 14901) The octagonal study where Samuel Clemens wrote some of his best-known books while a summer resident in the town. Nearby an exhibit contains photographs and Mark Twain memorabilia.

National Soaring Museum (607-734-3128; www.soaringmuseum.org; 51 Soaring Hill Dr., Elmira, NY 14903; Harris Hill, exit 51, Rte. 17) This aviation-orientation museum has a glider cockpit simulator, sailplane collection, and other exhibits.

National Warplane Museum (607-739-8200; www.warplane.org; 17 Aviation Dr., Horseheads, NY 14845; near Elmira-Corning Regional Airport) Here military aviation history comes to life through a series of exhibits and a collection of 23 vintage aircraft. You can watch old airplanes being restored, look inside the cockpits and gunners' areas, and walk under the wings of a PBY Catalina flying boat. Take a ride in *Fuddy Duddy*, a restored B-17 aircraft, with flights offered from May through October. The annual Wings of Eagles Air Show features more than 150 military aircraft in a thrilling two-day air show.

Trolley Tour (800-MARK TWAIN, leaves from Riverview Holiday Inn on E. Water St., Elmira) Ride in a turn-of-the-20th-century green-and-gold trolley on this guided 90-minute historic tour of the area. Stop at Mark Twain's study and Harris Hill.

RECREATION

GOLF

Mark Twain Golf Course (Harris Hill, 2275 Corning Rd., Elmira, NY 14903) An 18-hole Donald Ross–designed course with a large clubhouse and snack bar.

SHOPPING

Arnot Mall (607-739-8704; www.arnotmall.net; 3300 Chambers Rd. S., Horseheads, NY 14844) A major mall complex with more than 100 stores, several theaters, food court, and restaurants.

The Christmas House (607-734-9547; www.christmas-house.com; 361 Maple Ave., Elmira, NY 14904) This 1894 Queen Anne mansion features 15 rooms full of holiday ornaments and gifts. Santas, nutcrackers, decorated trees, and much more.

A Touch of Country (607-737-6945; 1019 Pennsylvania Ave., Elmira, NY 14904) A 17-room Victorian home filled with antiques, gifts, collectibles, and Christmas items.

CORNING

Thousands come to Corning each year to visit the **Museum of Glass**, which has expanded considerably over the past few years, and for this reason is called "The New Corning Museum of Glass." And it has become even more exciting: Now everyone can make a glass souvenir to take home.

Corning is also home to the **Hall of Science and Industry** and the **Steuben Glass Factory** as well as **Historic Market Street,** with more than 100 craft shops, artists' studios, gift stores, boutiques, cafés, and restaurants. This tree-shaded street and **Centerway Square** are listed on the National Register of Historic

Tree-shaded square off historic Market Street, Corning.

Places and are graced by period lighting, hanging baskets of flowers, brick walkways, and restored 19th-century buildings. The Market Street restoration has been cited as a benchmark for Main Street America, a national program.

Market Street and Centerway are the venues for many special events, including art and crafts fairs, street parties, jazz festivals, a festival of lights parade, and seasonal celebrations. The annual "Sparkle of Christmas" closes the streets to traffic so you can shop, take buggy rides, and enjoy the ice carving and live entertainment.

The old City Hall houses the **Rockwell Museum**, which was recently renovated and is now truly an amazing addition to the Corning scene. It contains a fabulous collection of art of the American West.

Complimentary shuttle bus service carries passengers from Market Street to the Corning Museum of Glass and other stops. This is a visitor-friendly town. You even get two free hours of parking.

LODGING

In addition to a number of chain hotels, including a **Holiday Inn, Radisson Hotel, Best Western,** and other chain properties, there are several inns and B&Bs.

Hillcrest Manor B&B (607-936-4548; www.corninghillcrestmanor.com; 227 Cedar Street, Corning, NY 14830) Innkeeper Dick Bright has furnished this historic seven-room B&B in true elegance. The 1890 neo-classic mansion is filled with antiques, art glass, western paintings, and bronzes. You can relax on the spacious veranda and enjoy a candlelit breakfast served on fine china. Hillcrest is within walking distance of area attractions and shopping.

Rosewood Inn B&B (607-962-3253; www.rosewoodinn.com; 134 E. First St., Corning, NY 14830) Suzanne and Stewart Sanders's lovely Victorian house is within walking distance of Market Street. The seven rooms have private baths; many of the rooms are decorated in soft warm colors like mauve and gray. The rooms are elaborately furnished with period antiques and memorabilia, and all rooms are air-conditioned. Most have queen beds and all feature luxurious 300-thread-count linens. A full breakfast is served in the formal dining room.

Villa Bernese (607-936-2633; www.southerntier.net/vb; 11860 Overlook Dr., Corning, NY 14830) Four rooms feature European-style amenities in a home that overlooks the Chemung River valley.

RESTAURANTS

Beauregard's Bakery and Café (607-962-2001; Market Street at Centerway Square, Corning, NY 14830) *The* place for wedding cakes, cookies, strudels, sticky buns, croissants, and other yummy desserts. It's also popular for lunch, where you eat in a cozy little café with brick walls, small counter, and booths. Sandwiches, box lunches, and soups are available.

DeClemente's Deli (607-937-5657; 30 W. Market St., Corning, NY 14830) Eat at wrought-iron tables outside or inside. This is one of the area's best delis.

Gaffer's Grille & Pub (607-962-4649; 58 W. Market St., Corning, NY 14830) The dining room offers superb contemporary cuisine in a Victorian atmosphere surrounded by scenes and sculptures of glass blowing by local artists. The taproom features casual dining, international beers, wine, spirits, specialty coffees, and late-night dining.

Green Shingles Inn Restaurant and Lounge (607-523-7784; Rte. 15, Lindley, NY 14858) Watch your favorite teams on a 50-inch big screen television while you eat your wings and burgers. Popular with sports fans.

The Glory Hole Pub (607-962-1474; 74 E. Market St., Corning, NY 14830) Located on Historic Market Street, this pub is dedicated to the history of glassmaking. Its name refers to the name of the furnace used to reheat the glass in the glassmaking process. Open Mon.–Sat. 4pm –1am. Serving food until midnight. Live entertainment weekly.

Jim's Texas Hots (607-936-1820; 8 W. Market St., Corning, NY 14830) There's no sign on the building, but there probably will be a line of customers outside to buy ice cream, hot dogs, and sandwiches. Texas Hots is hot.

London Underground Café (607-962-2345; 63 W. Market St., Corning, NY 14830) Serving regional American and European cuisine, this unique three-tiered restaurant has earned awards for its food and service. Everything is cooked in an open-style kitchen.

Market Brewing Pub (607-936-2337; 8 W. Market St., Corning, NY 14830) This establishment embodies the essence of the microbrew revolution. Serving six fresh beers brewed on premises as well as a diverse, delectable luncheon and dinner menu. Also offers rooftop seating, a *biergarten*, and dining room. Open daily, 11:30am–1am.

Old World Café and Ice Cream in Corning features an old-fashioned counter, tales, and chairs.

Old World Café and Ice Cream (607-936-1953; Market Street at Centerway Square, Corning, NY 14830) Most of the fixtures and furnishings, including the hand-carved mahogany woodwork, come from a circa-1800s ice cream parlor. There is an old-fashioned soda fountain counter, marble-topped round tables, tile floor, and pressed metal ceiling. In addition to ice cream, there are salads, sandwiches, wraps, soup, and other items. Open daily 10–6; Thurs. and Fri. 10–8

Pelham's Upstate Tuna Co. (607-936-TUNA; 73 E. Market St., Corning, NY 14830) If you want to cook your own fish or steak here, go for it. Pelham's features many unique items on its menu, but as you might guess, fish and seafood are big.

Sorge's Restaurant (607-937-5422; 66-68 W. Market St., Corning, NY 14830) This family-owned and -operated Italian American restaurant is known among the locals for its homemade pasta dishes and friendly service.

Spencer's Restaurant and Mercantile (607-936-9196; 359 E. Market St., Corning, NY 14830) A busy, fun place with pasta cooked to order, seafood, fish fry, and many other items served in an intimate rustic setting a bit off the beaten track.

ATTRACTIONS

Benjamin Patterson Inn Museum Complex (607-937-5281; www.cmog.com; 59 W. Pulteney St., Corning, NY 14830) Guides in period costume show you through this restored 1796 inn, 1784 log cabin, 1878 one-room schoolhouse, and a 19th-century agricultural exhibit. Open Mon.–Fri. 10–4.

Glass exhibit at the Corning Museum of Glass.

The Corning Museum of Glass (800-732-6845; www.cmog.org; 1 Museum Way, Corning, NY 14830) Take the day or more to explore this intriguing complex. Start with the 15-minute film for an introduction to glass and what you'll be seeing. Learn about the history of glassmaking, check out the Glass Innovation Center (where the mysteries of creating windows, optical glass, and vessels are revealed), and purchase glass items like a giant lightbulb lamp, a glass putter, or Christmas ornaments in one of the seven shops (even if you've seen the museum a hundred times, this is a great place to come for unique gifts).

A big stir has been created by the new Walk-in Workshop, where visitors can try making glass themselves. For a fee, you can try your hand at hot glass-working, flameworking, fusing, and sandblasting. Make a glass flower, a glass bead, or create an original design on a drinking glass. It's great fun for the whole family, and there are projects for children as young as two. The Studio at the Corning Museum of Glass also offers glassworking classes—for a day, a weekend, or weeklong.

One gallery displays a dazzling array of contemporary glass sculptures, from minute to towering; the studio provides instruction in all aspects of glass blowing and the Hot Glass Show enables you to watch master crafts-people transform gobs of molten glass into exquisite objects. Children and adults alike will enjoy the interactive exhibits.

A glass sculpture by Dale Chihuly, a 13-foot-high piece of green flamelike blown glass pieces inserted into a treelike structure is installed in the reception area. (Another of his works is in the park in front of the Monte Carlo Casino.) There are two places to eat, including an outdoor patio, and a shuttle that runs back and forth from the Market Street area every 15 minutes. And it seems they've thought of everything: Even the jitney path and sidewalk are heated to make sure things keep moving even in the winter. Open daily 9–5; in July and August, open 9–8.

The Fun Park (11233 E. Corning Rd. (Rte. 352) near the intersection of Gorton Rd., East Corning) This new family fun place on a 32-acre site offers indoor and outdoor 18-hole miniature golf courses, a 32-foot hydraulically operated climbing rock wall, roller racer track, bumper boat ride, video game arcade, a 250-yard golf driving range, trampoline basketball, and a concession stand.

Hands-On Glass (607-962-3044; www.handsonglass.com; 124 Crystal Lane, Corning, NY 14830) Experience glassmaking! Make your own paperweight, or blow your own Christmas ornament or glass Easter egg! Activities available year-round by appointment as well as summer workshops.

Rockwell Museum (607-937-5386; www.rockwellmuseum.org; 111 Cedar St., Corning, NY 14830) A major renovation project has been completed to show-case the largest collection of Western and Native American art east of the Mississippi. The exhibits include a nice mix of both traditional and contemporary art, ranging from paintings and sculptures to leatherwork and pottery. The museum also has a great kids program called Art Packs. Designed to help children understand, interpret and experience art, it is utilizes a backpack filled with activities, puzzles, and creative challenges related to the exhibits. It also includes a make-it and take-it project. Created for children ages 8–13, adults love the Art Packs, too. Artists represented include Frederic Remington, Thomas Moran, C. M. Russell, N. C. Wyeth, and painters from the Taos Society of artists. Special exhibits are designed to help children understand the importance of the heritage of the American West. Open Mon.–Sat. 9–5, Sun. noon–5.

SHOPPING

Market Street is a great place to get unique gifts and crafts. Then grab an ice cream or table in one of the small restaurants and ponder your purchases.

Bacalles Glass Shop (607-962-3339; 10 W. Market St., Corning, NY 14830) Everything glass, like oil lamps, crystal, jewelry, and other items.

Books of Marvel (607-962-6300; 94 E. Market St., Corning, NY 14830) This store buys and sells thousands of out-of-print books for young people as well as old issues of *National Geographic*. Enter through Glass Menagerie.

Comics for Collectors (607-937-GIFT; 60 E. Market St., Corning, NY 14830) *Superman, Wonder Woman,* and hundreds of other old-time favorites.

Connors Market Street Mercantile (607-962-6300; Market St., Corning, NY 14830) Corning's unique shopping experience, featuring Crabtree and Evelyn, Portmeiron, Boyds Collection, Mary Englebreit, the "Cat's Meow" and more. The interior has been restored to its original splendor of the early1900s.

The Glass Menagerie (607-962-6300; 37 E. Market St., Corning, NY 14830) Features hundreds of kaleidoscopes and paperweights along with crystal ornaments, jewelry, stained glass, bottles, animals, and other things.

Lost Angel Glass (607-937-3578; 79 W. Market St., Corning, NY 14830) Handcrafted glass in the contemporary mode.

Vitrix Hot Glass Studio (607-936-8707; 77 W. Market St., Corning, NY 14830) Glass artist Thomas Kelly works and sells his glass creations here.

West End Gallery (607-936-2011; 12 W. Market St., Corning, NY 14830) A fineart gallery, selling paintings, prints, and contemporary work.

ROCHESTER

As the 69th largest city in the United States, with a population of more than a million people, Rochester offers all the cultural attractions and facilities you'd expect from a major urban area. Home of companies like Bausch & Lomb, Kodak, and Xerox and with its own international airport, Rochester and its attractive suburbs are considered one of the nation's most desirable places to live.

As early as the mid-1800s, Rochester's thriving horticulture industry and gardens caused it to be called the "Flower City." Each May, the hundreds of varieties of lilacs planted in **Highland Park**—the largest public collection of lilacs in the world—are the focal point of the 10-day Lilac Festival.

Cultural attractions include the **Geva Theatre,** the **Rochester Philharmonic Orchestra**, the **Eastman School of Music**, the **George Eastman House** and **International Museum of Photography and Film**, the **Memorial Art Gallery**, the **Rochester Museum and Science Center** with its impressive planetarium, and the **Strong Museum**, a hands-on history center for families.

You can trace the history of the women's rights movement at the **Susan B. Anthony House and Museum**, see wild animals at the **Seneca Park Zoo**, and spend hours at the entertainment centers at **High Falls Complex,** one of Rochester's newest nightlife extravaganzas.

Among the many major players on the sports scene are the Rochester Redwings, an AAA baseball team, the Rochester Raging Rhinos, a champion soccer team, and the Rochester Americans hockey team, winner of several Calder Cups. With Lake Ontario on its northern boundaries and the many rivers and lakes in the region, Rochester residents enjoy a plethora of water sports. **Bristol Mountain** offers good downhill skiing, with a vertical drop of 1,200 feet, 22 trails, and 5 lifts. There are also many fine golf courses in the area, including **Greystone Golf Club, Locust Hill Country Club,** and **Oak Hill Country Club,** site of the 2003 PGA Championship.

Education plays a strong role in the city. Colleges include the Colgate Rochester Divinity School, Monroe Community College, Nazareth College of Rochester, Roberts Wesleyan College, Rochester Institute of Technology, and the University of Rochester.

Rochester was an important station on the Underground Railroad: **Maplewood Park** was where slaves boarded boats headed across Lake Ontario to Canada and freedom.

Famous residents include Frederick Douglass, African American orator, reformer, abolitionist, and publisher of the North Star newspaper; and George Eastman, who founded the Eastman Dry Plate Company, precursor to the Eastman Kodak Company. In 1888, the easy-to-use Kodak camera was introduced as well as a flexible film that would help launch the motion picture industry. Another famous Rochester citizen, Susan B. Anthony, founded the Women's Educational and Industrial Union. Anthony worked all her life to secure rights for women.

Several major events are held each year, including the aforementioned **Lilac Festival** in May with more than 1,200 lilacs in glorious bloom (585-256-4960); the annual **Corn Hill Arts Festival,** a juried art show in July representing more than 450 artists; **Oktoberfest** in September featuring two weekends of fun, music, food and entertainment (585-336-6070; and the **Clothesline Festival,** one of the nation's oldest outdoor juried art shows (585-473-7720).

LODGING

Most of the major hotel chains are represented in Rochester. There are also several small inns and bed & breakfasts in the area.

Avon Inn (585-226-8181; 55 E. Main St., Avon, NY 14414) This 19th-century country inn has 14 rooms with private baths as well as a restaurant.

B&B at Dartmouth House (585-271-7872, 800-724-6298; www.dartmouthhouse.com; 215 Dartmouth St., Rochester, NY 14607; in the historic Park/East Ave. District) Elegant accommodations in a convenient and quiet location.

Brookwood Inn Pittsford (800-396-1194; www.hudsonhotels.com/bipittsford; 800 Pittsford-Victor Rd., Pittsford, NY 14534) A modern 108-room hotel with all in-room amenities plus an indoor pool, sauna, exercise room, TV, and complimentary breakfast.

428 Mt. Vernon (800-836-3159; 585-271-0792; www.428mtvernon.com; 428 Mt. Vernon St., Rochester, NY 14620; at the entrance to Highland Park) This B&B, a gracious Victorian home, is set on 2 acres. All rooms have private baths, phones, and televisions. A full breakfast is served.

RESTAURANTS

Bacco's Ristorante (585-442-5090; 263 Park Ave., Rochester, NY 14607) Italian cuisine in the Northern style starts with complimentary bruschetta and homemade bread. Delicious.

Charlie's Frog Pond (585-271-1970; 625 Park Ave., Rochester, NY 14607) Serving breakfast, lunch, and dinner and offering an extensive menu in a pint-sized setting.

The Clark House (585-385-3700; 600 Whalen Rd., Penfield, NY 14526) Furnished in the colonial style and serving gourmet cuisine. The original structure, built in 1832, now houses the Blue and Clark Rooms.

Daisy Flour Mill (585-381-1880; 1880 Blossom Rd., Penfield, NY 14526) In a restored 1848 post-and-beam gristmill overlooking Irondequoit Creek, Daisy's featured items include Angus beef and seafood. Open for dinner.

Dinosaur Bar-B-Que (585-325-7090; www.dinosaurbarbque.com; 99 Court St., Rochester, NY 14604) Super ribs and Cajun and Cuban food have gained Dinosaur a solid reputation for great meals and value.

Edwards Restaurant (585-423-0140; www.edwardsrestaurant.com; 35 S. Washington St., Rochester, NY 14608) In the historic Greek-Revival Jonathan Child House, Edwards serves French and American cuisine in a rich British-club-style setting. Very elegant with excellent service, for lunch and dinner.

The Grill at Strathallan (585-454-1880; www.grill175.com; 550 East Ave., Rochester, NY 14607) Award-winning restaurant for fine dining and great for business lunches and dinners.

The Grill at Water Street (585-454-1880; 175 N. Water St., Rochester, NY 14604) Sophisticated yet casual, the Grill serves innovative American cuisine with flair.

The Olive Tree (585-454-3510; 165 Monroe Ave., Rochester, NY 14607) The Olive Tree, in a historic brick building, is known for its superb Greek cuisine.

Park 54 (585-442-8890; 54 Park Ave., Rochester, NY 14607) A creative menu combining American and Continental cuisine, art exhibits, and good service make this place a winner.

Richardson's Canal House (585-248-5000; www.canalhouse.org; 1474 Marsh Rd., Pittsford, NY 14534) On the roster of the National Register of Historic Places, this restored Erie Canal tavern offers a prix fixe meal featuring French and American regional food and a great location on the canal.

The Spring House (585-586-2300; 3001 Monroe Ave., Rochester, NY 14618) An early-19th-century four-story Southern Colonial–style inn with gardens and patio. Traditional American cuisine; an old favorite among locals.

Tapas 177 (585-262-2090; www.tapas177.com; 177 St. Paul St., Rochester, NY 14604) An eclectic menu of Mediterranean food served by candlelight along with music on weekends for a warm, romantic ambiance. Serving dinner.

Tokyo Japanese Restaurant & Steak House (585-424-4166; 2930 W. Henrietta Rd., Rochester, NY 14623) Great sushi, tempura, and other Japanese specialties.

2 Vine Restaurant (585-454-6020; www.2vine.com; 24 Winthrop St., Rochester, NY 14607) Serving French and Italian fare bistro-style in cozy intimate surroundings.

ATTRACTIONS

Center at High Falls (585-325-2030; 60 Brown's Race, Rochester, NY 14614) Built on the banks of the Genesee River, this new urban cultural park features interactive 3-D exhibits such as a room-sized "supermap," taxi tour, flour mill, and talking camera. There is the Triphammer Forge, with multilevel views of 1816 factory ruins and an art gallery.

Eastman School of Music's Eastman Theatre (585-274-1100, 585-274-1400; www.rochester.edu/Eastman; 26 Gibb St., Rochester, NY 14604) More than 700 concerts during the year are offered by students.

Genesee Country Village Museum (585-538-6822; www.geneseecountryvillage.org; 1410 Flint Hill Rd., Mumford, NY 14511) This is the third largest collection of historic buildings in the country, with 57 restored structures portraying life in the Genesee region from the 1790s to the 1870s. There are houses, schools, farms, blacksmiths, and stores, along with heirloom gardens and craftspeople, on 400 acres. Costumed villagers, restaurants, ships, and picnic areas. Open May–October; closed Monday.

George Eastman House (585-271-3361, www.eastman.org; 900 East Ave., Rochester, NY 14607) This 50-room historic turn-of-the-20th-century house, which George Eastman called home, is filled with important collections of films, cameras, books, and photography in changing exhibits. The house and gardens have been restored to their early 1900s appearance. Closed Monday and major holidays.

Geva Theatre (585-232-GEVA; www.gevatheatre.org; 75 Woodbury Blvd., Rochester, NY 14607) This professional regional theater produces a variety of performances, including comedies, musicals, and world premieres.

Memorial Art Gallery (585-473-7720; http://mag.rochester.edu; 500 University Ave., Rochester, NY 14607) This gallery contains an enormous collections of art work spanning 5,000 years including works by Edgar Degas, Mary Cassatt, Henry Moore, Jacob Lawrence, Hans Hofmann, the French impressionists, and many others. See revolving exhibits from the gallery's permanent collections plus exceptional art from leading contemporary and regional artists.

Museums of the Landmark Society (585-546-7029; www.landmarksociety.org; 123 S. Fitzhugh, Rochester, NY 14608) The Campbell-Whittlesey House Museum, an 1835 Greek-Revival home, brings to life the daily activities of a wealthy flour miller's household in the days when the Erie Canel was an important means of transport. The house has elegant parlors and a restored kitchen, pantry, and cold- storage room. Also visit the **Stone-Tolan House,** (585-546-7029; 2370 East Ave.), an early 1800s farmhouse and tavern.

New York Museum of Transportation/Rochester & Genesee Valley Railroad

Museum (New York Museum of Transportation: 585-533-1113; www.roch nrhs.org/rgvrrm.html; 6393 E. River Rd., West Henrietta, NY 14586; Rochester & Genesee Valley Railroad Museum: 585-533-1431; www.rgvrrm .mus.ny.us; 282 Rush-Scottsville Rd./Rte. 251, Rush, NY 14543) See historic rail cars and vintage vehicles, including a 1909 Erie Railroad depot, cabooses, trolleys, and a large HO model train. The two museums are connected by a railroad.

Rhoades Geologic Tours (585-271-7368; http://home.earthlink.net/~geologic tours; 57 Clovercrest Dr., Suite 100; mail: PO Box 18937, Rochester, NY 14618) This company features a full range of geologic and environmental tours throughout the Finger Lakes led by Mariana Rhoades.

Rochester Museum and Science Center (585-271-1880, www.rmsc.org; 657 East Ave., Rochester, NY 14607) This museum focuses on archaeology, science and technology, cultural heritage, and anthropology and features a computerized star theater and CineMagic 870 theater at the Strasenburgh Planetarium, plus a Seneca Iroquois display. Large-screen science/nature films are shown daily.

Rochester Philharmonic Orchestra (585-454-2620; www.rpo.org; Eastman School of Music's Eastman Theatre, 100 East Ave., Rochester, NY 14604) This

The Oak Hill Country Club was the site of the 2003 PGA Championship Golf Tournament.

critically acclaimed orchestra offers classical, pops, and special children's concerts, including traditional favorites like *The Nutcracker*.

Seneca Park Zoo (585-467-WILD; www.senecaparkzoo.org; 2222 St. Paul St., Rochester, NY 14621) River otters, polar bears, penguins, and other animals live in settings that approximate their natural environments. See elephants from Africa, orangutans from Borneo, wolves, kangaroos, and more than 300 other animals. Kids will love the new polar bear cub, Haley.

Strong Museum (585-263-2702; www.strongmuseum.org; 1 Manhattan Sq., Rochester, NY 14607) A great museum, with hands-on exhibits for kids who have fun while learning about history. Step onto Sesame Street, pilot a giant helicopter, shop for food in a king-sized supermarket, and board a whaling ship. See collections of dolls, toys, miniatures, a 1950s diner, a 1918 carousel, and an old-fashioned ice-cream fountain.

Susan B. Anthony House (585-235-6124; www.susanbanthonyhouse.org; 17 Madison St., Rochester, NY 14608) This redbrick house was the home for women's rights champion Susan B. Anthony from 1866 until her death in 1906. Today, the house is a museum filled with memorabilia from Anthony's life and the women's suffrage movement.

Seabreeze Amusement Park and Raging Rivers Waterpark (800-395-2500, 4600 Culver Rd., Rochester, NY 14622; off I-590N) Rides, slides, fun, games, soak zone, carousel, bumper cars, water park, giant Jack Rabbit roller coaster, food, entertainment. Four roller-coasters. Open weekends May to mid-June; daily mid-June to Labor Day.

Victorian Doll Museum (585-247-0130; www.rrlc.org/guide/arc47a.html; 4332 Buffalo Rd., N. Chili, NY 14514) If you love dolls, come here and browse through exhibits of thousands of collector's dolls of bisque, china, wood, wax, and paper. See Kewpie dolls, Noah's Ark toys, and a puppet theater.

RECREATION

CANAL CRUISES

Colonial Belle (585-223-9470; www.colonialbelle.com; 400 Packett's Landing, Fairport, NY 14450) A 246-passenger double-deck boat cruising the Erie Canal. On-board restaurant. Three cruises daily. Private charters.

Fairport Lady (585-223-1930, 10 Liftbridge Lane West, Fairport, NY 14450) An 80-passenger paddle wheeler offering lunch and dinner cruises along the Erie Canal. Charters available.

Sam Patch (585-262-5661; www.sampatch.org; Corn Hill Navigation, 12 Corn Hill Ter., Suite 7, Rochester, NY 14608) Canal cruises, including lunch, brunch, and dinner cruises, are offered aboard a replica of an authentic Erie Canal packet boat.

SHOPPING

More than 500 stores and services are at Rochester's four major malls: **East-View Mall, Greece Ridge Center, Irondequoit Mall,** and **Marketplace Mall.** Trendy **Park Avenue,** which runs from Alexander Street to Culver Road, contains a number of stylish shops, boutiques, and cafés. In the summer months, the street is a lively place with sidewalk cafés in full swing.

A. D. Flint Luggage and Leather Goods (585-325-5544; 111 Midtown Plaza, Rochester, NY 14604; 3400 Monroe Ave., Pittsford Colony Plaza, Rochester, NY 14618) This store sells top-quality leather goods, gifts, clocks, desk accessories, and travel items.

Irish Import Shop (585-225-1050; 3821 W. Ridge Rd., Rochester, NY 14626) This shop sells all things Irish, from Belleek china and Celtic brass to sweaters and Waterford.

Stever's Candies (585-473-2098; 623 Park Ave., Rochester, NY 14607) For more than 50 years, Stever's has been making homemade candy on the premises including chocolates, nuts, brittles, truffles, jellies, and sugar-free candy.

For More Information

Chemung County Commerce Center: 607-734-5137, 800-MARK TWAIN; fax 607-734-4490; www.chemungchamber.org; 400 E. Church St., Elmira, NY 14901.

Cortland County Convention and Visitors Bureau: 607-753-8463, 800-859-2227; www.cortlandtourism.com; 34 Tompkins St., Cortland, NY 13045.

Finger Lakes Tourism: 315-536-7488; www.fingerlakes.org; 309 Lake St., Penn Yan, NY 14527.

Greater Corning Area Chamber of Commerce: 607-936-3642, 866-463-6264; www .corningny.com; 1 Baron Steuben Pl., Corning, NY 14830.

Rochester Business Alliance: 585-244-1800; www.rochesterbusinessalliance.com; 150 State St., Rochester, NY 14614.

Steuben County Conference & Visitors Bureau: 607-936-6544, 866-946-3386; fax 607-936-6575; www.corningfingerlakes.com; 5 W. Market St., Corning, NY 14830.

Syracuse Convention and Visitors Bureau: 315-470-1910, 800-234-4797; fax 315-471-8545; www.visitsyracuse.org; 572 S. Salina St., Syracuse, NY 13202.

CHAPTER TEN
Finger Lakes Facts and Figures
INFORMATION

A fresh winter snow sits lightly on a Finger Lakes cottage.

This chapter contains facts and figures selected to enhance your Finger Lakes stay—a sampling of information from temperatures and newspapers to listings of annual events and visitors organizations.

AMBULANCE, FIRE, POLICE

Cayuga County Sheriff's Office: 315-253-1222.
Seneca County Sheriff's Office: 315-539-9241.
Steuben County Emergency Services/Control Center: 607-776-4099.
Tompkins County Sheriff's Office: 607-272-2444.
Tompkins County Ambulance/Fire: 607-273-8000.
Tompkins County City Police: 607-272-3245.
All other counties: 911.

BOOKS

BIKING AND HIKING

Biking & Hiking in the Central Destinations of the Finger Lakes Region features detailed routes for every lake region; 800-CALL-NYS. Free.

Take a Hike by Rich and Sue Freeman, Footprint Press, PO Box 645, Fishers, NY 14453; 1999. A fabulous resource for serious as well as novice walkers and hikers. Highly detailed descriptions of trails, how to get there, contact information, maps, photos, and historic information. $16.95.

Backroad Bicycling in the Finger Lakes Region by Mark Roth and Sally Walters with the TNMC Bike Club, Backcountry Guides, Woodstock, VT 05091, is a must-have for bicycle enthusiasts. Details include mile-by-mile directions, excellent maps, and history notes for each tour. $15.

HISTORY

Ontario County, compiled by Valerie Knoblauch, Ontario County Four Seasons Development Corp., 248 S. Main St., Canandaigua, NY 14424; 1989. A marvelous history of Ontario County, loaded with photos of notable people and places in the region's history and development.

As We Were, Volumes 1 and 2, compiled by the Seneca Falls Historical Society, 1979. A random collection of early-20th-century photographs of Seneca Falls. Available at the Seneca Falls Historical Society, 55 Cayuga St., Seneca Falls, NY 13148. $10.

In Homer you'll find Dave's veggies, one of many fruit and vegetable stands along Finger Lakes highways.

WINERIES

Touring East Coast Wine Country: A Guide to the Finest Wineries, by Marguerite Thomas, Berkshire House, and *Wineries of the Finger Lakes Region,* by Emerson Klees, Friends of Finger Lakes Publishing, PO Box 18131, Rochester, NY 14618. Excellent companions for exploring the wineries.

FINGER LAKES CULINARY BOUNTY

A new organization, Finger Lakes Culinary Bounty, promotes the use of regional cuisine using meats and produce from local farmers. A special logo designates which places specialize in preparing meals using these "home-grown" foods.

CLIMATE AND WEATHER

The climate in the Finger Lakes region can be fickle, indeed. June, July, and August are usually gloriously warm and sunny. Fall comes around mid-October or even earlier, providing all the wonderful color and bright-blue skies—perfect football weather. Snow usually comes in November but has arrived as early as mid-October. When snow rudely makes an early debut, it usually doesn't stay around long—kids have barely enough time to get their sleds out before the weather moderates, and the snow melts.

Winter usually delivers deep snow—blustery, huddle-around-the fire type stuff; temperatures can plunge below zero. The lakes often freeze. Some days the lakes are dotted with skaters and ice boaters.

One winter, driving above Skaneateles Lake, along Route 41 just outside of Scott—a small community of weathered buildings that time forgot—I came upon a breathtaking sight. Apparently others thought so, too, because drivers had parked their cars along the road to marvel at the icy wonderland suddenly created. Every twig, grass blade, and telephone wire was sheathed in a dazzling coat of ice that glistened in the sun.

The long-anticipated spring usually appears before Easter. But there have been years when the Easter bunny needed snowshoes and times when the lakes have still not thawed out.

Average Temperatures in the Finger Lakes

Summer: Day mid-80s; night 50s to 60s.
Fall: Day mid-60s; night mid-40s.
Winter: Day mid-30s; night teens to mid-20s.
Spring: Day mid-60s; night mid-40s.

(From the Finger Lakes Association)

In summer the temperatures are warm and balmy and in fact can get quite hot, sometimes into the 90s but seldom more than 100 degrees. Generally, the temperature average 75 degrees, and the lakes warm up mid-July. There are exceptions. In 1996 a heat wave in June warmed the lakes so fast that people were swimming before the parks were open and the rafts were out.

LAKE FACTS AND FIGURES

Each Finger Lake is unique; all are named after a Native American word or phrase. The list below goes from east to west.

Otisco

Length: 6 miles.
Depth: 66 feet.
Elevation: 784 feet.
Characteristics: Ringed by small lakeside camps and homes.
Meaning: "Waters much dried away."
Largest town: Amber.

Picking apples is fun for kids in the fall at Beak & Skiff Apple Hill in Lafayette.

Skaneateles

Length: 15 miles.
Depth: 350 feet.
Elevation: 867 feet.
Characteristics: Cold, clean water, shale base, steep hillsides at southern end;
    large homes and mansions hug northern shores.
Meaning: "Long Lake."
Largest town: Skaneateles.

Owasco

Length: 11 miles.
Depth: 177 feet.
Elevation: 710 feet.
Characteristics: More laid back than its neighbor Skaneateles.
Meaning: "Floating bridge" or "Crossing place."
Largest town: Auburn.

Cayuga

Length: 40 miles.
Depth: 435 feet.
Elevation: 384 feet.
Characteristics: Long and wide, can get very rough on windy days; large
    stretches of open rolling land between towns; many vineyards.
Meaning: "Boat Landing."
Largest town: Ithaca.

Seneca

Length: 36 miles.
Depth: 632 feet.
Elevation: 444 feet.
Characteristics: Deepest of the Finger Lakes and second deepest in the country;
    ringed by hills and vineyards.
Meaning: "Place of stone."
Largest town: Geneva.

Keuka

Length: 22 miles.
Depth: 187 feet.
Elevation: 709 feet.
Characteristics: Branches into a Y shape; many vineyards.

Meaning: "Canoe landing."
Largest town: Penn Yan.

Canandaigua

Length: 16 miles.
Depth: 262 feet.
Elevation: 686 feet.
Characteristics: Mostly lined by homes.
Meaning: "Chosen Spot."
Largest town: Canandaigua.

Honeoye

Length: 5 miles.
Depth: 30 feet.
Elevation: 818 feet.
Characteristics: Small; some nice houses.
Meaning: "Finger lying."
Largest town: Honeoye.

Canadice

Length: 3 miles.
Depth: 91 feet.
Elevation: 1,099 feet.
Characteristics: Highest elevation yet the smallest lake.
Meaning: "Long Lake."
Largest town: Canadice.

Hemlock

Length: 8 miles.
Depth: 96 feet.

More Finger Lakes Data

Hotel rates: Most range from $45 to $200.

Restaurant rates: Dinners range from $8 to $30 per person; lunches range from $5 to $20.

Family income: Average income ranges from $29,800 (Yates County) to $45,400 (Monroe County).

Average cost of family home: $68,000.

(From The Finger Lakes Association)

Elevation: 905 feet.
Characteristics: No motorized craft allowed on this pristine reservoir.
Meaning: Only lake named by white man; it refers to the Native American word "Onehda."
Largest town: Hemlock.

Conesus

Length: 9 miles.
Depth: 59 feet.
Elevation: 818 feet.
Characteristics: Small, quiet, and pretty; surrounded by meadows and woodlands.
Meaning: "Always beautiful."
Largest town: Lakeville.

MEDICAL FACILITIES

Auburn Memorial Hospital: 315-255-7011.
Cayuga Medical Center at Ithaca: 607-274-4011.

Syracuse

Community General Hospital: 315-492-5011.
Crouse Hospital: 315-470-7111.
St. Joseph's Hospital Health Center: 315-448-5111.
University Hospital: 315-464-5540.

Taylor-Brown Health Center, Waterloo: 315-787-4553.

NEWSPAPERS

Auburn, *The Citizen:* 315-253-5311.
Canandaigua, *The Daily Messenger and Sunday Messenger:* 585-394-0770; 800-724-2099.
Corning, *Corning Leader:* 607-936-4651
Dundee, Finger Lakes Media (The Dundee Observer **and** Watkins Review**):** 607-243-7600.
Elmira, *Star Gazette,* 800-836-8970
Geneva, *Finger Lakes Times and Sunday Finger Lakes Times:* 315-789-3333.
Ithaca, *Ithaca Times:* 607-277-7000.

Rochester, *Democrat and Chronicle:* 585-232-7100.
Skaneateles, *Press-Marcellus Observer:* 315-685-8338.
Watkins Glen, *Watkins Glen Review:* 607-535-1500.

Syracuse

Syracuse Post Standard: 315-470-0011.
Syracuse Herald Journal: 315-470-0011.
Sunday Herald American: 315-470-0011.
Eagle Newspapers: 315-434-8889; www.cnylink.com; 14 weekly newspapers in and around Syracuse.

RECREATION FACTS AND FIGURES

The extreme changes of climate, along with the dramatic landscape of hills, lakes, gorges, and meadows, have created a great range of recreational activities: sailing and boating, swimming, fishing, waterskiing, downhill and cross-country skiing, snowmobiling, climbing, hiking, biking, and ice skating. Hikers and bikers will find the Finger Lakes region laced with trails, both well traveled and off the beaten path. Some roads are still unpaved.

Hiking: The Finger Lakes Trail covers more than 559 miles, running south of the lakes from Allegheny State Park in southwestern New York State to the Catskill Mountains. Six spurs run from the main trail north, with a total of 238 miles. All these trails, and the campsites along the way, are maintained by the Finger Lakes Trail Conference. Many are good for cross-country skiing, biking, and horseback riding. Motorized vehicles are not allowed. (716-288-7191; www.finger lakes.net/trailsystem; PO Box 18048, Rochester, NY 14618.)

Biking: Cyclists can enjoy an excellent network of well-paved back roads as well as roads ringing the lakes. You can ride a loop around 10 of the lakes, with distances ranging from 12 miles (Canadice) to 90 miles (Cayuga). The terrain in the northern part of the lake is generally easier, more level, less rugged than the southern ends of the lakes. And cycling in the direction that the lakes run—north and south—is for the most part less strenuous than riding in an east-west direction.

Unless you have skis on your wheels, avoid cycling in the winter when icy roads and drifting snow make it slow going. Always bring a rain parka: You can start your ride in the blazing sun only to have a fast-moving storm take over. The weather in the Finger Lakes can be fickle, indeed.

Fishing: The lakes and rivers are a fisherman's paradise. Fed by underground streams and rivers that flow from Lake Ontario, the Finger Lakes harbor a variety of fish. Whether you troll, fly fish, or simply drop a line over the side of a boat, you can pull in rainbow trout, rock bass, sunfish, lake trout, perch, pan-

Other Useful Numbers

New York State

Empire State Bed & Breakfast Association of New York State: 585-882-6116; www.esbba.com.

NYS Canal Corporation: 800-4-CANAL-4.

NYS Department of Environmental Conservation: 518-457-3521 (for hunting and fishing information).

NYS Office of Parks, Recreation, and Historic Preservation: 518-474-0456.

NYS Parks: 800-456-CAMPS (for camping and cabin reservations).

NYS Thruway Information: 800-225-5697.

Rochester

Center City Visitor Information Center: 800-677-7282.

Cinemark IMAX: 585-426-2629.

City of Rochester Special Events: 585-428-6697.

The Dome Center: 585-334-4000.

Greater Rochester International Airport (585-464-6000; www.rocairport.com).

Fishing Advisory Hotline: 585-987-8800.

Rochester Events: 585-546-6810.

Rochester Information for the Deaf: 585-546-8484.

Rochester Riverside Convention Center: 585-232-3362.

Ticket Express: 585-222-5000.

Visitor Association Events Line: 585-546-6810.

Syracuse

Carrier Dome Box Office: 315-443-2121.

Empire Expo Center/NYS Fairgrounds: 315-487-7711, 800-475-FAIR; www.nys fair.org.

Fishing Information: 315-472-2111, ext. 2645.

Golf Information: 315-472-2111, ext. 3672.

Oncenter Complex: 315-435-8000; www.oncenter.org.

Onondaga County Parks & Recreation: 315-451-PARK.

ONTRACK: 315-424-1212.

Ski Information: 315-472-2111 x 7547.

Syracuse Events Hotline: 315-470-1978.

Syracuse Newspapers Newsline: 315-472-2111 (includes fishing, golf, and ski information).

Syracuse Hancock International Airport: 315-454-4330; www.syrairport.org.

Syracuse University Information: 315-443-5500.

Rental and Reservation Services

Bed and Breakfast Network of Central New York (315-498-6560, 800-333-1604; www.cnylodging.com) A referral service for B&Bs primarily in the Syracuse and Skaneateles areas.

The Finger Lakes Bed & Breakfast Association (800-695-5590; www.flbba.org) They offer travel packages specials.

Vacation Rentals (888-414-5253; www.rentalplus.com) A service providing a variety of rental properties in the Finger Lakes region including condominiums, B&Bs, cabins, and single houses.

---

fish, bluegills, pickerel, smelt, and other species that thrive in the cool clean lakes and feeder streams.

TOURISM ORGANIZATIONS

COUNTY TOURIST BOARDS

Cayuga County Office of Tourism: 315-255-1658, 800-499-9615; fax 315-255-3742; www.cayuganet.org/tourism; 131 Genesee St., Auburn, NY 13021.

Chemung County Commerce Center: 800-MARK TWAIN; fax 607-734-4490; www.chemungchamber.org; 400 E. Church St., Elmira, NY 14901.

Cortland County Convention and Visitors Bureau: 607-753-8463, 800-859-2227; www.cortlandtourism.com; 34 Tompkins St., Cortland, NY 13045.

Monroe County, Greater Rochester Visitors Association: 585-546-3070, 800-677-7282; fax 585-232-4822; www.visitrochester.com; 45 East Ave., Suite 400, Rochester, NY 14604.

Ontario County Tourism: 585-394-3915, 877-FUN-IN-NY; www.visitfinger lakes.com; 25 Gorham St., Canandaigua, NY 14424.

Schuyler County Chamber of Commerce: 607-535-4300; fax 607-535-6243; www.schuylerny.com; 100 N. Franklin St., Watkins Glen, NY 14891.

Seneca County Tourism: 315-539-1759, 800-732-1848; fax 315-539-1754; www.visitseneca.net; Box 491, Rte. 5 & 20, Seneca Falls, NY 13148.

Steuben County Conference & Visitors Bureau: 866-946-3386; 607-936-6544; fax 607-936-6575; www.corningfingerlakes.com; 5 W. Market St., Corning, NY 14830.

Onondaga County/Syracuse Convention and Visitors Bureau: 315-470-1910, 800-234-4797; fax 315-471-8545; www.visitsyracuse.org; 572 S. Salina St., Syracuse, NY 13202.

Tompkins County Convention and Visitors Bureau: 607-272-1313, 800-28-ITHACA; fax 607-272-7617; www.ithacaevents.com; www.visitithaca.com; 904 E. Shore Dr., Ithaca, NY 14850.

Yates County Tourism: 800-868-9283; fax 315-536-3791; www.yatesny.com; 2375 Rte. 14A, Penn Yan, NY 14527.

OTHER TOURISM ORGANIZATIONS

Bath Chamber of Commerce: 607-776-7122; 10 Pulteney Sq. W. Bath, NY 14810.

Camillus Chamber of Commerce: 315-488-1919; 4600 W. Genesee St.; Camillus, NY 13219.

Canandaigua Chamber of Commerce Tourist Center Information: 585-394-4400; fax 585-394-4546; www.canandaigua.com; 113 S. Main St., Canandaigua, NY 14424.

Greater Corning Area Chamber of Commerce: 866-463-6264; 607-936-3642; www.corningny.com; 1 Baron Steuben Place, Corning, NY 14830.

Finger Lakes Tourism: 800-548-4386; www.fingerlakes.org; 309 Lake St., Penn Yan, NY 14527.

Geneva Area Chamber of Commerce Information Center: 315-789-1776; fax 315-789-3993; www.genevany.com; 35 Lakefront Dr., PO Box 587, Geneva, NY 14456.

Greater Rochester Chamber of Commerce: 585-454-2220; 55 St. Paul St., Rochester, NY 14604.

Greater Syracuse Chamber of Commerce: 315-470-1800; fax 315-471-8545; http://chamber.cny.com; 572 S. Salina St., Syracuse, NY 13202.

Information Center of Corning: 607-962-8997; www.corningny.com; 1 Baron Steuben Pl., Corning, NY 14830.

Hammondsport Chamber of Commerce: 607-569-2989; http://nysfingerlakes.com/chamber; Box 539, Hammondsport, NY 14840.

Honeoye Chamber of Commerce: 585-229-4226; http://honeoye.com; PO Box 305, Honeoye, NY 14471.

Moravia Locke Chamber of Commerce: 315-497-1966; www.cayuganet.org/ml chamber; 102 Main St., Moravia, NY 13118.

Rochester Business Alliance: 585-244-1800; www.rochesterbusinessalliance.com; 150 State St., Rochester, NY 14614.

Skaneateles Chamber of Commerce: 315-685-0552; www.skaneateles.com; PO Box 199, Skaneateles, NY 13152.

Syracuse Convention and Visitors Bureau: 315-470-1910, 800-234-4797; fax 315-471-8545; www.visitsyracuse.org; 572 S. Salina St., Syracuse, NY 13202.

Trumansburg Area Chamber of Commerce: 607-387-9254; http://trumansburgchamber.com; PO Box 478, Trumansburg, NY 14486.

WINERY INFORMATION

New York Wine and Grape Foundation: 315-536-7442; www.nywine.com; 350 Elm St., Penn Yan, NY 14527.

WINE TRAILS

Four of the lake areas—Cayuga, Seneca, Keuka, and Canandaigua—have established wine trails, with maps and listings of the participating wineries. All sponsor wine-related events.

Cayuga Wine Trail: 800-684-5217; www.cayugawine.com.
Seneca Lake Wine Trail: 877-536-2717, 607-535-8080; www.senecalakewine.com.
Keuka Lake Wine Trail: 800-440-4898; www.keukawinetrail.com.
Canandaigua Wine: 877-386-4669; www.canandaiguawinetrailonline.com.

YEARLY EVENTS

Table decor for a New Year's gala.

SKANEATELES, OWASCO, AND OTISCO LAKES

MAY

Memorial Day Parade (Skaneateles) A hometown parade on Genesee Street, with veterans, scouts, and local dignitaries.

Memorial Day Parade (315-255-2211; Auburn) Floats, band and performers march along Genesee Street.

SUMMER

Annual Book Sale (315-685-5135; Skaneateles Library, 49 E. Genesee St., Skaneateles) Lots of books, old and new, for all ages.

Annual Summer Arts and Crafts Show (Marcellus; park off Rte. 175) Sale and exhibit of artwork by a variety of artisans.

Auburn Doubledays Home Games (315-255-2489; Falcon Park, 130 N. Division St. Auburn) Class-A professional baseball games.

Concerts at Emerson Park Pavilion (315-253-5611; Emerson Park, Rte. 38A, Auburn) Live entertainment through August, including concerts by bands such as the Dean Brothers and the Joe Whiting Band. Everything from rock 'n' roll to Irish step dancers.

Concerts in the Park (Skaneateles, Clift Park) Every Friday evening at 7:30pm throughout the summer outdoors in the park—or indoors at the Allyn Pavilion if it rains.

Concert Series (315-497-3825; Ethel Fuller Park, Rte. 38, Moravia) Free concerts at 7 pm.

Made in NY (315-255-1553; Schweinfurth Memorial Art Center, 205 Genesee St., Auburn) A juried show of artwork by artists and artisans living and working in New York State.

Polo Matches (Andrews St., Skaneateles) Held every Sunday through the summer at 3pm. Small parking fee.

JULY

Cayuga County Fair (315-253-0165; Cayuga County Fairgrounds, Rte. 31, Weedsport) Spend the day. There are farm animals, monster trucks, food concessions, midway games, live entertainment, and a demolition derby.

Skaneateles Classic and Antique Boat Show (315-685-0552; Clift Park and pier, Skaneateles) More than 60 antique and classic boats in and out of the water. Activities include concerts, boat parade, and shopping.

AUGUST

Skaneateles Festival (315-685-7418; Skaneateles) Twenty or so concerts are scheduled throughout August and September. They are held in a stone church and under the stars at Brook Farm.

SEPTEMBER

Labor Day Celebration & Field Days (Austin Park, Jordan St., Skaneateles) The town's largest parade is followed by barbecues, games, rides, and fireworks.

Quilt Exhibition (315-255-1553; Schweinfurth Memorial Art Center, 205 Genesee St., Auburn) Outstanding handmade quilts. Early November through early January.

DECEMBER

Skaneateles residents dress up in 19th-century garb for the annual Dickens Days holiday celebration.

Dickens Days (Skaneateles) The town is dressed for the holidays, and the townspeople are dressed as Dickens characters as they stroll Genesee Street. Very festive.

CAYUGA LAKE

MARCH

Maple Sugar Festival (607-273-6260; Cayuga Nature Center, 1420 Taughannock Blvd., Ithaca) See how maple syrup is tapped and made into sugar.

MAY

Cayuga Wine Trail Fresh Herb and New Wine Festival (800-684-5217; Cayuga Lake wineries) Visit participating wineries, taste new wines, sample foods made with fresh herbs, and take home potted herbs ready for planting.

JUNE

Annual Finger Lakes Carp Derby (315-568-5112, Peoples Park, Seneca Falls) More than $2,000 in prizes to catch the big one.

Annual Seneca County Fair (Seneca County Fairgrounds, Waterloo) A whole week of fun: tractor pulls, midway attractions, demolition derby, parades, barbecues, rides, animals, and more.

Canalfest (315-568-2906; Seneca Falls Canal Promenade) Arts and crafts show, with artisans, entertainment, food, antique boats, steamboats, and fireworks.

Ithaca Festival (607-273-3646, Ithaca) An enormous festival, with crafts, singing, theater, mimes, fireworks, food.

Old Home Days (607-532-8731; Interlaken) Great family fun, with parade, auctions, yard sales, entertainment.

Seneca Falls Canal Fest (Along the Canal Promenade, Seneca Falls) Fireworks, rides, arts and crafts, boat races, turtle race, food, and more.

Vintage Car Show (607-277-8979; On the Commons, Ithaca) Antique cars on display.

JULY

Finger Lake Grassroots Festival (607-387-5144; Trumansburg Fairgrounds, Trumansburg) Four days, usually the third weekend in July, of musical concerts on three stages.

AUGUST

Cayuga Wine Trail Chardonnay Weekend (800-684-5217; Cayuga Lake wineries) Taste and compare various styles of Chardonnay from participating wineries.

Empire Farm Days (585-526-5356; Rodman Ltd. & Sons Farm, Seneca Falls) A huge farm show.

OCTOBER

Apple Harvest Festival (607-277-8679; Ithaca) A gala weekend filled with local produce, including apples, cider, and pies; craft fair, entertainment, and storytellers.

DECEMBER

Cayuga Wine Trail Shopping Spree (800-684-5217; Cayuga Lake wineries) Taste wine, sample holiday hors d'oeuvres, and take home recipes.

Trumansburg Festival of Lights (607-387-6292; Trumansburg) The village Christmas tree is the center of attention as it is lit with a sing-along, music, crafts, horse and carriage rides, and dessert contest. Held the first weekend in December.

SENECA LAKE

FEBRUARY

Chocolate and Wine (315-536-9996; Seneca Lake wineries) Visit wineries, and taste gourmet chocolate delights paired with select wines; receive a gift, too.

APRIL

Spring Wine and Cheese Weekend (315-536-9996; Seneca Lake wineries) Follow a route around the lake, sipping wine and nibbling cheese and crackers as you go.

MAY

National Lake Trout Derby (315-789-8634, Seneca Lake, Geneva) Fish for prizes, fun. Memorial Day weekend.
Memorial Day Celebrations (315-568-2906, Waterloo) Parades, picnics, music, fairs in the "birthplace" of Memorial Day.

JUNE

Pasta and Wine, Seneca Lake Wine Trail (315-536-9996) Visit 21 wineries along Seneca Lake, and enjoy pasta dishes paired with wine.
Waterfront Festival (607- 535-4300, Seneca Harbor Park, Watkins Glen) Regatta, kayak rides, bands, chicken, BBQ.
Watkins Glen Historic Race (607-535-2481, Watkins Glen) Watkins Glen International, races with vintage cars.

SUMMER

Concerts in the Park (607-535-4300; Watkins Glen) Every Tuesday evening through mid-August.
Geneva Lakefront Park Concert Series (315-789-5005; Lakefront Park, Rte. 5 & 20, Geneva) Free concerts at 7pm through the summer.

JULY

American Legion Fireworks and July 4th Festival (315-789-5165; American Legion, Lockland Rd., Geneva) Festival of fun, games, food.
Dundee Day (downtown Dundee) Twenty-four miles of yard sales, arts and crafts, food, and fun. First Saturday after July 4th.
Finger Lakes Wine Festival (607-535-2481; Watkins Glen International Race Track, Watkins Glen, NY 14891) More than 60 wineries participate in this two-day event, which takes place under tents on the grounds of the Watkins Glen Race Track. Tastings, wine sales, a Taster's Banquet, Champagne Breakfast,

Kids enjoy a July 4th concert in Skaneateles' Clift Park.

live music and seminars, plus arts and crafts vendors add up to one great celebration of regional wines and produce.

Ontario County Fair (315-462-3168; Ontario County Fairgrounds) 4-H fair with
activities, stock car races, demolition derby, and more.

PBA's Classic Auto and Sports Car Show (315-789-1852; Lakeshore Park, Rte. 5
& 20, Geneva) More than 500 vintage cars on display, plus arts and crafts vendors, flea market, food, entertainment, vintage boat regatta, and fireworks.

St. Mary's Annual Festival (315-539-2944; Waterloo) Entertainment, fire engine
rides, games, and food under tents.

AUGUST

Pickin' in the Pasture (607-582-6363; Lodi NY) A celebration of bluegrass and
old-time music overlooking Seneca Lake.

Seneca Lake Whale Watch (315-781-0820; www.whalewatch.org; PO Box 226,
northern end of lake, Geneva Area Chamber of Commerce, Geneva) No
whales in this fresh-water lake but a weekend promising a whale of fun.
Crafts, games, food, water-ski show, boating excursions, musical performances, displays, fireworks, wine tastings. Third weekend of August.

SEPTEMBER

Ikepod Watkins Glen Grand Prix Festival and Zippo US Vintage Grand Prix
(607-535-3003; PO Box 65, Franklin St., Watkins Glen) Sports-car events, live
music, Concours d'Elegance (vintage and classic car show), race re-enactment of vintage cars from the 1948–1952 circuit, wine tastings, family fun, kid
racer school and derby, road rally, food vendors, and more.

NOVEMBER

Deck the Halls (315-536-9996; around the lake) Visit each of the wineries along
the Seneca Lake Wine Trail, and collect ornaments, recipes, and a wreath as
you go. Each place offers wine tastings and something to eat. Early reservations a must.

Christmastime.

KEUKA LAKE

FEBRUARY

Be Mine with Wine (800-440-4898; Keuka wineries) Each winery offers a
dessert paired with different wines.

APRIL

Easter Egg Hunt (607-569-2989; Village Square, Hammondsport) Children hunt for hidden eggs and prizes.

JUNE

Finger Lakes Historic Boats Show (800-868-9283, Fireman's Field, Penn Yan) Antique boat display, Finger Lakes–built boats.

JULY

Keuka Lake Art Association Show (607-569-2989; downtown Hammondsport) Local and regional artists show and sell their work.

AUGUST

Steuben County Fair (607-776-4801; Fairgrounds, Bath) This is the oldest continuously held annual agricultural country fair in the country.

SEPTEMBER

Buckwheat Festival (Penn Yan) Celebrates the importance of buckwheat in the area; with food, music, entertainment, and more.
4 AKC All Breed Dog Show (315-585-6669; Sampson State Park, Romulus) Obedience and agility trials.
The Genundowa Festival of Lights (607-569-2989; Village Square, Hammondsport) Native American dancing, drums, singing, storytelling, crafts, food, and art.

OCTOBER

Fall Foliage Festival (Cohocton) Family fun, fireworks, parade, games, food.
Rhineland Oktoberfest (800-440-4898; Keuka Lake wineries) Enjoy German music and food; taste world-class German-style wines at participating wineries.

OCTOBER

Keuka Holidays (800-440-4898; Keuka Lake wineries) As you visit each winery along the Keuka Lake Wine Trail, enjoy hearty winter foods and wine. Gift and recipe booklet also included.

CANANDAIGUA and Canadice, Conesus, Hemlock, and Honeoye Lakes

JANUARY

Festival of Lights (585-394-4922; Canandaigua) Grounds of Sonnenberg mansion filled with designs in lights; house and greenhouse decorated for holidays.

MARCH

Maple Sugaring (585-374-6160; Cumming Nature Center, Naples) Demonstrations in the process of maple sugaring.

MAY

Mercy Flight Balloon Festival (585-396-0584; Brickyard Rd., Canandaigua) Balloons, rides, helicopter rides, and crafts.

Naples Art and Music Festival (585-394-3915; Memorial Town Hall Park, Main St., Naples) An arts-and-crafts show, with more than 200 vendors. Food, plants, fiddlers contest, entertainment.

JUNE

Antique Market (585-394-1472; Granger Homestead, 295 N. Main St., Canandaigua) Antiques, treasure table, and bake sale.

Canandaigua Lake Trout Derby (585-394-4400; weigh-in stations at Inn on the Lake, Canandaigua) Prizes given for best catches.

SUMMER

Concerts in the Park (585-396-0300; Atwater Park, Canandaigua) Free concerts through the summer Fridays at 6:30.

Horse Drawn Carriage Rides (5585-394-1472; Granger Homestead, 295 N. Main St., Canandaigua) Forty-five-minute narrative rides through the city's historic neighborhoods on Friday afternoons.

JULY

Canandaigua Art Festival (585-396-0300; S. Main St., Canandaigua) Juried show with more than 300 art and craft exhibits and food vendors.

Civil War Re-enactment (585-396-1417; Bristol Woodlands Campground) Living encampment and scenarios, infantry, artillery, cavalry, battles, food. Ongoing through the month.

Hill Cumorah Pageant (315-597-2757; Rte. 21, Exit 43 NYS Thruway, Manchester, near Palmyra) Religion-based outdoor theatrical production, with a cast of 600 and recorded music from the Mormon Tabernacle Choir.

July 4th Celebration (585-396-5000; Kreshaw Park, Lakeshore Dr., Canandaigua) Family entertainment, activities, food, fireworks.

Native American Dance and Music Festival (Ganondagan Historic Site, 1488 Victor-Holcomb Rd., Victor) Native American foods, wonderful crafts and demonstrations, dance, and exhibits.

AUGUST

Pageant of Steam (585-394-8102; Gehan Rd., 5 miles east of Canandaigua) This weekend-long festival celebrates antique steam-powered vehicles. The 100-

acre site is the venue for a number of events, including sawmill demonstrations, parades, live music, a pedal tractor pull, grain threshing, shingle making, an antique car show, a garden tractor pull, and a giant craft and flea market.

Steuben County Fair (607-776-4801; Bath) Six days of fun, carnival, rides, livestock, exhibits, shows, truck pull, music, and demolition derby.

Waterfront Art Festival (585-383-1472; Kershaw Park, Lakeshore Dr., Canandaigua) More than 200 art and craft exhibits, demonstrations, cloggers, puppet shows, concerts, and face painting.

September

Naples Grape Festival (585-374-2240; www.naplesvalleyny.com; Memorial Town Hall Park, Main St., Naples) More than 250 exhibitors, live entertainment, juried arts and crafts, food, grape pie contest.

Ring of Fire Around the Lakes (Lakeside, Canandaigua/Honeoye Lakes) Residents light up the lakes with flares, signifying the end of the summer season.

October

Pumpkin Walk (585-394-6822; www.ontariopathways.org; Canandaigua) Hundreds of carved jack-o-lanterns twinkle in the dark along Ontario Pathways. Call for date.

Fall Festival (315-986-9821; Macedon) See Doug's giant straw-bale maze and pumpkin land, and ride hay wagons into the fields.

Haunted Gardens (585-394-4922; Sonnenberg Gardens, Canandaigua) Ghosts, vampires, goblins, and monsters lurk in the gardens and walkways of this turn-of-the-20th-century mansion.

November

Canandaigua Treaty Celebration (585-742-1690; www.ggw.org/ganondagan; Ontario County Courthouse, Canandaigua) Anniversary and celebration of the signing of the Canandaigua Pickering Treaty; held at 2pm.

Festival of Lights (585-394-4922; Canandaigua) Grounds of Sonnenberg mansion filled with designs in lights; house and greenhouse decorated for holidays. Through January.

Festival of Trees (585-394-1472; www.grangerhomestead.org; Granger Homestead and Carriage Museum, Canandaigua) Theme decorated Christmas trees, wreaths, mantel decorations, and other festive items.

Holidays at the Homestead (585-394-1472; www.grangerhomestead.org; Granger Homestead and Carriage Museum, Canandaigua) Craft show and bake sale.

December

Festival of Lights (585-394-4922; Canandaigua) Grounds of Sonnenberg mansion filled with designs in lights; house and greenhouse decorated for holidays. Through January.

HOST CITIES

Syracuse

MARCH

St. Patrick's Day Parade (downtown area, Syracuse) Wear green and watch the parade to celebrate this festive Irish holiday.

JUNE

Coors Light Balloon Fest (315-451-7275; Jamesville Beach, Syracuse) The sky fills with close to 50 colorful hot-air balloons. Rides, family activities, entertainment, food.

Jazz Fest (315-422-8284; Clinton and Hanover Squares, Syracuse) National and international jazz greats perform throughout the month. (Check for possible alternate sites.)

JULY

Pops in the Park (315-473-4330 ext. 3006; Hiawatha Lake Gazebo, Onondaga Park, Syracuse) Free concerts throughout the month and sometimes beyond.

AUGUST

Central New York Scottish Games and Celtic Festival (315-463-8876; www .cnyscots.com; Long Branch Park) Scottish and Celtic music and dancing, bands, clan genealogy.

Great New York State Fair (800-475-FAIR; www.nysfair.org/state_fair; 581 State Fair Blvd., Syracuse, NY 13209) Almost two weeks of fun and exhibits at the NYS Fairgrounds in late August–September, featuring car races, craft fairs, amusements, animals, horticulture, ethnic celebrations, food.

New York State Rhythm & Blues Festival (315-469-1723; www.nysbluesfest.com; Clinton, Armory and Hanover Squares and Hotel Syracuse/Radisson Plaza, Syracuse) Great performers entertain throughout several days.

SEPTEMBER

Golden Harvest Festival (315-638-2519; 8477 E. Mud Lake Rd., Beaver Lake Nature Center, Baldwinsville) More than 100 crafters join blues, folk, jazz, and reggae musicians, puppet shows, and pony rides for this fall celebration.

NOVEMBER–DECEMBER

Lights on the Lake (800-243-4797; Syracuse Chamber of Commerce, Syracuse) Flares are lit around the lake.

Cortland

APRIL

Central New York Maple Festival (Cortland) When the sugar maple sap starts running in early spring, it's time to celebrate. One of the highlights is a marathon.

JUNE

Apple Jazz Festival (Dwyer Memorial Park, Little York) Great music plus food and craft stands.

Firemen's Field Days (Homer) Games, fun, amusements, food and parade.

SEPTEMBER

McGraw Harvest Festival (607-836-6107; Recreation Center, McGraw) Crafts, parade, entertainment.

OCTOBER

The Great Cortland Pumpkinfest (800-859-2227; Courthouse Park, Cortland) Pumpkins everywhere, wagon rides, carving contests, food. Lots of fun for the whole family.

NYS Draft Horse Show and Sale (607-533-4160; Cortland County Fairground, Cortland) See draft horses strut their stuff.

NOVEMBER

Ice skating (Homer) On sunny winter days, the village green is filled with skaters of all ages.

Corning

MARCH

Spring Antique Show and Sale (607-937-5281; Greg Elementary School, Corning) Many vendors show and sell a wide assortment of furniture, glassware, memorabilia, and other old things.

Rochester

MAY

Lilac Festival (585-256-4960; www.lilacfestival.com; Highland Park, Highland Ave., Rochester) Thousands of lilacs and other spring flowers, plus a parade, races, arts and crafts, activities, entertainment, and horticultural exhibits.

JUNE

Maplewood Rose Festival (585-428-6697; www.ggw.org/~mna/rose.htm; Maplewood Rose Garden, corner Lake Ave. and Driving Park, Rochester) A three-day floral celebration centered around more than 5,000 roses. Tours, entertainment, and rose-culture workshops.

JULY

Corn Hill Arts Festival (585-262-3142; streets of Corn Hill neighborhood, Rochester) An eclectic variety of arts and crafts, live music, food, and entertainment.

Renaissance Festival (800-879-4446; http://sterlingfestival.com/renfest; Farden Rd., Sterling) Live jousting, food, period music and dance, knights in shining armor, stage and street performances, games and marketplace; through August.

The Rochester Music Fest (585-428-6697; www.rochestermusicfest.com; High Falls area, Rochester) A two-day festival of American music, featuring a variety of internationally known musicians from jazz to blues artists.

AUGUST

Monroe County Fair (585-334-4000; Monroe County Fairgrounds and Dome Center, corner E. Henrietta and Calkins Rds., Rochester) A good old country-style fair, with agricultural exhibits, rides, games, and entertainment.

Park Ave. Summer Art Fest (585-234-1909; along the 1-mile stretch of Park Ave., Rochester) Music, juried arts and crafts exhibits, outdoor dining, shopping.

SEPTEMBER

Clothesline Festival (585-473-7720; http://mag.rochester.edu/visit/clothes line; Memorial Art Gallery, 500 University Ave., Rochester) Hundreds of local and statewide artists sell and show their goods at one of the oldest and largest outdoor art show in the country.

OCTOBER

Rochester River Romance (585-428-6697; Genesee Valley Park and University of Rochester river campus waterways, Rochester) A weekend party along the city's waterways, with hiking, boating, special activities, and historical fun. On Sunday there is a collegiate invitational regatta for college rowing teams.

FUN THINGS FOR KIDS

Abbey Farm at Spring Hill (585-526-5420; www.abbeyhistoricalfarm.org; 1862 St./Rte. 5 & 20, Stanley, NY 14561) Experience what life was like on a farm in Victorian days with a tour from a costumed interpreter through the farmyard and barn. Pet and feed the animals, ride in a horse-drawn buggy.

Beak & Skiff Apple Hill (315-696-8683; Rte. 80, off Rte. 20 east of Skaneateles, LaFayette, NY 13084) Pick-your-own apples, ride farm's tractor-drawn wagon. Children will love the corn maze, and goat and sheep pen. There are picnic tables, a large retail store packed with apple-oriented and other items, from colorful candles to children's hand-knit garments, and a snack stand is open on weekends. (Call first for information on picking and snack stand operations.)

Beaver Lake Nature Center (315-638-2519; www.ongov.net/Parks/blnc.shtml; 8477 E. Mud Lake Rd., Baldwinsville, NY 13027) Explore forest, meadows, and wetlands along miles of trails and boardwalks. Paddle a canoe across the lake, learn about maple sugaring, go snowshoeing, and tour the visitor center.

Captain Bill's Seneca Lake Cruises (607-535-4541; 1 N. Franklin St., Watkins Glen, NY 14891) Captain Bill's white double-decker 150-passenger boat with its bright-blue awning is a picturesque sight as it cruises up and down Seneca Lake. Enjoy lunch, dinner, and sightseeing cruises as well as miniature golf located right outside Captain Bill's gift shop.

Copper Creek Farms (585-289-4441; 5041 Shortsville Rd., Shortsville, NY 14548) You can ride horseback or in a carriage along the trails on the property. Riding and lessons for all ages; pony rides for kids.

The Corning Museum of Glass (315-568-1510, 800-732-6845; www.cmog.org; 1 Corning Glass Center, Corning, NY 14830) Learn about glassmaking

Children learn about making objects out of glass at the Corning Museum of Glass walk-in workshop.

from prehistoric times to the present. See incredible glass sculptures and exhibits, and try your hand at making glass objects yourself at the new Walk-in Workshop.

Erie Canal Museum (315-471-0593; www.eriecanalmuseum.org; 318 Erie Blvd., E. Rte. 5 at Montgomery St., Syracuse, NY 13202) Find out about the history of the canal in the 19th-century Weighlock Building. You can view the story of Syracuse in the theater, take a historical walking tour, and explore the *Frank B. Thomson,* a 65-foot replica of an old canal boat.

Falcon Park (315-255-2489; 130 N. Division St., Auburn) See super baseball, and enjoy a hotdog in a 2,044-seat baseball stadium where the Auburn Doubledays, a Class-A farm team for the Houston Astros (in the NY–Penn League) play June–September. The team is named after Abner Doubleday, baseball's legendary founder, who grew up in Auburn.

Fillmore Glen State Park (315-497-0130; just off Rte. 38 south of Moravia; use the back parking lot) Near the south end of Owasco Lake, there are three 1.8-mile (one-way) moderately difficult dirt trails in this 938-acre magnificent gorge and valley. The Gorge Trail is a perfect one for young children, level and safe with smaller waterfalls and walls of layered shale all along the way—a "prehistoric library." The lower pool of water is great for swimming.

Navigating through a corn maze at the Beak & Skiff Apple Hill Orchards in Lafayette.

Hansen's Corn Maze (315-789-9327; 5268 Pre-Emption Rd, (6 miles south of Geneva on Rte. 6) Get lost in a 5-acre corn maze with stalks reaching up to 15 ft. Pick your own pumpkins, ride wagons, and eat farm-fresh food. Also a straw tower for kids and a giant sling shot.

Mid-Lakes Navigation Company (315-685-8500, 800-545-4318; www.mid-lakesnav.com; 11 Jordan St., PO Box 61, Skaneateles, NY 13152) Take a cruise on Skaneateles Lake or on New York State's canal system. On Skaneateles Lake, two boats, the *Judge Ben Wiles,* a double-decker and the

Barbara S. Wiles, a smaller classic wooden craft, feature lunch, dinner, and sightseeing cruises.

MOST: Milton J. Rubenstein Museum of Science and Technology (315-425-9068; www.most.org; 500 S. Franklin St., Syracuse, NY 13202) Buzzing with activity, this handsome brick building is filled with exhibits, many interactive. Go through the giant maze, thrill to dinosaurs, climb the rock wall, see how your lungs work as you navigate your way through the human body, stand inside a humungous bubble, and learn about the universe at the Silverman Planetarium.

National Warplane Museum (607-739-8200; www.warplane.org; 17 Aviation Dr., Horseheads, NY 14845; near Elmira-Corning Regional Airport) Here military aviation history comes to life through a series of exhibits and a collection of 23 vintage aircraft. Look inside the cockpits and gunners' areas, and walk under the wings of a PBY Catalina flying boat.

Plainville Farms Pioneer Learning Center (315-635-3427; 7830 Plainville Rd., Plainville, NY 13137) Tour a replica of a primitive log cabin and see items used by our early settlers. Indoor animal petting area with lots of live turkeys and favorite farm animals.

Rochester Museum and Science Center (585-271-1880; www.rmsc.org; 657 East Ave., Rochester, NY 14607) This museum focuses on archaeology, science, and technology, cultural heritage, and anthropology, and features a computerized star theater and CineMagic 870 theater at the Strasenburgh Planetarium, and a Seneca Iroquois display.

Rosamond Gifford Zoo at Burnet Park (315-435-8511; http://rosamond giffordzoo.org; 1 Conservation Place, Syracuse, NY 13204) See Siberian tigers, penguins and seals, a rainforest with birds, and 600 other animals that live in spacious, natural-looking environments. And don't miss the monkey house.

Roseland Waterpark (585-396-2000; www.roselandwaterpark.com; 250 Eastern Blvd., Rte. 5 & 20, Canandaigua, NY 14424) A 58-acre playground for family fun with water slides, giant wave pool, Adventure River, two body flumes, Splash Factory, three tube rides, a 30-acre private lake, river rafts, and playground.

Sciencenter (607-272-0600; www.sciencenter.org; 601 First St., Ithaca, NY 14850) It's a great place to spend a day, with more than 100 exhibits, many hands-on. See a boa constrictor, water flume, two-story kinetic ball, and explore the workings of a walk-in camera.

Seabreeze Amusement Park and Raging Rivers Waterpark (585-323-1900, 800-395-2500; www.seabreeze.com; 4600 Culver Rd., Rochester, NY 14622; off I-590N) Rides, slides, fun, games, soak zone, carousel, bumper cars, water park, giant Jack Rabbit roller coaster, food, entertainment. Four roller-coasters.

Seneca Museum of Waterways and Industry (315-568-1510; www.seneca museum.com; 89 Fall St., Seneca Falls, NY 13148) This marvelous museum just continues to grow and get better with new exhibits, hands-on presentations and an ongoing series of art and craft displays. A 35-foot mural depicts this canal along with original drawings, engineers' plans, and photographs.

Riding a stationary tiger at the Rosamond Gifford Zoo at Burnet Park in Syracuse.

Seneca Park Zoo (585-467-WILD; http://senecaparkzoo.org; 2222 St. Paul St., Rochester, NY 14621) River otters, polar bears, penguins, and other animals live in settings that approximate their natural environments. See elephants from Africa, orangutans from Borneo, wolves, kangaroos, and more than 300 other animals.

Watkins Glen State Park and Gorge (607-535-4511; Watkins Glen, NY 14891) Explore one of the Finger Lake's most beautiful parks, a deep rock-walled canyon with 19 waterfalls, many cascades, grottoes, and amphitheaters. There is an Olympic-sized swimming pool, picnic facilities, camping, and nonstop views.

IF TIME IS SHORT

The best thing of all would be to spend several days in the Finger Lakes with enough time to see and do everything you want to do as well as eat in the best restaurants and overnight in the greatest places in the area. In the real world, time is often much too short to accomplish all this. So if your trip to the region is all too brief, here is a quick list of my favorite places for you to consider. Please check out the listings in the book for more details.

HOTELS, INNS, AND B&BS

Eastlake Bed & Breakfast (866-222-1544; www.eastlakebb.com; 5305 E. Lake Rd., Conesus NY 14435) It's one of the best B&Bs in the area. Relatively new but built with a B&B in mind, Eastlake is set on a hill with views of Conesus Lake from the large windows and the wraparound porch. There is a generous-sized waterfront, with paddleboat and canoe.

Esperanza Mansion (315-536-4400; www.esperanzamansion.com; 3456 Rte. 54A; Bluff Point, NY, 14478) You'll revel in the views above Keuka Lake from the rooms and terrace of this elegant yellow Greek-Revival house. Each room is different and the restaurant is romantic.

Geneva on the Lake Resort (315-789-7190, 800-3-GENEVA; www.geneva onthelake.com; 1001 Lochland Rd., Geneva, NY 14456; on Rte. 14) A lovely European-style villa on Seneca Lake, with gardens, terraces, restaurant, pool, and waterfront. Each room is elegant, different. A favorite for romantic escapes.

Mirbeau (315-685-5006, 877-MIRBEAU; www.mirbeau.com; 851 West Genesee Street, Skaneateles, NY 13152) A luxurious inn with an old European ambiance and a Monet-style pond, just a five-minute walk from the lake, park and shops of Skaneateles, one of the regions loveliest towns. An exceptional spa and restaurant pamper privileged guests.

1795 Acorn Inn (585-229-2834; www.acorninnbb.com; 4508 State Road 64 South, Bristol Center, Canandaigua NY 14424) This 18th-century stagecoach inn features wonderful enclosed gardens and patios, fireplaces, floor-to-ceiling windows, and tastefully arranged antiques, Orientals, artwork, and period furniture. Truly a romantic setting of character without clutter.

The William Henry Miller Inn (607-256-4553; www.millerinn.com; 303 North Aurora St., Ithaca, NY 14850) Tudor styling, stained-glass windows, impressive antiques, and carved chestnut moldings create an elegant oasis in the heart of downtown Ithaca.

RESTAURANTS

Doug's Fish Fry (315-685-3288; 8 Jordan St, Skaneateles) The place is about the size of a one-car garage, but it's *the* place to come for fish and chips. The fish sandwich with slaw and fries ($6.25) is a huge seller.

Joe's Pasta Garage (315-685-6116; 28 Jordan St., Skaneateles) This new Italian-American bistro-style eatery, housed in a 19th-century stone building, has become one of the village's hottest restaurants. You can build your own pizza and pasta. Just about everything costs less than $10, and everything is made from scratch.

Lincoln Hill Inn (585-394-8254; 3365 East Lake Rd., Canandaigua) Gardens and terraces surround this 1804 farmhouse. Eat outdoors or in one of the candlelit dining rooms by the fireplace.

Maxie's Supper Club & Oyster Bar (607-272-4136; 635 West State St., Ithaca) Soul-satisfying Southern comfort food including New Orleans-style Cajun dishes have made this one of the hottest spots in town. Free music, good prices also help.

Moosewood (607-273-9610; Dewitt Building, 215 North Cayuga St., Ithaca) Vegetarian cuisine starring grains, fresh vegetables, and fruits along with bold salsas, fish, and seafood—yummy enough to be the subject of several best-selling cookbooks.

Rosalie's Cucina (315-685-2200; 841 West Genesee St., Skaneateles) Great Italian fare with a pedigree.

CULTURAL ATTRACTIONS

The Corning Museum of Glass (315) 568-1510, 800-732-6845; www.cmog.org; 1 Corning Glass Center, Corning, NY 14830) If you have time only for one museum, go to this one. Learn about glassmaking from prehistoric times to the present. See incredible glass sculptures and exhibits, and try your hand at making glass objects yourself at the new Walk-in Workshop.

Delavan Art Gallery (DAG) (315-425-7500; 501 W. Fayette St., Syracuse, NY 13204) This exciting new gallery in a converted warehouse showcases the work of more than 50 area artists, representing a wide spectrum of visual arts: ceramics, drawing, fiber design, glass, illustrations, multimedia painting, paper making, photography, sculpture, and woodworking.

Museum of Waterways and Industry (315-568-1510; www.senecamuseum.com; 89 Fall Street, Seneca Falls, NY 13148) This new museum gives you a crash course in the importance of the canals and waterways in the Finger Lakes. Current art exhibits are a bonus.

Sonnenberg Mansion and Gardens (707-255-1144; 585-394-4922; www

.sonnenberg.org; 151 Charlotte St., Canandaigua, NY 14424) This magnificent late-19th-century Victorian mansion with several formal gardens is perfect for any who love flowers and relish a glimpse as to how the rich used to live. With 40 rooms and 50 acres, you will have plenty to explore.

WINERIES

For History: **Pleasant Valley Wine Company/Great Western Winery** (607-569-6111; County Rte. 88, Hammondsport, NY 14840) Established in 1860, this was the first bonded U.S. winery. A large museum and magnificent buildings with huge wine cellars recall the early days of wine production. Still produces an award-winning bubbly.

For Wine Buffs: **Dr. Frank's Vinifera Wine Cellars & Chateau Frank** (800-320-0735; www.drfrankwines.com; 9749 Middle Rd., Hammondsport, NY 14840) This distinctive winery was founded by the man who upgraded the Finger Lakes wine by proving that prized European grape varieties could be grown in the region to produce world-class table wines. Makes a superb barrel-fermented Chardonnay and Pinot Noir.

For Creative Folks: **Bully Hill Vineyards** (607-868-3610; www.bullyhill .com; 8843 Greyton H. Taylor Memorial Dr., Hammondsport, NY 14840) With names like Space Shuttle Rose and Meat Market Red, you've got to appreciate the creativity of the founder, Walter Taylor, who has produced many award-winning wines as well as wine labels worth collecting. The Greyton H. Taylor Wine and Grape Museum and an excellent restaurant are also on the premises.

For Class: **Glenora Wine Cellars** (800-243-5513; www.glenora.com; 5435 Rte. 14, Dundee, NY 14837) Glenora enjoys a magnificent lakeside setting, spacious wine tasting room, restaurant, winery, and hotel. The barrel-fermented Chardonnay is very good.

RECREATION

Getting Close to Nature: The many spectacular parks in the region showcase deep gorges, waterfalls, and miles of hiking trails. Some of the best are **Watkins Glen State Park** at the south end of Seneca Lake; **Taughannock Falls State Park** on the southwestern side of Cayuga Lake and **Fillmore Glen State Park** in Moravia south of Owasco Lake.

Dinner and Canal Cruising: Take a lunch or dinner cruise on one of the lakes or cruise New York State's Canal system for a day or a week. Check out the *Introduction* chapter as well as the individual lake chapters for details.

SHOPPING

There are many shops and boutiques throughout the Finger Lakes. Some that come immediately to mind that are those located in downtown Corning, Ithaca, Skaneateles, and Armory Square in Syracuse. Some shops are so unusual that they're worth a side trip. These include **Arbor Hill, Bristol Springs** (Canandaigua Lake), where everything is grape-related; **Mehlenbacher's Taffy**, an old-fashioned candy store with hand-pulled candy in Hammondsport (Keuka Lake); **Weaver-View Farms**, selling Amish and Mennonite crafts, foods, and gifts (Seneca Lake); **MacKenzie-Childs** (Aurora/Cayuga Lake), a fantasy land of whimsically painted pottery, glass, and furniture; **Skyland Farm** (Seneca Lake), wonderful farm, garden, crafts shop, luncheon deli, and barn; and **Vermont Green Mountain Specialty Company**, Skaneateles, homemade candy and other goodies that are impossible to resist.

Index

LODGING BY PRICE CODE

RESTAURANTS BY PRICE CODE

RESTAURANTS BY CUISINE